Yugoslavia
a country study

Federal Research Division
Library of Congress
Edited by
Glenn E. Curtis
Research Completed
December 1990

On the cover: Muslim minaret, Skopje

Third Edition, First Printing, 1992.

Library of Congress Cataloging-in-Publication Data

Yugoslavia : a country study / Federal Research Division, Library of
  Congress ; edited by Glenn E. Curtis. — 3rd ed.
     p. cm. — (Area handbook series, ISSN 1057-5294)
  (DA pam ; 550-99)
     "Supersedes the 1982 edition of Yugoslavia: a country study,
  edited by Richard F. Nyrop."—T.p. verso.
     "Research completed December 1990."
     Includes bibliographical references (pp. 303-319) and index.
     ISBN 0-8444-0735-6
     1. Yugoslavia.   I. Curtis, Glenn E. (Glenn Eldon), 1946-
  II. Library of Congress. Federal Research Division. III. Area
  handbook for Yugoslavia. IV. Series. V. Series : DA pam ;
  550-99.
  DR1214.Y83   1992   91-40323
  949.7—dc20   CIP

Headquarters, Department of the Army
DA Pam 550-99

For sale by the Superintendent of Documents, U.S. Government Printing Office
Washington, D.C. 20402

Foreword

This volume is one in a continuing series of books prepared by the Federal Research Division of the Library of Congress under the Country Studies—Area Handbook Program sponsored by the Department of the Army. The last page of this book lists the other published studies.

Most books in the series deal with a particular foreign country, describing and analyzing its political, economic, social, and national security systems and institutions, and examining the interrelationships of those systems and the ways they are shaped by cultural factors. Each study is written by a multidisciplinary team of social scientists. The authors seek to provide a basic understanding of the observed society, striving for a dynamic rather than a static portrayal. Particular attention is devoted to the people who make up the society, their origins, dominant beliefs and values, their common interests and the issues on which they are divided, the nature and extent of their involvement with national institutions, and their attitudes toward each other and toward their social system and political order.

The books represent the analysis of the authors and should not be construed as an expression of an official United States government position, policy, or decision. The authors have sought to adhere to accepted standards of scholarly objectivity. Corrections, additions, and suggestions for changes from readers will be welcomed for use in future editions.

Louis R. Mortimer
Chief
Federal Research Division
Library of Congress
Washington, D.C. 20540

Acknowledgments

The authors are indebted to numerous individuals and organizations who gave their time, research materials, advice, and expertise on Yugoslav affairs to provide data, perspective, and material support for this volume.

The work of Steven L. Burg and Robert E. Bartos, authors of the Government and Politics and National Security chapters, respectively, of the previous edition of the Yugoslavia area handbook, supplied vital foundation material to the new authors of those chapters. Thanks also go to the Embassy of Yugoslavia and the Yugoslav National Tourist Office (New York) for supplying the editor with a large number of photographs from which to choose. The expert photography of Charles Sudetic and Sam and Sarah Stulberg has added timely and picturesque images of Yugoslavia. And, in the final stages of updating current events in Yugoslavia, the firsthand insights of Paul Pajic of the Library of Congress were invaluable.

Thanks also go to Ralph K. Benesch, who oversees the Country Studies—Area Handbook Program for the Department of the Army. In addition, the authors appreciate the advice and guidance of Sandra W. Meditz, Federal Research Division coordinator of the handbook series. Special thanks also go to Marilyn L. Majeska, who managed editing and production, assisted by Andrea T. Merrill; to Kimberly Lord, who designed the book cover; to Carlyn Dawn Anderson, who designed the illustrations on the title page of each chapter; to David P. Cabitto, who provided graphics support and, together with Harriett R. Blood and the firm of Greenhorne and O'Mara, prepared maps; and to Tim Merrill, who compiled geographic data. The following individuals are gratefully acknowledged as well: Sharon Costello, who edited the chapters, and Barbara Edgerton and Izella Watson, who did the word processing. Cissie Coy performed the final prepublication editorial review; Joan C. Cook compiled the index; and Linda Peterson of the Printing and Processing Section, Library of Congress, prepared the camera-ready copy, under the supervision of Peggy Pixley.

Contents

Chapter 2. The Society and Its Environment 59
Charles Sudetic

List of Figures

Preface

In the 1980s, Yugoslavia passed through a time of political, social, and economic transition that changed many of its basic institutions and threatened the very political structure of the nation. Events occurring after the death of Josip Broz Tito in 1980, and especially those at the end of the 1980s, demanded a new and updated version of *Yugoslavia: A Country Study*. Because Yugoslavia was already the most open of East European communist nations, large amounts of reliable information about events there have been available throughout the post-Tito period. A number of useful monographs and a host of scholarly articles and periodical reports have provided the basis for this new treatment of the country. The most useful of those sources are cited at the end of each chapter.

The authors of this edition have described changes in the last ten years against the historical, political, and social background of Yugoslavia. Each of the six Yugoslav republics and two provinces is treated separately in some respects, because of substantial differences in their social and political makeup and their history before 1918. The authors have attempted to describe the centrifugal impact of those differences on the history of the Yugoslav state, and especially on its current condition. With that in mind, several tables in the Appendix break down ethnographic and economic statistics by republic and province.

Yugoslav personal names are uniformly rendered in the Latin orthography used in Croatia and Slovenia, with the single exception that the spelling ''dj'' is used to replace the single letter that represents that sound in the Croatian system. As was not the case in the preceding edition, diacritics are supplied wherever appropriate. The spelling of geographical names conforms to that approved by the United States Board on Geographical Names, with the exception of commonly used international spellings such as Belgrade (Beograd) and Bosnia (Bosna). On maps English-language generic designations such as river, plain, and mountain are used. Organizations commonly known by their acronyms (such as LCY, the League of Communists of Yugoslavia) are introduced first by their full English names.

Measurements are given in the metric system; a conversion table is provided in the Appendix. A glossary and a bibliography are also included at the end of the book.

Country Profile

COUNTRY

Formal Name: Socialist Federal Republic of Yugoslavia.

Short Form: Yugoslavia.

Term for Citizens: Yugoslav(s).

Capital: Belgrade.

GEOGRAPHY

Size: Approximately 255,804 square kilometers.

Topography: Two principal regions. Successive mountain ranges run parallel to Adriatic coast, from Austrian border (northwest) to Greek border (southeast), occupying entire southern half of country. Second major region Pannonian Plains, occupying northeast section, extending from Austria (north) to Romania (east).

Climate: Generally temperate but varies from moderate Mediterranean along Adriatic coast to colder continental conditions in mountains and plains of east-central and northern sections of country.

SOCIETY

Population: 1990 estimate 23.5 million; 1990 annual growth rate 0.6 percent; 1988 population density 92.1 per square kilometer.

Languages: Serbo-Croatian, Slovenian, and Macedonian official state languages. Main national minority languages Albanian and Hungarian.

Ethnic Groups: Serbs, Croats, Muslim Slavs, Slovenes, Macedonians, and Montenegrins (all ethnically South Slavs, together constituting over 80 percent of total population) the main ethnic groups. Albanians and Hungarians (7.7 percent and 1.9 percent, respectively, according to 1981 census) the principal minority ethnic groups.

Education and Literacy: Education compulsory between ages seven and fifteen. Literacy estimated at 90 percent in 1990. Extensive growth in education system in post-World War II era through 1980; slower growth and restructuring in 1980s.

Health: Republic and province constitutions stipulate universal citizen rights to health care. General health insurance program covered most of population, with some exceptions in rural areas. Substantial expansion of health care resources beginning in 1960s, but disparities remained significant between rural and urban areas and between richer and poorer regions.

Religion: In 1990 Roman Catholic (30 percent), Serbian and Macedonian Orthodox (50 percent), Muslim (9 percent), Protestant (1 percent), and other (10 percent). Estimates of religious faiths vary widely.

ECONOMY

Gross National Product (GNP): Estimated at US$120.1 billion in 1990, or US$5,040 per capita. Average growth rate 0.5 percent in 1981–88 period. Economic growth slow throughout 1980s because of foreign debt and spiraling inflation.

Industry and Mining: Largest sector, accounting for 44.6 percent of GNP in 1988. Relatively broad base, with substantial petrochemical, metallurgy, automobile manufacture, and electronics. Substantial ferrous and nonferrous mining industries.

Agriculture: Consists of small, highly developed social sector and large private sector (95 percent of farm employment). Private farms averaged 3.5 hectares and fragmented. Main crops corn, rye, and wheat, with variety of additional produce. Livestock (pigs, horses, cattle, and sheep) more important than cropping but limited by fodder shortage.

Energy: National energy shortage despite large deposits of low-calorie coal (lignite) and some crude oil and gas.

Exports: US$13 billion in 1988, of which 31 percent machinery and transportation equipment, 42 percent semifinished and raw materials, and 9 percent agricultural commodities. Largest export markets Soviet Union, Italy, West Germany, and United States.

Imports: US$13.6 billion in 1988, of which 46 percent semifinished and raw materials, 27 percent machinery and transportation equipment, and 6 percent agricultural commodities. Largest import suppliers West Germany, Soviet Union, Italy, and United States.

Balance of Payments: Deteriorated during 1970s and 1980s. Remained serious constraint on growth in 1980s.

Exchange Rate: New "heavy" dinar established in 1990, worth 10,000 old dinars; 1990 exchange rate fixed at 7 dinars per West German deutsche mark. New rate January 1991 set at YD10.50 per US$1.

Inflation: In late 1989 about 1,950 percent; reduced to zero percent by reforms of 1990.

Fiscal Year: Calendar year.

Fiscal Policy: Governmental system highly decentralized. Federal budget expenditures, mainly for defense and administration, about one-quarter of total public sector budgeting. Economic reforms of 1990 used fiscal policy to eliminate inflation. Constitutional amendments aimed at stimulating private investment in formerly state-funded enterprises.

TRANSPORTATION AND TELECOMMUNICATIONS

Railroads: Total freight carried 83.6 million tons in 1978; total passengers 116 million in 1988. In 1990 total track about 9,300 kilometers, of which all was standard gauge, 3,800 kilometers electrified, and 10 percent double track.

Civil Aviation: In 1989 Yugoslav Air Transport operated 291 domestic and international routes. Major international airports at Belgrade, Zagreb, Ljubljana, Sarajevo, Skopje, Dubrovnik, Split, Titograd, Maribor, and Zadar.

Highways: 120,700 kilometers total, all but 15,100 kilometers hard surface in 1990. About 232 million tons freight transported in 1986.

Inland Waterways: 2,600 kilometers in 1982. About 16.2 million tons goods unloaded in 1988.

Ports: Nine major ports, of which Rijeka, Split, Bar, and Ploče most important; twenty-four minor ports. Total ocean freight 34.1 million tons in 1988. Belgrade most important river port.

Pipelines: 2,215 kilometers for crude oil; 2,880 kilometers for natural gas; and 150 kilometers for refined products (1990).

Telecommunications: Government-operated national direct-dial telephone system, including ten telephones per 100 residents in 1982. Yugoslav Radio and Television Network operated 250 stations, with national and local programming, in 1986. Two satellite dishes of International Telecommunications Satellite Organization (Intelsat) located in Yugoslavia.

GOVERNMENT AND POLITICS

Government: Federal system in which federal government and governments of six republics and two provinces (with limited autonomy) shared power and authority. After death of dictator Josip Broz Tito in 1980, head of state began annual rotation among members of eight-member State Presidency. Federal Executive Council (FEC) acted as cabinet; its president was prime minister and de facto head of government. Legislative branch was bicameral Federal Assembly (Skupština), representing republics and social organizations. Decision making slow, often cumbersome; proposals subject to veto by republics whose interests were threatened.

Politics: Until 1990, sole center of political power was League of Communists of Yugoslavia (LCY). Its split along republic lines coincided with growth of many noncommunist parties, mostly republic based, in late 1980s. First noncommunist republic government elected in Croatia in 1990. Multiparty elections held in all republics in 1990.

Foreign Relations: Maintained nonaligned international position after breaking with Soviet Union in 1948; remained a leader of world Nonaligned Movement through 1980s. Previously balanced relations with Soviet Union and West tilted toward West after economic and political crises in Soviet Union and Eastern Europe in late 1980s.

International Agreements and Memberships: Member of United Nations and most of its specialized agencies. Observer status in Council for Mutual Economic Assistance (Comecon). Also member of World Bank, International Monetary Fund (IMF), and General Agreement on Tariffs and Trade (GATT).

NATIONAL SECURITY

Armed Forces: Yugoslav People's Army (YPA) included army, air force, and navy, administered in four military regions. In mid-1990 army numbered 140,000 active-duty personnel (of which 90,000 conscripts); air force, 32,000 (4,000 conscripts); and navy, 10,000 (4,400 conscripts, 900 marines). Estimated 450,000 reservists available in wartime. Paramilitary Territorial Defense Forces (TDF) numbered 1 million to 3 million in 1990; 860,000 in regular training. TDF largely funded by and under peacetime control of republic governments; designated to fight either independently or under YPA command during an invasion.

Major Military Units: Major force structure change in army in 1990. Thirty brigades formed, including tank, mechanized, mountain infantry, and one airborne brigade. Naval submarines, corvettes, and frigates centered in Adriatic Fleet, administered from Split; smaller craft in both river and Adriatic commands; main mission Adriatic coastal defense. Air force operated over 400 combat aircraft (in twelve combat squadrons) and 200 helicopters. Main missions of air force to maintain air superiority over Yugoslavia and to support ground and naval operations. Substantial reliance on imported heavy military equipment; most aircraft and naval vessels manufactured domestically. Strong effort to expand domestic arms industry in 1980s.

Military Budget: In 1989 defense expenditures listed as equivalent of over US$4.4 billion, nearly 7 percent of GNP.

Internal Security Forces: State Security Service (an intelligence and secret police organization) monitored émigrés and domestic dissidents. People's Militia troops (15,000) used to quell domestic disorders beyond control of regular police. Militia (regular police, 40,000) used for routine law enforcement.

Figure 1. Administrative Divisions of Yugoslavia, 1990

Introduction

BY 1990 YUGOSLAVIA, "the land of the South Slavs," had become an international metaphor for ethnic strife and political fragmentation. Mikhail S. Gorbachev was described as attempting to keep the Soviet Union from becoming a "giant Yugoslavia" when Soviet republics began clamoring for independence in 1989. The metaphor was based on diversity in almost every aspect of Yugoslav national life—historical experiences, standard of living, the relationship of the people to the land, and religious, cultural, and political traditions—among the six republics and the two provinces that constituted the federal state.

In spite of ongoing conflict and fragmentation, many aspects of life in the country as a whole underwent significant improvement in the post-World War II period. A fundamentally agrarian society was industrialized and urbanized, and standards of living rose dramatically in most regions between 1945 and 1970. The literacy rate increased steadily, school instruction in the country's several minority languages became widespread, and the university system expanded. A national health care system was developed to protect most Yugoslav citizens, although serious defects remained in rural medical care. The traditional patriarchal family, once the most important social institution in most regions, lost its influence as Yugoslavs became more mobile and as large numbers of women entered the work force. In these same years, Yugoslavia adopted a unique economic planning system (socialist self-management) and an independent foreign policy (nonalignment) to meet its own domestic and security needs. In these ways, by 1980 Yugoslavia had assumed many of the qualities of a modern European state. In the following decade, as Western Europe moved toward unification, acceptance into the new European community became an important national goal for Yugoslavia.

The 1980s brought persistent challenges to the concept of federating the South Slavs. Although the unlikelihood of a union between "Catholic, westward-looking Croatia and Slovenia" and "Orthodox, eastward-looking Serbia" had been viewed as highly unlikely long before secession occurred and civil crisis escalated in 1991, arguments for preserving at least a loose Yugoslav confederation retained much of the logic of earlier decades. All regions of Yugoslavia were substantially interdependent economically throughout the postwar period. Although regions differed greatly in economic level, in 1991 many of the most profitable markets for all republics remained inside Yugoslavia. More important, in modern history only Montenegro and Serbia had existed as independent states, and no republic had been self-sufficient since 1918.

Nevertheless, in 1991 the six republics—Bosnia and Hercegovina, Croatia, Macedonia, Montenegro, Serbia, and Slovenia—and the two provinces, Kosovo and Vojvodina, moved decisively away from whatever unity had been achieved in the postwar period. Given the lack of common values between Orthodox Serbs in Belgrade and Muslim Slavs in Sarajevo, or between private entrepreneurs in Slovenia and Leninists in Montenegro, many experts argued that the survival and modernization of the postwar Yugoslav state had been the result of a unique, dominating personality, Josip Broz Tito, whose regime had orchestrated all the social, economic, and foreign policy changes. According to that theory, post-Tito separation of Yugoslavia's constituent parts was the natural course of events.

The fall of East European communism at the end of the 1980s intensified the forces of fragmentation in Yugoslavia by finally replacing the decrepit League of Communists of Yugoslavia (LCY—see Glossary), which had checked political expression of ethnic differences, with an open system that fostered such expression. But separation proved to be no less complex than continued federation. The first obstacle to dividing the federation was disagreement on the identity of its constituent parts—a result of centuries of ethnic intermixture and jurisdictional shifts. The second obstacle was the fact that the parts were not only diverse but also of unequal political and economic stature. Beginning in 1990, the Republic of Serbia, still run by a conventional communist regime, attempted to restrain fragmentation by reviving its historical tradition of geopolitical dominance in the Balkans. At the same time, the republics of Slovenia and Croatia used their economic superiority to seek independence on their own terms. The less endowed regions, caught between these contradictory aims, took sides or became pawns. The military and political events of 1991 then intensified the struggle of the diverse parts to achieve diverse aims. In the struggle, each of the political units had a different stake in, and a different perspective on, the theory that a post-Tito Yugoslav federation could work. Ominously, the intractable fighting of 1991 between Croats and Serbs was in many ways a continuation of their last bitter confrontation in World War II—supporting doubts that the Croats and Serbs could remain together in a single political structure.

The Yugoslav nation-state had begun as the dream of nineteenth-century idealists who envisioned a political union of the major South Slavic groups: the Croats, Serbs, Slovenes, and Bulgars. But by the twentieth century, each of those groups, as well as a number of smaller ethnic communities within their territories, had experienced centuries of very diverse cultural and political influences. Under these limitations, the Kingdom of the Serbs, Croats, and Slovenes (later renamed the Kingdom of Yugoslavia) was formed as a constitutional monarchy after World War I.

The interwar period was dominated by the competing claims of Serbian and Croatian politicians—the former dominating the government and supporting a strong centralized state, the latter agitating for regional autonomy. King Aleksandar, a genuine believer in the Yugoslav ideal, sought to unify his country by a variety of political measures, including dictatorship, but he was assassinated in 1934. Lacking a tradition of political compromise that might forge a national consensus, Yugoslavia remained divided as World War II began. More than three years of Nazi occupation yielded bloody fighting among three Yugoslav factions as well as with the invaders.

Two results of that war had particular impact on the postwar condition of Yugoslavia. The first was a vivid new set of memories to kindle hostility between Serbs and Croats, the majority of whom had fought on opposite sides in the occupation years; the second was the emergence of the unifying war hero Tito, who became dictator of a nonaligned communist federation. After declaring independence from the Soviet alliance in 1948, Tito also modified Yugoslavia's Stalinist command economy by giving local worker groups limited control in a self-management system. Although ultimately dominated by the party, this system brought substantial economic growth between the early 1950s and the 1970s and made Yugoslavia a model for the nonaligned world.

Two economic policies unknown in orthodox communist countries contributed greatly to this growth. Allowing laborers to emigrate to Western Europe as guest workers brought substantial hard currency (see Glossary) into Yugoslavia and relieved labor surpluses at home. And opening the country's many scenic beaches and mountains to Western tourists provided a second reliable source of hard currency, which proved especially useful when other parts of the economy declined during the 1980s.

In his later years, Tito began restructuring his government to prepare it for the post-Tito era. The last decade of the Tito regime paved the way for a power-sharing government-by-consensus that he saw as the best hope of binding the federation after his regime ended.

The 1974 Constitution gave substantial new power to the republics, which obtained veto power over federal legislation. This tactic also kept Tito's potential rivals within small local fiefdoms, denying them national status. Both the government and the ruling LCY became increasingly stratified between federal and regional organizations; by Tito's later years, the locus of political power was already diffused.

In the meantime, in 1966 the repressive national secret police organization of Aleksandar Ranković had been dismantled, yielding political liberalization that led to major outbursts of nationalism in Kosovo (1968) and Croatia (1971). Although Tito quelled such movements, they restated existing threats to a strong, Serb-dominated central government, a concept still cherished by the Serbs. The 1974 Constitution further alarmed the Serbs by giving virtual autonomy to Serbia's provinces, Kosovo and Vojvodina.

At Tito's death in 1980, the promising Yugoslav economy was in decline because of international oil crises, heavy foreign borrowing, and inefficient investment policies. Economic reform, recognized throughout the 1980s as an imperative step, was consistently blocked during that decade by ever more diametrically opposed regional interests that found little incentive to compromise in the decentralized post-Tito federal structure. Thus, Slovenia and Croatia, already long separate culturally from the rest of the federation, came to resist the central government policy of redistributing their relatively great wealth to impoverished regions to the south. By 1990 this resistance was both economic (withholding revenue from the federal treasury) and political (threatening secession unless granted substantial economic and political autonomy within the federation).

The decade that followed the death of Tito was a time of gradual deterioration and a period that saw ethnic hostility boiling just below the surface of the Yugoslav political culture. The 1980s in Yugoslavia was also a decade singularly lacking strong political leadership in the Tito tradition, even at the regional level. When the wave of anticommunist political and economic reform swept Eastern Europe in the late 1980s, a variety of noncommunist parties challenged the monolithic Yugoslav communist system in place since 1945. In 1990 the LCY gave up its stranglehold on national political power. Long-overdue economic reforms began promisingly in 1990 but then slowed abruptly as regions defended their vested interests in the status quo. Meanwhile, in 1989 the Serbian communist Slobodan Milošević had stepped into the Yugoslav power vacuum, striking a note of Serbian national hegemony that confronted a wide range of newly released nationalist forces in the other republics.

The Yugoslav republics were further separated by their varied reactions to the collapse of communism in Eastern Europe. Already pro-Western and economically dissatisfied, Slovenia and Croatia were the first republics to hold multiparty elections in early 1990; both elected noncommunist republic governments. Later in 1990, the republics of Macedonia and Bosnia and Hercegovina followed suit, but Serbia and Montenegro (Serbia's most loyal ally in the federation) gave decisive victories to the communists in their republic elections. By that time, the LCY had split along republic lines and renounced its role as the leading institution in Yugoslav society—a position that since 1945 had been the foundation of the party's legitimacy.

Already in the late 1980s, a large variety of small parties and factions had sprouted throughout the country. These groups advocated radical, nationalist, environmentalist, regional, and religious agendas. By the first republic elections in 1990, some of the new parties had formed coalitions. The largest of these in Croatia, the right-of-center Croatian Democratic Union, gained a solid parliamentary majority in that republic under Franjo Tudjman, who became president. In Slovenia, former communist Milan Kučan reached the presidency as leader of the diverse anticommunist Demos coalition. In general, although parties with very similar philosophies existed in two or more republics, issues of nationality prevented the union of such parties across republic borders.

Among Yugoslavia's postwar trouble spots, the Serbian province of Kosovo was the most enduringly problematic both economically and politically. Always the poorest region in Yugoslavia (in spite of significant mineral and fuel reserves), Kosovo also led by a wide margin in birth rates and unemployment rates. Its territory was claimed on valid historical grounds by two fiercely nationalistic ethnic groups—the Kosovo Albanians and the Serbs. Although they constituted a shrinking minority in Kosovo, the Serbs and Montenegrins controlled the province government and suppressed separatist movements in the province—adding to the resentment of the Albanian majority. Sporadic anti-Yugoslav propaganda from neighboring Albania reminded the Kosovo Albanians of their subservient position. Extensive federal economic aid programs throughout the 1970s and 1980s failed to eliminate the economic basis of discontent. In February 1989, units of the Yugoslav People's Army (YPA) and the federal militia were called in to quell the violence, and the province remained under occupation for the next three years.

The autonomy granted to Kosovo in the 1974 Constitution was virtually revoked by 1990. But resistance in Kosovo continued. Albanians boycotted the multiparty Serbian elections in December 1990, and in 1991 students and workers staged mass demonstrations against Serbianization of education and workplaces. Although Serbia had suspended the province legislature in mid-1990, Albanian delegates and intellectuals adopted a constitution for an independent republic of Kosovo, which was ratified in a referendum in September 1991. Meanwhile, Serbia had amended its constitution to abolish the remnants of self-rule in Kosovo and in Serbia's second province, Vojvodina. In 1990 drastic political reform in isolationist Albania gave Kosovo Albanians a new political option previously judged undesirable: joining Albania in a union of Greater Albania. By 1991 Kosovan separatist groups deemphasized the goal of republic status within Yugoslavia in favor of ethnic unity with their fellow Albanians. Such an eventuality threatened to spark war between Serbia and Albania as well as conflict with Macedonia, where over 25 percent of the population was Albanian in 1991.

The chaotic condition of Kosovo was a sensitive issue throughout postwar Yugoslav national politics. In the late 1980s, the issue assumed even greater dimensions, however. Milošević used the threat of Albanian irredentism in Kosovo to rally Serbian ethnic pride behind his nationalist faction of the League of Communists of Serbia. In doing so, he won the presidency of Serbia. By 1990 this single-issue strategy had made Milošević the most powerful political figure in post-Tito Yugoslavia. His open ambition for power and his assertion of Serbian hegemony soon added Macedonia and Bosnia and Hercegovina to the list of republics opposing Serbia in federal disputes. Despite widely held contempt for communism, however, opposition within Serbia remained fragmented and ineffectual until 1991. In the first multiparty elections in postwar Serbia, Milošević easily won reelection in December 1990. Because he controlled almost all the Serbian media, his campaign was able to ignore the chaotic Serbian economy.

In October 1990, internal and external conditions caused Slovenia and Croatia to seek independence in some form. Accordingly, the two republics proposed that Yugoslavia be restructured as a loose confederation of states, each with national sovereignty and its own army and each conducting its own foreign policy. Following the model of the European Economic Community (EEC—see Glossary), the formula included monetary uniformity and a common market. Serbia immediately blocked the plan, arguing that the large number of Serbs living in republics other than Serbia would become citizens of foreign countries. Beginning in 1990, groups from several Serbian enclaves in Croatia, some of which declared themselves the Krajina Serbian Autonomous Region in March 1991, skirmished with local police and Croatian security forces. Milošević was suspected of giving this movement substantial encouragement. By early 1991, large caches of illegally imported arms were held by both Serbs and Croats in multiethnic parts of Croatia, sharpening the threat of full-scale civil war.

Complex population patterns had been established in most of Yugoslavia by centuries of cultural, political, and military influences from outside—most notably the settlement policies of the long-dominant Habsburg and Ottoman empires. In fact, remaining ethnic patterns blocked a clean break from the federation by any republic except homogeneous Slovenia because large populations would be left behind unless borders were substantially redrawn. Even if Krajina had seceded from Croatia to join Serbia, for example, a substantial number of Serbs would have remained scattered in the Republic of Croatia.

Early in 1991, local conflicts in Krajina brought threats from Milošević to defend his countrymen from oppression, and tension mounted between Serbia and Croatia. In April 1991, Krajina declared itself part of Serbia; the Croats responded by tightening economic pressure on the region and by threatening to redraw their own boundaries to include adjacent parts of Bosnia inhabited by a Croatian majority. In early 1991, however, moderates on both sides managed to defuse numerous local crises and prevent a broader conflict.

Meanwhile, a major indication of Serbian political diversity appeared in March 1991 when anticommunist Serbs held a mass demonstration in Belgrade against the economic bungling and dictatorial practices of the Milošević government. When Milošević demanded that the YPA quell the uprising in his capital, half of the eight-member State Presidency of Yugoslavia (nominally commander in chief of the armed forces) voted against the measure. Repeating his frequent claim that an anti-Serb coalition was endangering Yugoslavia, Milošević secured the resignation of the other four members of the State Presidency (delegates from Serbia, Montenegro, Kosovo, and Vojvodina, all of whom he controlled). The crisis peaked when YPA troops mobilized but remained inactive, and Milošević soon instructed the four delegates to resume their positions.

This confrontation seemingly dealt Milošević a double blow: recanting his position toward the State Presidency was a major retreat for this most visible Yugoslav politician, and he lost substantial popularity among Serbs for his willingness to send the military against his own people. More important, the largely peaceful demonstrations set a precedent for public discussion of issues in Serbia, temporarily improving the prospects of a viable multiparty system in that republic.

In the months following the Belgrade demonstrations, the Serbs adopted a more conciliatory position in State Presidency-sponsored talks with representatives of the other republics on loosening the political structure of the federal system. Milošević continued railing against Croatian nationalist ambitions, hoping to provoke an incident that would justify YPA occupation of Croatia. In May 1991, violence in Krajina subsided when the State Presidency and the republic presidents reached an accord on jurisdictions and borders in areas disputed between Serbs and Croats.

At the same time, the Slovenes and Croats had continued the slow, steady brinkmanship of their relations with the federal government. In February 1991, both republic assemblies had passed resolutions to dissolve the Yugoslav federation into separate states as the next step after their 1990 declarations of the right to secede. The respective assemblies also passed constitutional amendments declaring republic law supreme over federal law and essentially overriding the authority of the federal Constitution.

Then in June 1991, Croatia and Slovenia declared their independence, which set off a new chain of events. Under orders from the Serb-dominated federal Secretariat for National Defense but without approval of the State Presidency, YPA units occupied strategic points in Slovenia on the pretext of defending Yugoslav territorial integrity against an illegal secession. After encountering unexpectedly stiff resistance from Slovenian territorial defense forces, the YPA withdrew from Slovenian territory. YPA embarrassment at this military failure was only partially averted by a three-month cease-fire arranged by the European Community (EC—see Glossary). When Slovenia reasserted its independence at the end of that time, the YPA made no response.

The cease-fire in Slovenia moved the conflict decisively from Slovenia to Croatia. Croatia's declaration of independence enabled Milošević to strengthen his position as defender of the Serbian minority in Croatia, which now seemed poised to absorb its Serbs into a separate state. Under the banner of anti-Croatian Serbian nationalism, economic failures and internal political differences became secondary; Milošević abandoned his conciliatory approach and regained his political foothold.

The first phase of the 1991 Serb-Croat conflict pitted Serbian guerrillas against Croatian militia in the regions of Croatia with large Serbian populations. The YPA intervened, ostensibly as a peacekeeping force preventing a wider conflict. The YPA role soon evolved into one of support for the Serbs and then into active occupation of Croatian territory, with no pretense of neutrality. Croatian forces besieged and captured YPA warehouses and garrisons, somewhat improving their decidedly inferior military position. Through the summer and fall of 1991, prolonged, sometimes siege-like battles raged in Croatia between Serbian guerrillas and the YPA on one side and the Croatian militia on the other. The areas of heaviest fighting were the population centers of Slavonia in eastern Croatia and the ports along the Adriatic coastline. Between August and December, fourteen cease-fires were arranged but were shortly violated by both sides. The EC, which feared the spread of ethnic conflict into other parts of Europe, arranged most of those agreements; Gorbachev was the broker of one. An estimated 10,000 people, the majority of them Croats, were killed in the conflict in the last four months of 1991, and about 600,000 people became refugees. During most of that time, Serbian and YPA forces occupied about one-third of Croatia.

Throughout the political and economic turmoil of the late 1980s and 1990, two national institutions survived: the YPA and the federal government. After World War II, the YPA had played the theoretical role of defender of the country's vaunted independent international position against attack from east or west. The YPA remained a bastion of conservative political influence after Cold War threats subsided and after electoral and legislative setbacks had sapped the unifying power of the LCY in 1990.

Led by an officer corps heavily Serbian and Montenegrin, the YPA took a dim view of rampant political diversification that threatened the power of the central government. Especially troubling were Slovenian and Croatian assertions of republic sovereignty over local military units, which threatened the very existence of the YPA organization. The failure of the old system also threatened the lifestyle of the YPA officer corps, which had enjoyed privileges such as summer houses on the Adriatic and generous pensions as part of their elite status in Yugoslav society.

Several times in 1990 and early 1991, Serbian and federal officials threatened to use YPA troops to restore order or protect federal property. In January 1991, Defense Secretary Veljko Kadijević, a Serb, threatened to send YPA forces into Croatia when that republic formed its own military establishment, and in March YPA units confronted mass demonstrations in Belgrade. After preliminary mobilization in the Belgrade crisis, a divided high command announced that it would not intervene in political disputes unless armed conflict erupted in one of the republics. Although this statement deferred the often-mentioned scenario of a military coup to hold the nation together, in the spring of 1991 the YPA intervened in dozens of battles between separatist Serbs and Croatian authorities in Croatia.

Forces of change began to affect the YPA by 1990. Disintegration of the LCY removed the ideological unity of the YPA (whose political power had been exercised through representation in party organizations) and negated its role as defender of the ruling party. LCY activity in the army was officially outlawed in late 1990, and all political organization in the military was to be banned in 1991 legislation. One response to depolitization was the formation in November 1990 of the League of Communists of Yugoslavia-Movement for Yugoslavia by a group of retired YPA officers to replace the old LCY as an advocate of preserving the existing federal structure. This party advocated continued socialism and condemned Slovenia and Croatia as capitalist puppets.

In February 1991, Slovenia and Croatia proposed that new, depoliticized professional military organizations be formed in each republic, and the two republics announced that they would slash support for the national military budget. At the same time, federal military spending decreased because of budget deficits, and the reliability of conscripts from Kosovo and other areas came increasingly into question. All republics save Serbia and Montenegro refused to provide recruits for the 1991 YPA action in Croatia; when draft evasion became a problem even in Serbia, the long-term future of the YPA became doubtful. Although the YPA was the fifth-largest armed force in Europe in 1991, its command structure and resource base were shown to be unreliable in combat. Nevertheless, as the authority of the Yugoslav federal government dwindled and arbitration of disputes faltered, the on-site power of the military often negated the civilian authority meant to restrain it. The unpredictability of YPA forces became a major obstacle for United Nations (UN) diplomats seeking an effective cease-fire between Serbian and Croatian forces at the end of 1991.

Economic reform remained a critical national and regional need in 1991. When economist Ante Marković became prime minister at the end of 1989, he inherited an inflation rate that had reached 2,600 percent that year and a national average personal income that had sunk to 1960s levels. Marković's two-step program began with harsh measures, such as closing unproductive plants, freezing wages, and instituting a tight monetary policy to clear away the remainder of the moribund state-subsidized system as soon as possible. Marković also avidly sought new economic ties with

Western Europe to reinvigorate Yugoslavia's traditional policy of multilateral trade.

Once inflation had been curbed, phase two (July 1990) continued tight monetary control but sought to spur lagging productivity by encouraging private and foreign investment and unfreezing wages. Marković applied his plan doggedly, convincing the Federal Assembly (Skupština) to pass most of its provisions. He was aided by the lack of workable alternatives among his critics, by the international credibility of his consultation with economists of the International Monetary Fund (IMF—see Glossary), and by his personal popularity. Inflation ended when the dinar (for value of the dinar—see Glossary) was pegged to the deutsche mark in December 1989, and new foreign loans and joint ventures in 1990 improved capital investment.

Although the end of inflation was very popular, however, plant closure and wage freezes were decidedly not so in regions where as many as 80 percent of plants were kept running only because of state subsidies. The Serbs opposed the plan from the beginning because their communist-dominated industrial management system was still in place, meaning that a new market economy would threaten many privileged positions. The Slovenes resented federalization of their funds to help run the program. In all republics, the immediate threat of mass unemployment blunted the drive to privatize and to peg wages to productivity. As in previous years, the republics saw a threat to their autonomy if they acceded to the requirements of such a sweeping federal program. By the fall of 1990, the optimism of Marković's first stage was replaced by the realization that many enterprises throughout the country either could not or would not discontinue their inefficient operations and would remain socially owned. Several major industries in Slovenia and Croatia were also still state controlled in 1991, although both republics drafted privatization laws that year.

The Serbian economy continued to decline at an especially rapid rate after the Marković reforms. In December 1990, the Serbian government illegally transferred US$1.3 billion from the National Bank of Yugoslavia to bolster the sagging republic economy—defying federal economic authority, further alienating the other republics, and exposing the failure of reform in the Yugoslav banking system.

The proportion of unprofitable enterprises in the national economy (about one-third) did not change between 1989 and 1990. By 1991 bankruptcy declarations by such firms had virtually ceased. Strikes decreased only slightly from a 1989 high of 1,900. A wave of strikes, mostly by blue-collar workers, slowed the economy in all regions of Yugoslavia at the end of 1990. At that point, inflation had risen to 118 percent per year and was expected to continue to rise into 1991, spurred by the Serbian bank transaction and unauthorized printing of money by republics in the last half of 1990. In mid-1991 inflation rose further when the federal government began printing more money to cover escalating military costs. By that time, the government had lost control of federal tax revenues, which were collected by the republics. Unemployment was close to 25 percent in January 1991, and no improvement in the standard of living was foreseen in the near future. Industrial production that month was down 18.2 percent from January 1990, the greatest such drop in forty years. The failure to devise a new banking system after the previous system collapsed increased black market financial activity and discouraged guest workers abroad from making deposits.

Marković warned consistently that continued chaos jeopardized economic reform and ultimately the federation itself. The IMF, for example, had joined the EEC in offering a combined loan of US$2 billion in early 1991, but continued unrest threatened that vital arrangement. Already in January 1991, the EEC postponed consideration of membership for Yugoslavia because of the internal situation. In early 1991, the United States cited human rights violations in Kosovo in threatening to end all bilateral economic aid. In the fall of 1991, the United States, the Soviet Union, and the EEC all threatened economic sanctions if diplomacy did not replace armed conflict in the Croatian crisis. The United States adopted sanctions against all the republics, but the EEC excluded Slovenia and Croatia.

Already seriously undermined by the constitutional power of the republics, the Yugoslav federal government apparatus was completely overshadowed in 1991. In December 1990, the Marković cabinet had drafted an eleven-point emergency program of basic legislation to keep the federation running until the State Presidency could agree on political reform. Four months later, however, the Federal Assembly was still debating some of those laws. Marković faced a delicate balance between using federal authority to hold the country together and heeding the demands of the economically vital Slovenes and Croats to loosen the federation. In early 1991, Marković criticized those republics for arming separate paramilitary forces and passing resolutions of separation from Yugoslavia. By April 1991, a substantial movement in the Federal Assembly sought to unseat Marković as prime minister. But the economic ties he had formed with the West were correctly seen by many politicians as the best way to save the Yugoslav economy, and Marković remained because his ouster would likely end the prospect for such aid.

Unlike most countries of Eastern Europe, Yugoslavia had begun major economic reform before making any changes in government structure. A round of constitutional amendments in 1990 dealt only with economic matters, leaving political power relationships untouched. Although Marković had planned to call elections for a Federal Assembly to begin work on a new constitution in 1990, he achieved no consensus on the timing or form of those elections. Among other changes, the new constitution presumably would have revamped Tito's unworkable system of rotating chief executives. In March 1991, special "professional working groups," including members from each republic, began drafting for the State Presidency proposals on political and economic issues for possible use as constitutional amendments. The first proposal outlined a new federal structure; the second proposed a new procedure for a republic to secede from the federation—two of the most volatile issues of the "transformation period."

The weakness of the national executive structure was revealed by the Belgrade demonstrations, when the eight-member State Presidency was essentially obliterated by walkouts and resignations orchestrated by Milošević. After the full membership was reestablished, fruitless constitutional discussions and "summit meetings" further damaged confidence in the State Presidency. By July 1991, unauthorized YPA actions in Slovenia and Croatia had removed de facto command of the military from the State Presidency, and national executive authority had virtually disappeared.

The events of 1991 forced all the republics to adjust their positions and defend their own interests first, lessening the probability of reversing regionalization and reestablishing a credible federal government backed by a reframed constitution. The diametrically opposed political blueprints of the centralist republics (Serbia and Montenegro) and the autonomist republics (Slovenia and Croatia, later joined by Macedonia and Bosnia and Hercegovina) meant that any attempt to redistribute power was very likely to be deadlocked.

While Serbia, Croatia, and Slovenia occupied center stage in 1991, the other three republics—Montenegro, Macedonia, and Bosnia and Hercegovina—divided their attention between local economic and social problems and the transformation crisis of the federation. After moving gradually toward supporting republic sovereignty, Macedonia and Bosnia and Hercegovina were forced by circumstances in the fall of 1991 to declare their own independence. Montenegro remained allied with Serbia in support of a strong central government. Unlike Slovenia and Croatia, those republics had little hope of surviving independently, and all contained precariously balanced ethnic mixtures (the Montenegrin population included a total of 20 percent Albanians and Muslim Slavs).

In December 1990, Bosnia and Hercegovina elected a multiparty assembly in which the noncommunist Muslim Party for Democratic Action (PDA) won a plurality of the 240 seats, and PDA president Alija Izetbegović became the first noncommunist president of the republic. The new assembly contained an ethnic mix representative of the overall population: 99 Muslim Slavs, 83 Serbs, and 50 Croats. Peaceful transition to a multiparty system in 1990 was considered a triumph of the three major ethnic parties and a promising indication that coalition building among them might work. In discussing the republic's position on a new federal structure in early 1991, the Serbian party advocated more centralism; the other two parties followed the Croatian and Slovenian recipe for a loose confederation. In the first year of his presidency, Izetbegović was a strong voice of conciliation on national constitutional issues, attempting to preserve political relations with all factions.

Because of its ethnic makeup, Bosnia and Hercegovina was a central point of contention between Serbs and Croats. Both sides had substantial territorial claims that threatened to destabilize the republic's internal politics. Serbs feared that Croatia would take Croatian-dominated parts of Bosnia and Hercegovina with it if it seceded; Croats feared leaving those parts to the mercy of the Serbs. The Muslim Slavs, in turn, remembered that Croatia and Serbia had split Bosnia and Hercegovina between them before World War II, so the Muslim Slavs feared reabsorption into those states. Within the six-member republic presidency, accusations and threats mimicked those exchanged by the factions in the federal executive branch.

In mid-1991 the central location of Bosnia and Hercegovina between Serbia and Croatia threatened to make it a second major military front in the Serb-Croat confrontation. When Croatian and Muslim Slav legislators sought to avoid a Serbian takeover by declaring the sovereignty of the republic in October, they antagonized their Serbian counterparts and exacerbated the threat of civil war. By that time, a large part of the population was armed and in the same explosive state as were the Serbian enclaves in Croatia a few months earlier.

Macedonia, least developed of the six republics, began 1991 in worsening economic condition (official unemployment was 26 percent, but likely much higher in reality, and per capita earnings were 70 percent of the national average) and with new manifestations of old problems: nationalism and ethnic tension. Politically, Macedonia had supported the Marković economic reforms wholeheartedly; in the republic elections of November 1990, all six major party platforms advocated a multiparty parliamentary system and a market economy. In voting for their reconfigured unicameral assembly of 120, Macedonians gave a plurality to the noncommunist nationalist coalition Internal Macedonian Revolutionary Organization-Democratic Party for National Unity, with the League of Communists of Macedonia a close second among the sixteen parties that posted candidates.

Anticommunism was much weaker in Macedonia than in Croatia and Slovenia. In 1945 Tito's recognition of Macedonia as a republic had freed the Macedonians from Serbian control and inspired strong loyalty to the Yugoslav federation. Nevertheless, in December 1990 a number of Macedonian leaders, including Macedonia's delegate to the State Presidency, Vasil Tupurkovski, and Ljupco Georgievski, head of the nationalist coalition, expressed solidarity with Slovenian and Croatian declarations of autonomy. At the same time, however, they cautioned that Macedonia was not ready for such a move. Because Macedonians had been treated as Serbs (and Macedonia had been part of Serbia) before World War II, the aggressive nationalism of Milošević brought alarm and hostility that was intensified by a new wave of Macedonian nationalism. Beginning in November 1988, a series of mass demonstrations demanded that Macedonia's Balkan neighbors, Greece and Bulgaria, recognize Macedonia's status as a Yugoslav republic (they had not done so because those countries had long-standing claims to parts of Macedonia) and treat their own Macedonian citizens as a separate minority. A significant faction in the republic advocated reuniting the Macedonians of all three countries in a new political entity.

Another ethnic issue also festered in 1991. The illegal influx of as many as 150,000 Albanian refugees from Kosovo to Macedonia brought resentment and calls for closing the borders. Especially in Skopje, Albanians were refused status as a separate nationality and barred from some types of employment; demonstrations were forbidden. But the Albanian Party for Democratic Prosperity elected seventeen delegates to the Macedonian assembly in the 1990 republic election. This significant departure from the total repression of the former communist regime in Macedonia brought hope that Albanian-Slav hostility would not spill over from Kosovo into Macedonia.

Montenegro had been the first Yugoslav republic where communist leaders held talks with the political opposition; in January

1990, Montenegro proposed a nationwide multiparty system for Yugoslavia. The talks grew out of the "Montenegrin Uprising" of 1989, in which mass demonstrations unseated the entire communist leadership and replaced it with a generation of younger communists seen as antibureaucratic reformers. But reformist zeal decreased in the next two years; republic multiparty elections were finally held in December 1990, but the League of Communists of Montenegro won 86 of the 125 assembly seats in a process marked by controversy and irregularities. Its candidate, Momir Bulatović, was elected president. Of the seven parties posting candidates in the election, four won seats.

In the first multiparty election, the major Montenegrin parties agreed on several key positions: a sovereign Montenegro within a united Yugoslav federation; conversion to a market economy, with partial or complete rejection of socialism; and integration of Yugoslavia into the EEC. Issues of dispute were the nature and pace of economic reform, the structure of the new federal Yugoslavia, and the advisable strategy for Montenegro should the federation dissolve. In spite of the reformist tendency of Montenegrin communists, the republic backed Milošević in most of his disputes with the northern republics. In March 1991, Prime Minister Milo Djukanović of Montenegro joined Milošević in a statement that expressed identical goals for Yugoslavia as a federation and for their respective republics. In the second half of 1991, Montenegro supported the Serbian diplomatic and military positions against Croatia, and YPA troops staged maneuvers against Croatia's Adriatic coastal cities from bases in Montenegro.

October 31, 1991

* * *

In the months following completion of this manuscript, Serbian guerrillas and YPA forces continued to advance into Croatia and pound Croatian strongholds in Vukovar, Dubrovnik, Osijek, and other locations. Vukovar, in northeastern Croatia, was designated for all-out defense by the Croats; after intense bombardment and almost complete destruction, the city surrendered in November. The medieval structures of Dubrovnik were threatened by heavy Serbian bombardment, arousing international protest. Croatian blockades of YPA garrisons and ostensible Croatian atrocities were the pretext for continued YPA action at the same time as Croatia requested that the EC or the UN negotiate a settlement.

De facto control of the YPA came into question in November, when Milošević and Tudjman both requested that a UN peacekeeping force separate the two sides, but continued fighting prevented such a force from being deployed. The failure of EC-arranged cease-fires between October and December brought speculation that the YPA was fighting independently for its own survival, beyond the control of either the federal government or Milošević's Serbian government. YPA spokesmen admitted that some units were moving outside the central command. Meanwhile, maintenance of the YPA effort put new stress on the already staggering national economy.

No agency of the federal government asserted influence over the struggle in Croatia at the end of 1991. The State Presidency, nominally in command of the YPA, lost its last vestige of ethnic balance when Croat Stipe Mešić resigned his position as president of the State Presidency in December, leaving the national executive in the hands of pro-Serbian delegates. In November one chamber of the Federal Assembly voted no confidence in Prime Minister Marković, and the second chamber threatened to force his resignation by following suit. Marković resigned in December to protest the proposed 1992 "war budget," over 80 percent of which was designated for the military.

Thus, control of events moved even further from the center to the republics, which showed no inclination to cede autonomy for the sake of reestablishing a credible central government. Instead, distrust and mutual hostility grew as each jurisdiction protected its own interests in the new power vacuum. Slovenia and Croatia entered 1992 anticipating recognition of their independence by the EC, while Montenegro, the strongest backer of Serbian military action in Croatia, established an independent position in favor of a peaceful resolution of the national crisis. In October Montenegro split from Serbia by supporting an EC call for transformation of Yugoslavia into an association of sovereign republics.

Croatia, meanwhile, had pressed hard for EC recognition as a key step toward gaining UN membership and full national status in possible UN-sponsored negotiations with the Serbs. In December 1991, the EC, under strong pressure from Germany, announced that it would recognize the independence of Slovenia, Croatia, and any other Yugoslav republic satisfying human rights and political requirements; the EC also officially named Serbia the aggressor in the Croatian conflict. Some EC members and the United States, however, feared that de jure Croatian independence would further inflame the conflict with Serbia or extend it into multiethnic Bosnia and Hercegovina.

Milošević reacted to the EC announcement by issuing charges that German expansionist ambitions were behind the EC position and that international recognition of Yugoslav republics would expand the civil war. At the end of 1991, Serbia sought to consolidate the advantages gained in recent months by settling Serbs in areas deserted by their Croatian populations, and plans were announced to make Krajina a separate Yugoslav republic.

At the beginning of 1992, most of Yugoslavia's major political and economic questions remained unanswered. One republic, Slovenia, seemingly had enough resources and a geopolitical position suitable to survival as an independent state. In 1991 it had already strengthened cultural and economic relations with West European nations, especially Austria and Germany, and had shed many of the remnants of the old Yugoslav centralized economic system—steps that promised rapid integration into Western market systems. In 1991 Slovenian officials, especially Foreign Secretary Dimitrij Rupel, traveled widely in the West to overcome international reluctance to recognize Slovenia. When initial Serbian resistance to its independence ended, Slovenia was completely free of political obligations to the Yugoslav federation.

Croatia, with its long history of nationalist independence movements and a relatively prosperous economy, remained entangled in the militant demands of its Serbian minority and ultranationalist Croats, its economy disrupted by the Serbian occupation, destruction of urban centers, and a massive refugee movement. A substantial radical nationalist faction threatened to overthrow Tudjman if he reached a compromise peace agreement with Serbia. This meant that the policy-making alternatives of both Tudjman and Milošević were narrowed by the extremist sentiments they themselves had aroused. Nevertheless, Croatia's hopes for true independence rested on international mediation in 1992 of its thorny territorial disputes with Serbia. Following the fifteenth cease-fire, imposed in December 1991, Serbia and the YPA agreed to allow a UN peacekeeping force to assume the role of protecting the Serbs in Croatia prior to final settlement and to remove all occupation forces from Croatian territory. The UN force headquarters was to be in Banja Luka, Bosnia, midway between the battle areas of Slavonia and the Adriatic coast. In January 1992, the main obstacle to introducing the UN force was continued military activity by irregular Serbian forces not controlled by the YPA or by any government.

Serbia's resources were increasingly taxed by the war with Croatia, by the decrepit state of its economy, and by growing isolation in Europe. Increased separatist activity in Kosovo threatened to open a second front for the YPA, and opposition groups also grew stronger in Vojvodina. For these reasons, Serbia revised its goals late in 1991 to include domination of a reduced Yugoslav federation. Serbian planners envisioned that the state would include most of the Serbian nationals in Croatia and Bosnia and Hercegovina, loyal ally Montenegro, and Macedonia. As 1991 ended, the Milošević government faced increased pressure from democratic opposition factions to end the war, reform the economy, and follow the other republics seeking the benefits of integration into the European community. At that time, 50 percent of Serbs polled described war against Croatia as a mistake. Although the Milošević government continued its anti-Croatian rhetoric, its conditions for a UN peacekeeping force had eased considerably by January 1992.

Meanwhile, to avoid being absorbed in the new Serbian federation, Macedonia and Bosnia and Hercegovina reaffirmed their 1991 declarations of sovereignty by requesting recognition by the EC, which promised to use human rights and commitment to democracy as the standards for recognition. European support was especially important for Bosnia and Hercegovina, where an uneasy peace among the Serbs, Croats, and Muslim Slavs was threatened by proposals to unite all Serbs in a single nation. Although some factions in Montenegro also showed discomfort at the prospect of Serbian domination, Montenegro did not leave the Serbian sphere by immediately seeking EC recognition. For all the actors, including Serbia, an important goal for 1992 was to cultivate a positive image and communication with the outside world. For the less powerful, this course could confer the recognition that might protect them from being swallowed into a new Greater Serbia. In designing their new policies, all five non-Serbian republics entered 1992 under competent popularly elected leaders: Tudjman in Croatia, Izetbegović in Bosnia and Hercegovina, Kiro Gligorov in Macedonia, Bulatović in Montenegro, and Kučan in Slovenia.

The Croatian conflict was the bloodiest war in Europe since World War II. Because the United States was far removed and the Soviet Union had ceased to exist, the military and political resolution of the conflict became an entirely European problem. The conflict accelerated a natural movement of the republics toward the economic stability of the EC and officially ended the era of Titoist nonalignment. Yugoslavia, a paragon of economic self-sufficiency twenty years before, had finally dissolved into units with sharply varying potential prosperity. Although these units had as little in common in 1992 as they had had in 1972, all of them, including Serbia, looked to Western Europe to help them salvage some of their postwar gains in the new and uncertain era that lay ahead in 1992.

January 1, 1992   Glenn E. Curtis

Chapter 1. Historical Setting

Patriarchal Monastery near Peć, Kosovo; from thirteenth to eighteenth century, served as seat of administration for Serbian Orthodox Church

YUGOSLAVIA IS THE COMPLEX PRODUCT of a complex history. The country's confusing and conflicting mosaic of peoples, languages, religions, and cultures took shape during centuries of turmoil after the collapse of the Roman Empire. By the early nineteenth century, two great empires, the Austrian and the Ottoman, ruled all the modern-day Yugoslav lands except Montenegro. As the century progressed, however, nationalist feelings awoke in the region's diverse peoples, the Turkish grip began to weaken, and Serbia won its independence.

Discontent with the existing order brought calls for a union of South Slav peoples: Slovenian and Croatian thinkers proposed a South Slav kingdom within the Austrian Empire, while Serbian intellectuals envisaged a fully independent South Slav state. By the end of the century, the Ottoman Empire was disintegrating, and Austria-Hungary, Serbia, and other powers vied to gain a share of the empire's remaining Balkan lands. The conflict of those ambitions unleashed the forces that destroyed the old European order in World War I.

The idea of a South Slav kingdom flourished during World War I, but the collapse of Austria-Hungary eliminated the possibility of a South Slav kingdom under Austrian sponsorship. Fear of Italian domination drove some leaders of the Slovenes and Croats to unite with Serbia in a single kingdom under the Serbian dynasty in 1918. Political infighting and nationalist strife plagued this kingdom during the interwar years. When democratic institutions proved ineffectual, Serbian dictatorship took over, and the kingdom collapsed in violence after the Axis powers invaded in 1941.

During World War II, communist-led Partisans (see Glossary) waged a victorious guerrilla struggle against foreign occupiers, Croatian fascists, and supporters of the prewar government. This struggle led to the rebirth of Yugoslavia as a socialist federation under communist rule on November 29, 1945. Under Josip Broz Tito, Yugoslav communists were faithful to orthodox Stalinism until a 1948 split with Moscow. At that time, a Soviet-led economic blockade compelled the Yugoslavs to devise an economic system based on socialist self-management. To this system, the Yugoslavs added a nonaligned foreign policy and an idiosyncratic, one-party political system. This system maintained a semblance of unity during most of Tito's four decades of unquestioned rule. Soon after his death in 1980, however, long-standing differences again separated the communist parties of the country's republics and provinces. Economic turmoil and the reemergence of an old conflict between the Serbs and the ethnic Albanian majority in Kosovo exacerbated these differences, fueled a resurgence of nationalism, and paralyzed the country's political decision-making mechanism.

Pre-Slav History

Ancient peoples inhabited the lands that now make up Yugoslavia for millennia before Rome conquered the region in the first century A.D. Archeological findings reveal that during the Paleolithic period (ca. 200,000–8000 B.C.) man's ancestors hunted and foraged in the mountains, valleys, and interior plains of today's Yugoslavia. In the Mesolithic period (8000–6000 B.C.), man expanded the use of tools and weapons and settled throughout the country. Farming came to the area at the dawn of the Neolithic period (6000–2800 B.C.) and spread throughout the region by 4000 B.C. Yugoslavia's Neolithic inhabitants planted cereal grains, raised livestock, fished, hunted, wove simple textiles, built houses of wood or mud, and made coarse pottery and implements.

Man began working with pure copper in the region in the third millennium B.C. During the Bronze Age (2800–700 B.C.), the population grew, settlements multiplied, and craftsmen began casting ornaments, tools, and weapons. After about 1450 B.C., smiths began working with locally mined gold and silver, horses and chariots became more common, and trade routes stretched to northern Europe and the Aegean. During the Iron Age (beginning 700 B.C.), trade flourished between the developing city-states of Italy and Greece and the region's first identifiable peoples: Illyrian-speaking tribes north of Lake Ohrid and west of the Vardar River (in present-day Macedonia), Thracian speakers in the area of modern Serbia, and the Veneti, who probably spoke an Italic tongue, in Istria and the Julian Alps (in present-day Slovenia and northwest Croatia).

Greeks set up trading posts along the eastern Adriatic coast after 600 B.C. and founded colonies there in the fourth century B.C. Greek influence proved ephemeral, however, and the native tribes remained herdsmen and warriors. Bardylis, a tribal chief of Illyria (present-day northwest Yugoslavia), assumed control of much of Macedonia in 360 B.C. Philip II and his son, Alexander the Great, later united Macedonia and campaigned as far north as present-day Serbia. In the fourth century B.C., invading Celts forced the Illyrians southward from the northern Adriatic coast, and over several centuries a mixed Celtic-Illyrian culture arose in much of modern Slovenia, Croatia, and Serbia, producing wheel-turned pottery, jewelry, and iron tools.

In the third century B.C., Rome conquered the west Adriatic coast and began exerting influence on the opposite shore. Greek allegations that the Illyrians were disrupting commerce and plundering coastal towns helped precipitate a Roman punitive strike in 229 B.C., and in subsequent campaigns Rome forced Illyrian rulers to pay tribute. Roman armies often crossed Illyria during the Roman-Macedonian wars, and in 168 B.C. Rome conquered the Illyrians and destroyed the Macedonia of Philip and Alexander. For many years, the Dinaric Alps sheltered resistance forces, but Roman dominance increased. In 35 B.C., the emperor Octavian conquered the coastal region and seized inland Celtic and Illyrian strongholds; in A.D. 9, Tiberius consolidated Roman control of the western Balkan Peninsula; and by A.D. 14, Rome had subjugated the Celts in what is now Serbia. The Romans brought order to the region, and their inventive genius produced lasting monuments. But Rome's most significant legacy to the region was the separation of the empire's Byzantine and Roman spheres (the Eastern and Western Roman Empires, respectively), which created a cultural chasm that would divide East from West, Eastern Orthodox from Roman Catholic, and Serb from Croat and Slovene.

Over the next 500 years, Latin culture permeated the region. The Romans divided their western Balkan territories into separate provinces. New roads linked fortresses, mines, and trading towns. The Romans introduced viticulture in Dalmatia, instituted slavery, and dug new mines. Agriculture thrived in the Danube Basin, and towns throughout the country blossomed into urban areas with forums, temples, water systems, coliseums, and public baths. In addition to gods of the Greco-Roman pantheon, Roman legionnaires brought the mystic cult of Mithras from Persia. The Roman army also recruited natives of the conquered regions, and five sons of Illyrian peasants rose through the ranks to become emperor. The Illyrian, Celtic, and Thracian languages all eventually died out, but the centuries of Roman domination failed to create cultural uniformity.

Internal strife and an economic crisis rocked the empire in the third century A.D., and two ethnic Illyrian emperors, born in areas now in Yugoslavia, took decisive steps to prolong the empire's life. Emperor Diocletian, born in Dalmatia, established strong central control and a bureaucracy, abolished the last Roman republican institutions, and persecuted Christians in an attempt to make them identify more with the state than the church. Emperor Constantine, born near Niš, reunited the empire after years of turmoil, established dynastic succession, founded a new capital at Byzantium in A.D. 330, and legalized Christianity.

In A.D. 395, the sons of Emperor Theodosius split the empire into eastern and western halves. The division, which became a permanent feature of the European cultural landscape, separated Greek Constantinople (as Byzantium was renamed in A.D. 330) from Latin Rome and eventually the Eastern Orthodox and Roman Catholic churches. It likewise separated the lands in what is now Yugoslavia, exercising a critical influence on the Serbs and Croats. Economic and administrative breakdown soon softened the empire's defenses, especially in the western half, and barbarian tribes began to attack. In the fourth century, the Goths sacked Roman fortresses along the Danube River, and in A.D. 448 the Huns ravaged Sirmium (now Sremska Mitrovica northwest of present-day Belgrade), Singidunum (now Belgrade), and Emona (now Ljubljana). The Ostrogoths had conquered Dalmatia and other provinces by 493. Emperor Justinian drove the invaders out in the sixth century, but the defenses of the empire proved inadequate to maintain this gain.

Slavic tribesmen poured across the empire's borders during the fifth and sixth centuries. The Slavs, characteristically sedentary farming and livestock-raising tribes, spoke an Indo-European language and organized themselves into clans ruled by a council of family chiefs. All land and significant wealth was held in common. In the sixth century, the Slavs allied with the more powerful Avars to plunder the Danube Basin. Together, they erased almost all trace of Christian life in Dalmatia and the northwestern parts of present-day Yugoslavia. In A.D. 626, these tribes surrounded Constantinople itself. The Avar incursions proved key to the subsequent development of Yugoslavia because they immediately preceded, and may have precipitated, the arrival of the Serbs and Croats.

Histories of the Yugoslav Peoples to World War I

Before Yugoslavia became a nation, the Slovenes, Croats, Serbs, Montenegrins, Bosnians, Macedonians, and Albanians had virtually independent histories. The Slovenes struggled to define and defend their cultural identity for a millennium, first under the Frankish Kingdom and then under the Austrian Empire. The Croats of Croatia and Slavonia enjoyed a brief independence before falling under Hungarian and Austrian domination; and the Croats in Dalmatia struggled under Byzantine, Hungarian, Venetian, French, and Austrian rule. The Serbs, who briefly rivaled the Byzantine Empire in medieval times, suffered 500 years of Turkish domination before winning independence in the nineteenth century. Their Montenegrin kinsmen lived for centuries under a dynasty of bishop-priests and savagely defended their mountain

Palace of Roman Emperor Diocletian, Split
Courtesy Sam and Sarah Stulberg

homeland against foreign aggressors. Bosnians turned to heresy to protect themselves from external political and religious pressure, converted in great numbers to Islam after the Turks invaded, and became a nuisance to Austria-Hungary in the late nineteenth century. A hodgepodge of ethnic groups peopled Macedonia over the centuries. As the power of the Ottoman Empire waned, the region was contested among the Serbs, Bulgars, Greeks, and Albanians and also was a pawn among the major European powers. Finally, the disputed Kosovo region, with an Albanian majority and medieval Serbian tradition, remained an Ottoman backwater until after the Balkan wars of the early twentieth century.

The Slovenes

The Slovenes, a Slavic people, migrated southwestward across present-day Romania in about the sixth century A.D. and settled in the Julian Alps. They apparently enjoyed broad autonomy in the seventh century, after escaping Avar domination. The Franks overran the Slovenes in the late eighth century; during the rule of the Frankish king Charlemagne, German nobles began enserfing the Slovenes, and German missionaries baptized them in the Latin rite. Emperor Otto I incorporated most of the Slovenian lands into the duchy of Carantania in 952; later rulers split the duchy

7

into Carinthia, Carniola, and Styria. In 1278 the Slovenian lands fell to the Austrian Habsburgs, who controlled them until 1918.

Turkish marauders plagued Carinthia, Carniola, and Styria in the sixteenth and seventeenth centuries. The Slovenes abandoned lands vulnerable to attack and raised bulwarks around churches to protect themselves. The Turkish conquest of the Balkans and Hungary also disrupted the Slovenian economy; to compensate, the nobles stiffened feudal obligations and crushed peasant revolts between 1478 and 1573.

In the tumult of the sixteenth century, German nobles in the three Slovenian provinces clamored for greater autonomy, embraced the Protestant Reformation, and drew many Slovenes away from the Catholic Church. The Reformation sparked the Slovenes' first cultural awakening. In 1550 Primoz Trubar published the first Slovenian-language book, a catechism. He later produced a translation of the New Testament and printed other Slovenian religious books in the Latin and Cyrillic (see Glossary) scripts. Ljubljana had a printing press by 1575, but the authorities closed it when Jurij Dalmatin tried to publish a translation of the Bible. Slovenian publishing activity then shifted to Germany, where Dalmatin published his Bible with a glossary enabling Croats to read it. The Counterreformation accelerated in Austria in the early seventeenth century, and in 1628 the emperor forced Protestants to choose between Catholicism and exile. Jesuit counterreformers burned Slovenian Protestant literature and took other measures that retarded diversification of Slovenian culture but failed to stifle it completely. Some Jesuits preached and composed hymns in Slovenian, opened schools, taught from an expurgated edition of Dalmatin's Bible, and sent Slovenian students to Austrian universities. Nonetheless, Slovenian remained a peasant idiom, and the higher social classes spoke German or Italian.

Slovenian economic links with Germany and Italy strengthened in the seventeenth and eighteenth centuries, and living conditions improved. The Vienna-Trieste trade route crossed through the Slovenian cities of Maribor and Ljubljana. Agricultural products and raw materials were exported over this trade route, and exotic goods were imported from the East. Despite his campaign to Germanize the Austrian Empire, Emperor Joseph II (1780–90) encouraged translation of educational materials into Slovenian. He also distributed monastic lands, workshops, and fisheries to Slovenian entrepreneurs.

By the end of the eighteenth century, Slovenian prosperity had yielded a self-reliant middle class that sent its sons to study in Vienna and Paris. They returned steeped in the views of the Enlightenment and bent on rational examination of their own culture. Slovenian intellectuals began writing in Slovenian rather than German, and they introduced the idea of a Slovenian nation. Between 1788 and 1791, Anton Linhart wrote an antifeudal, anticlerical history of the Slovenes that depicted them for the first time as a single people. In 1797 Father Valentin Vodnik composed Slovenian poetry and founded the first Slovenian newspaper.

After several victories over Austria, Napoleon incorporated the Slovenian provinces and other Austrian lands into the French Empire as the Illyrian Provinces, with the capital at Ljubljana. Despite unpopular new tax and conscription laws, Slovenian intellectuals welcomed the French, who issued proclamations in Slovenian as well as in German and French, built roads, reformed the government, appointed Slovenes to official posts, and opened Slovenian-language schools for both sexes. France strengthened the national self-awareness of the Slovenes and other South Slavs in the Illyrian Provinces by promoting the concept of Illyria as a common link among Slovenes, Croats, and Serbs. This concept later evolved into the idea of uniting the South Slavs in an independent state.

Austria reasserted its dominance of the Slovenes in 1813 and rescinded the French reforms. Slovenian intellectuals, however, continued refining the Slovenian language and national identity, while Austria strove to confine their activities to the cultural sphere. The pro-Austrian philologist and linguist Jernej Kopitar pioneered comparative Slavic linguistics and created a Slovenian literary language from numerous local dialects, hoping to strengthen the monarchy and Catholicism. France Prešeren, perhaps the greatest Slovenian poet, worked to transform the Slovenian peasant idiom into a refined language. In the 1840s, Slovenian audiences heard the first official public speech delivered in Slovenian and the first Slovenian songs sung in a theater. In 1843 Janez Blajvajs founded a practical journal for peasants and craftsmen that carried the cultural movement beyond the upper class to the masses.

Revolution convulsed Europe in 1848, and demonstrators in cities throughout the Austrian Empire called for constitutional monarchy. Crowds in Ljubljana cheered the apparent downfall of the old order. Intellectual groups drafted the Slovenes' first political platforms. Some programs called for an autonomous ''Unified Slovenia'' within the empire; others supported unification of the South Slavs into an Illyrian state linked with Austria or Germany. The 1848 revolutions swept away serfdom in the Austrian Empire, but the political movement of the Slovenes made little headway before the Austrian government regained control and imposed absolutist rule. In the 1850s and early 1860s, the campaigns of Slovenian leaders were again restricted to the cultural sphere.

Military defeats in 1859 and 1866 exposed the internal weakness of the Austrian Empire, and in 1867 Austria attempted to revitalize itself by joining with Hungary to form the Dual Monarchy (see Glossary). In the late 1860s, Slovenian leaders, convinced of the empire's imminent collapse, resurrected the dream of a united Slovenia. They staged mass rallies, agitated for use of the Slovenian language in schools and local government, and sought support from the Croats and other South Slavs. When the threat to the survival of Austria-Hungary waned after 1871, the Slovenes withdrew their support for a South Slav union and adapted themselves to political life within the Dual Monarchy. The conservative coalition that ruled Austria from 1879 to 1893 made minor cultural concessions to the Slovenes, including use of Slovenian in schools and local administration in some areas. Slovenes controlled the local assembly of Carniola after 1883, and Ljubljana had a Slovenian mayor after 1888.

In 1907 Austria instituted universal male suffrage, which encouraged Slovenian politicians that the empire would eventually fulfill the Slovenes' national aspirations. In October 1908, Austria annexed Bosnia and Hercegovina. The annexation sharpened the national self-awareness of the South Slavs and generated rumors of impending war with Serbia. Troop mobilization began. However, the main Slovenian parties welcomed the annexation as a step toward a union of the empire's South Slavs. Tensions eased after six months, but Austria-Hungary, fearing pan-Slavism (see Glossary), conducted witch hunts for disloyal Slavs. In 1909 Slovenian party leaders criticized Vienna for mistreating the Slavs, but the possibilities of a South Slav union within the empire declined. Demands rose for creation of an independent South Slav nation, and a socialist conference in Ljubljana even called for the cultural unification of all South Slavs. Such appeals began a heated debate on the implications of unification for Slovenian culture.

The Croats and Their Territories

Most historians believe that the Croats are a purely Slavic people who probably migrated to the Balkans from present-day Ukraine. A newer theory, however, holds that the original Croats were nomadic Sarmatians who roamed Central Asia, migrated onto the steppes around 200 B.C., and rode into Europe near the end of the fourth century A.D., possibly together with the Huns. The Sarmatian Croats, the theory holds, conquered the Slavs of northern Bohemia and southern Poland and formed a small state called

White Croatia near present-day Kraków. The Croats then supposedly mingled with their more numerous Slavic subjects and adopted the Slavic language, while the subjects assumed the tribal name "Croat."

A tenth-century Byzantine source reports that in the seventh century Emperor Heraclius enlisted the Croats to expel the Avars from Byzantine lands. The Croats overran the Avars and Slavs in Dalmatia around 630 and then drove the Avars from today's Slovenia and other areas. In the eighth century, the Croats lived under loose Byzantine rule, and Christianity and Latin culture recovered in the coastal cities. The Franks subjugated most of the Croats in the eighth century and sent missionaries to baptize them in the Latin rite, but the Byzantine Empire continued to rule Dalmatia.

Croatia emerged as an independent nation in 924. Tomislav (910–ca. 928), a tribal leader, established himself as the first king of Croatia, ruling a domain that stretched eastward to the Danube. Croatia and Venice struggled to dominate Dalmatia as the power of Byzantium faded, and for a time the Dalmatians paid the Croats tribute to ensure safe passage for their galleys through the Adriatic. After the Great Schism of 1054 split the Roman and Byzantine churches, Normans (probably with papal support) besieged Byzantine cities in Dalmatia. In 1075 a papal legate crowned Dmitrije Zvonimir (1076–89) king of Croatia.

A faction of nobles contesting the succession after the death of Zvonimir offered the Croatian throne to King László I of Hungary. In 1091 László accepted, and in 1094 he founded the Zagreb bishopric, which later became the ecclesiastical center of Croatia. Another Hungarian king, Kálmán, crushed opposition after the death of László and won the crown of Dalmatia and Croatia in 1102. The crowning of Kálmán forged a link between the Croatian and Hungarian crowns that lasted until the end of World War I. Croats have maintained for centuries that Croatia remained a sovereign state despite the voluntary union of the two crowns, but Hungarians claim that Hungary annexed Croatia outright in 1102. In either case, Hungarian culture permeated Croatia, the Croatian-Hungarian border shifted often, and at times Hungary treated Croatia as a vassal state. Croatia, however, had its own local governor, or *ban;* a privileged landowning nobility; and an assembly of nobles, the Sabor.

The joining of the Croatian and Hungarian crowns automatically made Hungary and Venice rivals for domination of Dalmatia. Hungary sought access to the sea, while Venice wished to secure its trade routes to the eastern Mediterranean and to use Dalmatian timber for shipbuilding. Between 1115 and 1420, the two powers waged twenty-one wars for control of the region, and Dalmatian cities changed hands repeatedly. Serbia and Bosnia also competed for Dalmatia. Serbia seized the coast south of the Gulf of Kotor on the southern Adriatic around 1196 and held it for 150 years; Bosnia dominated central Dalmatia during the late fourteenth century. Dalmatian cities struggled to remain autonomous by playing off one power against the others. Most successful in this strategy was Dubrovnik, whose riches and influence at times rivaled those of Venice. In the fourteenth century, Dubrovnik became the first Christian power to establish treaty relations with the Ottoman Empire, which was then advancing across the Balkans. Dubrovnik prospered by mediating between Europe and the new Ottoman provinces in Europe and by exporting precious metals, raw materials, agricultural goods, and slaves. After centuries as the only free South Slav political entity, the city waned in power following a severe earthquake in 1667.

In 1409 Ladislas of Naples, a claimant to the throne of Hungary, sold Venice his rights to Dalmatia. By 1420 Venice controlled virtually all of Dalmatia except Dubrovnik. The Venetians made Dalmatia their poorest, most backward province: they reduced Dalmatian local autonomy, cut the forests, and stifled industry. Venice also restricted education, so that Zadar, the administrative center of Dalmatia, lacked even a printing press until 1796. Despite centuries of struggle for dominance of the region and exploitation by Venice, Dalmatia produced several first-rate artists and intellectuals, including the sculptor Radovan, architect and sculptor Juraj Dalmatinac, writer Ivan Gundulić, and scientist Rudjer Bosković.

Ottoman armies overran all of Croatia south of the Sava River in the early sixteenth century and slaughtered a weak Hungarian force at the Battle of Mohács in 1526. Buda was captured in 1541, and then Turkish marauders advanced toward Austria. After Mohács, Hungarian and Croatian nobles elected the Habsburg Ferdinand I of Austria king of Hungary and Croatia. To tighten its grip on Croatia and solidify its defenses, Austria restricted the powers of the Sabor, established a military border across Croatia, and recruited Germans, Hungarians, and Serbs and other Slavs to serve as peasant border guards (see fig. 2). This practice was the basis for the ethnic patchwork that survives today in Croatia, Slavonia, and Vojvodina. Austria assumed direct control of the border lands and gave local independence and land to families who agreed to settle and guard those lands. The area that they settled became known as the Military Frontier Province. Orthodox border families also won freedom of worship, which drew stiff opposition from the Roman Catholic Church.

Turkish inroads in Croatia and Austria also triggered price increases for agricultural goods, and opportunistic landowners began demanding payment in kind, rather than cash, from serfs. Rural discontent exploded in 1573 when Matija Gubec led an organized peasant rebellion that spread quickly before panic-stricken nobles were able to quell it.

Religious ferment in Europe affected Croatian culture in the sixteenth century. Many Croatian and Dalmatian nobles embraced the Protestant Reformation in the mid-sixteenth century, and in 1562 Stipan Konzul and Anton Dalmatin published the first Croatian Bible. The Counterreformation began in Croatia and Dalmatia in the early seventeenth century, and the most powerful Protestant noblemen soon reconverted. In 1609 the Sabor voted to allow only the Catholic faith in Croatia. The Counterreformation enhanced the cultural development of Croatia. Jesuits founded schools and published grammars, a dictionary, and religious books that helped shape the Croatian literary language. Franciscans preached the Counterreformation in Ottoman-held regions.

Western forces routed a Turkish army besieging Vienna in 1683 and then began driving the Turks from Europe. In the 1699 Treaty of Karlowitz, the Turks ceded most of Hungary, Croatia, and Slavonia to Austria, and by 1718 they no longer threatened Dalmatia. During the Western advance, Austria expanded its military border, and thousands of Serbs fleeing Turkish oppression settled as border guards in Slavonia and southern Hungary. As the Turkish threat waned, Croatian nobles demanded reincorporation of the military border into Croatia. Austria, which used the guards as an inexpensive standing military force, rejected these demands, and the guards themselves opposed abrogation of their special privileges.

From 1780 to 1790, Joseph II of Austria introduced reforms that exposed ethnic and linguistic rivalries. Among other things, Joseph brought the empire under strict central control and decreed that German replace Latin as the official language of the empire. This decree enraged the Hungarians, who rejected Germanization and fought to make their language, Magyar, the official language of Hungary. The Croats, fearing both Germanization and Magyarization, defended Latin. In 1790, when Joseph died, Hungary was on the verge of rebellion. Joseph's successor, Leopold II, abandoned centralization and Germanization when he signed laws ensuring Hungary's status as an independent kingdom under an Austrian king. The next Austrian emperor, Francis I, stifled Hungarian political development for almost four decades, during which Magyarization was not an issue.

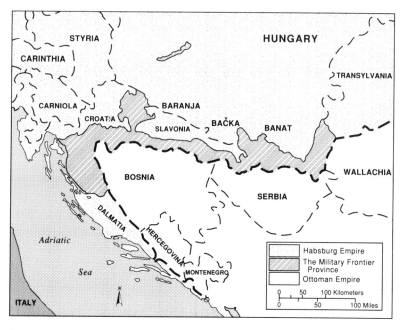

Source: Based on information from United Kingdom, Admiralty, Naval Intelligence Division, *Yugoslavia, 2: History, Peoples, and Administration,* London, 1944, 20.

Figure 2. Military Frontier Province Between the Habsburg and Ottoman Empires, ca. 1600–1800

Venice repulsed Ottoman attacks on Dalmatia for several centuries after the Battle of Mohács, and it helped to push the Turks from the coastal area after 1693. But by the late eighteenth century, trade routes had shifted, Venice had declined, and Dalmatian ships stood idle. Napoleon ended the Venetian Republic and defeated Austria; he then incorporated Dalmatia, Dubrovnik, and western Croatia as the French Illyrian Provinces. France stimulated agriculture and commerce in the provinces, fought piracy, enhanced the status of the Orthodox population, and stirred a Croatian national awakening. In 1814 the military border and Dalmatia returned to Austria when Napoleon was defeated; Hungary regained Croatia and Slavonia. In 1816 Austria transformed most of the Illyrian Provinces into the Kingdom of Illyria, an administrative unit designed to counterbalance radical Hungarian nationalism and co-opt nascent movements for union of the South Slavs. Austria kept Dalmatia for itself and reduced the privileges of the Dalmatian nobles.

The Croatian-Hungarian language conflict reemerged in the 1830s as Hungarian reformers grew more critical of Austrian domination. French-educated Croatian leaders, fearing Hungarian linguistic and political domination, began promoting the Croatian language and formation of a Slavic kingdom within the Austrian Empire. In 1832, for the first time in centuries, a Croatian noble addressed the Sabor in Croatian. With tacit Austrian approval, Ljudevit Gaj, a journalist and linguist, promoted a South Slavic literary language, devised a Latin-based script, and in 1836 founded an anti-Hungarian journal that called for Illyrian cultural and political unity. Hungary feared the Illyrian movement and banned even public utterance of the word ''Illyria.'' In 1843 the Hungarian assembly voted to make Magyar the official language of Hungary and Slavonia and eventually to make it the official language in Hungarian-Croatian relations. Croats called the law an infringement on their autonomy, saturated Vienna with petitions for separation from Hungary, and returned to Budapest all documents sent them in Hungarian.

Hungary rose against Austria during the revolutions that swept Europe in 1848. The Croats, rightly fearing Hungarian chauvinism and expecting union of Croatia, Slavonia, and Dalmatia, sided with Austria. Ban Josip Jelačić led an army that attacked the Hungarian revolutionary forces. His units soon withdrew, but Russian troops invaded Hungary to crush the revolution. Despite their loyalty to Austria, the Croats received only the abolition of serfdom. Rather than uniting the Slavic regions as promised, the emperor suspended the constitution and introduced absolutist rule and Germanization.

Austria ended absolutist rule in 1860, and a military defeat in 1866 brought the empire to the brink of collapse. In 1867 Emperor Franz Joseph entered the Dual Monarchy with Hungary, uniting the two states under a single crown. Conflicting interests kept Austria-Hungary from uniting the South Slavs: Croatia and Slavonia fell under Hungarian control, while Austria retained Dalmatia. In 1868 a Sabor dominated by pro-Hungarian deputies adopted the Nagodba, or compromised, which affirmed that Hungary and Croatia constituted distinct political units within the empire. Croatia obtained autonomy in internal matters, but finance and other Croatian-Hungarian or Austro-Hungarian concerns required approval from Budapest and Vienna. Hungarian leaders considered that the Nagodba provided ample home rule for Croatia, but Croatia opposed it strongly. A subsequent election law guaranteed pro-Hungarian landowners and officials a majority in the Sabor and increased Croatian hatred for Hungarian domination. Croatian members of the Hungarian assembly then resorted to obstructionism to enhance their meager influence.

After 1868 the Croatian leadership was divided between advocates of a South Slav union and nationalists favoring a Greater Croatia; a bitter rivalry developed between the Croats and Serbs. Bishop Josip Strossmayer dominated the Croatian South Slav movement and supported liturgical concessions to help reduce the religious differences dividing Croats and Serbs. In pursuit of a South Slav cultural union, he founded the South Slav Academy of Arts and Sciences in 1867 and the University of Zagreb in 1874. Ante Starčević opposed Strossmayer, pressed for a Greater Croatia, and founded an extreme nationalist party. In 1881 Austria-Hungary reincorporated the military border into Croatia, increasing the number of ethnic Serbs in Croatia to about 25 percent of its 2.6 million population. The change raised ethnic tensions. The Croats' ill will toward Hungary and ethnic Serbs deepened under Ban Karoly Khuen-Héderváry (1883–1903), who ignored the Nagodba and exploited the Croatian-Serbian rivalry to promote Magyarization. In 1903 Hungary rejected Croatian demands for financial independence, quelled demonstrations, and suppressed the Croatian press. After 1903 moderate Croats and ethnic Serbs found common ground, and by 1908 a Croatian-Serbian coalition won a majority in the Sabor and condemned Austria's annexation of Bosnia and Hercegovina. A new *ban*, hoping to split the coalition, brought bogus treason charges against ethnic Serbian leaders in Croatia; the subsequent trials scandalized Europe and strengthened the tenuous Croatian-Serbian coalition.

The Serbs and Serbia, Vojvodina, and Montenegro

Like the Croats, the Serbs are believed to be a purely Slavic people who originated in Ukraine. Some scholars now argue that the original Serbs were Central Asian Sarmatian nomads who entered Europe with the Huns in the fourth century A.D. The theory proposes that the Sarmatian Serbs settled in a land designated as White Serbia, in what is now Saxony and western Poland. The Sarmatian Serbs, it is argued, intermarried with the indigenous Slavs of the region, adopted their language, and transferred their name to the Slavs. Byzantine sources report that some Serbs migrated southward in the seventh century A.D. and eventually settled in the lands that now make up southern Serbia, Montenegro, Kosovo, and Bosnia and Hercegovina. Rival chiefs, or *župani*, vied to control the Serbs for five centuries after the migration. Zupan Vlastimir formed a Serbian principality under the Byzantines around 850, and the Serbs soon converted to Eastern-rite Christianity. The Serbs had two political centers in the eleventh century: Zeta, in the mountains of present-day Montenegro, and Raška, located in modern southwestern Serbia.

The *župan* of Raška, Stefan I Nemanja (1159–96), threw off Byzantine domination and laid the foundation for medieval Serbia by conquering Zeta and part of southern Dalmatia. His son and successor, Stefan II Nemanja (1196–1228), transformed Serbia into a stable state, friendly with Rome but with religious loyalty to Constantinople. In 1218 Pope Honorius III recognized Serbian political independence and crowned Stefan II. The writings of Stefan II and his brother (later canonized as St. Sava) were the first works of Serbian literature.

Later kings in the Nemanja line overcame internal rivalries and pressure from Bulgaria and Constantinople. They also rejected papal invitations to link the Serbian Orthodox Church with Rome, and they ruled their country through a golden age. Serbia expanded its economy, and Dalmatian merchants marketed Serbian goods throughout Europe and the Levant. The Nemanja Dynasty left to Serbia masterpieces of religious art combining Western, Byzantine, and local styles.

Serbia dominated the Balkans under Stefan Dušan (1331–55), who conquered lands extending from Belgrade to present-day southern Greece. He proclaimed himself emperor, elevated the archbishop of Peć to the level of patriarch, and wrote a new legal code combining Byzantine law with Serbian customs. Dušan had ambitions toward a weakened Byzantine Empire, but the Byzantine emperor suspected his intentions and summoned the Turks to restrain him. Dušan repelled assaults in 1345 and 1349 but was defeated in 1352. He then offered to lead an alliance against the Turks and recognize the pope, but those gambits also were rejected.

Rival nobles divided Serbia after the death of Dušan in 1355, and many switched loyalty to the sultan after the last Nemanja died in 1371. The most powerful Serbian prince, Lazar Hrebeljanović, raised a multinational force to engage the Turks in the Battle of Kosovo Polje on St. Vitus Day in 1389. The Turks barely defeated Lazar, and both he and the sultan were killed. The defeat did not bring immediate Turkish occupation of Serbia, but during the centuries of Turkish domination that followed, the Serbs endowed the battle with myths of honor and heroism that helped them preserve their dignity and sense of nationhood. Serbs still recite epic poems and sing songs about the nobles who fell at Kosovo Polje; the anniversary of the battle is the Serbian national holiday, Vidovdan (St. Vitus Day), June 28.

Civil war in the Ottoman Empire saved Serbia in the early fifteenth century, but the Turks soon reunited their forces to conquer the last Serbian stronghold at Smederjevo in 1459 and subjugate the whole country. Serbs fled to Hungary, Montenegro, Croatia, Dalmatia, and Bosnia, and some formed outlaw bands. In response to the activities of the latter, the Turks disinterred and burned the remains of St. Sava. By the sixteenth century, southern Hungary had a sizable Serbian population that remained after the Turks conquered the region in 1526. Montenegro, which emerged as an independent principality after the death of Dušan, waged continual guerrilla war on the Turks and never was conquered. But the Turkish threat did force Prince Ivan of Montenegro to move his capital high into the mountains. There, he founded a monastery and set up a printing press. In 1516 Montenegro became a theocratic state.

Social and economic life in Serbia changed radically under the absolute rule of the Turkish sultan. The Turks split Serbia among several provinces, conscripted Serbian boys into their elite forces, exterminated Serbian nobles, and deprived the Serbs of contact with the West as the Renaissance was beginning. The Turks used the Orthodox Church to mediate between the state and the peasantry, but they expropriated most church lands. Poorly trained Serbian priests strove to maintain the decaying national identity. In 1459 the sultan subordinated the Serbian church to the Greek patriarch, but the Serbs hated Greek dominance of their church, and in 1557 Grand Vizier Mehmed Pasha Sokolović, a Serb who had been inducted into the Turkish army as a boy, persuaded the sultan to restore autonomy to the Serbian church. Turkish maltreatment and exploitation grew in Serbia after the sixteenth century, and more Serbs fled to become mountain outlaws, or *hajduci*. Epic songs of the *hajduci* kept alive the Serbs' memory of the glorious independence of the past.

From 1684 to 1689, Christian forces attempted to push the Turks from the Balkans, inciting the Serbs to rebel against their Turkish overlords. The offensive and the rebellion ultimately failed, exposing the Serbs south of the Sava River to the revenge of the Turks. Fearing Turkish reprisals, the Serbian patriarch Arsenije III Carnojević emigrated in 1690 to Austrian-ruled southern Hungary with as many as 36,000 families. The Austrian emperor promised these people religious freedom and the right to elect their own *vojvoda,* or military governor, and incorporated much of the region where they settled, later known as Vojvodina, into the military border. The refugees founded new monasteries that became cultural centers. In Montenegro Danilo I Petrović of Njegoš (1696–1737) became bishop-prince and instituted the succession of the Petrović-Njegoš family. His efforts to unify Montenegro triggered a massacre of Muslims in 1702 and subsequent reprisals.

Austrian forces took Serbian regions south of the Sava from the Ottoman Empire in 1718, but Jesuits following the army proselytized so heavily that the Serbs came to hate the Austrians as well as the Turks. In the eighteenth century, the Turkish economy and social fabric began deteriorating, and the Serbs who remained under the Ottoman Empire suffered attacks from bands of soldiers. Corrupt Greek priests who had replaced Serbian clergy at the sultan's direction also took advantage of the Serbs. The Serbs in southern Hungary fared much better. They farmed prosperously in the fertile Danube Plain. A Serbian middle class arose, and the monasteries trained scholars and writers who inspired national pride, even among illiterate Serbs.

The eighteenth century brought Russian involvement in European events, particularly in competition with Austria for the spoils of the Turkish collapse. The Orthodox Serbs looked to the tsar for support, and Russia forged ties with Montenegro and the Serbian church in southern Hungary. In 1774 Russia won the diplomatic right to protect Christian subjects of the Turks; later it used this right as a pretext to intervene in Turkish affairs. When Russia and Austria fought another war with the Ottoman Empire in 1787 and 1788, Serbs fought guerrilla battles against the Turks. Austria abandoned the campaign, and the Serbs, in 1791. To secure their frontier, the Turks granted their Serbian subjects a measure of autonomy and formed a Serbian militia. Montenegro expanded in the late eighteenth and early nineteenth centuries. Bishop-Prince Petar I Njegoš (1782–1830) convinced the sultan to declare that the Montenegrins had never been Turkish subjects, and Montenegro remained independent through the nineteenth century.

In 1804 renegade Turkish soldiers in Belgrade murdered Serbian leaders, triggering a popular uprising under Karadjordje (''Black George'') Petrović, founder of the Karadjordjević Dynasty. Russia supported the Serbs, and the sultan granted them limited autonomy (see fig. 3). But internal discord weakened the government of Karadjordje, and the French invasion of Russia in 1812 prevented the tsar from protecting the Serbs. In 1813 the Turks attacked rebel areas. Karadjordje fled to Hungary; then Turkish, Bosnian, and Albanian troops plundered Serbian villages. The atrocities sparked a second Serbian uprising in 1815 that won autonomy under Turkish control for some regions. The corrupt rebel leader Miloš Obrenović (1817–39) had Karadjordje murdered and his head sent to the sultan to signal Serbian loyalty.

In 1830 the Ottoman Empire recognized Serbia as a principality under Turkish control, with Miloš Obrenović as hereditary prince. The sultan also granted the Serbian Orthodox Church

Figure 3. Expansion of Serbia, 1804–1913

autonomy and reaffirmed Russia's right to protect Serbia. Poor administration, corruption, and a bloody rivalry between the Karadjordjević and Obrenović clans marred Serbian political life from its beginning. After the sultan began allowing foreign governments to send diplomats to Serbia in the 1830s, foreign intervention further complicated the situation. Despite these obstacles and his autocratic manner, however, Miloš Obrenović stimulated trade, opened schools, and guided development of peasant lands. He abdicated in 1838 when Turkey imposed a constitution to limit his powers.

In the eighteenth and nineteenth centuries, Serbian culture made significant strides. Dositej Obradović, Vuk Karadžić, and other scholars accelerated a national renaissance. Through his translations and autobiography, Obradović spread the Enlightenment to the Serbs. Collections of Serbian folk songs and poems edited by Karadžić awoke pride in national history and traditions. Karadžić also overcame clerical opposition to reform the Cyrillic alphabet and the Serbian literary language, and he translated the New Testament. His work widened the concept of Serbian nationhood to include language as well as religious and regional identifications.

The European revolutions of 1848 brought more ferment in relations between the Serbs and their neighbors. As part of their revolutionary program, the Hungarians threatened to Magyarize the Serbs in Vojvodina. Some Serbs there declared their independence from Hungary and proclaimed an autonomous Vojvodina; others rallied behind the Austrian-Croatian invasion of Hungary. The Serbs nearly declared war, but Russian and Turkish diplomacy restrained them. The Serbs in Hungary gained nothing from helping Austria to crush the revolution. Vienna ruled Vojvodina harshly after 1850 and silenced Serbian irredentists there. When Austria joined Hungary to form the Dual Monarchy in 1867, Vienna returned Vojvodina and its Serbs to Hungary. Meanwhile, Petar II Njegoš of Montenegro (1830–51), who was also a first-rate poet, reformed his administration, battled the Turks, and struggled to obtain a seaport from the Austrians. His successor, Danilo II (1851–60), abolished the Montenegrin theocracy.

Prince Mihajlo Obrenović (1860–68), son of Miloš, was an effective ruler who further loosened the Turkish grip on Serbia. Western-educated and autocratic, Mihajlo liberalized the constitution and in 1867 secured the withdrawal of Turkish garrisons from Serbian cities. Industrial development began at this time, although 80 percent of Serbia's 1.25 million people remained illiterate peasants. Mihajlo sought to create a South Slav confederation, and he organized a regular army to prepare for liberation of Turkish-held Serbian territory. Scandal undermined Mihajlo's popularity, however, and he was eventually assassinated.

Political parties emerged in Serbia after 1868, and aspects of Western culture began to appear. A widespread uprising in the Ottoman Empire prompted an unsuccessful attack by Serbia and Montenegro in 1876, and a year later those countries allied with Russia, Romania, and Bulgarian rebels to defeat the Turks. The subsequent treaties of San Stefano and Berlin (1878) made Serbia an independent state and added to its territory, while Montenegro gained a seacoast. Alarmed at Russian gains, the growing stature of Serbia, and irredentism among Vojvodina's Serbs, Austria-Hungary pressed for and won the right to occupy Bosnia, Hercegovina, and Novi Pazar in 1878. Serbia's Prince Milan Obrenović

(1868–89), a cousin of Mihajlo, became disillusioned with Russia and fearful of the newly created Bulgaria. He therefore signed a commercial agreement in 1880 that made Serbia a virtual client state of Austria-Hungary. Milan became the first king of modern Serbia in 1882, but his pro-Austro-Hungarian policies undermined his popularity, and he abdicated in 1889.

A regency ruled Serbia until 1893, when Milan's teenage son, Aleksandar (1889–1903), pronounced himself of age and nullified the constitution. Aleksandar was widely unpopular in Serbia because of scandals, arbitrary rule, and his position favoring Austria-Hungary. In 1903 military officers, including Dragutin "Apis" Dimitrijević, brutally murdered Aleksandar and his wife. Europe condemned the killings, which, however, were celebrated in Belgrade. Petar Karadjordjević (1903–14), who knew of the conspiracy, returned from exile to take the throne, restored and liberalized the constitution, put Serbian finances in order, and improved trade and education. Petar turned Serbia away from Austria-Hungary and toward Russia, and in 1905 Serbia negotiated a tariff agreement with Bulgaria, hoping to break the Austro-Hungarian monopoly of its exports. In response to a diplomatic disagreement, Vienna placed a punitive tariff on livestock, Serbia's most important export. Serbia, however, refused to bend, found new trade routes, and began seeking an outlet to the sea. In 1908 Austria-Hungary formally annexed Bosnia and Hercegovina, frustrating Serbian designs on those regions and precipitating an international crisis. The Serbs mobilized, but under German pressure Russia persuaded Belgrade to cease its protests. Thereafter, Belgrade maintained strict official propriety in its relations with Vienna; but government and military factions prepared for a war to liberate the Serbs still living under the Turkish yoke in Kosovo, Macedonia, and other regions.

Bosnia and Hercegovina

In the seventh century, Croats and Serbs settled in the land that now makes up Bosnia and Hercegovina. Dominance of the regions shifted among the Croatian, Serbian, Bulgarian, and Byzantine rulers for generations before the Croatian and Hungarian crowns merged and Hungary dominated. Foreign interference in Bosnia and Hercegovina exacerbated local political and religious hostilities and ignited bloody civil wars.

The heretical Bogomil faith played an important early role in Bosnian politics. Ban Kulin (1180–1204) and other nobles struggled to broaden Bosnian autonomy, rejected the Catholic and Orthodox faiths, and embraced Bogomilism, a dualistic offshoot

Tombstones of heretical Bogomil sect, Bosnia
Courtesy Sam and Sarah Stulberg

of Christianity. The Bogomils enraged the papacy, and the Catholic kings of Hungary persecuted them to exterminate the heresy and secure Hungarian rule over Bosnia. Kulin recanted his conversion under torture, but the Bogomil faith survived crusades, civil war, and Catholic propaganda.

In the fourteenth century, Bosnia became a formidable state under the rule of Ban Stefan Tvrtko I (1353–91). Tvrtko joined Bosnia with the principality of Hum, forerunner of Hercegovina, and attempted to unite the South Slavs under his rule. After the Serbian Nemanja Dynasty expired in 1371, Tvrtko was crowned king of Bosnia and Raška in 1377, and he later conquered parts of Croatia and Dalmatia. Bosnian troops fought beside the Serbs at Kosovo Polje. After that defeat, Tvrtko turned his attention to forming alliances with Western states. Rival nobles and religious groups vied to gain control of Bosnia after the death of Tvrtko; one noble in Hum won the title of "Herzeg" (German for "duke"), whence the name "Hercegovina."

The fifteenth century marked the beginning of Turkish rule in Bosnia. Most of Bosnia was taken in 1463, Hercegovina in 1483. Many Orthodox and Roman Catholics fled, while Bogomil nobles converted to Islam to retain their land and feudal privileges. They formed a unique Slavic Muslim aristocracy that exploited its Christian and Muslim serfs for centuries and eventually grew fanatical and conservative. Turkish governors supervised Bosnia and Hercegovina from their capitals at Travnik and Mostar, respectively, but few Turks actually settled in these territories. Economic life declined, and the regions grew isolated from Europe and even Constantinople. As the sultan's military expenses grew, small farms were replaced by large estates, and peasant taxes were raised substantially. When the Ottoman Empire weakened in the seventeenth century, Bosnia and Hercegovina became pawns in the struggle among Austria, Russia, and the Turks.

The nineteenth century in Bosnia and Hercegovina brought alternating Christian peasant revolts against the Slavic Muslim landholders and Slavic Muslim rebellions against the sultan. In 1850 the Turkish government stripped the conservative Slavic Muslim nobles of power, shifted the capital of Bosnia to Sarajevo, and instituted centralized, highly corrupt rule. Austrian capital began to enter the regions, financing primitive industries and fostering a new Christian middle class. But the mostly Christian serfs continued to suffer the corruption and high rates of the Turkish tax system. In 1875 a peasant uprising in Hercegovina sparked an all-out rebellion in the Balkan provinces, provoking a European war. The Treaty of Berlin, which followed the Turkish defeat of 1878, gave Austria-Hungary the right to occupy Bosnia and Hercegovina to restore local order.

The Treaty of Berlin brought a period of manipulation by the Austro-Hungarian Empire. The empire suppressed Muslim and Orthodox opposition to the occupation and introduced an orderly administration. But it retained the feudal system because Bosnia and Hercegovina technically remained Turkish states. Seeking to increase the Catholic population of Bosnia, Vienna sent Austrian, Hungarian, Croatian, and Polish administrators and colonized northern Bosnia with Catholic Slavs and Germans. The administrator of the regions, Baron Benjamin Kállay (1882–1903), fostered economic growth, reduced lawlessness, improved sanitation, built roads and railroads, and established schools. However, Kállay, a Hungarian, exploited strong nationalist differences among the Muslim Slavs, Catholic Croats, and Orthodox Serbs.

At the turn of the century, nationalist differences reached the point of explosion. Fearful that Turkey might demand the return of Bosnia and Hercegovina after a revolutionary government was established in Constantinople, Austria-Hungary precipitated a major European crisis by annexing the regions in October 1908. Serbia, which had coveted the regions, mobilized for war. The crisis subsided a year later when Russia and Serbia bowed to German pressure and all Europe recognized the Serbian annexation as a fait accompli. Domination by Austria had embittered the ethnic groups of Bosnia and Hercegovina. Muslim Slavs resented Turkish withdrawal from the Balkans; the Croats looked initially to Vienna for support but were increasingly disappointed by its response; and the Bosnian Serbs, deeply dissatisfied with continued serfdom, looked to Serbia for aid.

Macedonia

In its earliest history, Macedonia was ruled by the Bulgars and the Byzantines, who began a long tradition of rivalry over that territory. Slavs invaded and settled Byzantine Macedonia late in the sixth century, and in A.D. 679 the Bulgars, a Turkic steppe people, crossed into the Balkans and directly encountered the Byzantine Empire. The Bulgars commingled with the more numerous Slavs and eventually abandoned their Turkic mother tongue in favor of the Slavic language. The Byzantines and Bulgars ruled Macedonia alternately from the ninth to the fourteenth century, when Stefan Dušan of Serbia conquered it and made Skopje his capital. A local noble, Vukašin, called himself king of Macedonia after the death of Dušan, but the Turks annihilated Vukašin's forces in 1371 and assumed control of Macedonia.

The beginning of Turkish rule meant centuries of subjugation and cultural deprivation in Macedonia. The Turks destroyed the Macedonian aristocracy, enserfed the Christian peasants, and eventually amassed large estates and subjected the Slavic clergy to the Greek patriarch of Constantinople. The living conditions of the Macedonian Christians deteriorated in the seventeenth and eighteenth centuries as Turkish power declined. Greek influence increased, the Slavic liturgy was banned, and schools and monasteries taught Greek language and culture. In 1777 the Ottoman Empire eliminated the autocephalous Bulgarian Orthodox Church and the archbishopric of Ohrid. Because of such actions, the Slavic Macedonians began to despise Greek ecclesiastical domination as much as Turkish political oppression.

In the nineteenth century, the Bulgars achieved renewed national self-awareness, which influenced events in Macedonia. The sultan granted the Bulgars ecclesiastical autonomy in 1870, creating an independent Bulgarian Orthodox Church. Nationalist Bulgarian clergymen and teachers soon founded schools in Macedonia. Bulgarian activities in Macedonia alarmed the Serbian and Greek governments and churches, and a bitter rivalry arose over Macedonia among church factions and advocates of a Greater Bulgaria, Greater Serbia, and Greater Greece. The 1878 Russo-Turkish War drove the Turks from Bulgarian-populated lands, and the Treaty of San Stefano (1878) created a large autonomous Bulgaria that included Macedonia. The subsequent Treaty of Berlin (1878), however, restored Macedonia to the Ottoman Empire, and left the embittered Bulgars with a much-diminished state.

The Bulgarian-Greek-Serbian rivalry for Macedonia escalated in the 1890s, and nationalistic secret societies proliferated. Macedonian refugees in Bulgaria founded the Supreme Committee for Liberation of Macedonia, which favored Bulgarian annexation and recruited its own military force to confront Turkish units and rival nationalist groups in Macedonia. In 1896 Macedonians founded the Internal Macedonian Revolutionary Organization (IMRO), whose two main factions divided the region into military districts, collected taxes, drafted recruits, and used tactics of propaganda and terrorism.

A 1902 uprising in Macedonia provoked Turkish reprisals, and in 1903 IMRO launched a widespread rebellion that the Turks could not suppress for several months. After that event, the sultan agreed to a Russian and Austrian reform scheme that divided Macedonia into five zones and assigned British, French, Italian, Austrian, and Russian troops to police them. Pro-Bulgarian and pro-Greek groups continued to clash, while the Serbs intensified their efforts in northern Macedonia. In 1908 the Young Turks, a faction of Turkish officers who promised liberation and equality, deposed the sultan. The Europeans withdrew their troops when Serbs and Bulgars established friendly relations with the zealous Turks. But the nationalist Young Turks began imposing centralized rule and cultural restrictions, exacerbating Christian-Muslim friction. Serbia and Bulgaria ended their differences in 1912 by a treaty that defined their respective claims in Macedonia. A month later, Bulgaria and Greece signed a similar agreement.

The Balkan Wars, World War I, and the Formation of Yugoslavia, 1912–18

The Balkan wars and World War I had dramatic consequences for the South Slavs. In the Balkan wars, Serbia helped expel the Turks from Europe and regained lands lost in medieval times. By 1914 the alliances of Europe and the ethnic friction among the South Slavs had combined to make Bosnia the ignition point, and Serbia one of the main battlegrounds, of World War I. When Austria-Hungary collapsed at the end of the war, fear of an expansionist Italy inspired Serbian, Croatian, and Slovenian leaders to form the new federation known as Yugoslavia, "the land of the South Slavs."

The Balkan Wars and World War I

In 1912 Turkish chauvinism and atrocities combined with Albanian insurgency to galvanize Serbia, Bulgaria, and Greece. In the First Balkan War, October 1912 to May 1913, these nations joined Montenegro to oust the Ottoman Empire from the Balkans. Besides capturing western Macedonia, Kosovo, and other Serbian-populated regions, Serbian forces moved through purely Albanian-populated lands to the Adriatic. Austria-Hungary convinced the major European powers to create an independent Albania to deny Serbia an Adriatic outlet, and it forced Serbia to remove its troops from Albanian territory. The Treaty of London (1913) awarded the Serbs almost all remaining Ottoman lands in Europe, but there was immediate conflict over the division of Macedonia. With Austro-Hungarian approval, Bulgaria attacked its erstwhile allies in June 1913, triggering the Second Balkan War. This time Serbia, Montenegro, Greece, Romania, and Turkey defeated Bulgaria and eliminated the possibility of Bulgarian participation in a South Slav state. Its victories filled Serbia with confidence and doubled its size. But the wars also weakened the country and left it with hostile neighbors and bitter Macedonian and Albanian minorities.

Serbian victories and the Serbs' obvious contempt for Austria-Hungary brought hostility from Vienna and anti-Habsburg sentiment in all the empire's South Slavic regions, especially Bosnia and Hercegovina. Confident behind German military protection, the high command of Austria-Hungary lobbied for war to eliminate Serbia. Serbia's alliance with Russia also encouraged the growth of expansionist, nationalist secret societies in the Serbian army. The most significant of these societies was the Black Hand, a group of army officers who dominated the army and influenced the government from 1911 to 1917.

In 1914 Archduke Franz Ferdinand, heir to the Habsburg throne and a longtime advocate of equality for the South Slavs in the empire, made an ill-prepared visit to Bosnia. On Vidovdan, Bosnian student Gavrilo Princip assassinated the archduke and the archduchess in Sarajevo. The Black Hand had armed and trained the assassin, but historians doubt that the rulers of Serbia had approved the plot. Nevertheless, on July 23 Austria-Hungary sent an ultimatum, threatening war unless Serbia allowed Vienna to join the murder investigation and suppress secret societies. Even the German kaiser felt that Serbia met the Austrian demands, but war was declared, the existing alliance structure of Europe went into force, and World War I began. The Central Powers—Germany, Austria-Hungary, and the Ottoman Empire—faced the Triple Entente—France,

Britain, and Russia. The Croats, Slovenes, and many Serbs in Austria-Hungary went to war against Serbia and Montenegro.

Despite overwhelming odds, Serbia twice cleared its soil of invading Austro-Hungarian armies early in the war, and late in 1914 plans were announced to unite the Serbs, Croats, and Slovenes in a South Slavic state. Italy joined the Triple Entente in 1915 and attacked Austria-Hungary; then Bulgaria joined the side of Austria-Hungary in the fall of that year. With French and Italian forces waiting in nearby Salonika, German, Austro-Hungarian, and Bulgarian forces attacked Serbia in October 1915. The Serbian army, weakened by typhus, escaped through Montenegro and Albania in midwinter, suffering heavy losses. After Italian units in Albania denied support, French ships evacuated the remaining Serbian forces to Corfu.

Austria-Hungary and Bulgaria occupied Serbia and Montenegro after the retreat. After recovering, the Serbian army helped the French and British capture Bitola in September 1916. Entente armies remained inactive there until the Central Powers began to disintegrate. They then routed the Bulgarians in September 1918, swept Austro-Hungarian and German forces from Serbia, and entered Hungary. In November Austria-Hungary collapsed, and the war ended. World War I destroyed one-fourth of Montenegro's population and several hundred thousand Croats and Slovenes. Serbia lost about 850,000 people, a quarter of its prewar population, and half its prewar resources.

Formation of the South Slav State

The idea of an independent South Slav state advanced during World War I, especially after Bolshevik Russia disclosed the secret 1915 Treaty of London, in which the Entente had promised to award Istria and much of Dalmatia and the Slovenian lands to Italy. Because they feared Italian domination, Ante Trumbić and other Dalmatian leaders formed the London-based Yugoslav Committee to promote creation of a South Slav state. In July 1917, Nikola Pašić of Serbia and Trumbić signed the Declaration of Corfu, which called for a union of Serbs, Croats, and Slovenes in one nation with a single democratic, constitutional, parliamentary system under the Karadjordjević Dynasty. The declaration promised equal recognition of the Latin and Cyrillic alphabets, the three national names and flags, and the three predominant religions. However, it did not indicate whether the new state would be centralized or federal. Pašić advocated a centralized state; Trumbić pressed for a federation.

The authority of Austria-Hungary over its South Slav lands ended in October 1918, and the National Council of Slovenes, Croats, and Serbs became the de facto government of the regions under Antun Korošec. On October 29, the Sabor in Zagreb annulled the union of Croatia with Hungary and gave the National Council supreme authority. In November Pašić, Trumbić, and Korošec signed an agreement in Geneva, providing for a joint provisional government but recognizing the jurisdiction of Serbia and the National Council in the areas under their respective control, until a constituent assembly could convene. But the war ended very rapidly, and Italy began seizing parts of Dalmatia. This prompted the National Council to seal a quick final agreement with Serbia, over the objections of Croatia's Peasant Party, without obtaining guarantees of regional autonomy. Leaders in Bosnia and Hercegovina and Vojvodina favored union; on November 24, the Montenegrins deposed the Njegoš Dynasty and declared solidarity with Serbia. On December 1, Prince Regent Aleksandar Karadjordjević and delegates from the National Council, Vojvodina, Bosnia and Hercegovina, and Montenegro announced the founding of the Kingdom of the Serbs, Croats, and Slovenes, to be ruled by Aleksandar. The Paris Peace Conference recognized the kingdom in May 1919.

The Kingdom of Yugoslavia

Ethnic hatred, religious rivalry, language barriers, and cultural conflicts plagued the Kingdom of the Serbs, Croats, and Slovenes (later renamed the Kingdom of Yugoslavia) from its inception (see fig. 4). The question of centralization versus federalism bitterly divided the Serbs and Croats; democratic solutions were blocked, and dictatorship was made inevitable because political leaders had little vision, no experience in parliamentary government, and no tradition of compromise. Hostile neighboring states resorted to regicide to disrupt the kingdom, and only when European war threatened in 1939 did the Serbs and Croats attempt a settlement. But that solution came too late to matter. The Kingdom of the Serbs, Croats, and Slovenes encompassed most of the Austrian Slovenian lands, Croatia, Slavonia, most of Dalmatia, Serbia, Montenegro, Vojvodina, Kosovo, the Serbian-controlled parts of Macedonia, and Bosnia and Hercegovina. Territorial disputes disrupted relations with Italy, Austria, Hungary, Bulgaria, and Albania. Italy posed the most serious threat to the new kingdom. Although it received Zadar, Istria, Trieste, and several Adriatic islands in the postwar treaties and took Rijeka by force, Italy resented not receiving all the territory promised under the 1915 Treaty of London. Rome

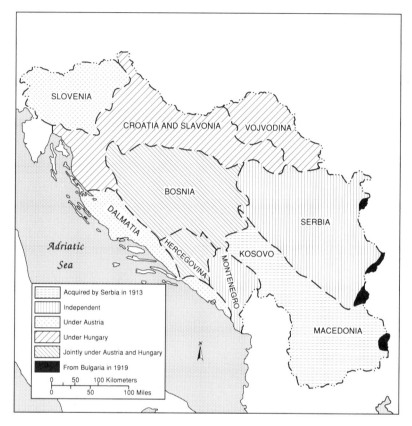

Source: Based on information from Gordon C. McDonald et al., *Yugoslavia: A Country Study,*
Washington, 1971, 44.

Figure 4. South Slav Territories at Formation of Yugoslav State, 1918–19

subsequently supported Croatian, Macedonian, and Albanian ex-
tremists, hoping to stir unrest and hasten the end of the new kingdom. Revisionist Hungary and Bulgaria also backed anti-Yugoslav
groups.

The creation of Yugoslavia fulfilled the dreams of many South
Slavic intellectuals who disregarded fundamental differences among
12 million people of the new country. The Serbs, Croats, and Slovenes had conflicting political and cultural traditions, and the
South Slav kingdom also faced sizable non-Slavic minorities, including Germans, Albanians, Hungarians, Romanians, and Turks,
with scatterings of Italians, Greeks, Czechs, Slovaks, Ruthenians, Russians, Poles, Bulgars, Sephardic and Ashkenazic Jews,
and Gypsies. The Orthodox, Roman Catholic, Islamic, Uniate,

Jewish, and Protestant faiths all were well established and cut across ethnic and territorial lines. Besides the divisiveness of a large number of minority languages, linguistic differences also split the Serbs, Croats, Slovenes, and Macedonian Slavs. Many people regarded the new government and its laws as alien, exploitative, and secondary to kinship loyalties and traditions.

Political Life in the 1920s

Serbia's Radical Party and Democratic Party and Croatia's Peasant Party competed with and allied with a large number of other ethnic and sectarian parties, so that no single party ever gained a majority. The Radical Party under Pašić, the strongest party in the country, drew backing from Serbia proper (see Glossary) and advocated strong central control under Serbian leadership. The Peasant Party under Stjepan Radić dominated Croatia and campaigned for an independent Croatian state and agrarian socialism. The Democratic Party found support mostly from Serbs outside Serbia; after initially advocating centralism, it turned to an opposition agenda.

The Serbian-Croatian rivalry, which was a clash of uncompromising advocates of central rule and regional autonomy, produced the main political conflict in Yugoslavia. In November 1920, voters chose delegates to a constituent assembly. The Radić party won nearly all Croatian seats but, adopting an obstructionist strategy that had been typical of Croatian politics under the Dual Monarchy, boycotted the assembly. When other anticentralist groups left the assembly in 1921, the Radicals and Democrats won by default the opportunity to adopt a centralist constitution. This document provided some liberties but allowed little room for local initiative or popular democracy, and it gave non-Serbs inadequate legal expression of their discontent. Communists attempted to assassinate King Aleksandar the day after the constitution took effect and murdered the interior minister a month later. The new Federal Assembly (Skupština) then passed broad security laws to suppress the Communist Party of Yugoslavia, which had gained considerable support with worker groups and poor peasants in the south.

Radić campaigned at home and abroad for Croatian autonomy, even seeking support in the Soviet Union—a country the kingdom did not recognize. The Peasant Party boycott of the Federal Assembly lasted until 1924, when a dissident coalition of Democrats, Slovenes, and Muslims forced the Radicals from power. King Aleksandar then appointed an anticentralist prime minister. Charges of corruption and Radić's harsh criticism of the Serbian establishment undermined the new cabinet. The Radicals soon regained power, arrested Radić for sedition, and threatened to ban his party.

Political realities, including the threat posed by fascist Italy to Croatia, induced Radić in 1925 to strike a deal with Aleksandar to recognize the monarchy and to join a government coalition led by Pašić. This union lasted until a corruption scandal forced Pašić to resign in 1926. Thereafter, weak coalitions failed to maintain stability, the Croats returned to obstructionism, and floor debates in the Federal assembly often became violent. In June 1928, a Montenegrin deputy shot Radić, who died two months later. Deputies from Croatia and Bosnia and Hercegovina soon left the assembly, demanding a federal state. Fearing anarchy, Aleksandar abrogated the constitution in January 1929, dissolved the assembly, banned political parties, and declared a temporary royal dictatorship.

While the Serbian-Croatian conflict occupied center stage, an equally bitter conflict arose between the Serbs and the ethnic Albanians in Kosovo. Serbs consider Kosovo to be hallowed ground, but their exclusive hold on the region slipped during the Ottoman tyranny in the late seventeenth century, and many Serbs fled Kosovo for Habsburg protection. After the mid-eighteenth century, Albanians became a majority in Kosovo and began oppressing the Serbs that remained. Between 1878 and 1912, Serbs left Kosovo in large numbers; in 1920 Belgrade began a drive to resettle Serbs in the region. Coercion, illegal expropriation of Albanian-owned land, and forced deportations marred this campaign. When Albanians attacked Serbian settlements and government institutions, the police seized Albanian property, imprisoned families, and destroyed homes. The government adopted a similar policy in Macedonia.

Economic Life and Foreign Policy in the 1920s

Yugoslavia inherited formidable economic problems after World War I. The new kingdom had to repair war damage, repay debts, eradicate feudalism by passing land reform, make up for shortages of capital and skilled labor, and integrate differing customs areas, currencies, rail networks, and banking systems.

The agricultural sector, which employed over 75 percent of the Yugoslav population, underwent a radical reform that failed to relieve nagging rural poverty. Before the war, German, Austrian, and Hungarian families owned sprawling estates in Slovenia, Croatia, and Vojvodina; Turkish feudalism remained in Kosovo and Macedonia; Muslim landlords in Bosnia owned large farms worked by Christian sharecroppers; some Dalmatians remained tenant farmers in a system devised in Roman times; and Serbia was a chaotic blend of independent small farms. The Yugoslav government erased remnants of feudalism, but the peasants received plots too small for efficient farming to support the rural population. Yields fell, and poverty and ignorance dominated most of the peasantry. Industrialization and emigration did not ease overpopulation.

In the industrial sector, Yugoslavia concentrated on extracting raw materials, expanding light industry, and improving its infrastructure. Insufficient domestic capital forced Yugoslavia to seek foreign investment. The government sold mining rights to foreign firms and borrowed heavily to build roads and rail lines, power plants, and a merchant marine. Despite steady economic growth based on the food industry, mining, and textiles, Yugoslavia remained substantially undeveloped and fell far behind the rest of Europe. Divergent economic interests and the widening differences in development of Croatia and Slovenia with the less developed southern regions exacerbated Serbian-Croatian tensions. The development disparity especially embittered many Serbs, who believed that their sacrifices in the war had benefited former enemies more than themselves.

Yugoslavia's foreign policy in the 1920s sought to counter threats from Italy, Hungary, and Bulgaria and to secure regional peace through a series of Balkan alliances. The young kingdom was a charter member of the League of Nations. In 1921 and 1922, Yugoslavia, Romania, and Czechoslovakia signed mutual defense and political treaties aimed at blocking a Habsburg restoration and blocking the ambitions of revisionist Hungary. This alignment, later known as the Little Entente, won support from France, which hoped to block Soviet expansion and contain Germany. In 1927 Yugoslavia and France signed a treaty of friendship. Though it was the focus of Yugoslav foreign policy for the next decade, this treaty included no military provisions and failed to relieve the fear of fascist Italy.

The Royal Dictatorship

After assuming dictatorial power, Aleksandar canceled civil liberties, abolished local self-government, and decreed strict laws against sedition, terrorism, and propagation of communism. The king named a Serb, General Petar Živković, as prime minister, officially changed the name of the country to the Kingdom of Yugoslavia in 1929, unified the six regional legal systems, and restructured the ministries. The king attempted to ease separatist pressures by replacing traditional provinces with a new territorial unit, the *banovina*. The dictatorship at first gained wide support because it seemed to make government more efficient and less corrupt.

The popularity of the dictatorship was short lived, however. Aleksandar's attempt to impose unity on the ethnic groups backfired, blocking the understanding of common national interests and unleashing more divisive forces. The royal dictatorship unified Croatian opposition to Serbian hegemony but fractured the once-unified Serbian parties. The police violently suppressed expressions of communism and ethnic dissidence. The state imprisoned Slovenian and Muslim politicians and tried Vlatko Maček, successor to Radić, for terrorist activity. Serbs also were oppressed, and the leader of Serbia's Democrats left the country in protest. Ultranationalist Croats also fled, and Italy granted asylum to Ante Pavelić, leader of the terrorist Ustaše (see Glossary).

In 1931 Aleksandar formally ended his personal rule by promulgating a constitution that provided for limited democracy. He legalized political parties but banned religious, ethnic, and regional groups and all organizations that threatened the integrity and order of the state. Hopelessly divided Serbian and Croatian opposition leaders could not even agree to issue a common statement on the new constitution. Only the candidates of Živković appeared on the ballot. Serbs protested the limitations on democratic liberties; the government imprisoned Maček, causing unrest in Croatia; and the ranks of the Ustaše grew. Despite the discontent, Aleksandar retained some popularity even in non-Serbian regions.

In 1931 the world economic crisis hit Yugoslavia hard. Foreign trade slumped, and the trade deficit rose. Collapsing world grain prices, the end of German reparations payments, and exhaustion of credit sources brought unemployment. Mines closed, bankruptcies increased, and severe weather conditions brought rural starvation. The economic crisis also brought charges that the Serbs were exploiting Croatia and Slovenia. Finally, French refusal of a badly needed loan shook the confidence of the Yugoslav government in its French ally.

Fearing Italy but doubtful of France, Aleksandar made unsuccessful offers to Mussolini in the early 1930s and attempted to build a Balkan alliance. In 1934 Yugoslavia, Romania, Greece, and Turkey signed a limited mutual defense agreement, later known as the Balkan Entente. Bulgaria refused to abandon its claims to Macedonia and did not join the pact, but tensions eased between Belgrade and Sofia. Fearing a vengeful, stronger Germany, France sought rapprochement with Italy in 1934, pressuring Yugoslavia to do likewise. But Yugoslavia began to turn to Germany instead to offset the threat from Italy.

The Regency

In October 1934, a Bulgarian assassinated Aleksandar in Marseilles. The assassin, an Ustaše agent, had received assistance from Italy and Hungary. Yugoslavs genuinely grieved for their king. Even Aleksandar's opponents feared that his death would result in the disintegration of Yugoslavia. Croats and Slovenes especially feared subjection to Italy.

Prince Pavle, cousin of Aleksandar, created a three-man regency to rule for Aleksandar's minor son, Petar II. Pavle hoped to liberalize the regime and reconcile the Serbs and Croats without altering the 1931 constitution. The government freed Maček and in 1935 held elections that revealed significant dissatisfaction. Pavle soon called on the Serb Milan Stojadinović to form a cabinet. His new government granted amnesty to political prisoners and permitted political parties additional leeway, but it refused to restore democracy and failed to solve the Croatian problem. Croatian separatists clashed with the police; communist-inspired student activists fomented disorder; and Croatian militia organizations formed. Maček and other Croatian leaders welcomed rising domestic and international tensions as positive forces that would bring about a federalist solution, and they refused to compromise or even enumerate their demands to the government. Stojadinović incurred the wrath of Serbian nationalists when he submitted an agreement with the Vatican on regulation of Catholic affairs; the Federal Assembly canceled the agreement, or Concordat, after Orthodox clergymen denounced it.

The assassination of Aleksandar deepened Yugoslav mistrust of Italy, but confidence in France and Britain also dropped after those countries refused to back a League of Nations censure of Italy for harboring the assassin. Fearing isolation, Yugoslavia strengthened its ties with Germany, which became the main trading partner of Yugoslavia after the latter voted in the league in 1935 to impose economic sanctions on Italy for invading Ethiopia. Under Stojadinović, however, movement began toward settlements with Bulgaria and Italy. In January 1937, Yugoslavia and Bulgaria signed an eternal-friendship pact, violating the provisions of the Little Entente and weakening the Balkan Entente. In March Yugoslavia and Italy followed up a 1936 trade agreement with a treaty of friendship. In December Stojadinović visited Mussolini and assured him that Yugoslavia would neither strengthen its relationship with Czechoslovakia and France nor recognize the Soviet Union. Still, Yugoslavia drew away from France only reluctantly, and public opinion remained firmly attached to the West.

Despite the support for democracy professed by the Stojadino-vić government, many Yugoslavs feared he aspired to become a fascist dictator. His supporters adopted the fascist salute and uniformed themselves in green shirts. The dictatorial air of Stojadi-nović, the Concordat, and accommodations with former enemies roused opponents in Serbia, with whom Maček struck up a quick friendship. Support for the prime minister dropped after the 1938 elections, and Pavle forced him to resign in February 1939. Dragiša Cvetković was then named prime minister.

Germany annexed Austria in March 1938 and smashed the Little Entente by partitioning Czechoslovakia later in the year; by 1939 it had gained a stranglehold on the Yugoslav economy. Pavle and Cvetković reaffirmed Yugoslavia's friendship with Germany and Italy but tried in vain to loosen Germany's economic grip with appeals to Britain and France. Belgrade again professed friendship with Berlin and Rome after Italy occupied Albania in April 1939; but Yugoslav popular opinion grew more adamantly pro-Western, and in May the government revealed its true colors by secretly shipping its gold reserves to Britain and the United States. Both Berlin and Rome suspected Yugoslavia's motives.

The Sporazum, Tripartite Pact, and Outbreak of World War II

Nationalist strife and portents of war induced Pavle to shore up national unity by reconciling the Serbs and Croats. On August 26, 1939, after months of negotiation, Cvetković and Maček sealed an agreement, the Sporazum, creating an autonomous Croatia. Under the Sporazum, Belgrade continued to control defense, internal security, foreign affairs, trade, and transport; but an elected Sabor and a crown-appointed *ban* would decide internal matters in Croatia. Ironically, the Sporazum fueled separatism. Maček and other Croats viewed autonomy as a step toward full Croatian independence, so they began haggling over territory; Serbs attacked Cvetković, charging that the Sporazum brought no return to democracy and no autonomy; Muslims demanded an autonomous Bosnia; and Slovenes and Montenegrins espoused federalism. Pavle appointed a new government with Cvetković as prime minister and Maček as vice prime minister, but it gained little support.

World War II began on September 1, 1939. The collapse of France in June 1940 crushed Yugoslav hopes of French support. When Greece repelled Italian attacks in October 1940, Mussolini requested aid from Germany. Berlin in turn pressed the Balkan countries to sign the Tripartite Pact and align themselves with the Axis powers—Germany, Italy, and Japan. Romania signed in November 1940, and Bulgaria in March 1941. Now virtually surrounded by enemies, neutral Yugoslavia desperately sought allies. It recognized the Soviet Union in 1940 and signed a nonaggression agreement with Moscow in 1941. When Germany redoubled pressure on Yugoslavia to sign the Tripartite Pact, Pavle and the cabinet stalled, hoping that Germany would attack the Soviet Union and ease the pressure on them. Time ran out for Yugoslavia on March 25. Convinced that the military situation of the country was hopeless, the government ignored pro-Western public opinion and signed a protocol of adherence to the Tripartite Pact. In return, Hitler guaranteed that Germany would not press Yugoslavia for military assistance, move its army into Yugoslav territory, or violate Yugoslav sovereignty.

On March 27, military officers overthrew the Cvetković-Maček cabinet, declared the sixteen-year-old Petar II king, and formed a new cabinet under General Dušan Simović. Anti-German euphoria swept Belgrade; Yugoslav, British, French, and United States flags flew; and crowds shouted anti-Tripartite slogans. The demonstrations, however, unnerved the new government, which affirmed Yugoslav loyalty to the Tripartite Pact because of the country's perilous position. But the declaration did not convince Hitler. On April 6, 1941, the Luftwaffe bombed Belgrade, killing thousands. Axis forces then invaded, the Yugoslav army collapsed, the king and government fled, and on April 17 remaining resistance forces surrendered unconditionally.

Yugoslavia in World War II, 1941–45

The Axis invasion caused panic in Yugoslavia as foreign occupiers partitioned the country and terrorized its people. Bloody encounters involved both invading and domestic forces throughout the four years of war. The communist-led Partisans (see Glossary) rose from near oblivion to dominate the country's resistance movement. They emerged from the war in firm control of the entire country.

Partition and Terror

Germany, Italy, Hungary, and Bulgaria dismembered Yugoslavia (see fig. 5). Germany occupied Serbia and part of Vojvodina. It created the puppet Independent State of Croatia (Nezavisna država Hrvatska—NDH) including Croatia and Bosnia and Hercegovina, and it annexed northern Slovenia. Italy won southern Slovenia and much of Dalmatia, joined Kosovo with its Albanian puppet state, and occupied Montenegro. Hungary occupied part of Vojvodina and Slovenian and Croatian border regions. Bulgaria took Macedonia and a part of southern Serbia.

Germany unleashed a reign of terror and Germanization in

Source: Based on information from Germany, Foreign Ministry, *Documents on German Foreign Policy, 1919–1945*, Washington, 1949.

Figure 5. Partition of Yugoslavia, 1941

northern Slovenia. It resettled Slovenes in Serbia, moved German colonists onto Slovenian farms, and attempted to erase Slovenian cultural institutions. The Catholic hierarchy collaborated with the authorities in Italian-occupied southern Slovenia, which suffered less tyranny than the north.

Germany and Italy supported the NDH and began diverting natural resources to the Axis war machine. When Maček refused to collaborate, the Nazis made Ante Pavelić head of the NDH. His Ustaše storm troopers began eliminating the 2 million Serbs, Jews, and Gypsies in the NDH through forced religious conversion, deportation, and extreme violence. The NDH was backed enthusiastically by some Croatian Catholic clergy, including the archbishop of Sarajevo; some Franciscan priests enlisted in the Ustaše and participated in massacres. The archbishop of Zagreb, Alojzije Stepinac, publicly welcomed and appeared with Pavelić while privately protesting NDH atrocities. Many Catholic priests, however, condemned the violence and helped Orthodox Serbs to practice their religion in secret. Even the Germans were appalled by Ustaše violence, and Berlin feared the bloodbath would ignite greater Serbian resistance. Italy reoccupied areas of Hercegovina to halt the slaughter there.

Jews and Serbs also were massacred in areas occupied by the Albanians and the Hungarians. Thousands of Serbs fled to Serbia, where the Germans had established a puppet regime under General Milan Nedić. Nedić considered himself a custodian rather than a collaborator and strove to limit the violence. In the south of Yugoslavia, many Macedonians welcomed Bulgarian forces, expecting that Sofia would grant them autonomy; but a harsh Bulgarianization campaign ended their enthusiasm.

Resistance in Yugoslavia developed mainly in dispersed units of the Yugoslav army and among Serbs fleeing genocide in Croatia and Bosnia and Hercegovina. Various armed groups in Serbia organized under the name Četnik (pl., Četnici—see Glossary), from the Serbian word for "detachment." Some Četnici supported Nedić, others the communist-led Partisan guerrillas. The best known Četnici were the followers of Colonel Draža Mihajlović, a Serbian nationalist, monarchist, and staunch anticommunist. Certain that the Allies would soon invade the Balkans, Mihajlović advised his Četnici to avoid clashes with Axis forces and prepare for a general uprising to coincide with the Allied push. In October 1941, Britain recognized Mihajlović as the leader of the Yugoslav resistance movement, and in 1942 the government-in-exile promoted him to commander of its armed forces.

The Resistance Movement

The communist-led Partisans eventually grew into Yugoslavia's largest, most active resistance group. The Communist Party of Yugoslavia (CPY) had sunk into obscurity after the government banned it in 1921. Police repression, internal conflict, and the Stalinist purges of the 1930s depleted party membership, and by the late 1930s its leadership in Moscow directed only a few hundred members inside Yugoslavia. The Partisan leader, Josip Broz Tito, son of a Croatian-Slovenian peasant family, had joined the Red Guards during the 1917 Bolshevik Revolution and become a party member after returning to Yugoslavia. Tito won membership in the Central Committee of the CPY in 1934, then became secretary general after a 1937 purge. In the four years before the war,

Tito directed a communist resurgence and built a strong organization of 12,000 full party members and 30,000 members of the youth organization. The party played some role in demonstrations in Belgrade against the Tripartite Pact, and it called for a general uprising after Hitler attacked the Soviet Union in June 1941. The Partisan slogan "Death to Fascism, Freedom to the People," combined with a pan-Yugoslav appeal, won recruits for Tito across the country—despite the fact that before the war the communists had worked for the breakup of Yugoslavia.

In July 1941, with some Četnik support, the Partisans launched uprisings that won control of much of the Yugoslav countryside. The Partisan leaders established an administration and proclaimed the Užice Republic in western Serbia. But in September the Axis struck back. Germany warned that it would execute 100 Serbs for every German soldier the resistance killed, and German troops killed several thousand civilians at Kragujevac in a single reprisal. Tito correctly reasoned that such actions would enrage the population and bring the Partisans more recruits, so he disregarded the German threat and continued his guerrilla warfare. He also arranged assassinations of local political figures and ordered attacks on the Četnici to coincide with German action against them. Mihajlović, however, feared that German reprisals would turn into a Serbian massacre, so he ordered his forces not to engage the Germans. After fruitless negotiations with Tito, the Četnik leader turned against the Partisans as his main enemy. Četnik units attacked Partisans in November 1941 and began cooperating with the Germans and Italians to prevent a communist victory. The British liaison to Mihajlović advised London to stop supplying the Četnici after the Užice attack, but Britain continued to supply Mihajlović.

In late 1941, the Partisans lost control of western Serbia, Montenegro, and other areas, and their central command withdrew into Bosnia. Despite the setbacks, Bosnian Serbs and other Yugoslavs flocked to the Partisans. The Serbian-based Četnici expanded into Montenegro, where they gained local and Italian support. Soviet dictator Joseph V. Stalin, fearing that Partisan action might weaken Allied trust of the Soviet Union and suspicious of revolutionary movements not under his control, reportedly instructed Tito to limit the Partisans to national liberation and antifascist activities. Moscow refused to supply arms to Tito, maintained relations with the government-in-exile, and even offered a military mission and supplies to the Četnici.

At Bihać in November 1942, the Partisan leaders, anxious to gain political legitimacy, convened the first meeting of the Antifascist Council for the National Liberation of Yugoslavia (Antifašističko veće narodnog oslobodjenja Jugoslavije—AVNOJ), a committee of communist and noncommunist Partisan representatives from all over Yugoslavia. AVNOJ became the political umbrella organization for the people's liberation committees that the Partisans established to administer territories under their control. AVNOJ proclaimed support for democracy, the rights of ethnic groups, the inviolability of private property, and freedom of individual economic initiative. Stalin reportedly barred Tito from declaring AVNOJ a provisional government. In 1943 Germany mounted offensives to improve its control of Yugoslavia in anticipation of an Allied invasion of the Balkans. The Partisans, fearing that an Allied invasion would benefit the Četnici, attacked Mihajlović's forces. In March the Partisans outmaneuvered the German army and defeated the Četnici decisively in Hercegovina and Montenegro. In May, however, German, Italian, Bulgarian, and NDH forces surrounded the Partisans and launched a final crushing attack. In fierce combat in the Sutjeska Gorge, the Partisans escaped encirclement. This proved a turning point in their fortunes; when Italy surrendered in September 1943, the Partisans captured Italian arms, gained control of coastal territory, and began receiving supplies from the Allies in Italy.

Tito convened a second session of AVNOJ in November 1943. This session, which included representatives of various ethnic and political groups, built the basis for the postwar government of Yugoslavia. AVNOJ voted to reconstitute the country on a federal basis; elected a national committee to act as the temporary government; named Tito marshal of Yugoslavia and prime minister; and issued a declaration forbidding King Petar to return to the country until a popular referendum had been held on the status of the monarchy. Tito did not notify Stalin of the November meeting, which enraged the Soviet leader. The Western Allies, however, were not alarmed because they believed that the Partisans were the only Yugoslav resistance group actively fighting the Germans. At Teheran in December 1943, Roosevelt, Churchill, and Stalin decided to support the Partisans. A month later, Britain stopped supplying the Četnici and threw full support to the Partisans. The first Soviet mission arrived at Partisan headquarters shortly thereafter. The United States kept a military mission with Mihajlović to encourage continued Četnik aid for downed American fliers.

In May 1944, German airborne forces attacked Tito's headquarters in Drvar, nearly capturing him. Tito fled to Italy and then established new headquarters on the Adriatic island of Vis. After throwing full support to the Partisans, Britain worked to reconcile Tito and Petar. In June 1944, at Britain's urging, Petar named

Ivan Subašić, former *ban* of Croatia, as prime minister of the government-in-exile. Subašić accepted the resolutions of the second AVNOJ conference, and Petar agreed to remain outside Yugoslavia. In September the king succumbed to British pressure and summoned all Yugoslavs to back the Partisans.

When the Red Army reached the Yugoslav-Romanian border in September 1944, Tito traveled secretly to Moscow, arranged for Soviet troops to enter Yugoslavia, and secured Stalin's word that the Red Army would leave the country once it was secure, without interfering in domestic politics. Soviet troops crossed the border on October 1, and a joint Partisan-Soviet force liberated Belgrade on October 20. The majority of the Red Army then continued into Hungary, leaving the Partisans and the Western Allies to crush remaining Germans, Ustaše, and Četnici. When the Partisans advanced into Croatia in the bloodiest fighting of the war, Ustaše leaders and collaborators fled to Austria with regular Croatian and Slovenian troops and some Četnici. The Partisans finally occupied Trieste, Istria, and some Slovenian enclaves in Austria, but they withdrew from some of these areas after the Allies persuaded Tito to let the postwar peace conferences settle borders. The Partisans crushed a small Albanian nationalist revolt in Kosovo after Tito and Albanian communist leader Enver Hoxha announced that they would return Kosovo to Yugoslavia.

World War II claimed 1.7 million Yugoslav lives, 11 percent of the prewar population—a mortality second only to that of Poland. About 1 million of those were killed by other Yugoslavs. The average age of the dead was twenty-two years. The country's major cities, production centers, and communications systems were in ruins, and starvation was widespread (see World War II and Recovery, ch. 3).

Postwar Yugoslavia
Communist Takeover and Consolidation

The communists under Tito emerged from the war as sole rulers of Yugoslavia, without major Soviet assistance. King Petar surrendered his powers to a three-member regency in late 1944, and under Allied pressure Tito and Subašić agreed to merge their governments. On March 7, 1945, a single provisional Yugoslav government took office with Tito as prime minister and war minister, Subašić in charge of foreign affairs, and Tito supporters occupying almost all cabinet posts. A communist-dominated Provisional Assembly convened in August, and the government held elections to choose a constituent assembly in November. New election

World War II concentration camp near Niš, Serbia
Courtesy Sam and Sarah Stulberg

laws barred alleged wartime collaborators from voting, and all candidates had to be nominated by the communist-controlled People's Front, the descendant of the wartime People's Liberation Front that encompassed all noncollaborationist political parties and organizations. The police harassed noncommunist politicians and suppressed their newspapers during the election campaign. Subašić and other noncommunist ministers resigned in protest, while Serbia's Radical Party, Croatia's Peasant Party, and other parties boycotted the election. People's Front candidates won 90 percent of the vote.

The newly elected constituent assembly dissolved the monarchy and established the Socialist Federal Republic of Yugoslavia on November 29, 1945. Two months later, it adopted a Soviet-style constitution that provided for a federation of six republics under a strong central government. In an effort to prevent Serbian domination of the new state, the regime made separate republics of Montenegro and Macedonia and created within Serbia itself the ethnically mixed Autonomous Province of Vojvodina and the mostly Albanian Autonomous Province of Kosovo. At a later date, the regime further divided Serbian territory by recognizing three ''nations'' (see Glossary), the Serbs, Croats, and Muslim Slavs, in an attempt to overcome competing Serbian and Croatian claims

43

to that republic. The constitution established a rubber-stamp Federal Assembly and a presidential council to administer the federal government. It also included restricted wording on the inviolability of the home, the right to work, and freedom of speech, association, and religion, among other rights. Tito headed the party, government, and armed forces; his party functionaries oversaw the industries and supervised republic and local officials.

Tito's government repaired wartime damage, instituted land reform, and established a Soviet-style economic system. United Nations deliveries of supplies prevented starvation and the spread of disease but did not solve the fundamental problem of rural poverty. In August 1945, the regime seized remaining large and medium-size landholdings along with property belonging to banks, churches, monasteries, absentee landlords, private companies, and the expelled German minority. It gave half the land to peasants and allocated the rest to state-owned enterprises. The authorities postponed forced collectivization but required peasants to sell any surplus to the state at below-market prices. Peasants received incentives to join newly founded state and cooperative farms. The CPY quickly implemented the Stalinist model for rapid industrial development; by 1948 it had nationalized virtually all the country's wealth except privately held land. State planners set wages and prices and compiled a grandiose five-year plan that emphasized exploitation of domestic raw materials, development of heavy industry, and economic growth in underdeveloped regions. The Yugoslavs relied on tax and price policies, reparations, Soviet credits, and export of foodstuffs, timber, minerals, and metals to generate capital. They redirected the bulk of their trade toward the Soviet Union and Eastern Europe (see Application of Stalinist Economics, ch. 3).

Between 1945 and 1948, the government punished wartime collaborators. British forces in Austria captured Ustaše members and Croatian and Slovenian collaborators along with innocent refugees. These were returned to Yugoslavia, where Partisans summarily executed thousands of innocent and guilty prisoners. The regime also imprisoned thousands of Četnici and executed Mihajlović and other Četnik leaders as collaborators after a show trial in 1946.

The communists often used collaboration charges to stifle political and religious opposition, as well as economic and social initiatives. The Roman Catholic Church bitterly opposed the new order. After the war, the authorities executed over 200 priests and nuns charged with participating in Ustaše atrocities. Archbishop Stepinac protested government excesses and the secularization of education, institution of civil marriage, and confiscation of church lands. In September 1946, the regime sentenced him to imprisonment for sixteen years for complicity with the Pavelić government. He served five years before the regime released him. Yugoslav-Vatican relations deteriorated during the imprisonment of Stepinac, and the government severed them in 1952 when Pope Pius XII named Stepinac a cardinal. The authorities permitted the funeral and burial of Stepinac in Zagreb in 1960, after which Yugoslav-Vatican relations gradually improved until diplomatic relations were reestablished in 1970.

The Yugoslav-Soviet Rift

Fearing that Soviet control of Eastern Europe was slipping, Stalin ceased advocating ''national roads to socialism'' in 1947 and ordered creation of a Soviet-dominated socialist alliance. In September the Soviet, East European, Italian, and French communist parties founded the Cominform (Communist Information Bureau—see Glossary), a successor to the prewar Comintern (Communist International) that Stalin had hoped to manipulate for the benefit of the Soviet Union.

Establishment of Cominform headquarters in Belgrade strengthened the image that Yugoslavia was the staunchest Soviet ally in Eastern Europe. Stalin, however, saw Yugoslavia's independent communists as a threat to his hold on Eastern Europe, and hidden resentment strained relations between the Yugoslav and Soviet leaders. Resentment had grown on the Yugoslav side during the war because of Stalin's objections to the Partisans' political initiatives, his refusal to provide the Partisans military aid early in the struggle, and his wartime agreements with Churchill and Roosevelt. After the war, Yugoslav leaders complained about Red Army looting and raping in Yugoslavia during 1944 and 1945 and about unfair trade arrangements. The Yugoslavs also resisted establishment of joint companies that would have allowed Moscow to dominate their economy.

In early 1948, the Soviet Union stalled negotiations on a Yugoslav-Soviet trade treaty and began claiming that the Red Army had liberated Yugoslavia and facilitated the Partisan victory. In March the Soviet Union withdrew its military and civilian advisers from Yugoslavia, charging the Yugoslavs with perversion of Stalinist dogma. The Yugoslavs rejected the charges, criticized the Soviet Union for recruiting spies within the Yugoslav party, military, police, and enterprises, and defiantly asserted that a communist could love his native land no less than the Soviet Union. This insubordination infuriated Stalin, and Yugoslav-Soviet exchanges grew more heated. Finally, at a special session in Bucharest that the

Yugoslavs refused to attend, the Cominform shocked the world by expelling Yugoslavia and calling upon Yugoslav communists to overthrow Tito.

At first the CPY responded to the Cominform measures with conciliatory overtures. Portraits of Stalin, Marx, Engels, and Tito hung side by side at the Fifth Party Congress in July 1948, and the delegates chanted pledges of support for Stalin and the Soviet Union. In a lengthy address, Tito refuted Soviet charges against Yugoslavia, but he refrained from attacking Stalin. The vast majority of Yugoslavs supported Tito. The press publicized Soviet attacks widely; Moscow appealed for loyalty, but its appeals were nullified by renewed claims that the Red Army had liberated Yugoslavia from fascism. A few prominent Yugoslav communists did defect, and for five years after 1948 the regime imprisoned thousands of suspected pro-Soviet communists.

The Yugoslav regime strove to prove its allegiance to Stalin after 1948. It answered Moscow's criticisms by supporting Soviet foreign policy and implementing additional Stalinist economic measures. In 1949 the Yugoslav government began collectivizing agriculture; over the next two years, it used a carrot-and-stick approach to induce 2 million peasants to join about 6,900 collective farms. The campaign, however, caused a decrease in agricultural output, and the use of coercion eroded peasant support for the government. Peasant resistance and a 1950 drought that threatened the cities with starvation soon stalled the collectivization drive. The government announced the program's cancellation in 1952.

In 1949 Yugoslavia stood isolated. Relations with the West worsened because of the bitter dispute with Italy over Trieste, the regime's refusal to compensate foreigners for nationalized property, continued Yugoslav support for the communists in Greece, and other issues. The Soviet alliance launched an economic blockade against Yugoslavia, excluding it from the Council for Mutual Economic Assistance (Comecon—see Glossary). The Soviet Union propagandized harshly against "Judas" Tito in Serbo-Croatian broadcasts, attempted to subvert CPY organizations, and sought to incite unrest among the Hungarian, Albanian, and Russian minorities in Yugoslavia.

Troop movements and border incidents convinced Yugoslav leaders that a Soviet-led invasion was imminent, requiring fundamental changes in foreign policy. In July 1949, Tito closed the Yugoslav-Greek border and ceased supplying the pro-Cominform Greek communists, and in August Yugoslav votes in the United Nations began to stray from the Soviet line. Welcoming the Yugoslav-Soviet rift, the West commenced a flow of economic aid in 1949, saved the country from hunger in 1950, and covered much of Yugoslavia's trade deficit for the next decade. The United States began shipping weapons to Yugoslavia in 1951. A military security arrangement was concluded in 1953, but the Western powers were unable to bring Yugoslavia into the North Atlantic Treaty Organization (NATO). Italy won control of Trieste in 1954.

Introduction of Socialist Self-Management

Faced with economic stagnation, a Soviet-led trade embargo, dwindling popularity, and a dysfunctional Soviet-style economic system, Yugoslav leaders returned to the core of their philosophy, the writings of Marx. Their aim was to reassess their ideology and lay the groundwork for a new economic mechanism called socialist (or workers') self-management. Enterprises formed prototype workers' councils in 1949, and the Federal Assembly passed laws in 1950 and 1951 to implement the system fully. These laws replaced state ownership of the means of production with social ownership, entrusting management responsibilities to the workers of each enterprise. The laws empowered enterprise workers' councils to set broad production goals and supervise finances, but government-appointed directors retained veto power over council decisions. The government also reformed economic planning and freed some prices to fluctuate according to supply and demand, but foreign trade remained under central control (see Socialist Self-Management, ch. 3).

The replacement of a command economy with a self-management system required the CPY to loosen its hold on decision making. At its Sixth Party Congress, in November 1952, the party renamed itself the League of Communists of Yugoslavia (LCY—see Glossary) to signal a break with its Stalinist past and a revision of its leading role in the country's political life. The congress declared that the party would separate itself structurally from the state. Instead of directing government and economic activity, the party was to influence democratic decision making through education, propaganda, and the participation of individual communists in political institutions, workers' councils, and other organizations. Free intraparty debate would determine party policy, but once the party had made a final decision, the principle of democratic centralism would bind all members to support it. By rejecting multiparty pluralism, the party retained a monopoly on political organization. Three months after the congress, the People's Front became the Socialist Alliance of Working People of Yugoslavia (SAWPY), an umbrella organization through which the party would maintain this monopoly. In addition, individual communists continued to occupy key government and enterprise-management posts.

In 1953 the Federal Assembly amended virtually the entire 1946 constitution to conform with the new laws on socialist self-management. On the federal level, the amendments created an administrative Federal Executive Council and reorganized the Federal Assembly. The amendments also reduced the already minimal autonomy of the individual republics, while local government retained power in economic and social matters.

In March 1953, the government began dissolving collective and state farms. Two-thirds of the peasants abandoned the collectives within nine months, and the socialist share of landownership sank from 25 percent to 9 percent within three years. In an attempt to mitigate the problem of peasant landlessness, the government reduced the legal limit on individual holdings from twenty-five or thirty-five hectares of cultivable land to ten hectares; this restriction would remain on the books for over three decades and would prevent the development of economically efficient family farms. The government also eliminated the system of compulsory deliveries, fixed taxes in advance, encouraged peasants to join purchasing and marketing cooperatives, and increased investment in the agricultural sector. As a result, Yugoslav agricultural output grew steadily through the 1950s, and its farms had record harvests in 1958 and 1959. Yugoslavia maintained its focus on industrial development through the 1950s, despite the government's new approach to economic planning and enterprise management. The industrial sector boomed after 1953; manufacturing exports more than doubled between 1954 and 1960; and the country showed the world's second highest economic growth rate between 1957 and 1960.

Living conditions, health care, education, and cultural life improved in the wake of the economic and political reforms. In the mid-1950s, the government redirected investment toward production of consumer goods, and foreign products became widely available. The regime also relaxed its religious restrictions, allowed for a degree of public criticism, curbed abuse of privileges by party officials, and reduced the powers of the secret police. Travel restrictions eased; Yugoslavs gained greater access to Western literature and ideas; artists abandoned "socialist realism" to experiment with abstractionism and other styles; and film makers and writers, including Nobel Prize-winner Ivo Andrić, produced first-rate works. But already in 1953, liberalization was an uneven, changeable phenomenon in Yugoslavia. A meeting of party leaders at the north Adriatic island of Brioni that year resolved to strengthen party discipline, amid growing concern that apathy had infected the rank and file since the Sixth Party Congress. Over the next several years, the party tightened democratic centralism; established basic party organizations in factories, universities, and other institutions; purged its rolls of inactive members; and took other measures to enhance discipline.

Milovan Djilas, one of Tito's closest confidants, disagreed with the Brioni decisions. In a number of articles in the foreign press, he criticized the party leadership for stifling democratic intraparty debate. He also exposed elitism in the private lives of leaders and suggested that the LCY dissolve itself as a rigid political party. This criticism exceeded Tito's tolerance, and his former comrades dismissed Djilas from his posts and imprisoned him. In 1957 Djilas published *The New Class,* in which he described the emergence of a new communist ruling elite that enjoyed all the privileges of the old bourgeoisie. The book won him international notoriety and prolonged his jail term. Publication of *Conversations with Stalin* in 1962 earned him more fame and a second prison term (see Djilas, Praxis, and Intellectual Repression, ch. 4).

Nonalignment and Yugoslav-Soviet Rapprochement

Yugoslav-Soviet relations showed signs of new life soon after Stalin died in March 1953. In an unprecedented gesture, Nikita S. Khrushchev, first secretary of the Communist Party of the Soviet Union (CPSU), visited Tito in Belgrade in 1955. Khrushchev expressed the regrets of the CPSU for the rift, although he did not blame it on Stalin directly. Tito rejected this explanation, and after formal discussions the Yugoslav and Soviet leaders decided to resume only state relations. In the final communiqué of the meeting, known as the Belgrade Declaration, the Soviet Union acknowledged the right of individual socialist countries to follow their own path toward socialism.

The LCY and CPSU restored relations in 1956, and at the CPSU's Twentieth Party Congress, Khrushchev blasted Stalin for his ''shameful role'' in the Yugoslav-Soviet estrangement. After a visit to the Soviet Union in June that deepened the rapprochement, Tito entertained hopes that all of Eastern Europe would adopt some version of Yugoslavia's model for socialist development. Movement toward liberalization in the Soviet alliance, however, ground to a halt with the 1956 Hungarian Revolution and the Soviet invasion that crushed it. Yugoslav-Hungarian relations cooled after the execution of Imre Nagy, the Hungarian revolutionary leader who had taken asylum in the Yugoslav embassy in Budapest. Yugoslav-Soviet relations were unstable in the years following the Hungarian invasion, but by 1961 they had entered a period of détente.

Nonalignment became the keystone of Yugoslavia's foreign policy in the 1950s. While isolated from the superpowers, Yugoslavia strove to forge strong ties with Third World countries similarly interested in avoiding an alliance with East or West and the hard choice between communism and capitalism. Tito found common ground with Egypt's President Gamal Abdul Nasser and India's Prime Minister Jawaharlal Nehru, and they worked together to organize a movement of Third World nations whose collective statements on international issues would carry greater weight than their individual voices. In 1961 Belgrade hosted the first major conference of the world's nonaligned nations. Tito used the prestige gained from the meeting and from his denunciations of neocolonialism to enhance the leverage gained by positioning Yugoslavia between East and West.

Reforms of the 1960s

Initial steps toward market socialism (see Glossary) and freer foreign trade in 1961 produced unacceptable inflation and a foreign-trade deficit, and emergency anti-inflation measures plunged Yugoslavia into recession in 1962. The recession produced an urgent debate on fundamental economic reforms, especially decentralization of investment decision making. During the debate, naturally conflicting interregional economic interests rekindled ethnic rivalries, and emotional nationalist claims reemerged to complicate economic discussions. Party leaders were unable to solve the widening economic gap between the country's more prosperous northern republics and the underdeveloped southern regions. Resentment grew from suspicions that some republics were receiving an unfair share of investment funds.

The government adopted stopgap recentralization measures to end the recession in 1962, but inflation and the foreign-trade deficit again rose sharply, renewing debate on economic reforms. Led by Eduard Kardelj and Vladimir Bakarić, party liberals (mostly from Slovenia, Croatia, and the Belgrade area) promoted decentralization measures and investment strategies that would benefit the wealthier republics. Conservatives (mostly from Serbia and Montenegro) supported maintaining or stiffening central controls and continuing investment in the less developed regions (see Overhaul in the 1960s, ch. 3).

In 1963 Yugoslavia established new constitutions at the national and republic level, expanding the concept of self-management beyond the economic sphere into social activity. This was achieved by creating local councils for education and culture, social welfare, public health, and political administration. The composition of the

President Tito with Nehru of India and Nasser of Egypt, at meeting of Nonaligned Movement leaders, Brioni, 1956
Courtesy Embassy of Yugoslavia, Washington

Federal Assembly was altered, simultaneous officeholding in the party and government was outlawed (except for Tito), and government tenure was limited and dispersed by the introduction of a regular rotation system (see The 1963 Constitution, ch. 4).

In the mid-1960s, the parliamentary institutions became more active, as Federal Assembly members criticized cabinet secretaries and amended bills and as liberal reformers used the assembly to advance their ideas. Between 1964 and 1967, the assembly reduced the role of the state in economic management and created the legislative foundation of market socialism. Reform also included external trade measures: Yugoslavia devalued its currency, obtained foreign loans, and joined the General Agreement on Tariffs and Trade (GATT—see Glossary).

The period immediately following this set of reforms brought stagnation, rising unemployment, unpopular price increases, illiquidity, increases in income disparity, and calls for new reforms. Leaders in Serbia, Montenegro, Macedonia, and elsewhere scrambled to stave off efforts to close unprofitable enterprises in their areas. Slovenes and Croats came to resent requirements for heavy investment in less developed republics at the expense of their own modernization. Yugoslav workers themselves eased unemployment by finding guest worker jobs in Western Europe (see Structure of the Economy, ch. 3). Foreign tourists and workers returning from abroad brought Yugoslavia much-needed foreign currency. A 1967 law allowed foreigners to invest up to 49 percent in partnerships with Yugoslav firms and repatriate their profits, and in 1970 Yugoslavia signed a long-sought commercial agreement with the European Economic Community (EEC—see Glossary). The postreform recession ended in 1969 as unemployment dropped and incomes and living standards rose, but inflation again gained momentum, and many enterprises remained unprofitable (see The Economic Reform of 1965, ch. 3).

Certain that the reforms would undermine party control and threaten Yugoslavia's survival, pro-centralist party leaders and mid-level bureaucrats attempted to obstruct their implementation. Again the centers of this movement were Serbia and Montenegro. The key opponent of reform was the hard-line Serbian vice president of Yugoslavia, Aleksandar Ranković, who also directed party cadres and the secret police. In 1966 the army intelligence unit, composed mostly of Croats, examined complaints that the secret police was mistreating Albanians in Kosovo. The investigation uncovered a wide range of unethical practices, including smuggling and surveillance of Tito himself. Tito purged the secret police, and Ranković was forced to resign (see Internal Security, ch. 5). But he remained the champion of Serbian nationalist groups, particularly on the issue of Kosovo.

After the defeat of the conservatives and adoption of additional party reforms, the party central organization lost its predominant position. Republic and province party leaders blocked action taken in Belgrade and gained control of party appointments, thus shifting the focus of party loyalty away from the center. New election laws brought direct multicandidate elections, often won by candidates who lacked party approval.

Party discipline softened when the ascendant liberals continued to argue that the LCY should influence rather than direct self-management decision making. The press and universities grew into centers of debate on an expanding list of taboo issues. Beginning in 1968, a group of intellectuals in Zagreb and Belgrade, known collectively as the Praxis circle, circulated unorthodox interpretations of Marx, supported student demonstrations, and criticized the rigidity of party positions. Despite official efforts to suppress it, the Praxis circle flourished and spoke out until 1975.

In 1968 attention moved back to foreign policy. Student unrest subsided, and Yugoslav-Soviet relations again sagged after Warsaw Pact nations invaded Czechoslovakia in August 1968. Tito, who had traveled to Prague before the invasion to lend support to Alexander Dubček's program of "socialism with a human face," denounced the invasion, and Moscow and Belgrade exchanged bitter criticism. The Yugoslavs warned that they would resist a Soviet invasion of their country, and Tito established a civil defense organization capable of mobilizing the entire country in such an event (see National Defense, ch. 5).

The quiet that the invasion of Czechoslovakia brought to the Yugoslav domestic scene was broken in November 1968 when ethnic Albanians in Kosovo and western Macedonia staged violent demonstrations to demand equality and republic status for Kosovo. Demonstrations and violent incidents continued through 1969. Among broad government concessions to the ethnic Albanians, a 1968 constitutional amendment allowed local economic and social planning and financial control in Kosovo. Serbian and Montenegrin intellectuals condemned the upgrading of Kosovo's status and accurately predicted that Albanian abuses would increase Serbian emigration from Kosovo. The creation of the separate Macedonian Orthodox Church and rising Muslim nationalism in Bosnia also irritated Serbian churchmen and intellectuals during this period.

After tough political bargaining, the Federal Assembly adopted constitutional amendments in 1971 that transformed Yugoslavia into a loose federation. The amendments limited federal government responsibilities to defense, foreign affairs, maintenance of a unified Yugoslav market, common monetary and foreign-trade policies, the self-management system, and ethnic and civil rights. The republics and provinces gained primary control over all other functions and a de facto veto power over federal decisions.

Unrest in Croatia and Its Consequences in the 1970s

Political, economic, and cultural tensions in the late 1960s sharply increased nationalist feeling in Croatia. In 1967 Croatian intellectuals, including Miroslav Krleža, the most respected literary figure in Croatia, signed a statement denying the validity of Serbo-Croatian as a historical language and promoting Croatian as a distinct language. The ensuing polemics escalated into a conflict over discrimination. Croatian historians recalled exploitation of Croatia by the Serb-dominated prewar government, and Croatian economists complained of disproportionate levies on Croatia for the federal budget and development fund. Party leaders in Zagreb won popularity by defending the economic interests of the republic, and nationalist leadership groups, including Matica Hrvatska, Croatia's oldest cultural society, began calling for constitutional changes to give the republic virtual independence. In November

1971, university students went on strike, and demonstrators marched through the streets. Tito pressed Croatian party leaders to quiet the nationalists, but the unrest continued. Finally, police and soldiers arrested hundreds of student leaders. The authorities disbanded Matica Hrvatska and purged "nationalists" and liberals from all Croatian organizations and institutions.

The rise of nationalism halted the liberal movement in the national party. Tito called for stricter adherence to democratic centralism and proclaimed that the LCY would remain the binding political force of Yugoslavia and that the party could not decentralize without endangering the country's integrity. He also called for the party to reassume its leading role and reestablish its control over the country's political and economic life. Through 1972 Tito overcame unprecedented local defiance to purge reformist party leaders in Serbia, Slovenia, Macedonia, and Vojvodina. He replaced them in most instances with antireform party veterans who had displayed less political talent than their predecessors but were considered more reliable politically. In 1974 the Tenth Party Congress elected Tito party president for life and proclaimed that Yugoslav "self-managed socialism" would remain under firm party control. The leadership muzzled the press, arrested dissidents, pressured universities to fire outspoken professors, and redoubled efforts to promote Tito's cult of personality.

The 1974 Constitution

In 1974 the government enacted a new Constitution, one of the world's longest, which created new representative bodies and a complex system of checks and balances, designed to enhance party power and limit the influence of professional enterprise managers. The new Constitution replaced direct election of representatives to legislative bodies, substituting a complex system of indirect elections by delegates representing associated labor, sociopolitical organizations, and local citizens in general. The leadership heralded the new system as "direct workers' democracy," but the mechanism actually allowed the central party leadership greater control of the Federal Assembly and republic and local assemblies. Despite recent nationalist unrest and conservative backlash, the Constitution retained the 1971 amendments that shifted power from the federal government to the republics.

In his last years, Tito virtually ignored worsening economic conditions and worked domestically to strengthen collective leadership and prevent a single individual or group from accumulating excessive power. In foreign affairs, Cuba threatened Yugoslav leadership of the Nonaligned Movement by pushing the movement toward

*Gathering of world dignitaries for President
Tito's funeral, May 1980
Courtesy United Press International*

a pro-Soviet position at the 1979 Conference of Nonaligned Nations in Havana. Tito condemned the Soviet invasion of Afghanistan that year. Despite the weakening of the Nonaligned Movement by the influence of Cuban dictator Fidel Castro, in the 1970s Yugoslavia largely succeeded in maintaining friendly relations with all states, regardless of their political and economic systems. Tito died on May 4, 1980, and Yugoslavia's collective presidency assumed full control in a smooth transition. Most Yugoslavs genuinely mourned the loss of their longtime leader, who had been their country's strongest unifying force. The presence of forty-nine international leaders at his funeral showed the wide respect that Tito had gained around the world.

In 1980 Yugoslavia entered a new era after the death of the most effective leader the South Slavic nation had ever had. The history of the country had featured division much more prominently than unification; over the centuries, the constituent parts of the modern Yugoslav state had alternated between independence, federation with other states, and domination by larger powers. Each of the republics of the modern federation underwent its own historical and cultural development, very often in conflict with the territorial or political goals of its Slavic and non-Slavic neighbors. Although the South Slavic state was a longtime dream of many, initial efforts to establish such a state were very problematic. After two disastrous world wars, the nation held together in a relatively calm period of development, but after Tito the threat of economic and political disharmony again appeared.

*　　*　　*

There is a wealth of informative, well-written English-language sources on the history of Yugoslavia and its many peoples. An excellent short work is Fred Singleton's *A Short History of the Yugoslav Peoples. Black Lamb and Grey Falcon* by Rebecca West is a classic popular history and personal memoir of a tour through Yugoslavia on the eve of World War II. Robert Lee Wolff's *The Balkans in Our Time* describes the emergence of Yugoslavia and the other Balkan countries and their development to the postwar period. An excellent study of Yugoslav foreign policy of the 1920s and 1930s is J.B. Hoptner's *Yugoslavia in Crisis, 1934–1941.* The works of Francis Dvornik on the migrations, conversion, and cultural development of the Slavs devote considerable attention to the Slovenes, Croats, Serbs, and Bulgars. Two excellent examinations of postwar Yugoslavia development are Dennison Rusinow's *The Yugoslav*

Experiment, 1948–1974 and *Conflict and Cohesion in Socialist Yugoslavia* by Steven L. Burg. (For further information and complete citations, see Bibliography.)

Chapter 2. The Society and Its Environment

Folk dancers

THE MANY FACETS of the ethnic lens through which Yugoslavs view the universe have magnified the divisions in Yugoslav society and obscured its few unifying elements. The obvious cultural and economic contrasts were only the starting point of differences that existed on many levels. In the alpine north, baroque Catholic altars reflected Slovenia's cultural affinity with Austria and Italy, but modern glass-and-steel skyscrapers revealed Slovenia's aspirations toward a role in modern Europe. In the Balkan south, the ancient stone churches of Macedonia reflected a rich Byzantine tradition, while acute poverty and a low literacy rate were part of the legacy of Ottoman domination that had insulated Macedonians from the influences of the Renaissance, the Enlightenment, and the Industrial Revolution. The forces of war and external threat bound Slovenia, Macedonia, and the patchwork of cultures between them into a single country, but they allowed scant opportunity for consideration of how ethnic differences could be overcome.

Despite the ethnic and cultural cleavages that continued to divide Yugoslavia in 1990, the country made great social progress after World War II. On the eve of the war, Yugoslavia was a backward, predominantly peasant land with a few developing basic industries mostly located in its northern regions. Paved roads were rare, schools few, and almost half the people illiterate. Infectious disease was frequent, infant mortality was very high, doctors were few, and hygiene, medical facilities, and child care were poor, especially in rural areas. The strong kinship ties that undergirded society were the only social welfare system available to most people. Meanwhile, rural overpopulation fragmented landholding, and poverty frayed the fabric of the family. While educated citizens in the northern cities might watch ancient Greek drama in theaters, many of their compatriots in the southern mountains actually lived according to Homeric traditions of blood vengeance: buying, selling, and stealing brides; practicing rituals of blood brotherhood; and reciting epic poems to the music of a crude single-string instrument.

Before World War II, Yugoslavia's small upper class was composed of a Serb-dominated bureaucracy and military and a few professionals, entrepreneurs, and artisans. Like the Habsburg and Ottoman domination of earlier centuries, the Serbian hegemony established after World War I frustrated the autonomy of the country's other major nationalities. Preoccupation with issues of nationalism prevented effective solutions to the country's grave social problems. Animosities among the Yugoslav peoples exploded in civil war after the Nazis occupied the country in 1941. World War II claimed 1.7 million Yugoslav lives and inflicted deep wounds on all national psyches. Atrocities were committed by all sides, and more than half of Yugoslavia's war dead were killed by other Yugoslavs.

After World War II, Yugoslavia's communist government promoted the slogan Brotherhood and Unity and moved energetically to smooth over ethnic antagonisms. Josip Broz Tito and his revolutionary regime eradicated wartime collaborators along with many innocents, ousted what remained of the old Serb-dominated elite, nationalized private property, and established a new party-based governing class. Membership in the wartime Partisans (see Glossary), rather than competence or education, became the key to a successful career. The new government, led by a ruling circle steeped in Marxism and Leninism, undertook radical steps to modernize the country: first reconstruction, then rapid industrialization. Modernization continued apace after the Yugoslav communists ended their alliance with the Soviet Union in 1948 and introduced socialist self-management, a unique version of socialism. Thousands of peasants migrated to urban areas in the decade following World War II. Patriarchal extended families broke down at an accelerated rate, and women began to find jobs and a new identity outside the home. New schools and hospitals opened, and universities began training teachers, doctors, and engineers.

Although Yugoslavia's economy expanded rapidly, by the mid-1960s it could not absorb the large number of individuals emerging from the education system. Tito opened the borders to emigration, and within a decade about a million Yugoslavs had left to take jobs in Western Europe. Massive capital redistribution from relatively rich northerly regions to the less-developed south did not mitigate the huge differences in development between them. The economic downturn of the late 1970s and 1980s slowed the entry of qualified individuals into the working and managing classes. In the 1970s, the northern republics began to complain about the contributions to development in the southern regions mandated by the central government. An entrenched bureaucracy sabotaged economic and social reforms in the 1970s and 1980s, and by the late 1980s economic and political stagnation had eroded many of the earlier improvements in Yugoslavia's standard of living. As the concept of the centrally planned economy waned throughout Eastern Europe, Yugoslavia turned to the West, causing further tension between tradition and change. In 1990 political victories by noncommunist parties in Slovenia and Croatia promised a fresh approach to old and new social tensions and regional disparities. Such changes portended a complete restructuring of the Yugoslav federation.

Geography and Population

Varied and often breathtaking, Yugoslavia's landscape allows outside access to the country from virtually every direction, but it seriously hampers internal movement from one region to the next. Throughout history, Yugoslavia's topography has exposed the country to foreign invaders, frustrated internal commerce and political cohesion, and preserved the extraordinarily complex ethnic mosaic created by successive invasions and migrations. The ruggedness of their terrain is one reason Yugoslavs have often won renown as soldiers but seldom as merchants.

Topography

Rugged mountains dominate the 255,804 square kilometers of Yugoslavia. Mountains separate the fertile inland plain from a narrow, rocky Adriatic coastline. Yugoslavia's three main mountainous regions occupy about 60 percent of its territory. The Julian Alps of Slovenia, an extension of the Italian and Austrian alps, include Yugoslavia's highest peaks. The Dinaric Alps rise dramatically along the entire 1,500-kilometer Adriatic coast. Finally, spurs extend southward from the Carpathian and Balkan mountains through Serbia from the Danube River's Iron Gate near the Romanian-Bulgarian border, intersecting with the Dinaric Alps in Macedonia (see Drainage Systems, this ch.).

The composition of Yugoslavia's mountains varies. The Dinaric Alps, like the offshore Adriatic islands, are chiefly cracked limestone strata that form long valleys and contain topographical oddities such as magnificent caves, disappearing rivers, and a freshwater lake (on the north Adriatic island of Cres) deeper than the Adriatic seabed. In some areas east of the coast, erosion of the limestone has exposed the crystalline rock outlayers of the Rhodope Massif, which is the primeval core of the Balkan Peninsula. From Bosnia southeastward, areas of crystalline rock are interspersed with alluvial sedimentary rock. Serbia's mountains contain a variety of rock types, including volcanic rock and exposed crystalline formations. Geological fault lines in southern Yugoslavia have caused occasional earthquakes; the most serious in recent times killed over 1,000 people at Skopje in 1963.

North and west of Belgrade are the Pannonian Plains, which include all of the Serbian province of Vojvodina. These plains were the floor of a huge inland sea during the Tertiary period (65 million to 2.5 million years ago). Here eons of sedimentary and wind-blown deposits have created layers of fertile soil that are over 160 meters deep in some places.

Yugoslavia possesses about 1,500 kilometers of convoluted Adriatic coastline, not including its many islands. From the coast, access inland is easiest through four passages. The Postojna Gate, used for millennia by merchants and armies crossing between the Adriatic and Central Europe, is Yugoslavia's northernmost passage through the coastal mountains. Farther south, the Neretva River is a centuries-old trading link between the Adriatic and Bosnia. Below the Neretva, the Gulf of Kotor is a spectacular fjord long considered a strategic port. Finally, the port of Bar connects with the interior of Montenegro and Serbia by means of the Belgrade-Bar Railroad, giving Serbia access to the Adriatic.

Drainage Systems

The Pannonian Plains are drained by the Danube and its four major tributaries, the Drava, Tisa (Hungarian spelling Tisza), Sava, and Morava (see fig. 6). The Danube, extremely wide and deep at some points, varies greatly between high- and low-water seasons. The former is from March or April until May or June, the latter from mid-July to late October. The Danube also drains the interior highlands. The Vardar River and its tributaries drain the southeastern region into the Aegean Sea, and the Neretva drains the south-central region into the Adriatic. The western alpine slopes parallel to the coast are drained into the Adriatic by surface and underground streams. Underground streams are formed when water seeps through the limestone of the alps into channels, then empties into the Adriatic below its surface.

Climate

Yugoslavia lies in the southern half of the northern temperate zone, but the climate of its mountains, interior plain, and seacoast varies dramatically according to elevation, prevailing winds, and distance from the sea. The mountain regions fall under the influence of continental air currents and Mediterranean air masses. Snow blankets most of the highlands during the winter, but temperature and precipitation differ with elevation. For example, Montenegro's capital, Titograd (elevation 210 meters) enjoys an average monthly temperature ten degrees warmer than that of Cetinje (3,530 meters), which is only 40 kilometers to the west; and Crkvica (5,776 meters),

Figure 6. Topography and Drainage

a town 32 kilometers north of Cetinje, averages 4,623 millimeters of annual rainfall, three times more than Titograd. The interior plain has a continental climate featuring hot, humid summers. A dry wind, the Košava, brings freezing air from central Eurasia in the winter, but snowfall is usually light. The Dalmatian coast enjoys mild Mediterranean weather. Summers on the coast are hot and dry with turquoise blue skies; a fair sea breeze, the Maestral, cools the land during mornings and afternoons. Winters are cool and rainy. A chilling winter wind known as the Bura sweeps down through gaps in the coastal mountains; and a southwest wind, the Jugo, brings winter rains. Warm winds blow up the Vardar Valley from the Aegean into Macedonia, making subtropical agriculture possible in some parts of that republic.

Pollution

After World War II, industrialization and urban development progressed rapidly in Yugoslavia. As in other East European countries, the environmental effects of such growth went unrecognized for many years. In the 1980s, a constitutional amendment and numerous environmental protection laws were passed, but they had little initial effect on pollution of the air, soil, and water. A small green movement struggled to bring the problem onto the political agenda, but it had achieved little political influence as of 1990. Yugoslavia's air suffered from sulfur dioxide pollution caused by vehicle emissions, trash fires, and the burning of high-sulfur lignite (soft coal) in power plants and home heating units. Oil spills frequently appeared on the Sava River; dangerous levels of phenol in the Ibar River occasionally required the town of Kraljevo to shut off its water supply; and the artificial lake above the Djerdap Hydroelectric Station on the Danube was referred to as the dump of Europe. Nuclear waste from Yugoslavia's only nuclear electric plant, at Krško in Slovenia (a main target of the green movement), had almost filled its subterranean nuclear waste storage facilities in 1990. Deforestation increased soil erosion problems, and mounds of trash littered the roadsides in most eastern and southern rural areas.

Population

Yugoslavia's resident population was estimated at 23.4 million people in 1987, up from 15.7 million in 1948 and 22.4 million in 1981. In addition, over a million Yugoslavs lived and worked for long periods of time in other European countries. The country's population density grew from 62 persons per square kilometer in 1948 to 92 per square kilometer in 1988.

Between 1961 and 1981, Yugoslavia's annual population growth (1.0 percent) was about the same as that of the world's developed countries. By 1990, the rate had dropped to 0.6 percent. The population growth rate in Yugoslavia's economically less-developed regions, however, was significantly higher than that in the developed regions. For example, in 1986 the respective annual growth rates of Kosovo and Macedonia were 2.5 percent and 1.5 percent. By comparison, the respective rates in industrialized Vojvodina and Slovenia were only 0.5 percent and 0.9 percent. The annual growth rate of the country's working-age population was 1.3 percent, indicating that an increasing proportion of that group was found in the less developed regions.

The average age of Yugoslavia's population in 1986 was 33.9 years. Men averaged 32.6 years of age; women, 35.1. The average age of the Yugoslav population increased over the last half century because the birth rate declined and life expectancy increased over that period (see table 2; table 3, Appendix). Between the 1921 and 1981 censuses, the Yugoslav population as a whole moved from the demographic category of population maturity toward the oldest category, demographic old age. The demographic aging of the population varied in different parts of the country, however, and in 1981 Yugoslavia's republics and provinces fit into different categories of demographic aging. The populations of Vojvodina, Serbia proper (see Glossary), and Croatia were in demographic old age; those in Montenegro and Slovenia were on the threshold of demographic old age; those in Bosnia and Hercegovina and Macedonia had reached demographic maturity; the population of Kosovo, however, was still in demographic youth.

Life expectancy began to increase in 1918, lengthening from about 35 years to 67.8 years for men and 73.5 years for women in 1982. After World War II, the mortality rate in Yugoslavia declined precipitously. In 1984 the country had a mortality rate of about 9.3 per thousand, down from 12.8 per thousand in 1947. In Kosovo the mortality rate dropped from 13 per thousand in 1947 to 5.8 in 1984, while in Slovenia it dropped from 13.5 to 10.9 per thousand.

Yugoslavia's infant mortality rate, a key indicator of a population's social, economic, health care, and cultural levels, dropped from 118.6 infant deaths per thousand births in 1950 to 28.9 per thousand in 1984. In 1984 Vojvodina (12.0 infant deaths per thousand births), Slovenia (15.7), and Croatia (15.8) reported Yugoslavia's lowest infant mortality rates, while Kosovo (63.1) and Macedonia (49.5) reported the highest. In spite of higher living standards and health care, however, in 1985 Yugoslavia's infant mortality rate ranked only above Albania among European countries.

In Slovenia, Croatia, Vojvodina, and Serbia proper, birth rates declined together with the mortality rate. But in Bosnia and Hercegovina, Macedonia, and Montenegro, a rapid drop in the birth rate came only after 1960, while Kosovo's birth rate dropped only slightly through 1990. By 1980 the population explosion among Kosovo's ethnic Albanians had become Yugoslavia's most pressing demographic problem. Between 1950 and 1983, the population of Kosovo grew by about 220 percent, while the Yugoslav total increased by only 39 percent. Kosovo's high annual birth rate (about 29 births per thousand in 1988, the highest in Europe) and the increased life expectancy of the population spurred this demographic growth. Although Kosovo's birth rate declined somewhat during the 1980s, the absolute number of births increased while the mortality rate declined. By 1980 Kosovo had become the most densely populated part of Yugoslavia (146 persons per square kilometer), although it remained the country's least-developed region.

In the mid-1960s, the government began actively supporting family planning practices to control population growth. In 1969 the Federal Assembly (Skupština) passed a liberalized abortion law. At the same time, the government passed a resolution on family planning that urged expansion of free programs in family planning and modern contraceptive techniques. The resolution also emphasized the role of the social services and other national institutions in sex education and planned parenthood. After 1969 the obvious failure of family planning in Kosovo produced calls for greater dissemination of birth control information and devices and establishment of family planning counseling services. The winning party in Croatia's 1990 republican elections, however, ran on a platform that called for banning abortion. The party's victory raised the possibility of antiabortion legislation in that republic.

Yugoslavia's Peoples

Modern Yugoslavia had its genesis in a nineteenth-century Romantic idea that the South Slavs, chiefly the Serbs, Croats, Slovenes, and Bulgars, should be united in a single independent state. Except for the existence of an independent Bulgaria, the Yugoslavia created after World War I was a virtual realization of this idea. With the creation of the South Slav state, however, the Yugoslavs had to face the fact that besides similar languages, similar ancient ethnic roots, and the shared experience of foreign oppression, they had rather little in common.

Ethnographic History

The South Slavs lived for centuries on two sides of a disputed border between the Eastern and Western Roman Empires, between the Eastern Orthodox and the Roman Catholic churches, between the Islamic crescent and the Christian cross. Those on the Eastern side (today's Serbs, Montenegrins, Muslim Slavs, and Macedonians) had lived under Byzantine and Turkish influence; those on the Western side (the Slovenes and Croats) had lived under the religious authority of Rome and the secular authority of Vienna, Budapest, and Venice. Besides the South Slavs, the Yugoslav state contained a mélange of minority peoples, many of them non-Slavic, who professed different religions, spoke different languages, and had different and often conflicting historical assumptions and desires. With over twenty-five distinct nationalities, Yugoslavia had one of the most complex ethnic profiles in Europe. Over seventy years after Yugoslavia's creation in 1918, serious doubts remained that a federation of such disparate elements could continue as an integrated state.

The Constitution of 1974 divided the country's ethnic groups into two categories: nations (see Glossary), or ethnic groups whose traditional territorial homelands lay within the country's modern boundaries, and nationalities, or ethnic groups whose traditional homelands lay outside those boundaries. The Yugoslav nations were the Croats, Macedonians, Montenegrins, Muslim Slavs, Serbs, and Slovenes (see fig. 7). Yugoslavia's main nationalities were the Albanians, Bulgars, Czechs, Hungarians, Italians, Romanians, Ruthenians, Slovaks, Turks, and Ukrainians (see table 4, Appendix). Other nationalities included the Austrians, Germans, Greeks, Gypsies, Jews, Poles, Russians, and Vlachs (a Romanian group). The other nationalities besides these totaled less than 0.1 percent of the country's population and did not enjoy special constitutional status as nationalities; as individuals, however, they were entitled to the same rights and freedoms guaranteed all other Yugoslavs in the national Constitution.

Ethnic Composition

Serbs constituted more than a third of the total population in the 1981 census. They were followed by the Croats (19.7 percent), Muslim Slavs (8.9 percent), Slovenes (7.8 percent), Albanians (7.7 percent), Macedonians (6.0 percent), Montenegrins (2.6 percent), and Hungarians (1.9 percent). In the 1981 census, about 1.2 million people, or 5.4 percent of the country's population, declared themselves to be ethnic Yugoslavs, a fourfold increase since 1971. Yugoslav scholars disagree about the reason for this rise in avowed Yugoslavism. Demographers have attributed the increase to an upswing in popular identification with Yugoslavia as a state following the death of Tito in 1980 and to minority group members declaring themselves Yugoslav nationals. Given the national tensions of the late 1980s, analysts eagerly awaited the 1991 census for new trends in Yugoslav national identification.

Yugoslavia's overall ethnic makeup did not change drastically in the seventy years after the country was founded, despite the fact that the population grew by more than 70 percent during that time. Exceptions to this pattern of stability were the marked increase of the Albanian population and a steep decline in the numbers of Jews, ethnic Germans, and Hungarians after World War II.

Most of Yugoslavia's six republics and two provinces showed significant ethnic diversity. Only Serbia proper, Slovenia, and Montenegro were largely homogeneous. Croatia had a substantial Serbian minority of nearly 12 percent. Macedonia had Turks, Vlachs, and a fast-growing Albanian population. Muslim Slavs, Serbs, and Croats made up the population of Bosnia and Hercegovina, but no single group predominated. Kosovo was predominantly Albanian with Serbian, Montenegrin, and Muslim Slav minorities; and a Serbian majority shared Vojvodina with Hungarians (at 19 percent, the largest minority in that province), Croats, and many less numerous groups (see table 5, Appendix).

Complicating the ethnic situation was the fact that most nationalities were not confined within the borders of the country's republics, provinces, or districts (*opština,* the next largest jurisdiction). For example, in 1981 about 98 percent of all Yugoslavia's Slovenes lived in Slovenia, and about 96 percent of its Macedonians lived in Macedonia; but only 60 percent of the Serbs lived in Serbia proper, and only 70 percent of the Montenegrins lived in Montenegro. In the postwar era, the share of a republic's population that belonged to that republic's dominant national group generally declined. Thus, in Slovenia, where Slovenes accounted for 98 percent of the population in 1948, they accounted for only about 90 percent in 1981.

Yugoslavia's federal and republican constitutions guarantee equal rights for all ethnic groups, including the right to participate in public life, government, and the armed forces. Minority nationalities have the right to organize groups to exercise their cultural rights and promote their national interests. Article 119 of the federal criminal code, however, prohibits propaganda and other activities aimed at inciting or fomenting national, racial, or religious intolerance, hatred, or dissension between nations and nationalities. The federal and republican constitutions also provide for proportional representation of the nations and nationalities in assemblies, commissions,

Figure 7. Ethnic Groups

the highest levels of the army's officer corps, and other government institutions.

Languages

According to the 1974 Constitution, the three official languages of Yugoslavia were Serbo-Croatian, Slovenian, and Macedonian. Serbo-Croatian has an eastern and a western variant; it is written in the Latin alphabet in Croatia and in the Cyrillic alphabet (see Glossary) in Serbia and Montenegro (see fig. 8). Both alphabets are used in Bosnia and Hercegovina. Ironically, the Croatian literary variant is closer to the language spoken by most Serbs and Montenegrins than to that spoken by most Croats. Like Serbo-Croatian, Slovenian, which uses the Latin alphabet, became a literary language in the nineteenth century. Macedonian, which has elements of both Bulgarian and Serbo-Croatian, obtained a standardized Cyrillic-based alphabet and orthography only after World War II.

In order of usage, Yugoslavia's most significant minority languages included Albanian, Hungarian, Turkish, Bulgarian, Romanian, Italian, Vlach, Czech, Slovak, Ruthenian, and Romany, the language of the Gypsies. The Constitution guaranteed members of the nationalities the right to use their own language and alphabet, including the right to use it in public affairs and in addressing government agencies. The nationalities also received the option of education in their native language through high school or vocational school (see Education, this ch.). Children attending such schools were required to study one of the three official Yugoslav languages. In 1990 the government of Serbia filled a gap in this guarantee by opening the first Romany-language primary school in the world. In the 1970s, the government eliminated the requirement that schoolchildren study a second official Yugoslav language; this change caused a steep drop in the number of Slovenian and Albanian students who learned Serbo-Croatian and threatened to isolate some Slovenian and Albanian communities.

The Yugoslav Nations

In 1990 national identity remained a vital characteristic in Yugoslavia, and distrust across ethnic boundaries persisted. Second only to the government bureaucracy, nationalism and ethnically based discrimination provided the universal explanation for all evils befalling the Yugoslav peoples. Kosovan Albanians complained that Macedonians purposely built their province's roads badly; Serbs complained that the Slovenes exploited their economy and that they were the victims of plotting Croats, Slovenes, and Islamic-fundamentalist ethnic Albanians; Croats and Slovenes feared Serbian domination and complained of the lack of discipline of their fellow Yugoslavs to the south.

The deepest and oldest national rivalry in Yugoslavia was the one between the Serbs and Croats, who despite their shared language possessed different social and value systems and political cultures. Two sayings illustrated these animosities and the essential difference in the inherited political styles of both peoples. The first says: The very way of life of a Serb and Croat is a deliberate provocation by each to the other. The second, a self-complimentary Serbian stereotype, says: In a conflict with authority, the Serb reaches for the sword and the Croat for his pen. The Serbian stereotype refers to the tradition of the *hajduk*, the idealized mountain renegade who responded violently to the oppressive anarchy of the Ottoman Empire during its last two centuries; the Croatian stereotype reflects

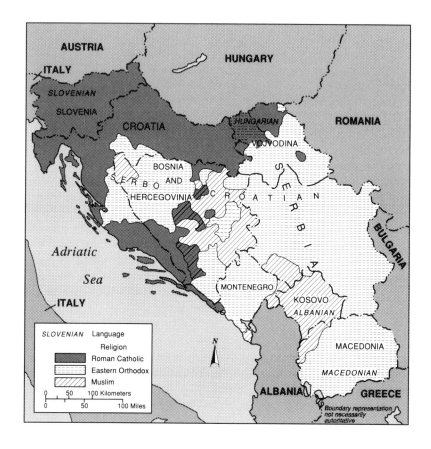

Figure 8. Principal Languages and Religions

the cultural influence of responding through the legal system to the Habsburgs' highly bureaucratized infringements on national and individual freedoms in Croatia.

Serbs

The demographic distribution and ethnic outlook of the Serbs exerted paramount influence on the shape of the modern Yugoslav state from the very beginning. The Serbs were Yugoslavia's most populous and most dispersed nationality. Although concentrated in Serbia proper, in 1981 they also accounted for substantial portions of the population of Kosovo (13.2 percent), Vojvodina (54.4 percent), Croatia (11.5 percent), and Bosnia and Hercegovina (32.0 percent). Historically, the first cause of this scattering was the severe oppression of Serbs under Ottoman occupation, which led to migration to the unoccupied territory to the west. After World War II, Yugoslavia's first communist government tried to define the country's postwar federal units to limit the Serbian domination believed largely responsible for the political turmoil of the interwar period. This meant reducing Serbia proper to achieve political recognition of Macedonian and Montenegrin ethnic individuality and the mixed populations of Vojvodina, Kosovo, and Bosnia and Hercegovina (see Formation of the South Slav State, ch. 1).

The Serbs' forefathers built a rich kingdom during the thirteenth and fourteenth centuries, then suffered under Ottoman occupation for 370 years (1459-1829). During the Ottoman era, the Serbian Orthodox Church preserved the Serbs' sense of nationhood and reinforced the collective memory of past glory. The church canonized medieval Serbian kings; fresco painters preserved their images; and priests recited a litany of their names at daily masses. Until the nineteenth century, virtually all Serbs were peasants; the small percentage that lived in towns as traders and craftsmen wore Turkish costume and lived a Turkish life-style. Until the twentieth century, peasant Serbs lived mainly in extended families, with four or five nuclear families residing in the same house. An elder managed the household and property (see The Family, this ch.).

The independence movement of the nineteenth century brought significant cultural changes to the Serbs. During that century, the scholars Dositej Obradović and Vuk Karadžić overcame stiff opposition from the Orthodox Church to foster creation of the modern Serbian literary language, which is based on the speech of the ordinary people. Karadžić adapted the Cyrillic alphabet to create the form still used in Yugoslavia.

After World War I, the Serbs considered themselves the liberators of Croatia and Slovenia—nations whose loyalty the Serbs found suspect because they had seemed unwilling or unable to rise against Austria-Hungary in the independence struggles that preceded World War I. The Serbian political elite of the interwar Kingdom of Yugoslavia was extremely centralist and accustomed to wielding unshared power. On the eve of World War II, the Yugoslav army officer corps and the civilian bureaucracy were dominated by Serbs (2 Croats and 2 Slovenes were generals; the other 161 generals were either Serbs or Montenegrins). Serbian hegemony in interwar Yugoslavia triggered a militant backlash in Croatia, Macedonia, and Kosovo; during World War II, Croatian nationalist fanatics butchered Serbs, Jews, and Gypsies with a brutality that appalled even the Nazis (see Partition and Terror, ch. 1).

The Serbs' memories of their medieval kingdom, their 1389 defeat by the Ottoman Turks, their nineteenth-century uprisings, and their heavy sacrifices during twentieth-century wars contributed significantly to their feeling that they had sacrificed much for Yugoslavia and received relatively little in return. In the late 1980s, a passionate Serbian nationalist revival arose from this sense of unfulfilled expectation, from the postwar distribution of the Serbs among various Yugoslav political entities, and from perceived discrimination against the Serbs in Kosovo in the 1970s and 1980s (see Serbia, ch. 4). In this process, the Serbian Orthodox Church reemerged as a strong cultural influence, and the government of Serbia renewed celebrations of the memories of Serbian heroes and deeds. These events caused leaders in Slovenia and Croatia to fear a resurgence of the Serbian hegemony that had disrupted interwar Yugoslavia (see Regional Political Issues, ch. 4).

The Serbian-Albanian struggle for Kosovo, the heartland of Serbia's medieval kingdom, dominated Serbia's political life and café conversation in the 1980s. Between 1948 and 1990, the Serbian share of Kosovo's population dropped from 23.6 percent to less than 10 percent, while the ethnic Albanian share increased in proportion because of a high birth rate and immigration from Albania. The demographic change was also the result of political and economic conditions; the postwar Serbian exodus from Kosovo accelerated in 1966 after ethnic Albanian communist leaders gained control of the province, and Kosovo remained the most poverty-stricken region of Yugoslavia in spite of huge government investments (see Regional Disparities, ch. 3; Kosovo, ch. 4). After reasserting political control over Kosovo in 1989, the Serbian government announced an ambitious program to resettle Serbs in Kosovo, but the plan attracted scant interest among Serbian émigrés from the region.

In the republics of Croatia and Bosnia and Hercegovina, the Serbs' situation was more complex and potentially more explosive than in Kosovo. Despite denials from the governments of both republics, Serbs in Croatia and Bosnia and Hercegovina complained bitterly in the late 1980s about ethnically based discrimination and threats. The Serbian government reacted with published exposés of World War II atrocities against Serbs and the Croatian chauvinism that had inspired them.

Montenegrins

A robust mountain people with a warrior tradition, the Montenegrins were the smallest in population of Yugoslavia's nations. In 1981 they made up 68.5 percent of Montenegro's population,

1.4 percent of Serbia proper's, 2.1 percent of Vojvodina's, and 1.7 percent of Kosovo's. The Montenegrins and the Serbs shared strong political and cultural ties, including the Eastern Orthodox faith, the Cyrillic alphabet, the Serbo-Croatian language (different dialects), and a history of bloody struggle against the Ottoman Turks. Many historians maintain that the Montenegrins are Serbs. Montenegro's most renowned poet and ruler, the nineteenth-century bishop-prince Petar II Njegoš, considered himself a Serb; likewise, the founder of Serbia's medieval kingdom, Stefan I Nemanja, was born in Podgorica, now Titograd, capital of Montenegro.

For centuries Montenegrin society was composed of patrilineally related extended families organized into clans. The extended family tradition lasted well into the twentieth century. Loyalty to kin and protection of family honor were the paramount values. Civic responsibility was a foreign notion, and pragmatism was a sign of weakness. Scratching out a living in the remote, rocky hills, the Montenegrins stubbornly defended their independence against incursions by the Ottoman Turks. Personal tenacity and combat skills were the most valued male virtues; women tended the fields and livestock, maintained the home, nursed the wounded, and nourished the next generation of warriors. Stories of ancestral courage and honor were passed from one generation to the next by bards who recited epic poems to the accompaniment of a *gusle,* a simple, single-string instrument. Practices such as bride theft and blood brotherhood were common, and blood vengeance survived late in the twentieth century.

After World War I, political forces in Montenegro were deeply divided between the Greens, who supported an independent Montenegro, and the Whites, who advocated unification with Serbia. The Whites prevailed, and in censuses taken during the interwar period Montenegrins were classified as Serbs. Montenegrins played a significant role in the defense forces of the interwar Kingdom of Yugoslavia.

Montenegrins enlisted in the communist Partisans in large numbers during World War II and were disproportionately represented in the Communist Party of Yugoslavia (CPY) and the government after the war. Although a large number of Montenegrin communists were expelled from the CPY for pro-Soviet sympathies after Yugoslavia broke with the Soviet Union in 1948, Montenegrins remained overrepresented in the Yugoslav bureaucratic and military services. In the early 1970s, Montenegrins made up roughly 5 percent of the population. But about 15 percent of the leaders of federal administrative bodies were Montenegrins, nearly 20 percent of the generals in the Yugoslav People's Army (YPA) were Montenegrin, and their presence in the overall officer corps was also disproportionately high (see The Military and Society, ch. 5). The Montenegrins' postwar loyalty to the CPY yielded plentiful development funds for their republic. For this reason, Montenegrin industries developed dramatically, although often without rational distribution of resources. Much investment was inordinately capital intensive and wasted, and the republic suffered from low prices for the raw materials it sold to other republics.

Croats

The Croats, a people with long-frustrated national ambitions, have seen themselves for decades as cultured West Europeans shackled to the backward Balkans. Yugoslavia's second most numerous ethnic group, the Croats accounted for 75.1 percent of Croatia's population, 18.4 percent of Bosnia and Hercegovina's, 1.4 percent of Montenegro's, 2.9 percent of Slovenia's, 0.5 percent of Serbia proper's, and 5.4 percent of Vojvodina's, according to the 1981 census. Small enclaves of Croats were as far removed as Kosovo and Romania. As the 1990s began, however, the Republic of Croatia anticipated radical changes in its relations with the rest of Yugoslavia potentially leading to the first independent Croatian state since medieval times.

The Croats enjoyed their own medieval kingdom for several centuries before a long period of Hungarian rule from 1102 to 1918. Most Croats lived under Hungarian kings until 1526 and under Habsburg monarchs thereafter; the Croats of Bosnia and Hercegovina and Slavonia lived under Ottoman rule for several hundred years; and the Croats of Dalmatia passed from Hungarian to Venetian to Austrian rule. With the help of Roman Catholic clerics, the Croats maintained a strong collective memory of their former statehood despite their centuries of foreign domination. Two pivotal events in the Croats' social development were the birth of modern Croatian national sentiment after a brief period of Napoleonic rule in the early nineteenth century and the emancipation of the serfs in 1848. Writers, scholars, merchants, and wealthy landowners led the Croatian national movement, which was triggered by resistance to Hungary's drive to impose Magyar (the national language of Hungary) as the language of public life in Croatia in the mid-nineteenth century (see The Croats and Their Territories, ch. 1).

Before the 1848 revolution against the Austrian Empire, the Croats' social structure was rigidly stratified. The peasantry consisted of serfs bound to the land, semi-serfs who held land on condition of labor and other payments, and landless peasant-nobles.

Croats in native costume,
Smotra Folk Festival, Zagreb
Courtesy Sam and Sarah Stulberg

At the end of the nineteenth century, only a very small proportion of Croatia's total population was employed in industry. The landowner class kept the peasants uneducated to ensure easy exploitation. Among the peasants in Croatia, traditional extended families gradually gave way to individual family farms after the abolition of serfdom in the Austrian Empire in 1848, but rural overpopulation and land fragmentation brought hunger to many areas by the turn of the century. During the late 1800s, many Croats emigrated to the Americas and Australia.

After 1868 Croatian nationalists actively protested Hungary's Magyarization campaigns; later, between the world wars, they spoke against Serbian hegemony and for a loose Yugoslav federation or complete independence for Croatia. During World War II, Hitler established a puppet fascist regime, run by the terrorist Ustaše (see Glossary), to rule a greater Croatian state whose population was roughly half Serb. Substantial numbers of Croatian nationalists and clergy took part in this regime. The Ustaše were vehemently Roman Catholic, anti-Serb, and anti-Semitic; their avowed policy was to obliterate the Serbs from their territory by conversion, deportation, or execution. The regime closed all Serbian Orthodox primary schools, outlawed the Cyrillic alphabet, and ordered Serbs to wear colored arm bands.

After 1945 Yugoslavia's communist regime worked to snuff out manifestations of Croatian nationalism wherever they appeared, labeling advocates of Croatian national interests as neo-Ustaše. National aspirations reached a brief peak in 1971 in what was called the Croatian Spring, but their threat to the federation caused Tito to crack down severely in 1972. In 1990 the sweeping victory of Franjo Tudjman's anticommunist Croatian Democratic Union in the republican parliamentary elections brought a new rush of Croatian nationalism. Croats campaigned to distinguish Croatian as a separate language, and new Slavic-root words were introduced to replace words borrowed from foreign languages. Old Croatian national symbols reappeared, and in October 1989, a statue of revolutionary patriot Josip Jelačić was restored to Zagreb's central square, forty-two years after its removal by federal authorities.

Slovenes

The Slovenes were among the most westernized but least numerous of the Slavs. About 2 million strong, they lived almost exclusively in the mountainous Republic of Slovenia and in enclaves in Austria and Italy bordering Slovenia. The Slovenes never possessed an independent state but lived within German-dominated

A canal in Ljubljana
Courtesy Sam and Sarah Stulberg

empires from Charlemagne's day to the end of World War I. From the thirteenth to the twentieth century, they were ruled by the Austrian Habsburgs. Centuries of exposure to a strong Germanic, Roman Catholic culture fostered qualities that distinguish the Slovenes from the Croats, who lived under the Hungarians, and the Serbs, who lived under the Turks, during the same period. The tenacity of the Slovenian drive for ethnic and cultural survival was evident under German cultural hegemony and surfaced again when the Slovenes spearheaded the drive for democratic reforms in communist Yugoslavia in the late 1980s.

Slovenian cultural self-awareness dates from the Protestant Reformation and the Catholic Counterreformation. Propagandists for both sides made use of the Slovenian language, which at the time was exclusively a peasant idiom. This bolstering of the Slovenes' linguistic identity laid the foundation for the later growth of a Slovenian sense of national identity, which began in earnest after Napoleon's armies occupied Slovene-populated regions in the early nineteenth century and promoted the idea of a Slovenian nation. One of the few monuments to Napoleon outside France remains in Ljubljana, as evidence of Napoleonic influence on the Slovenes. Intellectuals trained by the Catholic clergy led the Slovenian national movement through the nineteenth century. Led by the Romantic poet France Prešeren, they established Slovenian as a literary language and produced a rich national literature. Slovenian leaders sought political and cultural autonomy under the Habsburgs rather than territorial independence. Although they sympathized with their coreligionist Croats, the Slovenes had no interest in uniting with the Orthodox Serbs until World War I.

The Slovenes were by far the most economically advanced of the South Slavs at the close of the nineteenth century, and Slovenia maintained that position in the interwar years. Widespread primogeniture (land inheritance by the oldest son) in Slovenia limited the land fragmentation that plagued the Balkans. Credit and marketing cooperatives saved rural Slovenian families from the chronic indebtedness that afflicted other regions in the 1920s and 1930s. The Slovenes' readiness to negotiate and compromise also served them well in the interwar era. Their most important contribution to interwar Yugoslavia's parade of coalition governments was Monsignor Antun Korošec, leader of the conservative Populist Party. Korošec, an effective spokesman for Slovene interests, headed several Yugoslav ministries in the late 1920s and early 1930s. The Slovenes' linguistic distinctiveness and distance from Belgrade kept their republic free of the Serbian bureaucrats who gained strong influence over other republics during the interwar years.

Slovenia's level of prosperity remained higher than that of the other Yugoslav republics throughout the socialist era. Because its per capita income was highest, the republic contributed a higher per capita share to Yugoslavia's federal funds than any other republic. The Slovenes complained that the less developed republics exploited them and that as a result their standard of living slipped precipitously relative to that in the neighboring regions of Austria and Italy. Nevertheless, among the Yugoslav republics, Slovenia had the highest proportion of its population employed in industry, the lowest rate of unemployment, and the highest value of exports per capita. Slovenia also boasted one of Europe's highest literacy rates in the 1980s. Throughout the turbulent late 1980s, the Slovenes maintained a strong sense of cultural continuity and a devout belief in Roman Catholicism.

Muslim Slavs

Beginning in the late 1960s, the Yugoslav government recognized the Muslim Slavs of Bosnia and Hercegovina as a particular nation and not merely as a religious group. Belgrade granted this recognition in an effort to resolve the centuries-old struggle in which Serbs and Croats claimed ethnic ties with the Muslim Slavs to gain a political majority in the disputed republic of Bosnia and

Hercegovina. Muslim Slavs lived in every Yugoslav republic and province, but by far the largest concentration was in Bosnia and Hercegovina (39.5 percent of the population). In the 1980s, Montenegro was 13.4 percent Muslim Slavs, Serbia proper 2.7 percent, and Kosovo 3.7 percent.

Controversy surrounds the geographic and ethnic origins of the Muslim Slavs. The best-known theory holds that during the Middle Ages Slavs in Bosnia and Hercegovina embraced a heretical form of Christianity known as Bogomilism, then converted in large numbers to Islam when the Ottoman Turks conquered them. A second theory says that the Muslim Slavs were Serbs who embraced Islam and settled in Bosnia. A third is that the Muslims were Turkish settlers from Anatolia who adopted the Serbo-Croatian language. In any case, Islamization brought tangible economic and social benefits to those who converted while the Turks ruled their territory; by 1918 Muslim Slavs accounted for 91 percent of Bosnia's landowners and a large portion of its merchants. Many emigrated to Turkey, however, after the end of Ottoman rule, and the Yugoslav land reforms of 1918 impoverished previously prosperous Muslim Slav landowners.

Islamic culture dominated Bosnia for centuries, and the region now boasts a wealth of mosques, *medreseler* (Islamic schools), *tekkeler* (dervish monasteries), Turkish inns and baths, graceful stone bridges, covered bazaars, cemeteries, and ornate Turkish-style homes. Modern Western culture penetrated Bosnia and Hercegovina only after Austria occupied the region in 1878, but most Muslims saw its influence as alien and a portent of a Roman Catholic resurgence. Gradually, Latin and Cyrillic scripts replaced the Arabic that was used for centuries to write Turkish, Arabic, and Persian literature. After 1918 secular education began supplanting Islamic schools, and education became available to women. Many Muslim Slav landowners became urban tradesmen and craftsmen after losing their properties in the interwar land reform. Long after World War II, the Muslim Slavs engaged predominantly in traditional crafts and modern services such as automobile and electronics repair.

In need of inexpensive oil supplies in the 1970s, the Tito government encouraged relations between Yugoslavia's Muslim Slavs and their coreligionists in the oil-rich Arab countries, especially Libya. But by raising the status and visibility of its Muslim Slavs, Yugoslavia created another potential nationalist issue within its borders. In 1983 a dozen persons were convicted of fomenting religious and national hatred and planning to turn Bosnia into a religiously pure Islamic state. The likelihood of major upheaval sponsored by Muslim fundamentalists abroad was considered small, however, because

Mostar and the Neretva River
Courtesy Sam and Sarah Stulberg

most of Yugoslavia's Muslim population belonged to the Sunni branch of Islam not in sympathy with the main fundamentalist groups of the Middle East (see Islam, this ch.).

Macedonians

Beginning in the seventh century A.D., the area of the modern Republic of Macedonia was overwhelmingly populated by Slavs; and in the ninth century, Macedonia produced the first flourish of Slavic literary activity. Unresolved, however, is the specific nationality to which Macedonia's Slavs now belong. The Bulgars, the Serbs, and the Greeks claim them. Bulgaria recognized the Macedonian minority in the Pirin region that it retained after World War II. In the late 1980s, however, neither Bulgaria nor Greece recognized a Macedonian nationality: Bulgaria insisted that Macedonia's Slavs were Bulgars; Greece maintained that the adjective "Macedonian" was only a territorial designation, and that the inhabitants of Aegean Macedonia were not Slavs at all but ethnic Greeks who happened to speak a Slavic language. By contrast, beginning in the 1960s the Yugoslav government gave the Macedonians the nominal status of a separate nation, to forestall Greek and Bulgarian claims. In 1981 Yugoslav statistics showed about 1.3 million ethnic Macedonians in Yugoslavia, 250,000 in Pirin Macedonia (southwestern Bulgaria), and over 300,000 in Aegean Macedonia (northern Greece). According to the 1981 census, Macedonians made up 6 percent of Yugoslavia's total population, 67 percent of Macedonia's, and 0.5 percent of Serbia proper's.

Macedonia was the first of the Yugoslav lands to fall under the Ottoman Turks and the last to be freed from Ottoman rule. The dark centuries of Ottoman domination left the region's Slavs backward, illiterate, and unsure of their ethnic identity. In the nineteenth century, Bulgarian, Serbian, and Greek clergy established church schools in the region and worked to spread their respective national ideologies through education. Families often compromised by sending one child to each type of school, and whole villages frequently passed through several phases of religious and national reorientation. After the end of Ottoman rule, control of Macedonia became the most inflammatory issue of Balkan politics. After a period of guerrilla warfare, terrorism, and savage reprisals ending with Bulgaria's defeat in the Second Balkan War in 1913, an anti-Bulgarian campaign began in the areas of Macedonia left under Serbian and Greek control. Bulgarian schools and churches were closed, and thousands of Macedonians fled to Bulgaria, which then was viewed as a place of refuge. The process was repeated after Bulgaria's World War I occupation of Macedonia ended. In the interwar period,

Macedonian terrorist groups, with intermittent Bulgarian support, continued armed resistance against the Yugoslav government. The Yugoslavs refused to recognize a Macedonian nation, but many Macedonians accepted Yugoslav control in the 1930s and 1940s. Bulgarian occupation in 1941, first greeted as liberation, soon proved as offensive as the Yugoslav assimilation program it replaced; the sense of confused allegiance among Macedonians thus continued into the postwar period.

After World War II, the Yugoslav government recognized Macedonian nationhood and established a separate republic, energetically nurturing Macedonian national consciousness and the Macedonian language. The first standardized Macedonian grammar was published in 1948. Federal support for Macedonian cultural institutions, including a university in Skopje, furthered the program of national recognition. In 1967 Belgrade underscored the Macedonians' ethnic individuality by supporting the independence of the Macedonian Orthodox Church, which for years afterward enjoyed a more favored position than any of Yugoslavia's other churches.

Albanians

Yugoslavia's ethnic Albanians lived mainly in Kosovo (about 77.4 percent), Serbia proper (1.3 percent), Macedonia (officially about 19.8 percent but probably much higher), and Montenegro (about 6.3 percent). In recent decades, a search for work drew ethnic Albanians to the country's larger cities as well as to Western Europe and North America. Despite the fact that the 1.7 million ethnic Albanians counted in the 1981 census exceeded the populations of Macedonians and Montenegrins in Yugoslavia, Albanians were not recognized as a nation under the 1974 Constitution because, according to the Yugoslav government, their traditional homeland was outside Yugoslavia. In general, Albanian culture was practiced more openly in Yugoslavia than in Albania, where the remains of Stalinist suppression limited many aspects of self-expression. Thus, ironically, Yugoslavia was the only place where some Albanian traditions were preserved.

Albanians were once a mostly Roman Catholic people. After the Ottoman Turks conquered them in the fifteenth century, many Albanian families gained economic and social advantages by converting to Islam. By 1990 only about 10 percent of Kosovo's ethnic Albanians were Catholic.

In the late eighteenth century, Albanians held important posts in the Ottoman army, courts, and administration. Feudal economic relations survived among the ethnic Albanians of Kosovo and Macedonia until Serbia took those regions from the Ottoman Empire in 1913. After World War I, the Serbian government made repeated attempts to colonize Kosovo with the families of its officer corps. Under Serbia, Albanians enjoyed no voice in local administration, no schools, and no publications in their own language in the interwar period. Serbs and Montenegrins dominated the administration of Kosovo from 1946 to 1966, despite the numerical superiority of the Kosovan Albanians, their postwar recognition as a distinct nationality, and the introduction of Albanian-language schools and publications.

In 1966 Aleksandar Ranković, the Serbian head of the Yugoslav secret police, fell from power, and Kosovan Albanians assumed a dominant position in the province. After 1968 Albanians were permitted to display the national flag of Albania in Kosovo and adopt the official Albanian literary language, which is based on the dialect of Albania rather than that spoken in Kosovo. Cultural exchanges introduced teachers from Albania and textbooks printed in Albania. Yugoslavia's 1974 Constitution gave Kosovo virtually the same rights as the country's constituent republics; nowhere in Europe had such far-ranging concessions to national rights been granted in a region considered so potentially separatist. After that time, however, the clash of extreme Serbian and Kosovan nationalist ideologies caused a Serbian nationalist backlash that revoked many of those concessions (see Kosovo, ch. 4).

For centuries, ethnic Albanian villagers in Kosovo lived in extended families of 70 to 100 members ruled by a patriarch. Although the traditional extended family structure eroded steadily after World War II, in 1990 extended families of 20 to 40 members still lived within walled compounds. Blood vengeance, arranged marriages, and polygamy were not uncommon. Many Albanian women lived secluded in the home, subordinate to male authority, and with little or no access to education.

In 1990 Yugoslavia's ethnic Albanians had the highest birth rate in Europe, and more than half of Kosovo's Albanians were under twenty years old in the late 1970s. The birth rate strained the region's already desperate economy and depressed the Albanians' standard of living in every area. The ethnic Albanians also had Yugoslavia's lowest literacy rate: 68.5 percent of individuals over age ten were able to read in 1979. In 1981 only 178,000 of 1.5 million Albanians in Kosovo were employed; one in four of those employed held nominal bureaucratic positions. Meanwhile, the student population of 470,000 was a constant source of political unrest and potentially higher unemployment upon graduation.

Gypsies

Yugoslavia had one of the largest Gypsy populations in the world. The 1981 census officially recorded 168,099 Gypsies in the country, but unofficial counts estimated the Gypsy population as five to six times larger. The Gypsies suffered many serious social problems, and intolerance of Gypsies by other ethnic groups was still prevalent in the northern parts of Yugoslavia in the 1980s. A high percentage of Gypsies were illiterate or had only a few years of primary education. Despite government attempts to lure them into schools and paying jobs, many Gypsies continued to live a nomadic existence as traders, beggars, and fortune-tellers. During the 1980s, large conventions periodically demanded full recognition of Yugoslav Gypsies as a separate nation; the federal government reached no decision on their proposals, although some concessions were made. Meanwhile, the Gypsies undeniably added a unique element to Yugoslav culture: Gypsy musicians played at most weddings, and Gypsy street bands played music for handouts on holiday weekends.

Social Groups

Although Yugoslavia's ethnic landscape remained relatively stable during the twentieth century, its socioeconomic structure underwent especially profound changes after World War II. On the eve of the war, Yugoslavia was a predominantly agricultural land with slowly developing basic industries. Society's broad base was the peasantry, which made up over 80 percent of the population. The country had a minuscule working class; government bureaucrats and a few entrepreneurs, professionals, merchants, and artisans made up the elite. After World War II, Yugoslavia's communist rulers ordered rapid industrialization, and peasants left their farms in droves to fill industrial and office jobs in the cities. The communists brushed aside the prewar elite, nationalized about 80 percent of their property, and established a new class of government bureaucrats. For several decades, party membership and education were the keys to upward mobility in Yugoslav society. But the economic downturn of the 1970s and 1980s brought nagging unemployment and stifling bureaucracy that seriously impeded entry into the working and managing classes, even for educated and skilled individuals. Yugoslavia's immense postwar social transformation brought profound changes to the family structure, the lives of women, young people, and the elderly.

The Peasantry

Under the post-World War II communist regime, Yugoslavia

experienced one of the quickest transformations from an agricultural to an industrial society that history has ever witnessed. The agricultural population shrank from 86.1 percent of the total population in 1921 to 67.1 percent in 1948 and to 16.7 percent in 1984. By comparison, it took the United States ninety years to drop from a 72 percent farm population in 1840 to 32 percent in 1930. Aside from government economic policies that intentionally deprived agriculture of resources after World War II, social factors also pushed peasants off the land (see Application of Stalinist Economics, ch. 3). The lack of pension benefits for peasants, the absence of social benefits for their children, limited availability of state housing in rural areas, and isolation from the lively cultural and social life of the urban centers accelerated the process.

Despite their dramatic shift from agricultural to nonagricultural activities, Yugoslavs remained linked to the soil in many ways. The country's agricultural population still numbered 4.3 million in 1981; of that number, 2.2 to 2.9 million tilled small private plots, including about 1.5 million people who held regular jobs elsewhere. Even before the economic turmoil of the late 1980s, many city dwellers, especially retirees with inadequate pensions, supplemented their income and their diet by selling or consuming produce they grew or livestock they raised on small plots in nearby villages.

The average age of Yugoslavia's peasant population rose rapidly after World War II. Moreover, given the outward migration of young men, by the 1970s women accounted for 60 percent of the agricultural work force. In 35 percent of farm households, no children remained to operate the farm when the older generation retired. In 1990 the federal government proposed a law to provide pensions for individual peasant farmers and to give young people greater incentive not to abandon the land for city jobs.

The Soviet-style agricultural collectivization program began in Yugoslavia in 1949 and ended less than four years later. Abandonment of collectivization left the country's prewar patchwork of small private landholdings virtually intact. Peasants accounted for 95 percent of the agricultural work force and owned about 82 percent of Yugoslavia's arable land in 1989. The average peasant farm had eight or nine parcels of land totaling about 3.4 hectares. Constitutional amendments adopted in 1988 raised the ceiling on landownership from ten to thirty hectares in flatland areas and sixty hectares in hilly and mountainous regions.

Conditions on the average Yugoslav peasant farm changed dramatically after 1945; significant differences remained, however, between peasant life in the more developed northwestern parts of the country and that in the less developed southeastern regions.

Lake Bled, Slovenia
Courtesy Sam and Sarah Stulberg

In 1990 electricity was available virtually everywhere, and many peasant households had artificial lighting, refrigeration, freezers, radios, and televisions. Few peasants, however, had telephones. The number of tractors had risen, but fragmented landownership made large-scale mechanized farming impossible in most areas. Mechanization of farm activities in more developed regions reduced the necessity for human toil, but the overall efficiency of Yugoslav farms lagged far behind that of farms in the West. On the average, one Yugoslav farmer produced enough agricultural goods for five people, whereas in Western industrial countries average production fed sixty-five people.

In part the exodus from agricultural life in Yugoslavia was driven by a desire to cast off ways of life that peasants themselves often considered obsolete. Older villagers, frequently painfully aware of their backwardness, wished to see their children and grandchildren find a life for themselves in what they called the wide world. Yugoslavia's peasant villages, however, shed many traditions only very slowly. In 1990 older men and women still wore folk costumes in some parts of Hercegovina, Macedonia, and Kosovo. Peasant dances, handicrafts, and powerful locally distilled beverages remained part of everyday life. Priests baptized most newborns and buried most of the dead, but villagers in many areas still visited traditional folk healers and fortune-tellers, who read the future in coffee grounds. While all was amiable on the surface, behind the scenes family and neighborhood animosities persisted through the generations, and villagers squabbled bitterly over scarce resources and inheritances. Cafés were filled with old men during the day and younger men at night. Alcoholism commonly afflicted both men and women, and alcohol-related road and farm accidents claimed an inordinate number of lives.

Transportation improvements after the war gave many peasants the opportunity to work away from the family farm and still retain close links with their homes. Uprooted peasants accounted for about half the Yugoslav guest workers in Western Europe (see Guest Workers, this ch.). By 1970 some 1.5 million peasants, about 25 percent of the economically active rural population, held jobs outside agriculture, and about half of Yugoslavia's rural population lived in households with at least one member who held an industrial job. Money sent home by guest workers abroad created a boom in new rural home building, even in some of the least accessible mountain areas. In eastern Serbia, this prosperity was expressed in the building of extravagant cemetery monuments, including graveside cottages.

The Workers

The Yugoslav industrial working class grew exponentially after World War II, when the communist regime launched its drive for rapid industrialization. From 1947 to 1952, industrial employment grew by 75.2 percent as peasants left their farms for jobs in the cities. From 1954 to 1975, industrial jobs grew at an average annual rate of 4.3 percent, and the industrial working class grew from 1.1 million in 1947 to 6.3 million in 1985. In the mid-1980s, the social sector (see Glossary) of the economy employed about 98 percent of the country's workers.

Several years after Yugoslavia's 1948 economic break with the Soviet Union, the government instituted a comprehensive economic reform that transformed state ownership of enterprises into social ownership and theoretically turned over control of the enterprises to the workers who labored in them (see Socialist Self-Management, ch. 3). Socialist self-management remained a sacrosanct tenet of the Yugoslav political culture for the next thirty-five years, until economic turmoil forced structural reform in 1989.

Under self-management, workers who were permanent employees in enterprises were virtually guaranteed a job for life. If a worker terminated employment with an enterprise, however, he or she almost always lost the possibility of finding another position within the social sector. Under the Law on Associated Labor of 1976, each worker belonged to a basic organization of associated labor (BOAL) assigned according to his or her precise role in the production process. The BOALs elected workers' councils, which in turn appointed executive bodies to set wages and production goals and recommend investment policy. The executive body appointed a director or board responsible for day-to-day operation of the enterprise.

Despite the profoundly egalitarian ideology on which it was based, practical operation of self-management reflected the stratification of the industrial work force. Skilled and educated workers occupied a disproportionately large number of seats on workers' councils. From the mid-1950s to the mid-1970s, skilled workers (roughly a third of enterprise employees) regularly won half the workers' council slots; the percentage of semiskilled or unskilled workers declined during the same period. Workers' council presidents also came disproportionately from the ranks of skilled workers or white-collar employees. Workers with advanced educational degrees accounted for nearly two-thirds of all workers' council presidents. The composition of executive bodies reflected the same trend.

The enterprise director and the director's staff wielded considerable influence. Access to and control of information about business conditions and overall operation of the enterprise gave the director an advantage in steering workers' council decision making. Workers exercised more influence on policies directly affecting working conditions and wages; over the years, they left investment and production decisions and daily operation of the enterprise to the director.

Self-managed enterprises responded to market conditions differently than firms in capitalist countries, and the relationship of the interests of management and skilled and unskilled workers also differed. Policies geared toward enhancing the enterprise's efficiency and competitiveness conflicted with socially guaranteed higher wages and job security for workers. Economic downturns generally caused reductions in investment rather than layoffs or reduced wages. An enterprise could reduce its labor force only with the workers' consent. This normally meant long, tedious legal procedures and finding alternative employment or job training to prevent workers from becoming unemployed.

The economic restructuring that followed the turmoil of the 1980s radically changed the fortunes of the working class. Strikes reached epidemic proportions by the end of the decade. Large numbers of workers returned their membership cards in the League of

Communists of Yugoslavia (LCY—see Glossary), and by 1985 party membership included only one of eleven semiskilled workers and one of five skilled workers (see League of Communists of Yugoslavia, ch. 4).

Lacking organizational autonomy, the official trade unions failed to protect the workers' living standards, and workers generally regarded the unions as irrelevant (see Trade Unions, ch. 4). In the late 1980s, unofficial unions began forming in Slovenia and the other republics after the government lifted restrictions on forming independent organizations.

Laws restricting private business ownership became increasingly ineffectual in the late 1980s. Most often ignored were tax statutes and restrictions on the number of workers employed in private enterprise. Workers outside the social sector frequently worked sixty or more hours per week and earned much better wages than those paid for the same work in the social sector. Private employers often employed skilled workers illegally, especially after the normal closing hour of socially owned enterprises (3:00 P.M.), and many workers employed in the social sector moonlighted in their free time.

In the 1980s, unemployment became a serious threat to the Yugoslav working class. Between 1965 and 1985, the number of officially unemployed persons rose from 237,000 to 1,039,000. Unemployment rates varied widely among regions. Slovenia consistently had the lowest, Kosovo by far the highest unemployment. The comprehensive economic reform of December 1989 led to elimination of redundant workers in Yugoslav firms and brought another steep increase in national unemployment (see Living Standards, ch. 3). In the initial aftermath of the reform, government planners relied on expansion in the private sector to re-employ workers who lost their jobs. In the first year, however, unemployment continued to rise.

The Political Elite and Intellectuals

During the nineteenth and early twentieth centuries, a tiny intelligentsia dominated the process of social and political change that transformed Yugoslav society. South Slavic writers, journalists, and scholars articulated popular aspirations and acted as catalysts for the rising nationalism of the peoples enclosed by the Austro-Hungarian and Ottoman empires. In interwar Yugoslavia, despite the prevalence of revolving-door cabinets, a group of about forty to fifty educated and politically experienced figures formed a semipermanent ruling circle. The bureaucratic and professional class was a broader middle stratum of about 200,000 white-collar workers concentrated in urban centers. Government service, which

Harbor at Dubrovnik
Courtesy Sam and Sarah Stulberg

required secondary and university schooling, was virtually the only employment opportunity available for ambitious individuals.

Yugoslavia's interwar ruling elite represented the tip of a very broad-based social pyramid. Society was overwhelmingly rural and uneducated; only about half of the population could read, and less than 10 percent lived in cities. The elite was drawn from the sons of the middle and upper strata: large landowners and bureaucrats and a handful of industrialists, financiers, and military officers. No rising industrial bourgeoisie threatened their hold on the state apparatus. The elite was also overwhelmingly Serbian; most Croatian intellectuals and the minuscule number of educated Macedonians and Albanians were excluded. Their exclusion from the only path to upward mobility—the government bureaucracy—exacerbated the bitter nationalism and separatism of the era (see Political Life in the 1920s, ch. 1).

The turmoil of World War II and political takeover by the CPY brought radical changes to Yugoslavia's ruling circle. The communists ousted the prewar elite and replaced it with a new ruling class chosen by party loyalty. During the war, the party was composed largely of peasants and workers. Party leadership was significantly more rural than the prewar elite; in 1945 only 5 percent of CPY leaders came from Belgrade, the former bastion of power. In 1952 Yugoslavia's communist political leadership class numbered about 51,000; it grew to 93,000 in the 1960s and added another 100,000 members in the mid-1970s after constitutional redefinition of the self-management system.

In the immediate postwar period, service in Tito's anti-Nazi Partisan forces or pre-1941 membership in the CPY were the main prerequisites for a successful elite career. Over 75 percent of pre-1941 party members pursued professional political or military careers following World War II. They also tended to linger in their positions. Active and retired persons with pre-1941 party membership accounted for less than 0.5 percent of total party membership in the late 1960s, but they held over 15 percent of the leading positions in the party and society at large. By the 1980s, the LCY had lost its working-class base and had become a party of state employees. Party members accounted for 94.1 percent of the Croatian parliament in 1982. Communists accounted for over 95 percent of all government administrators until the LCY abandoned its monopoly of power in 1990. Until that date, nomination of delegates to fill positions at all levels of the government—which led to automatic election—was based on support from the party elite. The party monopoly led to formation of uncontrollable and nonelected oligarchies in each of Yugoslavia's eight federal units (see Local Government and the Communes, ch. 4).

With few exceptions, the men who took power in Yugoslavia after World War II were the sons of peasants and workers. This pattern persisted through the 1960s, when 68.4 percent of Yugoslavia's political leaders had fathers who had been peasants or workers and more than 75 percent had grandfathers from those backgrounds. The same pattern applied to the country's professional classes as a whole. In 1960 nearly one-third of all white-collar workers had been peasants themselves in 1946, and nearly three-fourths came from peasant or worker families.

As the Partisan generation aged, education became more important in professional advancement. By the early 1970s, about 90 percent of the country's professionals had gained their positions at least nominally on the basis of educational credentials. Older employees upgraded their job qualifications through continuing education programs. Expanding opportunities in higher education, liberal admissions standards, and substantial public financing for education all contributed to upward mobility in the 1960s and 1970s. As many more Yugoslavs received formal educational training and reached privileged positions, however, mobility declined. The probability that children of workers or peasants would become university students fell compared with the chances of the children of professionals.

The rise of a substantial technical intelligentsia was a major social development in postwar Yugoslavia. The technical intelligentsia, which provided scientific and management support for industrialization, came to enjoy considerable popular prestige. Although they could find higher-paying jobs in the West, relatively few members of this class joined the massive worker emigration to Western Europe that began in the late 1960s. Before Tito's death in 1980, the technical elite—who supported enterprise autonomy—had a hostile relationship with party and government officials who favored democratic centralism. In the mid-1960s, party hard-liners attacked the technocrats for their petit bourgeois mentality and labeled them class enemies who subverted self-management.

The communist regime's relationship with artists and scholars was likewise a troubled one. Artists and scholars were constantly at odds with the government's efforts to control nationalism and free expression. Numerous Croatian intellectuals lost their jobs or were imprisoned after the Croatian Spring of 1971, and trials of dissident writers and scholars took place regularly for the next two decades throughout the country (see Djilas, Praxis, and Intellectual Repression, ch. 4). Intellectuals came to the fore again in the late 1980s, when national differences divided the LCY. Albanians were the most manifestly disaffected intellectuals in the 1980s, as they fought Serbian restrictions on autonomy for Kosovo. The Kosovo issue also drew Serbian intellectuals into the political arena. A memorandum written by leading members of the Serbian Academy of Sciences and leaked to a Belgrade newspaper in 1986 described the Serbian nation as being in greater jeopardy than at any time since World War II. Likewise, Slovenian intellectuals led the push for democratic reforms that swept over the country from Slovenia southward in the late 1980s (see Intellectual Opposition Groups, ch. 4).

The Family

Despite the massive changes of the socialist era, society in Yugoslavia remained oriented around family and kin. Rights and duties were defined by family relationships much more rigorously than in contemporary Western societies. For example, the 1962 Basic Law on Relations Between Parents and Children defined the material support legally due one's parents, children, siblings, grandparents, and other relatives. The law obliged citizens to support needy or incapacitated relatives and specified the order in which aid and assistance should come from both lineal and collateral relatives.

The *zadruga* (pl., *zadruge*), a kin-based corporate group holding property in common, was the traditional basis of rural social organization throughout the Balkans. From the feudal era onward, customary and formal law enshrined the rights and obligations of *zadruga* members. Throughout rural Croatia, Serbia, Montenegro, Hercegovina, Macedonia, Kosovo, and much of Bosnia, the *zadruga* persisted as a formally constituted kin group until well after World War II. Its most common form was a group of patrilineally related males, along with their spouses and children. Members of a *zadruga* generally owned and farmed land in common.

The *zadruga* survived because membership in a corporate group conferred clear advantages on the individual peasant family. For the Balkan peasantry, the *zadruga* made it possible to endure wars, foreign rule, exploitation of new lands, conversion from pastoralism to agriculture, and seasonal off-farm employment. Precise configuration of the kin group varied during the past five centuries in response to regional changes in political, economic, and geographic conditions. The *zadruga* maintained cultural integrity during centuries of foreign domination, and it protected the peasant against the predations of state and bandit. Religious practices centered on the individual *zadruga* and not on the parish church. Even among Muslim Slavs, each *zadruga* had a patron saint; the saint's day celebration, the *slava,* remained the high point of the calendar for many families late in the twentieth century.

Large multifamily households enjoyed significant advantages, especially in rural areas, well into the twentieth century. A substantial adult labor force permitted family members to specialize and to engage in a variety of subsidiary operations to supplement agricultural income. The burden of agricultural labor could be spread at peak seasons, men were freed to engage in politics, and women had time for handicrafts. An extended family's wealth almost always exceeded that of two to three nuclear households of comparable size. The *zadruga* also provided a refuge for the orphaned, the widowed, the infirm, and the elderly.

The composition of the extended family changed with the increasing life expectancy realized in the twentieth century. The number of generations in a given household rose from two to three or even four, while the number of collateral relatives—brothers, cousins, and second cousins—decreased. Patriarchal authority, often overbearing within the traditional *zadruga,* grew more so as the life expectancy of the parents increased. The wars of the twentieth century and

Albanian man and boy in oda, *traditional family room, Kosovo*
Courtesy Charles Sudetic

migration away from rural areas after World War II caused a decline in joint ownership of property by extended families.

Under communist rule, the extended family became a cooperative rather than a formally corporate kin group; but family loyalty and a general feeling of responsibility toward kin persisted. Individuals relied on relatives for mutual aid and support in a wide variety of social and economic contexts. Family solidarity eased the shock of urbanization and industrialization throughout the 1960s and 1970s; relatives provided urban housing for students from the countryside and employment advice and assistance for the recent rural migrant. Migrants to the city maintained ties with their kin in the country, periodically helping with agricultural or construction tasks. Among the country's technical and managerial elite, kinship strengthened the relationship between commune and enterprise and reinforced local and familial loyalties.

Nominal kinship in the form of godparenthood, or *kumstvo,* cut across the familial focus of South Slavic social relations. *Kumstvo* and marriage were the two institutions by which the *zadruga* formed ties with other kin groups. Traditionally, the godparent-godchild relationship formed a permanent link, inherited patrilineally, between two *zadruge.* Although *kumstvo* observance was less elaborate among Muslim Slavs, they did observe rituals such as the cutting of a child's umbilical cord and the first hair cutting. The relationship implied few specific obligations between the *zadruge* besides a general expectation of friendship and assistance.

With urbanization, the number of large and extended families declined. From the 1948 census to the 1981 census, average family size dropped from 4.37 to 3.67 members. The decline was steepest in the developed regions. In Kosovo, approximately three-quarters of all households had five or more members in the early 1970s, and over a quarter had ten or more members. As late as 1953, about one-third of all Yugoslav households were classified as extended families. The percentage of extended families dropped precipitously by the early 1970s. Smaller domestic groups appeared to be more advantageous in an urban setting; in both developed and less-developed regions, only about one-fourth of all urban households were extended families by 1980.

The Role of Women

Traditionally, women played subservient roles in Yugoslavia's patriarchal families, especially in the country's backward mountainous regions. In the interwar period, specific legislation protected women's subservient status within the family. Rapid industrialization and urbanization in the communist era broke down traditional family patterns in varying degrees among the landless inhabitants of rural and mountainous areas. This trend was most pronounced in the more developed northern and western urban areas. The number of women employed outside the home rose from about 400,000 in 1948 to 2.4 million in 1985. As women began working away from home, they developed a more independent identity.

After World War II, women in Yugoslavia won complete civil and political rights and gained access to education, employment, social welfare programs, health care, and political office. Although women became better educated and increasingly employed, however, they did not generally win full equality in the job market or advancement to high social and political positions. In the 1980s, the percentage of women in low-level political and management positions was quite representative, but their representation declined toward the top of the administrative pyramid.

Women accounted for 38 percent of Yugoslavia's nonagricultural labor force in 1987, up from 26 percent thirty years earlier. The participation of women in the Yugoslav work force varied dramatically according to region. In Slovenia women made up 43.9 percent of the work force; in Kosovo, 20 percent. In 1989 Yugoslav women worked primarily in three fields: cultural and social welfare (56.3 percent of the persons employed in the field), public services and public administration (42 percent), and trade and catering (41.8 percent). Almost all Yugoslavia's elementary school teachers were women.

Although women's groups had formed in Ljubljana, Zagreb, and Belgrade and a number of female political columnists had advocated the feminist cause, as of 1990 the women's movement had yet to achieve significant power in Yugoslavia. Feminist commentators observed that Yugoslavia's rapid industrialization had not eradicated traditional patriarchalism but had instead created a new form of patriarchal society in which women were treated as sex objects exploited in the workplace and at home. Those allegations were backed by the wide availability of hard-core pornography everywhere in the country and the fact that most working women were still expected to do traditional household chores.

Students and Youth

Students were a perennial source of concern for Yugoslavia's communist regime. They often assumed the viewpoint of pure Marxism in criticizing the inequality of the socialist self-management system; in general, students far surpassed their elders in demanding reform. Student unrest erupted in 1968 at several universities, in 1971 at the University of Zagreb, and in 1981 at the University of Priština. In 1968 students in Belgrade, Zagreb, Ljubljana, and Sarajevo protested the bourgeois quality of Yugoslav socialism and the failure of socialist self-management to create an egalitarian society. The later unrest in Zagreb and Priština was largely an expression of the respective nationalistic goals of the Croats and the Kosovans.

In the late 1980s, youth publications, especially in Slovenia, provided an important public platform for frank debate of sensitive issues and taboo topics, such as nuclear energy, government corruption, and resistance to military service (see The Media, ch. 4). With the collapse of communism throughout Eastern Europe in the late 1980s, student activists on Yugoslav campuses focused on issues of ecology, nationalism, women's rights, and peace. Polling data, however, showed a high degree of apathy among Yugoslavia's young people. In a youth opinion poll conducted in the port city of Split, 83 percent of the respondents said that nepotism and connections were essential to success; 53 percent answered that knowledge and intelligence had no influence whatsoever on social status, advancement, or success in life.

Pensioners

Between 1965 and 1988, the number of Yugoslavs receiving old-age and disability pensions and survivor benefits rose steeply (see table 6,

Appendix). The annual rate of increase was 4 to 7 percent, depending on the republic or province. This growth was considerably higher than the growth in the employment rate, which averaged 2 percent to 4.5 percent annually in the same period. The number of pensioners grew as a result of broader coverage by old-age pension plans, an aging population, and the high disability rate of laborers. The number of persons receiving survivor benefits also increased between 1965 and 1988 as a result of the relatively high accident mortality rate.

In the late 1980s, retirement and disability pensions covered all employed individuals and all self-employed persons outside the agricultural sector. Pensions also were available to private farmers under a voluntary payment plan, and private farmers nearing old age were offered pensions in exchange for the sale of their land to an agricultural cooperative. Retirement age was set at sixty years after at least twenty years of service for men and fifty-five years after at least fifteen years for women. Retirement became mandatory in the early 1970s. The economic crisis of the 1980s jeopardized Yugoslavia's pension system, and in 1990 pensions often went unpaid for months.

Urbanization and Housing

Despite massive post-World War II migration from rural villages to cities, Yugoslavia still ranked as one of Europe's least urbanized countries in 1990. At the war's end, almost 80 percent of the Yugoslav population lived in villages. Over the next twenty-five years, about 4.6 million people, equivalent to 20 percent of the country's 1981 population, migrated to cities. The urban population grew by 80 percent between 1953 and 1971; by the mid-1970s, slightly over one-third of all Yugoslavs lived in urban centers.

Housing

Obtaining adequate housing was a major problem in all Yugoslav cities, especially for rural migrants. For years, single male migrants resorted to dormitory-style accommodations that many enterprises maintained for their workers. Migrants from urban areas fared better in finding housing in cities because of their greater experience with urban life and generally higher education or professional level. The quality of migrant housing usually improved with length of residence, and acquisition of satisfactory housing became a mark of a migrant's success in a new location.

Although Yugoslavia had a total of 6.7 million housing units in 1984, housing remained in short supply in every urban area, and cost began to increase dramatically in the 1970s. In 1987 the price of a housing unit with sixty square meters of floor space equaled about twenty average annual incomes. While the urban population grew in the 1970s, housing construction in Yugoslavia's cities actually dropped. Urban centers received 10,000 fewer new housing units in 1978 than in 1975, a decline that was sharpest in the six largest cities. In Slovenia this fall resulted in part from the republic's effort to promote the simultaneous growth of several urban centers. In Yugoslavia's other republics, however, the drop reflected shortages of building materials, rising construction costs, and administrative problems in the self-managed housing system.

Yugoslavia's housing system offered two methods of obtaining long-term accommodations: through private initiative, using bank, enterprise, or private loans; or through allocation of socially owned apartments. A person's chances of receiving housing loans or a socially owned apartment generally were proportional to his or her social standing.

About two-thirds of Yugoslavia's housing units were privately owned, and about 80 percent of housing construction was done by private enterprise. In nearly all cases, private housing construction was a long-term, pay-as-you-go ordeal involving contribution of significant labor by the homeowner. The outskirts of all Yugoslav cities featured rows of occupied and unoccupied homes at various stages of completion. Private housing consisted mostly of village houses, private apartments, and homes built on the periphery of major cities.

Socially owned apartments were allocated by the state without investment by the occupant; rent and maintenance payments were nominal. Although apartments were technically social property, occupants had de facto property rights. Enterprises deducted funds for social apartments from the general employee payroll; thus, all employees paid for socially owned housing, whatever type of housing they occupied. Apartment allocation was based on a complex set of criteria, including family size, work seniority, age, and position. The wait for a socially owned apartment could last decades, and bitter disputes arose among candidates for a long-sought apartment.

Graft was endemic in the Yugoslav housing system. Partly for this reason, workers had the least chance of obtaining socially owned housing, while professionals and members of the bureaucracy had the greatest. Reform plans for the early 1990s called for occupants of socially owned apartments to begin buying them outright by adding a monthly principal payment to their maintenance fees, but in 1990 reforms awaited a government decision on redefinition and distribution of social property.

Urban Problems

Yugoslav cities grew without adequate planning. Regardless of region, people with tenure in socially owned apartments lived mostly in the city centers, while privately owned homes were located farther out. The chronic housing shortage resulted in the development of sizable unplanned settlements on the periphery of large cities. These settlements often lacked paved streets, running water, or sewer lines. Gypsy shantytowns also surrounded many urban areas. City inspectors were reluctant to evict the inhabitants of these areas because eviction would cause a public outcry and appear to be discrimination against the poor.

Yugoslavia's speedy urbanization brought many problems associated in the West with life in big cities. Drug use, although still relatively uncommon, grew steadily in the 1980s. Drug traffickers frequented Yugoslavia's main roadways, carrying heroin and other drugs to Western Europe from sources in the Middle East. Some of these drugs found their way into Yugoslavia's drug underground. Urban treatment facilities registered about 2,000 drug addicts, but the total number of drug abusers was estimated at 10,000 in 1988. The Yugoslav government's antidrug program consisted of a campaign to interdict drug shipments, treat drug abusers, and prevent drug abuse.

Guest Workers

Besides urbanization, a second important migration trend in Yugoslav society after World War II was the emigration of Yugoslav guest workers and their dependents. The departure of Yugoslavs seeking work began in the 1950s, when individuals began slipping across the border illegally. Economic expansion in Western Europe in the 1960s created a demand for labor that domestic labor supplies could not fill; at the same time, Yugoslav industries could not absorb all the workers in the country's labor pool, including educated and highly skilled individuals. In the mid-1960s, Yugoslavia lifted emigration restrictions, and the number of émigrés increased rapidly. By the early 1970s, Yugoslavia had Europe's second-highest emigration rate, and 20 percent of the country's labor force was employed abroad. In 1973 about 1.1 million workers and dependents were living and working outside Yugoslavia's borders; 900,000 of these were living in Western Europe. Restrictions on guest workers in Western Europe curtailed the outflow of Yugoslavs in 1973 and 1974, and the somewhat reduced movement has remained steady since. In 1985 about 600,000 Yugoslavs were working abroad, accompanied by about 400,000

Street in Kaludjerica, a town of Serbian refugees from Kosovo, near Belgrade
Courtesy Charles Sudetic

dependents. In 1987 the rate of permanent return to Yugoslavia was about 40,000 workers per year.

In the early 1970s, a disproportionate number of émigré workers came from Yugoslavia's economically developed northern and western regions, including Croatia, Slovenia, eastern Vojvodina, and northeastern Serbia. The 1981 census, however, showed an increase in the number of guest workers from Serbia proper, Montenegro, and Kosovo. Overall, only 30.9 percent of émigré workers came from cities and towns. A 40 percent drop in the number of reported Croatian guest workers caused speculation that many Croats were adopting permanent foreign residency.

Higher wages in West European countries at first attracted mostly city-dwelling, mature male Yugoslav workers with specific job skills. By the mid-1970s, the attraction had spread to peasants, unskilled workers, and women in rural areas. In the 1970s, guest workers were more likely to have completed elementary school and voca-·tional training than the Yugoslav population as a whole. The outflow of skilled workers slowed growth in a variety of Yugoslav industries. Hotels and restaurants in Yugoslav resort areas often faced seasonal shortages of trained caterers and waiters. Waiters would work a single season on the Dalmatian coast to gain experience and savings, then they would emigrate to Austria, Switzerland, or France. Adriatic hotels usually trained a new staff each season; ironically, some employed guest workers of their own from Poland and Czechoslovakia.

About one-third of all guest workers were women, a proportion that corresponded to their share in Yugoslavia's overall domestic work force. But striking disparities in the rates at which women emigrated from Yugoslavia's various regions reflected the influence of the country's ethnic diversity. Slightly more than 40 percent of all emigrants from Vojvodina and Slovenia were women, as were over a third of those from Serbia proper and Croatia. Women from Kosovo emigrated least, accounting for less than 5 percent of all émigrés from that region.

Guest workers returned to Yugoslavia not only for economic reasons but also because of emotional connections with their birthplace, family, and traditions and because of a desire by parents to educate their children in their homeland. With the reunification of Germany and the economic downturn created by the Persian Gulf crisis of 1990, Yugoslavia faced a possible large-scale return of guest workers from Western Europe. Many observers predicted that a return of skilled workers would have a positive effect on Yugoslavia's economy. The 1981 census showed that the bulk of the returning guest workers (81.7 percent) continued to work; only 3.2 percent became unemployed officially. Most former peasants and agricultural workers returned from abroad to find new employment in nonagricultural sectors of the economy, indicating that they had acquired other skills and job experience during their years abroad. Returning guest workers unable to find work were entitled to some unemployment compensation if they paid into an unemployment compensation fund during their stay abroad. Prior to German reunification, guest workers in the Federal Republic of Germany (West Germany) automatically contributed to such funds in accordance with a bilateral agreement.

Religion

Religious affiliation in Yugoslavia was closely linked with the politics of nationality; centuries-old animosities among the country's three main religions—Eastern Orthodoxy, Roman Catholicism, and Islam—remained a divisive factor in 1990. Forced conversions of Orthodox Serbs to Roman Catholicism by ultranationalist Croatian priests during World War II had made a lasting impression; more recently, Serbian official spokesmen often characterized Serbian conflicts with Kosovan nationalists as a struggle between Christianity and Islam. Religious tension existed even in the most prosperous regions: in the 1980s, local politicians delayed construction of an Orthodox church in Split and a mosque in Ljubljana, both predominantly Roman Catholic cities.

Demography and Distribution

The distribution of Yugoslavia's major religions followed the country's internal borders only roughly. Serbia and Montenegro were under the ecclesiastical authority of the Serbian Orthodox Church. Macedonia had its own Macedonian Orthodox Church after 1967, but that republic also included many Muslim ethnic Albanians. Croatia and Slovenia were predominantly Roman Catholic, but many Orthodox Serbs also lived in Croatia, and the Muslim Slav and ethnic Albanian populations of Slovenia were growing. Bosnia and Hercegovina contained Muslim Slavs, Orthodox Serbs, and Catholic Croats. Vojvodina had significant numbers of Eastern Orthodox, Roman Catholic, and Protestant believers; Kosovo was predominantly Muslim, although about 10 percent of the province's ethnic Albanians were Roman Catholic, and virtually all its Serbs were Eastern Orthodox (see fig. 8).

Besides Eastern Orthodoxy, Roman Catholicism, and Islam, about forty other religious groups were represented in Yugoslavia. They included the Jews, Old Catholic Church, Church of Jesus Christ of the Latter-Day Saints, Hare Krishnas, and other eastern religions. Major Protestant groups were the Calvinist Reformed Church, Evangelical Church, Baptist Church, Methodist Church, Seventh-Day Adventists, Jehovah's Witnesses, and Pentecostal Church of Christ.

The connection between religious belief and nationality posed a special threat to the postwar communist government's official policies of national unity and a federal state structure. Although postwar constitutions provided for separation of church and state and guaranteed freedom of religion, church-state relations in the postwar period were often tense when the government attempted to reduce church influence. From 1945 to the early 1950s, the authorities carried out antichurch campaigns that imprisoned, tortured, and killed many members of the clergy. The government subsequently established a general policy of rapprochement, but until the 1980s the state still exerted pressure on many religious communities. Yugoslavs who openly practiced a religious faith often were limited to low-paying, low-status jobs. After Tito's death in 1980, the Yugoslav government no longer pursued a consistent policy toward the country's churches. After that time, each republic and province followed policies toward religion that were acceptable at home but sometimes unacceptable in other parts of the country.

Political liberalization in the late 1980s brought Yugoslavia's religious communities a level of freedom unprecedented in the postwar period. The spring of 1990 marked the beginning of a religious revival throughout the country. On Easter 1990, television stations throughout the country covered Eastern Orthodox and Roman Catholic services for the first time; two weeks later, Belgrade television broadcast prayers marking the end of Ramadan, the Muslim holy month. With the rebirth of Western-style democracy in Yugoslavia, fundamental amendments were expected in laws banning church involvement in politics, education, social and interethnic affairs, and military training.

Religious belief declined significantly in Yugoslavia after World War II, but the drop was not uniform throughout the country. In the censuses of 1921 and 1948, religious believers accounted for over 99 percent of the population. Secularization followed closely the postwar government programs of modernization, urbanization, and vigorous antireligious propaganda. A 1964 survey (Yugoslavia's last nationwide study of religion through 1990) described 70.3 percent of Yugoslavs as religious believers. The areas with the highest percentage of religious believers were Kosovo (91 percent of the population) and Bosnia and Hercegovina (83.8 percent); those with the lowest were Slovenia (65.4 percent), Serbia (63.7 percent), and Croatia (63.6 percent). Although hard figures were not available, in the late 1980s signs indicated a resurgence of religious belief, especially among young people.

Eastern Orthodoxy

Since Byzantine times, the Eastern Orthodox churches have had an almost symbiotic connection to individual nation-states such as Greece and Russia. Yugoslavia had two main Orthodox churches: the Serbian Orthodox Church, present since the Middle Ages, and the Macedonian Orthodox Church, which split from the Serbian church in 1967. The Romanian Orthodox Church was also present in Vojvodina. An estimated 11.5 million Yugoslavs, primarily Serbs, Montenegrins, and Macedonians, were Eastern Orthodox by family background.

The self-governing Serbian Orthodox Church was founded in the thirteenth century by St. Sava Nemanja, brother of the first Serbian king. In the centuries after its founding, the church served a series of kings and emperors, and it acted as the repository of Serbian culture during the centuries of Ottoman domination (1459–1829). The Serbian church supported the Karadjordjević Dynasty that ruled the Kingdom of Yugoslavia between the world wars. The brutal religious persecution of Orthodox priests in World

Examples of Yugoslav religious architecture
Courtesy Charles Sudetic

War II enhanced the church's popular standing throughout Serbia. After the war, the communist regime took advantage of the Serbian church's loyal support of the Yugoslav state to gain legitimacy in the eyes of the Serbian population. But the church soon came into direct conflict with the communist regime's policy on nationalities and lost its secular role and influence. One result of this conflict was the refusal of the Serbian church hierarchy to recognize the Macedonian Orthodox Church, given self-governing status by the Yugoslav state in 1967.

In 1987 the Serbian Orthodox Church, headquartered in Belgrade, included about 2,000 parishes; 2,500 priests, monks, and nuns; 180 monasteries and convents; four seminaries; and one school of theology. It also published ten periodicals. The Serbian church was very active in defending the Serbian and Montenegrin minorities in Kosovo. Following the upswing of ethnic tensions in Kosovo in the 1980s, identification as an Orthodox churchgoer became more popular in Serbia. In 1985 completion of the long-delayed Cathedral of St. Sava in Belgrade received government approval. When finished, the cathedral was to be the largest Eastern Orthodox church in the world.

At various times before World War I, the Eastern Orthodox diocese in Macedonia was under the jurisdiction of Serbian, Bulgarian, and Greek Orthodox authorities. Between the world wars, the Serbian church was in control. Until 1958 the Serbian, Bulgarian, and Greek Orthodox hierarchies recognized no distinct Macedonian nation or independent Macedonian Orthodox Church. In 1958, however, the Serbian Orthodox hierarchy recognized the Macedonian dioceses by consecrating a Macedonian bishop. Shortly thereafter the Macedonian Orthodox Church came into official existence, but it remained under the authority of the Serbian Orthodox Church. In 1967 Macedonian clergy proclaimed their church independent, prompting the Serbian Orthodox Church to refuse all further relations with it. Aware that a self-governing Macedonian church would enhance the sense of Macedonian nationhood within the Yugoslav federation, political authorities gave the church their full support. Without recognition from the Serbian hierarchy, however, the Macedonian church remained isolated from the world's other Eastern Orthodox churches. By the mid-1980s, the Macedonian Orthodox Church had six dioceses in Yugoslavia and two abroad, 225 parishes, 102 monasteries, about 250 priests and about 15 monks, and one school of theology.

Roman Catholicism

The Roman Catholic Church was Yugoslavia's most highly

organized religious community. About 7.5 million Catholics—mainly Croats, Slovenes, Hungarians, and ethnic Albanians—lived in Yugoslavia. The church had eight archbishoprics, 13 bishoprics, 2,702 parishes, 182 monasteries, 415 convents, two schools of theology, and about 4,100 priests, 1,400 monks, and 6,600 nuns. It also published several dozen newspapers and periodicals whose combined circulation far surpassed that of the rest of the country's religious press.

The Roman Catholic Church had uneasy relations with Yugoslavia's communist regime throughout the postwar period. This was partly because its hierarchy was loyal to Rome and partly because the Catholics supported Croatian nationalism in the early 1970s. Many Yugoslavs retained a strong, emotional association between Catholicism and the war crimes, forced conversions, and deportations by the Croatian fascist state in World War II.

Soon after the war, the government's agrarian reform appropriated church land. Catholic schools were closed, and formal religious instruction was discouraged. Between 1945 and 1952, many innocent priests were shot or imprisoned in retribution for wartime atrocities. The arrest and 1946 trial of Alojzije Stepinac, archbishop of Zagreb, led to the low point of Catholic-Yugoslav relations in 1952. At that point, Tito severed relations with the Vatican in response to the elevation of the recently released Stepinac to cardinal. Stepinac, tried for war crimes, had actually been held guilty of refusing to adapt the Vatican's stand on social issues such as divorce and education to conform with the secular requirements of the communist state of Yugoslavia. Stepinac also had enraged Tito by protesting arbitrary postwar punishment of Catholic clergy. After Yugoslavia's break with the Soviet Union in 1948, religious repression gradually decreased as Tito sought the approval of the West. The state-approved funeral and burial of Stepinac in 1961 signaled a new modus vivendi between the Yugoslav government and the Roman Catholic Church of Yugoslavia.

In 1966 Yugoslavia and the Vatican signed a protocol in which Belgrade pledged to recognize freedom of conscience and Rome's jurisdiction over ecclesiastical and spiritual matters for Yugoslav Catholics. In return, the Vatican agreed to honor the separation of church and state in Yugoslavia, including prohibition of political activity by clergy. In 1970 Yugoslavia and the Vatican resumed full diplomatic relations. Nonetheless, opportunities for conflict remained. Franjo Cardinal Kuharić, primate of Croatia, touched off a major controversy in Serbia in 1981 by proposing rehabilitation of Stepinac; subsequent appeals for canonization of the cardinal met strong Serbian resistance.

Islam

Yugoslavia's Islamic community, the largest in any European country west of Turkey, was concentrated among three ethnic groups: Muslim Slavs, located in Bosnia and Hercegovina and Kosovo; ethnic Albanians, primarily in Kosovo, the enclave of Novi Pazar in Serbia, and Macedonia; and Turks inhabiting the same regions as the Albanians. Most of the Muslim Slavs and Albanians converted to Islam in the early stages of Ottoman occupation to gain the higher social status that Ottoman policy afforded to converts. They were the only groups in the European provinces of the Ottoman Empire to convert in large numbers.

In 1930 Yugoslavia's separate Muslim groups united under the authority of a single ulama, the Rais-ul Ulama, who enforced Islamic religious and legal dogma and managed the affairs of the Islamic community. Headquartered in Sarajevo, Yugoslavia's Islamic community included about 3,000 religious leaders and 3,000 mosques in the 1980s. Some Yugoslav Muslim officials studied at Islamic institutions abroad. Financial contributions from Islamic countries such as Libya and Saudi Arabia helped fund many of the 800 mosques constructed in Yugoslavia after World War II. In 1985 a grand mosque was opened in Zagreb after years of delay. The only Islamic school of theology in Europe was located in Sarajevo, and Islamic secondary schools operated in Sarajevo, Skopje, and Priština. A religious school for women, attached to the Islamic secondary school in Sarajevo, had a capacity of sixty. The Islamic community of Yugoslavia published a variety of newspapers and periodicals.

Relations of the postwar communist government with the Islamic community were less troubled than those with the Orthodox or Roman Catholic churches. Yugoslavia's Islamic leaders generally had kept a low profile during World War II, although the authorities condemned the mufti of Zagreb to death for allegedly inciting Muslims to murder Serbs. In the 1960s and 1970s, Tito used Yugoslavia's Islamic community to maintain friendly relations with oil-producing Arab countries because Yugoslavia needed access to inexpensive oil. But after the 1979 fundamentalist revolution in Iran, the Yugoslav government reviewed its policy on potentially destabilizing contacts between Yugoslav Muslims and Middle Eastern governments. The ulama responded by disavowing all connection with the pan-Islamic movement.

Besides mainstream Sunni Islam, the Yugoslav Muslim population also included several small groups such as the Bektashi dervishes. Founded in the thirteenth century, the Bektashi sect was one of the official religions of Kosovo under the tolerant policy of the Ottoman Turks. Its practice disregarded much of traditional Islamic ritual and contains some Christian elements, especially in areas where Christianity is the prevalent religion. After Turkey dissolved its Bektashi orders in 1925, the sect survived only in the Balkans.

Other Faiths

During the Protestant Reformation, a number of Protestant communities arose in regions now included in Yugoslavia. Many initial Protestant conversions were later reversed in the Counterreformation, especially in Slovenia and Croatia. The most notable exceptions were the Calvinist communities of Vojvodina. The surviving Calvinist Reformed Church in Vojvodina was mostly Hungarian in membership. In 1987 it had forty-three parishes, ninety-two affiliated offices, about sixty churches and prayer houses, and over forty ministers trained at theological schools in Austria, Hungary, and Switzerland. In the twentieth century, numerous Protestant faiths, including newer groups such as the Seventh-Day Adventists and Jehovah's Witnesses, also found a foothold in Yugoslavia.

Much of Yugoslavia's prewar Jewish community was destroyed in the Holocaust, and many of the survivors emigrated to Israel after 1948. Yugoslavia's 1931 census recorded a Jewish population of 68,405. By contrast only 6,835 persons identified themselves as Jews by nationality in the census of 1948, and in 1981 the number of Jews had shrunk to 5,638. The remaining Jewish community was organized into twenty-nine communes affiliated with the Belgrade-based Federation of Jewish Communities of Yugoslavia.

Education
History of Yugoslav Education

Primary schooling in interwar Yugoslavia was a four-year course. Although enrollments more than doubled between 1919 and 1940, on the eve of World War II only about 27.3 percent of Yugoslav young people between the ages of five and twenty-four were enrolled in school or receiving some kind of instruction. Only about 4 percent of the pupils who completed primary school went on to secondary schools. Muslim parents remained suspicious of education for women, and many rural areas had no schools at all. In the late 1930s, about 40 percent of the population over ten years of age was illiterate. Striking regional disparities existed in levels of literacy. While over three-quarters of all Slovenes and Croats could read and write, only a tenth of Kosovo's ethnic Albanians were literate. Yugoslavia's interwar education system was highly centralized, and instruction was exclusively in Serbo-Croatian. Macedonians and Croats especially resented Belgrade's dominance of education; many Croatian teachers enlisted in the pro-Nazi Ustaše forces during the war. World War II decimated Yugoslavia's teacher corps and heavily damaged its education facilities. In 1953 about 14.5 percent of the active nonagricultural population had not finished four grades of elementary school, while 63.5 percent had not completed the eighth grade.

In the postwar period, the Yugoslav government invested heavily in rebuilding the national education system. Besides building new schools, libraries, and other facilities, the government took energetic steps to enhance the qualifications of Yugoslavia's teaching cadres. By 1989 the majority of teachers in primary and secondary schools held university degrees. In addition, schools began employing a variety of teacher aides and specialists, including librarians, media specialists, medical personnel, special-education instructors, vocational-training specialists, and computer programmers—most of whom were university graduates. Within thirty years after adoption, such measures radically changed the educational base of the Yugoslav population. By 1981 only 2.7 percent of the active nonagricultural population had less than three years of primary school; the portion that had completed the eighth grade had risen to 81.1 percent; and 58.1 percent of that group had at least a high school diploma. Of the overall population, 25.5 percent had completed a secondary program, and 24.2 had completed eight years of a primary program (see table 7, Appendix).

Primary Schools

A 1958 education law lengthened the country's primary education sequence to eight years and made attendance compulsory for children from seven to fifteen years of age. Between 1945 and 1981, elementary school enrollment rose from 40 percent to 98.6 percent of all children between ages seven and ten and 92 percent of those between eleven and fourteen. In the same period, the number of elementary school teachers increased more than fivefold, and the student-teacher ratio fell from 59 to 1 to 20 to 1. Primary education in Yugoslavia's less developed regions improved dramatically, and instruction in the languages of Yugoslavia's ethnic minorities increased. In Kosovo the number of primary school students rose tenfold between the end of World War II and 1981. In 1986 the student-teacher ratio for primary instruction in the languages of Yugoslavia's ethnic minorities was 18.8 to 1, better than the Yugoslav average overall.

Secondary Education

Secondary education also improved noticeably in the postwar decades. Between 1947 and 1981, the number of students in secondary and postsecondary schools rose more than sixfold, and by 1984 more than 90 percent of the pupils who completed primary school continued their education on the secondary level. In 1989 the secondary school student-teacher ratio in Yugoslavia overall reached 15 to 1, although the ratio varied by region.

A comprehensive curriculum reform in 1974 offered students a choice of postprimary instruction paths. The motivation for reform was to contribute more skilled workers to Yugoslav industry. The reform basically combined separate college preparatory and vocational schools into giant standard secondary schools in which the first two years of instruction were uniform for all students. In the third year, students were expected to choose a general career path from college preparatory and vocational options.

Critics complained bitterly that the new curriculum failed to prepare students adequately to meet the country's needs. University officials asserted that students spent too much time in vocational instruction; enterprise directors complained that the vocational track still did not prepare enough young people to fill skilled jobs. Critics on both sides called for a return to completely separate four-year college-preparatory and vocational schools. In 1990 another round of reforms was imminent, but Yugoslavia's economic woes delayed funding. Between 1977 and 1984, spending on education had already fallen from 5.9 percent to 3.5 percent of total national income.

The amount of secondary school instruction conducted in minority languages rose rapidly after World War II. In 1945 only 4,233 students received such instruction; in 1985–86 the number was 85,892. In addition to Serbo-Croatian, Slovenian, and Macedonian, secondary school instruction was conducted in Albanian, Bulgarian, Czech, Hungarian, Italian, Romanian, Russian, Slovak, Turkish, and Ukrainian (see table 8, Appendix). Government officials hoped that increasing the average education level in Kosovo would reduce future population growth in the region. According to the 1981 census, 55.5 percent of Kosovo's population over age fifteen had completed elementary school; this figure was only 5.2 percent in 1953. In 1981 Slovenia had the highest literacy rate of the republics and provinces (99.2 percent), and Kosovo had the lowest (82.4 percent) (see table 9, Appendix).

Higher Education

Yugoslavia also made significant progress in university education in the postwar period. Until 1987 the system was available to all who could qualify. At that time, however, fiscal problems caused a cut in student acceptance by 7 percent, and course offerings were cut. The number of universities, art academies, and advanced vocational schools rose from 26 in 1939 to 322 in 1987, and the number of students attending them increased from 20,000 to 347,000 in the same period. Higher education in Yugoslavia also faced serious problems at the beginning of the 1990s. University dropout rates were high, and students who remained in school took an average of seven years to complete a four-year degree and five years to finish a two-year program. High tuition and living expenses made it difficult for many students to attend full time and put university education beyond the reach of other Yugoslav families.

Health Care and Social Welfare

Before World War II, medical care in Yugoslavia was generally very poor. The country had only one physician for every 750 urban residents; in rural areas, the ratio was almost twenty times worse. In 1990, despite overall strides in the nation's health care system, a wide disparity remained between urban and rural areas in the delivery of health care.

Disease and Mortality

The most frequent causes of death in Yugoslavia in 1984 were diseases of the circulatory system (45.2 percent of total deaths for men and 56 percent for women) and cancer (16.1 percent for men and 13.3 percent for women). Death from circulatory diseases was more than twice as likely in the country's developed regions as in the less developed areas, while in Kosovo the share of infectious diseases still accounted for 7.8 percent of male deaths and 10.1 percent of female deaths in the 1980s. Increasing environmental pollution and cigarette smoking possibly were reflected in a steep increase in deaths from cancer and circulatory problems between 1975 and 1986. Accidents, especially traffic accidents, accounted for 41.2 deaths per 100,000 inhabitants, while the suicide rate rose by almost a quarter between 1975 and 1989.

Development of the Health Care System

Poor nutrition and ignorance of hygiene and child care were normal conditions in Yugoslavia before World War II. As a result,

Yugoslavia suffered Europe's highest death rate from tuberculosis; malaria, diphtheria, typhus, syphilis, dysentery, and whooping cough also ravaged the country.

After World War II, the Yugoslav state took direct control of the country's health care system and established a general health insurance program. In the early years of the program, coverage was inconsistent for a substantial portion of the population; private farmers and their families were not covered until 1959. In recent decades, however, improvements in health care and the delivery of health services were dramatic. Overall coverage rose from a quarter of the population in 1952 to over 80 percent in 1984. The number of physicians rose to 45,869 in 1987, and the number of hospital beds reached 142,427 (see table 10, Appendix). In 1990 the system included about 280 hospitals. Health education and increased access to health care reduced the outbreak of infectious diseases to a fraction of earlier levels. Diphtheria was eradicated completely; the incidence of typhus fell from 3,022 in 1955 to 160 in 1986; of syphilis from 7,248 to 300; of whooping cough from 28,066 to 2,978; and of tuberculosis from 37,945 to 15,891. Maternity-related deaths and birth-related infant deaths also plummeted between the 1950s and the 1980s.

In 1987 farmers and farm workers used health care facilities about one-fourth as often as industrial workers. Job openings at rural health care facilities went unfilled despite the fact that few jobs for health care workers existed in the cities. Between 1965 and 1970, one-third of all medical school graduates left the country to find work. Disparities in health care between Yugoslavia's developed and less developed regions also were dramatic. In 1983 Slovenia had one doctor for every 434 persons, compared with one per 1,141 persons in Kosovo. Likewise, Slovenian hospitals had one bed per 128 persons in the republic; Kosovo had one bed per 334 persons. In Slovenia 99.7 percent of all births took place with professional medical care; in Kosovo professional care attended only 60.5 percent of births.

The Contemporary Health and Welfare Systems

Yugoslavia's 1974 Constitution requires the organization of self-managed communities of interest for health care to manage the health care system (see Socialist Self-Management, ch. 3). The communities of interest represented both the users and the employees of health care facilities. Thus, such groups included delegates from the workers' council of the health care facility, local citizenry served by the facility, and delegates from local enterprises contributing funds to the facility. Generally, each commune had a health center, although cooperative use of facilities was possible through agreements among individual communes. Health stations—less equipped facilities available for primary first aid—were more numerous. In 1988 health centers numbered 450, health stations 2,550.

The federal Constitution entitles all Yugoslav citizens to health care in a variety of situations. Infectious diseases and mental illnesses judged dangerous to society received automatic treatment. Workers were guaranteed care for occupational diseases or work-related injuries. Pregnant women, infants, and preschoolers received comprehensive medical care. Children younger than fifteen, students younger than twenty-six, and citizens over sixty-five were entitled to general medical care. The health care system distributed contraceptive devices, and free abortions were available up to ten weeks after conception or later under special circumstances. Federal law required that women receive uninterrupted paid maternity leave beginning at least 28 days before expected delivery and ending at least 105 days afterward. By 1990 some republics had increased minimum maternity leave to as much as one year. Working mothers also received income compensation for time taken from work to care for sick children.

Yugoslavia's social welfare system nominally provided services for destitute persons and families, physically and mentally handicapped persons, broken families, alcoholics and drug addicts, and elderly persons without relatives to care for them. In 1986 about 3 percent of the population received services from the social welfare system. In 1984 Yugoslavia operated 340 social work centers, including shelters, juvenile homes, care centers for handicapped children, foster home placement agencies, nursing homes, and facilities for care of the mentally handicapped and mentally ill. Altogether, the system employed about 2,100 social workers and 1,000 other professionals in the mid-1980s. Self-managing communities of interest managed the centers, which provided services to 687,000 Yugoslavs in 1984. In the socialized planning of the postwar period, the Yugoslav education, health, and social welfare systems reached substantially higher standards. The average citizen benefited from these improvements, but social protection and opportunity remained unequally dispensed among the republics in 1990.

*   *   *

Contrasts in Emerging Societies, edited by G.F. Cushing et al., is an anthology of primary-source material describing socioeconomic conditions in southeastern Europe in the nineteenth century. It provides an excellent glimpse of life in the Yugoslav lands during that period. *The National Question in Yugoslavia* by Ivo Banac is an exhaustive treatment of the disparate Yugoslav peoples and their relations in the years immediately before and after the formation of the Yugoslav state. Steven L. Burg's *Conflict and Cohesion in Socialist Yugoslavia* and Pedro Ramet's *Nationalism and Federalism in Yugoslavia, 1963–1983* discuss Yugoslavia's national question in later decades. Stella Alexander's *Church and State in Yugoslavia since 1945* describes the relations between the postwar communist regime and the Serbian Orthodox and Roman Catholic churches. *The Yugoslavs* by Dusko Doder is an insightful and entertaining description of the virtues and foibles of the Yugoslav peoples in the 1970s. *Kosovo: Past and Present,* edited by Ranko Petković, presents an official, pro-Serbian assessment of the Kosovo problem, while *Studies on Kosova,* edited by Arshi Pipa and Sami Repishti, presents the Albanian side of the conflict. *Jugoslavija, 1945–1985,* edited by Dušan Miljković, contains a wealth of statistical comparisons of socioeconomic indicators for the Yugoslav republics that a non-reader of Serbo-Croatian can easily decipher with the help of a dictionary. (For further information and complete citations, see Bibliography.)

Chapter 3. The Economy

Woman factory worker

AFTER WORLD WAR II, Yugoslavia established a one-party communist regime and an economic system modeled on that of the Soviet Union. In 1948, however, the Soviet-led international communist alliance Cominform (see Glossary) ousted Yugoslavia and imposed an economic blockade. At this time, the Yugoslav leadership reevaluated Marxist doctrine and set out to develop a unique system of economic administration, which it labeled socialist self-management. This system was seen as a more accurate realization of the Marxist theory that the means of production should be owned and operated by the people. By comparison, Yugoslavs considered the Soviet system to be statist because the Soviet state had simply replaced the capitalists of the West in exploiting the worker class.

Under the strong hand of Josef Broz Tito, most aspects of the Yugoslav economy prospered from 1950 to 1979. The gross material product (GMP—see Glossary) rose rapidly, millions of peasants were given jobs in the social sector (see Glossary), industrial production expanded rapidly, and export of manufactured products increased substantially. Living standards also improved as personal incomes increased, social services were extended and improved, and supplies of consumer goods expanded. In the 1960s, Yugoslavia's market-economy reforms positioned the country as an economic leader of the Nonaligned Movement.

The 1980s, however, brought a grave economic crisis. Beginning in 1979, the Yugoslav economy entered an extended downturn because of increases in oil prices in 1973 and 1979, the world recession that began in 1979, and careless investment and borrowing policies pursued in Yugoslavia's rapid postwar industrialization. Inflation soared out of control, reaching an annual rate of 2,600 percent by the end of 1989. Personal income, consumption, and labor productivity fell, and unemployment exceeded 16 percent by the end of the 1980s. These problems were especially serious in the poorer regions of Yugoslavia such as Macedonia and Kosovo. Foreign loans dried up at the same time, as Yugoslavia was forced to reschedule its US$20 billion foreign debt. Patchwork attempts to solve these problems generally failed.

In January 1990, the government of Prime Minister Ante Marković introduced a reform package. This program included monetary reforms designed to combat inflation and give the federal government more control over macroeconomic policy. It drastically reformed currency, wage, and price policy. Despite doubts by many domestic and foreign economists and domestic opposition to painful austerity measures, the Marković program began to stabilize the economy in the first six months of 1990. The new program was a significant break with the decade of economic policy stagnation that had crippled Yugoslavia's growth since 1979.

Economic History

World War II and Recovery

Before World War II, Yugoslavia was one of Europe's most underdeveloped countries. The eradication of feudalism after World War I left over 75 percent of the population living in poverty and dependent on small, inefficient peasant farms. Economic growth, though steady, was modest. In 1938 per capita income was 30 percent below the world average.

The 1941 German invasion of Yugoslavia and the subsequent partition of the country among Germany, Bulgaria, Hungary, and Italy destroyed all semblance of normal economic life. The Germans built new factories in Slovenia and Croatia and converted remaining plants to produce military equipment. The peasants continued to farm, but over 50 percent of livestock and 80 percent of equipment were destroyed or confiscated during the occupation. The communications network was sabotaged, and over half the railroads and rolling stock was demolished. Inflation was rampant, and barter became the prime means for transacting business. The most devastating blow to Yugoslavia fell on its people: over 11 percent of the prewar population was killed; another 25 percent was left homeless.

Postwar reconstruction in Yugoslavia was financed by aid from the United Nations Relief and Rehabilitation Administration. The administration provided a total of US$60 million of aid in food, clothing, medical supplies, seed, livestock, jeeps, and railroad stock. By the end of 1946, Yugoslav national income was restored to its 1938 level.

Application of Stalinist Economics

With the victory of Tito and the People's Front in November 1945, post-World War II Yugoslavia became a one-party communist state. The Communist Party of Yugoslavia (CPY) was strictly Marxist-Leninist in economic outlook and fiercely loyal to the centralized economic program of Soviet dictator Joseph V. Stalin. Supporting the Soviet Union's foreign policy in most issues and imitating its domestic policy, the party labeled itself the vanguard of the proletariat. Nationalization of industry, redistribution of private land, and collectivization of agriculture (see Glossary) were at the core of Yugoslav domestic economic policy as the 1950s began.

Under the land reform of 1945, over 1 million hectares of land were confiscated from private owners and institutions. A state-controlled land fund was established to hold and redistribute the land to peasants and state farms. Local authorities set the exact amount of land peasants could retain, within the state parameters of twenty to thirty-five hectares. Despite the state landholding limits, a large share of agricultural activity remained in the private sector. The state extracted a share, however, by requiring delivery of surplus products to state enterprises.

Following the example of the Soviet constitution of 1936, the Yugoslav constitution of 1946 initiated the process of bringing all sectors of the economy under state control. At the program's inception, all mineral wealth, power resources, means of communication, and foreign trade were nationalized. By 1948 all domestic and foreign-owned capital, excluding some retail trade and small craft industries and most of agriculture, had been brought into the social sector.

Forced collectivization of agriculture was instituted in January 1949, bringing the last privately owned portion of the economy under state control. At the program's inception, 94 percent of Yugoslav agricultural land was privately owned; but by the height of the collectivization drive in 1950, nearly 96 percent was under the control of the social sector. Yugoslav planners expected that rapid collectivization and mechanization of agriculture would increase food production, improve the people's standard of living, and release peasants to work in industry. The result, however, was a poorly conceived program that was abandoned three years later.

The First Five-Year Plan

All economic activity for the period of the First Five-Year Plan (1947–52) was directly managed by the Federal Planning Commission, which, in turn, was closely supervised by the party. The objectives of the plan were to overcome economic and technological backwardness, strengthen economic and military power, enhance and develop the socialist sector of the country, increase the people's welfare, and narrow the gap in economic development among regions.

Economic development in the first half of the planning period was relatively successful; from January 1947 through June 1949, the plan was approximately on schedule. Then, in late 1949, agricultural and industrial development began to fall behind planned rates. The targets set were very ambitious and did not take into account Yugoslavia's inadequate power resources and limited range of indigenous raw materials. Primarily because of poor investment policy, agriculture had no hope of reaching its target of 52 percent growth over 1939 levels. Only 7 percent of total investment was earmarked for achieving that ambitious goal. The rapid industrialization foreseen in the plan required vast imports of fuel, food, and raw materials. Because Yugoslavia's sparse and low-quality exports could not finance such acquisitions, it was forced to run a large trade deficit, most of which was financed by credits and loans from Western Europe and the United States.

Following Yugoslavia's 1948 ouster from the Cominform (Communist Information Bureau—see Glossary), Cominform members instituted an economic boycott against the country, further slowing Yugoslavia's economic growth. Many treaties and trade agreements among the Soviet Union, Eastern Europe, and Yugoslavia were abrogated, loans were canceled, and nearly all trade was halted. In 1948 trade with the Soviet Union and Eastern Europe made up approximately 50 percent of Yugoslavia's imports and exports, but that figure was reduced to zero by 1950. Yugoslavia suffered doubly in the many instances when it did not receive goods, particularly machinery and capital goods, for which it had already paid.

However disastrous the effects of the Cominform blockade, Tito himself estimated that it accounted for less than 20 percent of the damage to the Yugoslav economy during the second half of the First Five-Year Plan. The droughts of 1950 and 1952 were an even greater economic disaster than the boycott. Another formidable burden was the need to divert substantial resources to rebuilding the Yugoslav military and arms industry.

By the end of the First Five-Year Plan, Yugoslavia had become acquainted with the economic problems that would eventually become chronic in the 1980s: an oversized balance of payments deficit, significant foreign debt, low labor productivity, and inefficient use of capital. But the comprehensive, long-term, centrally directed planning approach was able to mobilize national resources to achieve rapid postwar development in Yugoslavia. Although inefficient, the high rate of investment in the First Five-Year Plan ensured increased output throughout the Second Five-Year Plan (1957-61). From 1950 to 1960, industrial output rose faster in Yugoslavia, in both per capita and total output, than in almost any other country in the world over the same period.

Launching Socialist Self-Management

The aim of the Yugoslav shift from Stalinist economics was to redefine the party as a source of ideological guidance, eliminating its political power over the economy. This would follow the true spirit of Marxism by giving the people control over their economic destiny. "The factories to the workers" was the slogan of the decade.

In 1950 the Basic Law on the Management of State Economic Enterprises by Working Collectives was introduced to establish workers' participation in the management of their own enterprises. The basic law decentralized planning, turning it over to local communes and workers' councils and incorporated the principles of socialist, or workers', self-management into all aspects of public life. Central authorities outlined only general economic guidelines rather than imposing mandatory targets from a centralized command structure. The state retained control over the appointment of enterprise directors and the allocation of investment resources, however, thereby retaining considerable de facto control over the economy.

In agriculture the failure of collectivization led to abandonment of that experiment in 1952. By that date, one-fifth of the 7,000 agricultural collectives already had been dissolved. In March 1953, peasants were officially allowed to leave the collectives, and most of them did so. Later the same year, the state ended compulsory delivery of agricultural products to state enterprises. Peasants were left to produce what they could and to sell surpluses on the open market.

The "Perspective" Five-Year Plan

In the five years between the first and second five-year plans, the Yugoslav economy followed ad hoc annual plans. During this interval, a high rate of investment and savings was maintained. In 1957 the government introduced the Second Five-Year Plan, called the "Perspective Plan" because its stated goals were not strictly mandatory. The primary purpose of this plan was to incorporate the principles of socialist self-management. The plan specified scope, expected trends in demography and productivity, volume and allocation of investment, and increases in production on the federal level. But enterprises, communes, and republics were left to their own devices in reaching production levels. They devised their own plans, then submitted them to the Federal Planning Commission. That body then consulted with republic planning institutes and drew up the final plan according to federal government policies.

Yugoslav economists consider the Second Five-Year Plan the most effective postwar Yugoslav economic plan. Its achievements came, however, at the expense of negative impact on the international balance of payments, uneven domestic investment patterns (which once again allocated insufficient investment resources to agriculture), growing unemployment, inflation, and cash-flow problems. Nonetheless, fulfillment of the plan was declared ahead of schedule in 1960.

Overhaul in the 1960s

A movement toward greater market freedom in Yugoslavia spurred economic reforms in the 1960s. The Third Five-Year Plan, begun in 1961, was abandoned the next year because of a growing economic crisis and failure to meet any plan targets at the end of the first year. The basic goals of that plan were to increase personal consumption, production growth, and labor productivity through loosened government controls on wages and higher investment in the production of energy, steel, nonferrous metals, chemicals, and capital equipment. Particular attention went to investment in the less developed republics and to mechanization of agriculture.

Economic planning in the 1960s strove to make Yugoslavia more competitive on the world market and to expose the economy to the beneficial influence of free international trade. A more liberal trade policy eliminated multiple exchange rates, devalued the dinar (for value of the dinar—see Glossary), and reduced tariffs and import restrictions. In addition, the Yugoslav tourist industry received government support, and Yugoslavs were allowed to work as guest workers abroad (see Guest Workers, ch. 2). Hard-currency (see Glossary) remittances from tourism and guest workers became important sources of relief for Yugoslavia's weak balance of payments. Unfortunately, these changes were poorly prepared and badly implemented. Not long after the Third Five-Year Plan was abandoned in 1962, industrial production fell to half its 1960 level, imports spiraled, exports stagnated, and inflation increased because wages increased faster than productivity.

After the Third Five-Year Plan failed, the government reverted to a system of ad hoc annual plans similar to those implemented between 1952 and 1957. Beginning in December 1962, Yugoslavia's leading economists and politicians launched a two-year series of debates to identify and correct economic flaws, adjusting the roles of the federal government, enterprises, planning, and the market in economic growth and development policy. The conservative minority feared that decentralized control over investment and overemphasis on market forces would lead to the loss of socialist

Fifth International Technical Exposition, Belgrade, 1961
Courtesy Yugoslav National Tourist Office, New York

values. Liberals, however, saw decentralized decision making and a greater role for market forces as the only way out of Yugoslavia's economic stagnation.

The new constitution of 1963 introduced market socialism (see Glossary), a system that basically reflected the views of the liberals in the debates of 1962 and 1963. Decision making was decentralized, market forces were allowed greater play, and the federal government further loosened its control over investment, prices, and incomes. The federal government was only to intervene with emergency measures in times of crisis. The self-management system thereby received more power and responsibility in the economic development of the country.

The Economic Reform of 1965

The reform of July 1965 consisted of thirty laws that formed the legislative framework for market socialism. An important goal of this framework was to allow enterprises to keep a larger share of their earned income, much of which was previously paid to the government. The five major components of the reform were lower taxes; limited state control of investment allocations; removal of price controls and large adjustments to product prices, to bring domestic prices closer to world price levels; devaluation of the dinar

129

and reduction of customs duties and export subsidies; and permission and credit for peasant landowners to buy farm machinery.

Economic performance in the 1950s and early 1960s was strong primarily because of consistently heavy investment policies. Between 1954 and 1965, GMP increased by an average of 8.4 percent per year. In the same period, gross industrial output increased at a yearly average of 12.2 percent; industrial employment, 6.6 percent; social sector employment, 5.9 percent; exports, 11.7 percent; and fixed investments, 9.2 percent per year. In the mid-1960s, however, these rates began to fall because the 1965 reform caused excessive demand on resources, growing inflation, continuing balance of payments problems, and expanded unemployment. From 1965 to 1974, average annual GMP growth dropped to 6.4 percent, gross industrial output to 7.7 percent, industrial employment to 3.3 percent, social sector employment to 2.9 percent, exports to 5.6 percent, and fixed investments to 8.2 percent per year.

Adjustments in the 1970s

Yugoslavia entered the 1970s in an economic crisis. Growth was slowing because more investment was needed to achieve each additional unit of growth. At 34 percent, Yugoslavia's rate of inflation was the highest in Europe in 1974, and the government reimposed the price controls that had been relaxed under the 1965 reform. Growing unemployment prompted large numbers of Yugoslav workers to migrate to Western Europe. The government wholeheartedly supported this trend because the hard-currency earnings brought into Yugoslavia by the guest workers mitigated the effects of increased foreign debt and export stagnation. The disappointing results of the reform and nationalist uprisings in Croatia and Kosovo between 1968 and 1972 led Tito to end the market socialism experiment by putting economic policy making back under party control in 1974.

The new Constitution of 1974 and the Law on Associated Labor of 1976 reorganized the economy from top to bottom. Large and medium-sized enterprises were dissolved into smaller, self-contained units called basic organizations of associated labor (BOALs). Under this system, workers gained more control over management decisions, banks, and social services. At the same time, Yugoslavia became more federalized as party authority was decentralized to republic and provincial governments and local communes (see Political Innovation and the 1974 Constitution, ch. 4). The new statutes introduced a system of self-management agreements to coordinate interaction among basic organizations of associated labor and social compacts to coordinate interaction between economic and political bodies.

As this new system went into place, the economy was hit by a severe increase in world petroleum prices. Because Yugoslavia depended heavily on imported petroleum products, this development aggravated existing inflation and foreign debt. Nevertheless, Yugoslavia tried to overcome its balance of payments problems by placing even stronger emphasis on output growth, increased spending (particularly on nonproductive investment and consumption), and foreign borrowing. The result was a dramatic rise in foreign indebtedness and inflation and a decline in living standards. When petroleum prices rose again in 1979 and the world entered an economic recession, Yugoslavia could no longer afford to maintain its debt burden. Foreign loans became inaccessible, and inflation continued to climb. By 1980 these conditions clearly called for slowing the pace of development and adjusting the system so as not to jeopardize future growth.

The Economic Management Mechanism
Socialist Self-Management

The system of socialist self-management remained the distinctive element of the Yugoslav economy in 1990. Following the slogan "the factories to the workers," policy makers established the system in the 1950s as a way of transferring economic management from the state to the workers. The organization of enterprises operating under socialist self-management was elaborated further in the 1974 Constitution and the Law on Associated Labor of 1976.

The original self-management concept redesignated enterprises as work organizations of associated labor and divided them into smaller units at the level of factory departments. Each smaller unit, a BOAL, was a self-managed entity, financially and commercially independent. As members of basic organizations, workers had the right to attend general meetings and elect and serve on workers' councils. The councils were elected bodies that formulated business policy and plans, made investment and borrowing decisions, approved enterprise accounts, and gave final approval to directors and management boards. Despite these extensive nominal powers, however, decisions by the workers' councils were heavily influenced by enterprise directors, who were appointed by the League of Communists of Yugoslavia (LCY—see Glossary), as the CPY was called after 1952. Only one-third of the committees nominating enterprise directors could come from the councils; the remainder were members of local communes and trade unions, all still controlled by the LCY in 1990. In the final step, the workers' council chose from the nominating committee's list of candidates, but in most cases the list contained only one name at that stage.

Work communities were developed for white-collar clerical, administrative, and technical workers of the labor organizations. Also self-managed, the work communities resembled the BOALs but provided fewer rights and responsibilities to their members. Self-managed communities of interest were established by basic organizations to provide transportation, communications, education, and health services for production workers (see Health Care and Social Welfare, ch. 2). Complex organizations of associated labor provided vertical and horizontal integration to improve cooperation and specialization among work organizations and their component units.

Another unique element of the Yugoslav economic system was the use of self-management agreements and social compacts. Self-management agreements were binding contracts among self-management organizations in the social sector; they were enforceable in court if a party failed to fulfill its obligations. The contracts provided for allocation among the member organizations of joint income between wages and investment and for the sharing of risks. Social compacts were written among basic organizations, communities of interest, government economic agencies, and trade unions. They specified criteria for income distribution, foreign trade relations, employment policy, and ranking of priorities.

Capital Ownership and the Market

In 1990 most enterprises, government institutions, social services, and banks operated under the system of socialist self-management. All institutions employing this system were considered to be owned by society and not by the state, which is the owner in most centrally planned economies. In spite of their nominal control, however, workers had no rights of ownership of the assets they used.

Agriculture also was decentralized in the 1950s. Forced collectivization was officially abandoned in 1952, and most agricultural land was returned to small peasant farmers. Small-farmer agriculture dominated Yugoslavia's socialist market economy through the 1980s. In 1984 private farmers accounted for 83 percent of tilled land, 84 percent of all livestock, and 72 percent of net agricultural output in Yugoslavia.

Throughout the postwar period, official Yugoslav policy was hostile to private enterprise, or the "small economy." In theory, only small entities such as peasant farms, urban artisans and tradesmen, retail

Street market, Belgrade, stocked with produce from private farm plots
Courtesy Charles Sudetic

businesses, restaurants, and tourist facilities were permitted independent ownership and operation. In the late 1980s, many prominent Yugoslav economists recommended that private enterprise be given full recognition and incentive and that maximum private ownership of land be increased from ten to thirty hectares. These proposals were based on the belief that the entrepreneurial spirit would encourage greater efficiency and higher productivity in an economy long hampered by the political constraints of government control.

In spite of Tito's retrenchment in the mid-1960s, Yugoslavia moved slowly for three decades toward toleration of market forces in a system that originally attempted to operate in total isolation from the world economy. This trend toward market liberalization, however, gradually slowed in the 1970s because of the movement toward federalism and the introduction of the social compact system in the 1974 Constitution. Consensual by definition, social compacts restricted independent decision making, which in turn limited competition among basic organizations of labor in communes and republics. Decentralization of economic decision-making power to the republic level prevented enterprises from expanding markets beyond their own region; by the late 1980s, this tendency had weakened the market system significantly.

In January 1990, Yugoslavia began a new stage in the incorporation of a Western-style market economy into the system of workers' self-management. According to the 1990 reforms, enterprises were to operate on the basis of profitability, and unprofitable firms previously protected by the state now risked bankruptcy. Enterprises critical to national welfare, such as steel, energy, and defense-related industries, were excepted in the first stage of the reform. Although most enterprises remained in the social sector, the 1990 program allowed workers to become shareholders in their firms and legalized worker strikes. Strikes had been tolerated in the late 1980s, but their legality had never been established. Some economic experts predicted that by the time all the 1990 reforms were in place, the Yugoslav economy would differ from Western capitalism only in the larger proportion of state-owned enterprises in Yugoslavia. In 1990 the estimated gross national product (GNP—see Glossary) was US$120.1 billion, or US$5,040 per capita.

Planning and Pricing

In 1990 the Yugoslav economy ostensibly operated on a new system of economic planning. Throughout the 1960s and the early 1970s, planning was "indicative": federal authorities handed down plans with detailed, specific goals to be achieved, with little input from below. In 1976 a radically new system of voluntary planning, called "social planning," was established. Plans of five years or longer were formulated from the bottom up, with the participation and agreement of all parties concerned.

The planning process started when federal authorities announced the timetable for the overall plan and major intermediate goals. Following the general government program, enterprises and their subordinate organizations drew up microplans, while macroplans were formulated within and among all the local governments and self-managed communities of interest. This was done simultaneously at all levels without any hierarchical approval system. Individual plans were modified through discussion with all parties concerned; the result was then written into binding social contracts. Enterprises and other bodies constructed self-management agreements that addressed specific aspects of the plan, such as the supply of materials and the amount of new capacity required. Annual assessments and adjustments provided adaptability to changing conditions. The Yugoslav economy's dependence on imported technical equipment for growth meant that changing world markets often made such adjustments necessary.

The consensual approach to planning proved ineffective in Yugoslavia. It was time consuming and, because social compacts were voluntary and therefore unenforceable, plans were largely ignored except in rare instances of federal government intervention. Extreme decentralization of planning also meant that cooperative projects among republics and provinces were not well coordinated. This inefficiency particularly hindered development of national solutions for maintaining the energy balance and distributing foreign exchange.

Until the 1960s, price controls were set at particular points in the chain of production. Such control points were the initial sale of a raw material and the release of a final product for sale on the retail market. Intermediate prices were determined by supply and demand. This combined pricing system worked fairly well to moderate inflation until many price controls were removed in 1964. By the late 1980s, pricing again was moving distinctly toward free market determination. The 1990 reforms removed price controls on 85 percent of all commodities. Price controls remained only on essentials such as electricity, gasoline, oil, coal, some raw metals and nonmetal minerals, medicines, and railroad, postal, and telephone services.

Trade Unions

In the 1980s, membership in trade unions was officially voluntary, but most workers were members and had dues deducted directly from their pay. Trade union officials usually were LCY members and, because the self-management system had no evident division between employers and employees, officials had relatively little responsibility. Their one official function was to nominate members of workers' councils (see Trade Unions, ch. 4).

Before 1990, strikes, or "work stoppages" as they were euphemistically called, officially were neither legal nor illegal. The idea of a strike in a self-management system was theoretically contradictory, because technically workers would be striking against themselves. Hence, Yugoslav work stoppages took the form of political protest against the system rather than conflict between employer and employees. The reforms introduced in January 1990 officially declared the workers' right to strike.

Strikes were relatively rare until the late 1970s, when soaring inflation and falling personal incomes generated widespread discontent. In 1987, 1988, and 1989, government-imposed income freezes set off waves of major strikes, each lasting several weeks. In the first nine months of 1987 alone, 1,000 strikes were called, involving over 150,000 workers. The 1989 strikes involved over 900,000 workers. Demands almost always included higher pay and often the replacement of management as well.

Traditionally, trade union officials opposed strikes; but in the late 1980s they modified this stand. In 1985 some union leaders broke tradition by suggesting that when workers' demands were justified and no other solution existed, the trade union should take the lead in organizing a strike. As of early 1990, no union had taken such action, however, and many union officials remained on record as opposing strikes.

Government Revenue and Spending

Most federal revenue was collected in the form of turnover taxes and assessments by local and federal self-management communities of interest, which had financial management responsibility for social services such as education, health, and pensions. Because a large portion of the national budget was committed to social services, levies by the communities of interest were an important part of the tax structure. The republics and provinces and the communes also levied taxes; their main revenue sources were the same as those of the federal government, but they also taxed income and personal property. The last two categories provided little income because the minimum income level on which income tax was collected was very high. Personal property taxes were collected mostly on private homes (see Housing, ch. 2). Peasants and private businesses were taxed on assessed incomes, often at very high rates that discouraged individual economic initiative. Constitutional reform aimed at restructuring the tax system to eliminate such restrictions.

In 1987 the government purchased 41 percent of Yugoslavia's GMP through large expenditures on defense, government administration, and social services (see table 11, Appendix). Social services received an unusually large allotment for a country of Yugoslavia's modest resources. Defense took about 46 percent of federal outlays budgeted for 1990 because of Yugoslavia's policy of maintaining security and integrity as a nonaligned state (see Threat Perception; Military Budget, ch. 5). Other major federal expenditure categories were education and aid to underdeveloped regions.

The 1974 Constitution virtually eliminated direct federal expenditures on investment. Partly for this reason, in 1990 the federal government accounted for only one-quarter of total government spending in Yugoslavia. The remainder was disbursed by authorities at the republic or commune level.

Banking

The banking sector was crucial to Yugoslavia's efforts to constrain domestic demand, to shift resources toward export-producing sectors, and to increase investment efficiency. Laws introduced in 1985 effectively created a new banking system and sought to bolster financial discipline, improve investment selection, and strengthen the commercial banks.

Almost all financial assets and savings in Yugoslavia were held in banks or kept in cash in the form of dinars or foreign currency. The financial institutions within Yugoslavia included the central banking system, which consisted of the National Bank of Yugoslavia and the national banks of the six republics and two autonomous provinces; the commercial banking system, including 166 basic banks and 9 associated banks; and other financial institutions such as internal banks and the Yugoslav Bank for International Economic Cooperation (YBIEC).

The central banking system was responsible for planning and implementing monetary policies. But in the 1970s, the federalized status of the National Bank of Yugoslavia limited its control over the commercial banks and made it relatively powerless to carry out national monetary policy. Because the credit policies of commercial banks were relatively unchecked and because they were organized on a republic basis, those banks were very powerful in maintaining the serious imbalance of investment and development among the regions of Yugoslavia. The reforms of January 1990, however, gave the National Bank of Yugoslavia more control over the operations and policies of commercial banks.

Day-to-day commercial banking activities were carried on by the self-managed business or basic banks. They were local or regional organizations that were nominally controlled by their founding local enterprises or communities of interest. In reality, because bank managers were politically appointed, they were heavily influenced by local party and government organizations. Two or more basic banks could form an associated bank through a self-management agreement. The major functions of associated banks were to pool resources and handle foreign exchange operations on behalf of their member basic banks.

Banks, enterprises, and other financial organizations were audited by the Social Accounting Service. All banks were required to be members of the Yugoslav Banking Association (YBA). The function of the YBA was to initiate and organize cooperation among member banks through self-management agreements. A typical agreement of this type established uniform interest rates on deposits for all Yugoslav savings banks.

Internal banks were financial service organizations established through self-management agreements among basic organizations of associated labor. Not considered financial institutions per se and not subject to monetary regulation, internal banks were important as a cooperative source of funding to facilitate investment of their member basic organizations. Only member basic organizations and their workers were allowed to deposit in internal banks.

The YBIEC was established in 1979 to provide financial support for foreign transactions. Owned by over 300 major capital goods and services exporters, the YBIEC's main responsibility was to extend export credit and insurance to exporters and joint ventures. In 1989 a new law transformed the organization into a joint stock company and expanded its ownership to include state and banking institutions. The YBIEC received funding from its members, basic and associated banks, the National Bank of Yugoslavia, and foreign borrowing and issue of securities.

Structure of the Economy

Labor and Unemployment

Unemployment was a major problem for Yugoslavia in the late 1980s. During that period, over 875,000 Yugoslavs worked abroad, and up to 25 percent of the workers employed in the productive social sector at home were classified as surplus labor; nevertheless, more than 1.2 million people were registered as unemployed in 1988. This was about one-sixth of the total working-age population of Yugoslavia that year.

Yugoslav unemployment statistics were based on the number of people who registered with the government as job seekers in the social sector. Several factors caused inaccuracies in such figures, however. Students often registered as job seekers in order to receive better health benefits; many workers registered if they were seeking a job better than the one already held; and some of the unemployed did not register because they saw no prospect of getting a job.

Because unprofitable Yugoslav enterprises often were supported by the government and prevented from going into bankruptcy, workers in the social sector rarely lost their jobs before the reforms of 1990. Therefore, a large proportion of job seekers in the 1980s were young people. In 1988 over 92 percent of the unemployed were under age forty, and nearly 57 percent were under age thirty. Yugoslav unemployment also tended to be long term: according to official statistics for 1988, although almost one-quarter of the unemployed were able to find work in less than six months, almost 62 percent were without a job for over one year, many for more than three years. A third characteristic of Yugoslav unemployment was the large regional difference in unemployment rates. In 1986 Slovenia was at virtually full employment while the underdeveloped province of Kosovo had more than one job seeker for every two workers employed in the social sector.

Several factors interacted to raise unemployment in Yugoslavia in the 1980s. Immediately after World War II, peasants made up about four-fifths of the population. Rural workers increasingly were forced into the cities to seek jobs, better health care, improved earning potential, and pensions. Two government policies stimulated this movement. Following traditional Marxist development patterns, Yugoslavia concentrated investments in heavy industry, directing capital away from agriculture and further impoverishing the peasants. And the policy of discouraging nonfarm private business eliminated a potential alternative economic activity. Marxist ideology obliged social sector enterprises to absorb extra labor, even if it meant redundancy and decreases in labor productivity. Between 1975 and 1988, labor distribution remained relatively stable among the major enterprise categories (see table 12, Appendix).

The economic reforms of the 1960s gave market forces more influence in enterprise management decisions, which helped eliminate excess labor. Fortunately for Yugoslavia, at this time several West European countries required imported labor; Yugoslav workers were encouraged to leave the country for temporary jobs in Western Europe. Then the oil price shock and worldwide recession beginning in 1979 dropped labor demand in Western Europe and forced many Yugoslav guest workers to return home. Domestic enterprises returned to conditions of surplus labor and low productivity. By the late 1980s, however, the guest worker force was again contributing substantial amounts of hard currency to the Yugoslav economy.

In the late 1980s, measures such as improved health care and pensions attempted to raise the rural standard of living and draw some of the unemployed out of the cities; but in 1990 prospects for stemming unemployment still seemed poor. The primary goal of the 1990 economic reforms was to reduce Yugoslavia's runaway inflation. But the new anti-inflation policies aggravated the unemployment problem, even as they improved labor productivity (see The Reforms of 1990, this ch.).

Industry

After World War II, Yugoslav development policy emphasized growth in the industrial sector. All means of production were completely nationalized and remained so through 1990. The high rate of investment in industry in the First Five-Year Plan followed the slogan "heavy industry at any cost." The cost was a serious imbalance in economic development that the Yugoslav government was still trying to rectify in 1990 (see fig. 9).

Postwar Policy

Between 1949 and the late 1970s, the fastest growing industrial branches were oil and gas extraction and refining and manufacture of machinery for electric power generation, transport equipment, chemicals, and electric power. These branches received high priority because their production levels were very low at the end of World War II. Other priority branches that were already better developed in the late 1940s—such as mining of coal and ferrous and nonferrous metals—expanded output significantly, but growth rates were considerably lower than those of the top-priority industries. Several nonpriority branches, such as furniture, paper, raw materials for construction, and the traditional food and beverage industries, expanded faster than the overall industrial average (see table 13, Appendix).

After the war, industry was concentrated in the traditional manufacturing regions of northern Yugoslavia. Beginning in 1961, industrial policy stressed locating new manufacturing facilities closer to sources of raw materials. This meant greater national investment in the underdeveloped economies of Montenegro and Macedonia, which in turn caused discontent in Slovenia and Croatia, the much richer northern republics required to contribute large shares to the national investment program (see Regional Disparities, this ch.).

The Fifth Five-Year Plan (1976–80) promoted primary production: development in all energy-producing sectors accelerated, and domestic oil and gas exploration was intensified to reduce Yugoslavia's dependence on imported fuels and minimize the effect of the oil crises of the 1970s. This step was also a prerequisite for further growth in industries with high energy consumption such as iron and steel, nonferrous metallurgy, and chemicals. In the late 1970s, a renewed commitment to self-sufficiency in ferrous and nonferrous metallurgy was based on exploitation and processing of domestic raw materials. Greater attention also went to machine-building industries that produced capital equipment necessary for the development of heavy industry.

The Sixth Five-Year Plan (1981–85) continued the industrial strategy of the previous plan. Priority industries for investment were metallurgy, base chemicals, and machinery. At the same time, the plan limited expansion of production facilities in other manufacturing industries.

Shipbuilding

In 1987 Yugoslavia ranked third in the world in shipbuilding. Construction and repair of ships contributed heavily to the domestic economy by bringing in hard currency. In the late 1980s, the shipbuilding industry was the only Yugoslav industry exporting more than half its output; in 1987 thirty-seven of forty-three ships built in Yugoslav shipyards were sent abroad. The ninety ships planned for export between 1986 and 1990 were to earn about US$2 billion. Seagoing, rivergoing, fishing, and engineering ships went to Liberia, the Soviet Union, Czechoslovakia, Norway, Finland, and Sweden. Receiving countries used Yugoslav ships for a variety of purposes, from transport of fruits and vegetables to outfitting the Soviet navy. Major shipyards were the Uljanik Shipyard at Pula, the May 3 Shipyard at Rijeka (the largest in Yugoslavia), the Split Shipyard, and the Dunavbrod Association of inland shipyards, based in Zagreb. Jugotanker, a firm based at Zadar, had one of the world's largest tanker fleets.

Metallurgy

Among major metallurgical facilities were the Trepča Metallurgical Combine in Kosovo, which produced zinc, tin, and refined silver and gold; the Metal Semifinished Products Industry at Slovenska Bistrica in Slovenia, specializing in alumina processing; the Smederevo Metallurgical Combine, known for microalloys and automobile steel important in replacing imported metals; the Zorka Plant at Šabac in western Serbia, which produced sheet and finished metals; and the Topola Foundry, also in western Serbia, important for cast iron and modular metals for the automobile industry. In 1987 the metallurgy industry contributed one-third of Yugoslavia's total exports (US$4.2 billion). In the 1980s, however, many of Yugoslavia's steel-producing industries faced stagnation because of hard-currency shortages that curtailed the import of cold-rolled steel used in finishing. Outdated extraction technology and weak infrastructure hindered enterprises that relied on domestic materials.

Automotive Industry

The extensive Yugoslav automotive industry was dominated by the Red Banner (Crvena zastava) group of plants, located in Kragujevac and several other cities. Red Banner produced passenger automobiles such as the Yugo, Zastava, Una, and Florida; commercial and delivery vehicles; and machine tools. In 1989 half the enterprise's production was exported, primarily to France,

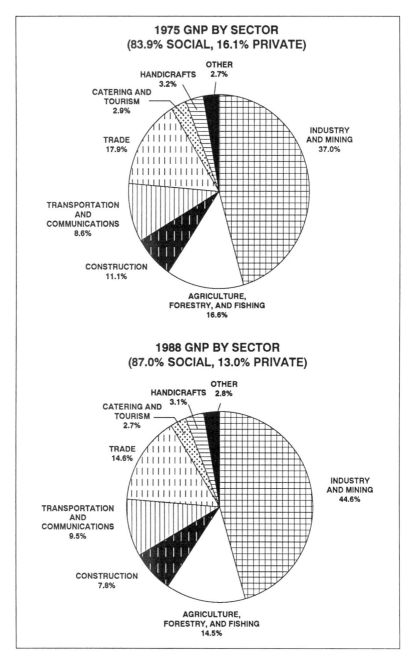

Source: Based on information from Yugoslavia, Savezni zavod za statistiku, *Statistički godišnjak Jugoslavije, 1989,* Belgrade, 1990, 101.

Figure 9. Gross National Product (GNP) by Sector, 1975 and 1988

Poland, the Soviet Union, the German Democratic Republic (East Germany), and the United States. In joint production agreements with firms in France, Poland, the Soviet Union, Italy, and East Germany, Red Banner contributed vehicle components, machine tools, and spare parts.

Chemicals

Production of chemical fertilizers, rubber, plastics, ammonia, liquefied gas, coke, and petroleum byproducts was vital to Yugoslav self-sufficiency in the 1980s. The large petrochemical and oil-refining facility built by Dow Chemical on the north Adriatic island of Krk became the chief Yugoslav petroleum processing plant. Although Yugoslavia had little prospect of independence from foreign oil suppliers, the Krk plant enhanced its independence at the petrochemical processing stage. Other major petrochemical and chemical facilities included the Chemical Industry at Pančevo, the Petroleum Industry of Zagreb, and the Chemical Production Industry at Prahovo in eastern Serbia. The main customers for Yugoslav chemicals and petrochemicals in the late 1980s were the Soviet Union and Eastern Europe, with some sales to Britain, Italy, France, Belgium, Greece, the Netherlands, Luxembourg, and the United States.

The Industrial Structure in 1990

By the 1980s, four decades of intensive investment had yielded significant expansion in the range and depth of Yugoslav industrial output. In 1986 the largest proportions of national industrial output came from production of electrical energy (12.5 percent); food processing, machinery, and transport equipment (each almost 11 percent); textiles (over 10 percent); metalworking (8.2 percent); and chemicals (6.9 percent). Because industrial policy in the 1970s emphasized domestic self-sufficiency in manufactured goods, domestic markets received larger proportions of industrial output from that time; Yugoslav industry was able to meet a high percentage of domestic demand for consumer goods under these conditions.

Despite its impressive growth, Yugoslav industry in 1990 was beset by a number of problems. Imbalances in investment since the 1950s had resulted in an inadequate supply infrastructure for electric power, water, and transport. In addition, many domestic firms were unable to meet customer demand because of shortages in raw materials, components, and spare parts for machinery. In some industries, low quality precluded export of Yugoslav goods. Decentralization of investment decision making in the 1960s frustrated interregional investment. Neither federal nor republic authorities had sufficient investment funds to finance expansion of basic industries, and enterprises were reluctant to place funds outside their home republics. In this way, republics and provinces became economically isolated from one another. The 1990 reforms were designed to improve capital mobility and structural imbalances by giving the federal government more power in macroeconomic policy-making areas such as investment targeting.

By the end of the 1980s, the agricultural predominance of the 1940s had given way to an industrial system whose diversity resembled that of the developed West. In 1987 one-quarter of the country's population was employed in agriculture, compared with three-quarters in 1945. In 1987 agriculture and fishing contributed only 11 percent of the Yugoslav GMP, compared with 45 percent from manufacturing and mining.

Agriculture

Yugoslavia has abundant fertile farmland. Throughout the postwar period, the private sector predominated in both amount of land tilled and production. In 1987 the 2.6 million privately owned farms in Yugoslavia accounted for 84 percent of all agricultural land. The social sector in agriculture included large agroindustrial complexes, or combines, which also processed the food they produced and dominated the food processing industry. The agricultural social sector also included state farms, owned and operated directly by the state, and general agricultural cooperatives. Most of the farms in the social sector were located in the north, in the Pannonian Plains of Vojvodina and eastern Croatia. All government agricultural investments and subsidies were reserved for state farms and general agricultural cooperatives; this meant that social sector farming was usually more technologically advanced than private sector farming. Nevertheless, private farms far exceeded those in the social sector in overall basic equipment, livestock holdings, and land cultivated (see table 14, Appendix).

Over 65 percent of arable land in Yugoslavia was devoted to the cultivation of cereals, particularly corn, wheat, and rye. The principal nonfood crop was tobacco, which supplied the domestic cigarette industry; hemp, cotton, and hops also were widely cultivated and processed domestically. Almost all the cotton and more than half of the tobacco came from Macedonia, while more than 60 percent of hops were grown in Slovenia. Collective farms on the Pannonian Plains produced corn, wheat, sugar beets, potatoes, and sunflowers. All regions of the country produced wine, each area with its own characteristic varieties. Yugoslavia was also known

Collective dairy farm, Bečej Vojvodina
Courtesy Charles Sudetic

for cultivation of orchard fruits, particularly plums, apples, pears, and peaches.

Pigs, sheep, horses, and cattle were the main types of livestock raised in Yugoslavia. Pigs and poultry were raised for meat, cattle for meat and dairy products, and sheep mainly for wool. Serbia was the largest pig-breeding area; the large Muslim populations of Bosnia and Hercegovina and Kosovo limited pig breeding in those regions. Sheep raising was centered in the uplands of Serbia and Macedonia; beef and dairy cattle were raised in all the northern republics. Live animals and meat products were two of Yugoslavia's largest export items in the late 1980s.

Irrigation, flood control, drainage works, and facilities for the distribution and storage of produce were adequate only in some regions of Yugoslavia in 1990. Construction of such agricultural infrastructure required heavy capital expenditure that was often unavailable because of the chronic undercapitalization of Yugoslav agriculture. Thus, Yugoslav farming enterprises remained highly vulnerable to weather conditions in the 1980s. For this reason, and because of population growth and higher nutritional expectations after World War II, Yugoslavia was a net importer of agricultural products through the entire postwar period. The United

States, the Soviet Union, Australia, and Canada were Yugoslavia's main suppliers of food, mostly grain.

In the 1980s, the Yugoslav agricultural sector performed inefficiently. The food distribution system was weak, farm incomes were low, and until the 1990 reforms agricultural prices were under strict control. Moreover, because most investment funds were earmarked for the social sector, state farms showed higher yields than farms in the much larger private sector. State agricultural investment policy thus prevented application of modern agricultural methods in over 80 percent of agricultural activity, resulting in inefficient use of large amounts of agricultural machinery and artificial fertilizers. The long-standing imbalance of agricultural investment and the importance of the private sector were recognized in the 1980s by the federal government's Green Plans (see Glossary), which devoted special attention and funding to agriculture and officially recognized the private sector as the most important supplier of farm produce. The Green Plans did increase crop yields somewhat, but in the late 1980s they were unable to overcome the inherent weakness of investment and infrastructure policy.

Energy and Mineral Resources

Energy policy in the late 1980s was aimed at reducing dependence on foreign sources and utilizing domestic power resources more fully. For conventional power generation, the Yugoslav power industries began replacing heavy oil with coal in thermoelectric generators and relying more heavily on hydroelectric stations. Development of nuclear power generation was limited by public resistance (especially after the Chernobyl' disaster in 1986) and by lack of domestic technology and nuclear fuel.

The southern portions of Yugoslavia were richer in lignite (soft coal) and hydroelectric potential, while the more prosperous northern areas produced all the country's crude petroleum and one-third of its total electrical power (see fig. 10). Yugoslavia always had an overall shortage of energy resources: natural gas and oil reserves were meager, low-caloric lignite (soft coal) was by far the predominant type of coal, and other fuel deposits remained unexploited because of insufficient funding for exploration and equipment. In 1990, because of poor funding support and conflicting regional interests, Yugoslavia still lacked a complete nationwide electric transmission grid. Industry regularly experienced power shortages caused by weaknesses in the transmission system and lack of generating capacity. Periodic emergency measures to restrict energy consumption included limits on use of private automobiles and stricter speed limits. In the late 1980s, the Croatian power industry was near bankruptcy, and the Yugoslav oil industry faced collapse.

In 1989 Yugoslav wells supplied only 26 percent of domestic raw petroleum requirements; the main foreign suppliers were the Soviet Union, Iraq, and Libya. Significant amounts of domestic petroleum and natural gas came only from wells in the sedimentary rock of the Pannonian Basin. Lack of proper equipment and up-to-date technology limited exploration of several large deposits believed to exist in that area. In 1968 extensive natural gas prospecting and some oil prospecting began in the Adriatic Sea, assisted by heavy foreign investment. In 1988 Southern Adriatic I near Ulcinj in Montenegro became the first offshore oil well to go into operation with support from a domestic interrepublican investment group. Despite declining foreign participation and lower international oil prices, Adriatic exploration continued in 1990 because of Yugoslavia's strong need to improve the balance of domestic versus imported fuel supply. The Adria Pipeline was the major supply line of petroleum connecting the Adriatic port at Krk Island to industries and refineries in the interior of the country.

Production of natural gas increased significantly in the 1980s with the opening of the Molve field in Croatia in 1985 and three wells in the northern Adriatic in 1989. Molve increased national production by one-third, yielding 1 billion cubic meters annually. Yugoslavia remained heavily dependent on the Soviet Union for natural gas in 1990, although Adriatic exploration continued. In 1985 construction began on a pipeline connecting the Soviet Union with Macedonia; in 1986 the Yugoslav natural gas distribution system included about 2,880 kilometers of pipeline.

Coal was the most important fuel for Yugoslav energy generation in the late twentieth century; 75 percent of domestic coal went to thermoelectric plants. Total coal reserves were estimated at 22 billion tons in 1985, and total production remained around 70 million tons yearly in the late 1980s. In 1990 hard coal production was less than in the 1960s, but production of lower-quality brown coal and lignite remained steady through the 1980s. The center of the lignite industry was the Tito Mines complex at Tuzla in the Pannonian Basin. Yugoslavia's only deposits of high-grade bituminous coal were in relatively small reserves in Istria in northwest Croatia, eastern Serbia, and Bosnia. Potential new reserves had been located but not yet evaluated in 1990.

In spite of the importance of coal to the Yugoslav economy, inefficiency in managing power resources led to significant waste in the coal industry. Shaft mine output increased throughout the 1980s, but at the expense of decreased productivity rates, wasted resources,

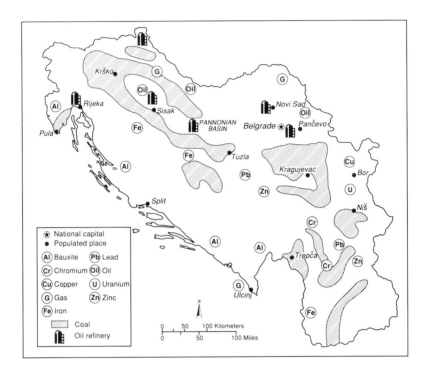

Figure 10. Industrial Centers and Natural Resources, 1990

abnormal wear on equipment, and unusually high production costs. Surface mining of Yugoslavia's lignite reserves also was mismanaged. Although Kosovo contained the largest lignite field in Europe and 50 percent of Yugoslavia's coal reserves, inefficiencies in energy planning limited Kosovo's contribution to 15 percent of the country's actual coal supply in 1988.

The potential for developing hydroelectric power in Yugoslavia in the 1980s was greater than for development of fossil fuels. From 1956 through the 1980s, production of electricity from hydroelectric sources exceeded that from all other sources. Despite heavy investment in this area, however, only an estimated 20 percent of Yugoslavia's hydroelectric potential was in use in 1990. Many obstacles hindered access to resources in mountainous watersheds of the Drina, Bosna, and Neretva rivers (see fig. 6). Costs were very high for building power stations in difficult terrain and for transmitting power across hundreds of miles of mountains to consumers. In the 1980s, the largest provider of hydroelectric power to Yugoslavia was the joint Yugoslav-Romanian Djerdap Hydroelectric Station on the Danube River.

Krško, Yugoslavia's first nuclear power station, was designed by the United States firm Westinghouse; it began transmitting power from its site in eastern Slovenia in 1982. In 1987 Krško produced about 5 percent of Yugoslav domestic electric power. After its construction, however, further nuclear development became problematic. Although Yugoslav uranium deposits in eastern Serbia were believed sufficient to fuel additional nuclear reactors, policy makers feared the results of Yugoslav dependence on foreign nuclear fuel suppliers. In 1990 the Krško plant still imported all its nuclear fuel from the United States. At the other end of the generation process, Yugoslavia had no good sites for nuclear waste disposal.

In 1986 Yugoslavia began looking for foreign credits to build four new nuclear plants. However, environmental and political factors and the prospects of increasing the foreign debt made this an unpopular program by the late 1980s. Policy makers feared that new plants would divide the country into western and eastern nuclear spheres, exacerbating Serbian-Slovenian economic and political disputes. The Krško plant and a projected plant in Prevlaka in western Yugoslavia were financed by Western partners; three other projected plants in Serbia, Macedonia, and Montenegro were to be financed by the Soviet Union. Hot interregional disputes postponed building of these plants into the 1990s and weakened national resolve to continue a program of nuclear power generation.

Yugoslavia was endowed with a wide variety of ferrous and nonferrous ores. About 80 percent of the country's iron ore reserves were located at Vareš and Ljubija in Bosnia and Hercegovina, with other major deposits in Slovenia and Macedonia. A poor transportation network and lack of suitable fuels near the highest grade deposits hindered exploitation of those ores. Yugoslavia could probably have been self-supporting in iron ore if resources were fully exploited, but in 1990 the country was still a net importer of iron ore, scrap, and semifinished steel.

Yugoslavia also was rich in several nonferrous metals. Bosnia and Hercegovina produced 56 percent of the country's bauxite, while Kosovo's Trepča Metallurgical Combine, the largest lead-and-zinc center in the country, enabled that province to produce 47 percent of Yugoslavia's lead and zinc ores. Kosovo also supplied a substantial part of Yugoslav chromium. The Bor and Majdanpek areas of Serbia were the only copper sources in the country, and Serbia also provided most of Yugoslavia's antimony. Macedonia contributed chromium, manganese, and uranium, and the most productive mercury mines in Europe were located at Idrija in the Julian Alps of Slovenia.

Many of Yugoslavia's mineral deposits were in inaccessible areas remote from sources of energy. Massive capital investments were needed for the roads and communications necessary to reach many untapped reserves. But Yugoslav industry often lacked the capacity to absorb available mineral resources, and much raw and semifinished material was exported in return for manufactured goods.

Transportation and Telecommunications

The reconstruction period of 1945–47 emphasized repair of the transportation network destroyed during World War II. Even in 1990, road and rail communications in many regions, particularly the mountainous areas of Kosovo, eastern Bosnia, and southern Serbia, were still inadequate (see fig. 11). In addition, the Dinaric Alps, running along the Adriatic coast, were an obstacle to efficient transport of interior resources to the coast for shipping. Only two main rail lines, the Zagreb-Split line and the Sarajevo-Ploče line, cut from the interior to seaports. These deficiencies had a profound effect on the ability of Yugoslavia to develop its mineral and hydroelectric resources.

Transportation lines in the northern lowlands and southward along the Vardar and Morava rivers were better developed because they served international traffic and linked the republic capitals of Ljubljana, Zagreb, Belgrade, and Skopje. Routes from Italy and Austria converged at Ljubljana, and several important road and rail lines ran north into Hungary from the area between Zagreb and Belgrade.

The tourism boom that began in the 1960s led to the construction of a number of new highways, most important of which was the Adriatic Coastal Highway running from Rijeka to the Albanian border. From that highway several link roads were built into the interior. In 1990 plans called for the interior roads to link the Adriatic Coastal Highway with the Brotherhood and Unity Highway, which ran from Yugoslavia's northern border with Austria through Ljubljana, Zagreb, Belgrade, and Skopje and across the southeastern border into Bulgaria. Two-thirds of the highway were to be open as a six-lane road in the mid-1990s, with the southern portion remaining a two-lane road. In 1990 about 106,000 kilometers of Yugoslav roads had hard surfaces, and another 15,100 kilometers had dirt surfaces. In 1987 some 3 million passenger automobiles and 207,000 trucks were registered in Yugoslavia.

In 1990 the country had about 9,300 kilometers of rail lines, of which about 3,800 kilometers were electrified. All rail lines were

Trepča Metallurgical Combine, Kosovo
Courtesy Charles Sudetic

standard-gauge, 1.435-meter track; 10 percent of them were double track in 1988. Yugoslavia had 184 usable airports in 1988, of which 54 had permanent-surface runways and 23 were longer than 2,440 meters. The largest international airports were in Belgrade, Zagreb, Ljubljana, Sarajevo, Skopje, Dubrovnik, Split, Titograd, Maribor, and Zadar. The Yugoslav national airline, Yugoslav Air Transport (Jugoslovenski Aero Transport—JAT) flew 5.8 million passengers in 1986.

In 1988 the Yugoslav merchant marine included 269 ships, totaling 5.4 million deadweight tons; Yugoslavia also owned twenty-one ships, totaling 347,000 deadweight tons, registered in Liberia and Panama. The merchant marine fleet included 134 cargo, 72 bulk, 15 container, 14 roll-on roll-off ships, and 9 petroleum tankers. Yugoslavia also had 1,194 river craft, which navigated inland on 1,620 kilometers miles of rivers, 640 kilometers of canals, and lakes Scutari and Ohrid. The major Adriatic ports were Rijeka, Split, Bar, and Ploče; Belgrade was the major inland port, located on the Danube.

In the 1980s, telecommunications in Yugoslavia were quite advanced in comparison with the national transportion systems. The Yugoslav Radio and Television Network (Jugoslovenska Radio-televizija) operated 250 radio and television stations in 1986; its

151

main broadcasting centers were in Belgrade, Ljubljana, Sarajevo, Novi Sad, Priština, Skopje, Titograd, and Zagreb. Both national and local programming were offered, and Radio Koper also broadcast in Italian. In 1986 about 4.8 million radios and 4.1 million television sets were in use in Yugoslavia. Two multipurpose satellite dishes of the International Telecommunications Satellite Organization (Intelsat) were located in Yugoslavia, supporting international telex, television, and telephone communications. The government-operated national telephone system included ten phones per 100 residents in 1982; all phones were direct dial by 1980 and were evenly divided between business and residential installations.

Foreign Trade

Unlike other East European countries, Yugoslavia had no centralized foreign trade plan, nor was trade controlled by a central foreign trade ministry or a small number of state trading organizations. Although the government encouraged production for export, enterprises themselves took part in making trade policy. The Law on Associated Labor of 1976 established self-managed communities of interest for foreign economic relations in each republic and province; those organizations determined what goods their jurisdiction should import. The communities of interest included representatives of local basic organizations of associated labor, banks, and other organizations involved in trade. Their principal missions were to maximize export profits and to limit imports to comply with the federal deficit ceiling.

Historical Background

Adherence to the Soviet model after World War II meant that foreign trade was controlled entirely by the state, contact with the Western industrialized countries was kept to a minimum, and domestic resources were used as much as possible in the process of industrial development. Therefore, exports were viewed merely as a device for obtaining essential imports, and many items were manufactured within the country although they could have been imported much more cheaply. In 1948 foreign trade amounted to less than 10 percent of Yugoslavia's GNP. Most trade activity was bilateral commodity exchange with other socialist countries. Over two-thirds of pre-World War II Yugoslav foreign trade had been with Western Europe, but by 1948 over 50 percent of imports and exports involved Cominform countries.

Immediately following Yugoslavia's expulsion from Cominform in 1948, trade with socialist countries dropped to zero. This sudden change meant that between 1948 and 1950 the total value of

Figure 11. Transportation and Pipeline Systems, 1990

154

Yugoslav exports fell by nearly 50 percent and imports by 25 percent. Yugoslavia was forced to turn to the Western industrialized nations to obtain capital equipment, fuel, and raw materials for the intense industrial development called for in the first two five-year plans. Throughout the 1950s, United States and West European credits and grants were vital in sustaining industrial growth in Yugoslavia.

As early as 1961, new foreign exchange and foreign trade policies stressed liberalization and decentralization. The driving motivation of the reform of 1965 was to bring Yugoslavia into the world market. This meant removal of foreign trade barriers and open economic competition with foreign enterprises. Theoretically, those developments would spur greater efficiency in the domestic market and make Yugoslav goods more competitive on the world market. As a result, Yugoslavia could sell its competitive goods on the international market and halt production of items that could be imported more cheaply. The domestic market remained under the protection of partial government price support until Yugoslavia could be fully transformed to a market economy and the dinar made convertible to Western currency.

Trade in the 1970s was greatly influenced by Yugoslavia's dependence on oil imports and a worsening balance of payments. Increases in world oil prices in 1973 and 1979 accelerated import costs, whereas export growth was slow. The Fifth Five-Year Plan (1976–80) failed to transfer emphasis to technologically advanced industries able to replace imports and expand exports. Balance of payments constraints slowed domestic activity in 1972, in 1975–76, and in 1979–81. In addition, the world recession at the end of the 1970s caused net interest payments on foreign debts to increase considerably, net receipts from Yugoslavs working abroad to decline, and foreign lenders to withdraw.

In 1980 Yugoslavia owed over US$18 billion to Western creditors. Because the only way to shift the debt was to increase exports, the slogan adopted for trade policy in the 1980s was "export by any means." Exports accelerated, and prices for them dropped. By 1986 the Yugoslav trade deficit with the European Economic Community (EEC—see Glossary) had dropped to US$1 billion from its 1980 level of US$4 billion. But this drop was more a function of decreased non-oil imports, required to conserve hard currency reserves, than of increased exports.

Trade with the industrialized West dropped sharply in the mid-1980s, from a 55.6 percent share in 1978 to 43.3 percent in 1984. During this period, debt owed to Western Europe reached 60 percent of the total Yugoslav debt. In response, a piecemeal policy rescheduled some debt, sought loans from new Western sources, and continued repayment of at least the interest on existing debts.

After massive devaluations in the dinar in 1989, that currency was pegged to the West German deutsche mark and declared convertible in January 1990. Set at seven dinars to the deutsche mark, the dinar was to move parallel with the DM against other Western currencies. This provision allowed citizens as well as enterprises to convert dinars to Western currency upon demand. At the beginning of the 1990s, economists predicted that the value of Yugoslav exports would continue to rise to record levels and the foreign debt would be manageable; in the early stages of the reform, the "new" dinar proved more stable than most economists had expected.

Exports and Imports

Yugoslavia's exports in the late 1980s consisted mainly of manufactured goods, ores, and simple processed goods. Over one-quarter of goods sold abroad were machinery and transportation equipment (see table 15, Appendix). This was a relatively high proportion of sophisticated exports, considering that among European nations Yugoslavia ranked low in per capita income. Main export customers were Italy, the Soviet Union, France, Austria, Czechoslovakia, the United States, and the Federal Republic of Germany (West Germany). Live horses and meat products were Yugoslavia's most important agricultural exports. The largest single meat export, veal, was shipped primarily to Greece. Meat export declined in the late 1970s because of EEC trade barriers, a rise in domestic meat consumption, and feed shortages; but between 1985 and 1987, total meat product exports more than doubled, rising well beyond the 1980 level. Yugoslavia ran trade deficits in merchandise of US$1.5 billion in 1985, US$2.2 billion in 1986, US$1.4 billion in 1987, and US$619 million in 1988.

Throughout the postwar period, Yugoslavia was a net importer of raw materials, fuels, iron and steel products, and capital equipment (see table 16, Appendix). Chief suppliers of petroleum products were the Soviet Union, Iraq, Libya, and Algeria. Machinery and transportation equipment, also imported in large amounts, came principally from West Germany, Italy, the United States, the Soviet Union, Britain, and Czechoslovakia. In the category of raw materials other than petroleum, Yugoslavia bought oilseeds and coal from the United States; wool from Australia; cotton, coal, and iron ore from the Soviet Union; and cotton from Egypt.

Mostar loop, part of the Belgrade highway system
Courtesy Yugoslav National Tourist Office, New York

Trading Partners

Yugoslavia's trade policy followed the complete realignment of its foreign policy after expulsion from the Cominform in 1948. By the 1960s, structural reform and entry into the international market had broken down many economic and social barriers between Yugoslavia and the outside world. Although the Soviet Union remained Yugoslavia's largest trading partner throughout the 1980s, the emergence in 1986 of West Germany as Yugoslavia's top source of imports typified increased emphasis on trade with Western Europe (see table 17, Appendix). Beginning in the 1980s, Yugoslavia traded with developing countries more selectively than it had in previous decades, when the Yugoslav economy was more able to absorb the commercial losses associated with such ventures.

Yugoslavia's growing trade deficit greatly influenced its trade with Western industrialized nations in the 1980s. Many measures were adopted to cut all but essential imports from the West and encourage import-substituting domestic industries. But the import of expensive Western technology often was a prerequisite for establishing such industries. On the export side, over half of Yugoslav exports still went to the East European members of the Council for Mutual Economic Assistance (Comecon—see Glossary) in the

1980s, but only the more demanding Western markets (and limited Third World transactions) paid hard currency for Yugoslav goods.

The Industrialized West

Yugoslavia became a member of the General Agreement on Tariffs and Trade (GATT—see Glossary) in 1965, when Tito's reform program brought tariff and trade regulations into line with international practice. The International Monetary Fund (IMF—see Glossary) began substantial loan support to Yugoslavia in 1965. Although the United States provided Yugoslavia substantial financial aid throughout the postwar years, Yugoslavia's trade with the industrialized West focused on Western Europe. In the 1980s, economic relations with that region, which was also the greatest source of foreign loans to Yugoslavia, became even more important. A 1981 agreement with the EEC allowed Yugoslavia to sell 70 percent of its industrial goods duty free in EEC markets. This concession led to a Yugoslav policy of large-scale below-cost export to Western Europe and to resentment from EEC members whose products were undercut. The quality of Yugoslav products often remained unsatisfactory to West European markets, however, and competition increased as EEC members granted concessions to their former colonies in the 1980s. Overall trade between Yugoslavia and the EEC fell by 15 percent between 1980 and 1985. The trade deficit with the EEC was cut by 75 percent in the same period (from US$4 billion to US$1 billion), but only because of severe cuts in imports associated with Yugoslavia's overall economic decline.

The Common Agricultural Policy of the EEC, designed to protect EEC farmers from low-priced outside competition, excluded most Yugoslav agricultural products from that market in the 1980s. In the late 1980s, Yugoslavia's trade imbalance crisis brought EEC concessions in the sale of specific products such as wine and veal, but clothing, textiles, and most produce remained subject to EEC duties.

Full membership in the EEC became a goal of Yugoslav economic policy in the late 1980s, and the media discussed the prospect constantly; in 1990 Prime Minister Ante Marković officially declared that recent economic and political reforms qualified his country for inclusion. In response, the EEC strongly encouraged Yugoslav emulation of Western market economics and extended favorable financial terms wherever possible. Nonetheless, formidable reasons remained to delay full membership. One major obstacle, the Yugoslav trade deficit with the EEC, had virtually disappeared by 1989. But Yugoslavia would also have to eliminate all duties and accept all EEC standards to include itself in the EEC free trade zone; the Yugoslav economic structure did not permit such changes in 1990.

Politically, in 1990 Yugoslavia was still far from the genuine national multiparty system required of EEC members, and continued regional conflict jeopardized the long-term credibility of overtures by the Marković government. Yugoslavia's strongly neutral international position also was a negative factor until Austria, neutral but wealthy, applied for EEC membership in 1989. Meanwhile, Yugoslavia had established special trading relationships with EEC members West Germany and Italy (accounting for 70 percent of Yugoslavia's EEC trade in 1989), as well as most members of the neutralist European Free Trade Association (EFTA—see Glossary). In 1988 the EEC granted a five-year extension of Yugoslavia's special commercial status. West European experts generally agreed that if it remained politically stable, Yugoslavia would be admitted to the EEC ahead of former Comecon members such as Poland and Hungary.

The Soviet Union and Its Allies

Seven years after the embargo of Yugoslavia by the Soviet Union and its allies, trade relations with the Soviet Union began to improve. In 1955 and 1956, the Soviet Union, Czechoslovakia, Poland, and East Germany granted credits to Yugoslavia totaling US$40 million, at rates considerably below standard World Bank (see Glossary) rates. By 1964 Yugoslavia had gained observer status in Comecon, and some meetings of that organization were held in Belgrade. Because trade with the Soviet Union consisted mainly of exchanging Yugoslav consumer goods, machines, ships, and transportation equipment for critical Soviet oil, Yugoslavia was at the mercy of its larger partner. In the 1980s, the Soviet Union first raised the price of oil independently of world prices, then arbitrarily reduced imports of Yugoslav consumer goods. Continuation of Soviet oil supply arrangements into the 1990s also damaged Yugoslavia's image as a nonaligned country qualified for inclusion in Western economic groupings. Soviet oil supply became less reliable in 1990 when the Soviet economy experienced a domestic oil shortage and cut foreign deliveries. And the machinery and equipment that Yugoslavia exported to Comecon countries required raw and semifinished materials bought with hard currency, making the Comecon connection an indirect hard-currency drain in this respect. Buying oil from the Soviet Union, however, required no hard currency and provided a market for low-quality Yugoslav consumer goods. For Comecon members, trade with nonaligned Yugoslavia was a convenient way of obtaining Western products whose technological restrictions made them unavailable by direct purchase.

The Third World

As a founding member of the Nonaligned Movement, Yugoslavia established and maintained commercial relations with a large number of Third World countries (see Nonalignment, ch. 4). But trade with the underdeveloped countries never approached the level of trade with Western Europe or the Soviet Union. In 1987 total trade volume with Iraq, Yugoslavia's largest Third World partner, was about one-sixth that with the Soviet Union and one-fifth that with West Germany. Between 1979 and 1987, both imports from and exports to Third World countries declined slightly as a proportion of the respective Yugoslav totals.

In the 1980s, two factors increasingly defined Yugoslavia's trade policy with the Third World: the need for hard currency and the need to limit dependency on Soviet oil by keeping other channels open. Both considerations encouraged commercial activity with oil-rich countries such as Iraq, Iran, Libya, Algeria, Angola, and Indonesia. Because those countries also sold oil to the West, they were able to pay their Yugoslav partners in hard currency.

In the 1980s, Yugoslav energy and machine-building industries were especially active in start-to-finish construction of electric power plants and hydroelectric stations, power transmission lines, irrigation systems, and other major construction projects in selected Third World countries. Two firms, Energoinvest of Sarajevo and Energoproekt of Belgrade, represented groups of Yugoslav enterprises that acted as contractors in such cases. In 1988 Yugoslav construction services abroad were valued at US$1.4 billion. In 1990 Yugoslav fuel industries were active in joint oil and natural gas exploration in Syria, Tunisia, Libya, Angola, and Algeria.

Yugoslav consumer goods, most notably consumer electronics from the Niš Electronics Industry, vehicles from the Red Banner auto plants, and footwear, also went to Third World markets. Major customers were India, Egypt, Iran, and Iraq.

Guest Workers and Tourism

Beginning in the 1960s, Yugoslavia earned considerable hard-currency income from so-called "invisibles": remittances from Yugoslav guest workers working abroad and from tourists visiting from countries whose currency was convertible into dinars. These remittances were important to the Yugoslav budget, particularly in the mid-1970s when they bridged the gap in the trade balance and produced surpluses in the balance of payments. Beginning in the

Beach at Dubrovnik, one of Yugoslavia's major tourist areas
Courtesy World Bank (Hilda Bijur)

early 1970s, changes in financial laws encouraged Yugoslavs working abroad to deposit foreign currency savings in Yugoslav banks. Remittances, which averaged US$2 billion in the late 1970s, became the richest source of hard-currency income for the Yugoslav economy. In the late 1980s, unofficial hard-currency income played a visible role in stimulating activity such as construction of private housing. Through 1990 about 375,000 workers had invested in Yugoslav firms after returning, and another 160,000 had started private businesses.

Yugoslavia was already an exporter of surplus labor before World War II. The Tito government actively discouraged that practice until the early 1960s, however, when growing unemployment altered official policy. Beginning with the reform of 1965, government policy encouraged workers to go abroad. In 1981 there were 875,000 Yugoslavs working abroad, mostly in West Germany and Austria (see Guest Workers, ch. 2).

Generally speaking, heavy reliance on tourism is not wise policy for a developing country because that industry is highly sensitive to seasonal fluctuations and uncontrollable economic and political events. But from 1961, when 1 million tourists visited Yugoslavia, the figure increased steadily to over 9 million in 1988, under government support for the tourist industry that had begun

960s. Besides its monetary contributions to the na-
e of payments, tourism produced a quick return for
ed in the hotel, restaurant, and service industries. In
real terms, income in those industries increased about 1.7 times
between 1965 and 1988. Tourism also stimulated the building,
transportation, food manufacturing, and handicrafts industries.

Foreign Exchange

Because Yugoslavia's industrial strategy did not stress exports,
few domestic enterprises were established to satisfy export demand.
This meant a scarcity of foreign exchange throughout the postwar
years, especially in the 1980s. Such a condition presented two major
problems: allocation of scarce foreign exchange reserves and maintainance of a positive balance of payments. The Yugoslav government experimented with various ways to allocate foreign exchange.
Until 1986 the retention ratio system allowed exporters to retain
only a share of their foreign exchange earnings, requiring the rest
to be diverted to the National Bank of Yugoslavia. This system
created much discontent because enterprises that generated a considerable amount of foreign currency frequently had to apply for
administrative allocations, which they frequently did not receive.
At the same time, because Slovenia and Croatia earned much of
Yugoslavia's foreign currency, the retention ratio system allocated larger proportions of the receipts to those two republics. This
exacerbated disparities in economic development and nationalist
conflicts between the richer and poorer republics. Moreover, allocation from above conflicted with the principle of independence
inherent in socialist self-management.

A new system established in 1986 was directed toward establishing a free market in foreign exchange. All foreign exchange
receipts were to be surrendered to authorized banks at official exchange rates. Enterprises needing foreign exchange to pay for imports then applied to the banks, which determined the amount each
enterprise needed by its use of foreign exchange the previous year
and export performance in that year. This system never worked
because there was never enough foreign currency to satisfy demand.

In 1987 the government tried to apply a law under which foreign exchange was allocated by a system of functional priorities.
The top priority was the servicing of foreign debts and other foreign contracts. This was followed by needs of net exporters, priority needs of federal agencies and organizations, imports of fuel,
and, lastly, imports of consumer goods. To compensate firms for
their loss of retention rights under the previous ratio system, the
federal government set up a system of export subsidies. This system

destroyed incentives to export, which in turn cut the influx of foreign currency. In 1987 the Yugoslav government failed for the first time to pay interest on its foreign debt. As part of its agreement in May 1988 to reschedule Yugoslavia's foreign debt and provide new loans, the IMF forced the Yugoslav government to relax foreign exchange controls and open an effective foreign exchange market. Foreign exchange reserves amounted to US$7.5 billion in early 1990.

Managing the Crisis of the 1980s

Between 1975 and 1980, the Yugoslav social product fell, and inflation reached an annual rate of 50 percent. When the international oil shock of 1979 hit, policy makers realized they could not continue an economic development strategy based on heavy foreign borrowing and inefficient investment at home. In 1983 the Long-Term Economic Stabilization Program was released by the government's Krajgher Commission. The commission reexamined Yugoslavia's development priorities and formulated a revised strategy for the 1980s. Self-management would remain at the center of the system, but substantial reorientation would occur. Important elements were coordination of investment between industrial and agricultural sectors, diversification of energy resources, greater investment in technical development, and improved incentives for the private sector, now recognized as the most efficient part of the national economy. Workers, whose wages had increased faster than their productivity under the self-management system, would be subject to wage austerity programs to restore the balance.

Although the party overwhelmingly endorsed the long-term program, influential conservatives blocked practical application of Krajgher Commission programs. In 1983 the Federal Assembly (Skupština) passed only eight of twenty-five major legislative proposals; it postponed decision on the remainder, many of which would have activated parts of the long-term program. The events of 1983 set a precedent for a new round of economic bickering and regional finger pointing that delayed meaningful reform another seven years.

Inflation and Foreign Debt

Inflation continued to spiral during the 1980s. In 1987 it had reached 150 percent annually; by early 1989 it had reached 1,950 percent. In the same period, foreign debt rose, unemployment remained high, living standards fell, and regional economic disparities widened.

ugoslavia had the highest per capita foreign debt in
ling over US$20 billion (see table 18, Appendix). In
he Yugoslav government signed an agreement with
the IMF that provided new foreign loans and rescheduled the debt,
in return for which the government agreed to cut inflation by carefully limiting expansion of domestic bank credits. This was the first
attempt to use monetary policy to control Yugoslav inflation.

Living Standards

When the world recession of 1979 forced many Yugoslav guest
workers to return home, strong political pressure forced social sector
enterprises to take up the slack by hiring surplus workers. This
caused social sector productivity to fall by 20 percent from 1979
to 1985; real personal income of social sector employees dropped
25 percent and, despite the forced overemployment, unemployment in this sector increased from 14 percent in 1984 to nearly
20 percent in 1989. In 1989 an estimated 60 percent of Yugoslav
workers lived at or below the minimum income level guaranteed
by the state, and the standard of living had fallen by 40 percent
since 1982—returning that indicator to the level of the mid-1960s.
Average monthly take-home pay for an employee in the social sector
was the equivalent of US$170 in 1989. Yugoslav officials estimat-
ed that closing unprofitable enterprises under the 1990 reforms
might cause 2 million more workers to lose their jobs in the early
1990s.

Regional Disparities

The substantial autonomy given subnational governments in
managing their own economic development prevented the six
republics and two provinces from developing cross-boundary economic relationships, and the political fragmentation of Yugoslavia's uniquely loose federal structure stymied efficient exchange
of goods and services. Stark economic disparities among regions
remained unmitigated throughout the 1980s despite numerous federal programs to redistribute wealth by integrating the natural
wealth of poorer regions (such as the coal and minerals of Kosovo)
into the national economy.

The three northern republics, Slovenia, Croatia, and most of
Serbia, emphasized high technology in building production capacity
and attracting foreign investment. By contrast, the less developed
southern regions, especially Kosovo, Macedonia, Montenegro, and
southern Serbia, stressed traditional, labor-intensive, low-paying
economic activity such as textile manufacture, agriculture, and handicrafts. This contrast produced sharp differences in employment,

investment, income potential, and social services among the eight political units of the federation. For example, in the late 1980s average personal income per social sector worker in Macedonia was half that of a similar worker in Slovenia. Especially in Kosovo and Macedonia, poor economic and social conditions exacerbated longstanding ethnic animosities and periodically ignited uprisings that threatened civil war (see Regional Political Issues, ch. 4).

Meanwhile, the federal government continued to divert the earnings of prosperous Slovenia and Croatia into its Fund for Underdeveloped Regions in the late 1980s. The Slovenes, who contributed 25 percent of Yugoslavia's hard-currency export earnings in 1989, were especially irritated by the requirement to pay as much as 20 percent of the republic's income to subsidize nonproductive enterprises in other republics; this issue fueled the drive for Slovenian secession. In 1990 Slovenian leaders announced curtailment of their contribution to the Fund for Underdeveloped Regions because they had lost hope that the mismanaged central government would ever invest their earnings profitably and because the local economy was declining. Croatia threatened similar action if the federal government did not make concessions. By this time, economic autonomy and membership in the EEC had become attractive and plausible alternatives for Slovenia and Croatia (see Slovenia; Croatia, ch. 4).

The Reforms of 1990

In December 1989, the Marković government presented an economic reform package. The program was actually a continuation of a 1989 reform that attempted to introduce a "united market economy" compatible with the existing self-management system. Of the twenty-four laws included, the Federal Assembly passed seventeen outright; six remained provisional. At the heart of the program's monetary reform was a new "heavy" dinar, worth 10,000 old dinars, pegged to the deutsche mark, and convertible with all Western currencies.

Wages were frozen and income pegged to rates 18 to 32 percent higher than wage rates of December 15, 1989. Price controls were removed on 85 percent of commodities. The only exceptions were essential categories such as electricity, fuels, medicine, raw metals and minerals, and rail, postal, and telephone services, which remained under government control.

The program strengthened existing bankruptcy and liquidation laws forbidding state subsidy of enterprises and banks operating at a loss, and bankrupt enterprises no longer received bank loans. At the time of the 1990 reforms, one-quarter to one-third of

165

Yugoslavia's 27,600 enterprises were showing losses, and the debts of 100 Yugoslav banks totaled US$2 billion to US$3 billion. To mitigate the inevitable effects of massive layoffs from enterprise closings, the program allotted US$150 million in aid to the poorest regions, primarily in the south, and US$100 million for social security and unemployment compensation. An anticipated foreign loan of US$500 million was to pay for those allotments. The West contributed US$1 billion in 1989 to cancel the deficit in the banking system and implement the new reforms, and as much as US$4 billion more was promised if the program took effect.

Although Marković's entire package was not accepted by the Federal Assembly, the new program had immediate effects and received mostly positive reactions in Yugoslav society. By April 1990, the monthly inflation rate had dropped to zero, from its December 1989 monthly rate of 64.3 percent. The revaluation of the dinar was credited with an export increase of 21 percent and an import increase of 32 percent in the first four months of 1990, as well as an increase of US$3 billion in foreign currency reserves in the first six months of 1990. By mid-1990 the government was claiming 1,200 new joint investment deals with foreign firms, worth an estimated US$588 million, and a total of 10,200 new enterprises formed. Industrial productivity fell by 8.7 percent, however, because of the extreme monetary controls used to decrease the money supply and stop inflation and because of the large number of unprofitable enterprises closed by the reforms. Domestic investment slowed drastically, but the reforms brought much less civil unrest than anticipated. Some industries continued paying wages unrelated to productivity, nullifying the incentive effect of federal wage restrictions.

The initial phase of the Marković reform package was a six-month preliminary step. When phase two began in mid-1990, policy makers began seeking nonmonetary controls for inflation, encouraging banks to keep interest rates down, funding an agency for development of small and medium-sized enterprises, and reshaping investment incentives. The overall goal of these steps was to mitigate the initial shock effect of the austerity program and gradually allow market forces to stimulate a new round of investment geared to private enterprise. The next round of constitutional amendments, introduced in 1990, included provisions to facilitate large-scale changes of public to private ownership, to reform tax policy to encourage private investment, and to create a new credit distribution role for the National Bank of Yugoslavia. After the first stage of reform, progress was uneven; in 1990 many industries remained under obstructionist political appointees who had no stake in overall economic progress. Resistance was especially strong in Serbia, where one in three enterprises was unprofitable at the end of 1990. Even the optimistic Marković cautioned that future steps in economic reform would cause additional social discomfort, but in 1990 Yugoslav economic planning finally had made a discernible break with its ineffectual past.

*   *   *

Several useful books and essays on the Yugoslav economy are available in English. *The Economy of Yugoslavia* by Fred Singleton and Bernard Carter, though dated, provides a comprehensive historical and structural view of the Yugoslav economy. Harold Lydall's *Yugoslavia in Crisis* fully analyzes the economic situation of Yugoslavia at the end of the 1980s and the systemic problems that created that situation. Several chapters of *Yugoslavia in the 1980s,* edited by Pedro Ramet, analyze the economic crisis of the early 1980s, forecast future developments, and provide abundant statistics. *Yugoslavia: A Fractured Federalism,* edited by Dennison Rusinow, contains two chapters that describe the causes and results of Yugoslav political-economic policy making in the 1980s. The Yugoslav government's *Statistički godišnjak Jugoslavije* (Statistical Yearbook of Yugoslavia), published in Serbo-Croatian with an English key, lists exhaustive statistics on all sectors of the economy, as well as economic indicators since 1970. (For further information and complete citations, see Bibliography.)

Chapter 4. Government and Politics

Josip Broz Tito

THE SOCIALIST FEDERAL REPUBLIC of Yugoslavia (Socijalistička Federativna Republika Jugoslavija—SFRJ) came into existence in 1945 as a state with nominally socialist political institutions, dominated until 1990 by a single communist party. In that forty-five-year period, the country's political structure evolved in three major stages: as an orthodox member of the monolithic Soviet-led communist alliance (1945–48); as a nonaligned communist dictatorship (1948–80) whose slogan was "brotherhood and unity" among its constituent republics; and as a decentralized federation, with no dominant leader and most aspects of political power centered at regional levels.

During the last two stages, Yugoslav political life emphasized "development from below," a principle that gave substantial economic and political decision-making power to local communes and self-managed industrial enterprises. This feature, unique to Yugoslavia and present even during the powerful dictatorship of Josip Broz Tito (1945–80), focused political power in official and unofficial local groupings. Also unique to Yugoslavia was the concept of statutory autonomy in nearly all governmental functions for each of the six republics in the federation. The inefficiency of the national political system was masked until 1980 by the charisma of Tito, who provided enough national unity for economic and political reforms to be accomplished when necessary.

As early as 1948, the Yugoslav system experimented with political configurations unknown in previous Marxist or Stalinist practice. Although Yugoslavia began political reforms far ahead of other European communist states, opposition political parties only became legal in the late 1980s, a development stimulated partly by reform elsewhere in Eastern Europe. The League of Communists of Yugoslavia (LCY—see Glossary) retained substantial control over the government's appointive and legislative functions, but innovations made party control of the country's diverse ethnic and economic groups problematic as early as the 1960s; the political management of economic reform, urgently needed by 1980, was complicated by the same factors.

Tito was aware that without him the Yugoslav political system would be a fragile entity. Therefore, in his last years of power he attempted to restructure the system. His preparations for the regime that would follow him emphasized decentralization of power to accommodate the unique structure of the Yugoslav federation: six republics and two provinces of widely varying political and ethnic backgrounds, as well as contrasting economic levels. To prevent yet another occurrence of the hostile fragmentation for which the Balkans had become a symbol, Tito tried to equalize the political power of the republics, minimizing the potential for domination by one republic that might stimulate others to secede from the federation.

The institutionalized political balance that followed Tito's thirty-five years in office had several effects. Regional power meant that federal decision making required unanimous consensus among the republics. The veto power of each republic promoted pressure politics and negotiations outside statutory institutions in the process of reaching consensus; public accountability for decisions was thus obscured. At the same time, the unanimity requirement and equal rotation of top government positions among the republics and provinces fostered regional participation, provided an image of national unity, and prevented the emergence of a new dictator. In fact, no strong national leader emerged in Yugoslavia throughout the 1980s. The system gave the six republics free exercise of formal and informal political leverage on behalf of their own agendas, which often clashed.

Historical regional animosities and ambitions resurfaced in the first post-Tito decade. Serbia, with the strongest leadership of any republic, revived the concept of a strong centralized state under Serbian domination; but other republics, defending their sovereignty in a decentralized Yugoslavia, used Tito's consensual policy-making apparatus to block Serbian ambitions. In the process, the LCY, sole legal all-Yugoslav party for forty-five years, split in 1990 over the question of how much political diversity should be tolerated at the national level. At that point, the viability of the federation (whose demise was widely predicted as early as 1980) came under even more serious scrutiny.

Political Evolution after 1945

From 1945 to 1980, Josip Broz Tito was the only leader of the Socialist Federal Republic of Yugoslavia. His influence on Yugoslav politics began several years before the war and remained formidable a decade after his death. Tito presided over a series of political experiments that separated Yugoslavia from the Stalinist model of centralized decision making. Tito's political culture replaced that model with autonomous grass-roots political institutions; nonetheless, it retained the external trappings and ideology of a monolithic Marxist state. Before the end of Tito's regime, however, the inherent contradiction of that combination began to erode national institutions, including the LCY.

Breaking with the Soviet Union

Several years before World War II, Tito had survived Joseph V. Stalin's purge of Yugoslav communists in the Soviet Union. In fact, Stalin had sent him back to Yugoslavia to reinvigorate the party there. After the war, Tito was able to unite the country because his leadership of the Partisan (see Glossary) forces against the Nazis had made him a charismatic national hero and put his followers in a position to assume power. Under Tito's patronage, an entire generation of wartime Partisans became the postwar ruling class of Yugoslavia.

In 1948 Yugoslavia received international attention as the first country to break from Stalin's monolithic communist alliance, and the country subsequently maintained an independent foreign policy that made it a prototypical postwar "nonaligned nation." Shortly after his break with Stalin, Tito began a process of guaranteeing political equality to the constituent republics. At that time, Tito deemed a degree of regional autonomy necessary to maintain his own internal political support because the external backing of the communist alliance no longer provided legitimacy to his regime.

Tito's first constitution (1946) was modeled on the Soviet constitution of 1936. This constitution included direct communist party control over all aspects of state activity, no recognition of the constituent republics as political entities, and no stipulation of individual civil liberties. Tito refused to make his country fully subservient to the Soviet alliance, however, and in 1948 Stalin ejected Yugoslavia from the Cominform (Communist Information Bureau—see Glossary). From that time, Tito fashioned an independent political leadership that soon moved away from the rigid state domination of Stalinism.

The Sixth Party Congress (1952) was a watershed of Yugoslav political change, driven primarily by the need to prove that Yugoslavia could create a form of socialism superior to the Stalinist version from which it had recently split. In that meeting, liberal forces led by Milovan Djilas (a long-time close adviser of Tito) created a constitution that partially separated party and state political functions and restored some political rights to the constituent republics and some civil rights to individuals. At that time, constitutional foundations were also built for workers' control over enterprises and expanded local government power. The Federal People's Assembly established by the 1953 constitution contained two houses—the Federal Chamber, directly representing the regions, and the

Chamber of Producers, representing economic enterprises and worker groups. The federal government executive branch (the Federal Executive Council—FEC) included only the five secretariats dealing with national affairs and foreign policy. Foreign policy became the most important function of the FEC. The LCY retained exclusive political control, based on the Leninist credo that the state bureaucracy would wither away and that a multiparty system would only bring more cumbersome bureaucratic institutions.

Through the remainder of the 1950s, the economic decentralization of the 1953 constitution increased friction among the republics, which sought advantages in national allocation and resource redistribution policy. By 1960 this friction generated a new wave of constitutional change, aimed at preserving regional autonomy while restoring economic policy decisions to the federal level.

The 1963 Constitution

The regional divisions that prompted constitutional change also delayed concrete action by two years, as the constitution's framers sought language satisfactory to all political factions. By 1963 a new constitution had been prepared under the guidance of Eduard Kardelj, Tito's chief theoretician, with substantial input from liberal legal scholars. The new document reflected the perceived need for recentralization: the parliamentary Federal Assembly (Skupština) was divided into one general chamber, the Federal Chamber, and four chambers given specific bureaucratic responsibilities. In an effort to end regional conflict and promote national representation of the Yugoslav people, the constitution directed that individual republics be represented only in the Chamber of Nationalities, a part of the Federal Chamber. This provision was especially important in ensuring continued contributions from all regions to federal development funds for the poorer republics.

Other provisions of the new constitution increased decentralization instead of reducing it. Tito retained his position as president of the federation but renounced his state position as president of the FEC, a change that further separated party and state functions. The 1963 constitution also introduced the concept of rotation, which prohibited the holding of higher or lower level executive positions for more than two four-year terms. Other notable provisions extended human and civil rights and established constitutionally guaranteed court procedures. All these provisions were unique among the constitutional systems of contemporaneous communist states.

Although the 1963 constitution reflected the liberal leanings of Yugoslav leadership in those years, substantial power existed outside the institutional structure. Aleksandar Ranković, state secretary in charge of the secret police, led an obstructionist bloc that opposed economic reform in the 1960s and advocated a return to the pre-1953 strong party role. In the many deadlocks between the liberal and obstructionist groups in this period, Tito was always the final arbiter. He generally supported economic reform but resisted decentralization of state power.

Post-Ranković Diversification

In 1966 the party's liberal majority convinced Tito to oust Ranković by proving that the security chief had grossly abused his power. With secret police activity reduced and the conservatives lacking a leader, new political forces blossomed in Yugoslavia. In 1967 a series of constitutional amendments, instigated by Bosnia and Hercegovina, enlarged the role of the Chamber of Nationalities in federal decision making. The amendments specified separate functions for that chamber and canceled the centralizing force the 1963 constitution had exerted on the Federal Assembly. A new generation of younger, more pragmatic leaders began replacing conservative, older party members, and issues of nationalism and economics now were debated hotly and openly in the LCY. With politicians no longer allowed to hold concurrent federal and party positions, the bodies of state government grew more independent of party domination. (In the next twenty-plus years, however, national leaders moved constantly from party to state positions and back, thus largely preserving the connection.)

After 1966 the Yugoslav media more openly criticized government and party policy, and economic enterprises became more truly "self managing." In 1967 and 1968, the party openly debated whether delegates to the Federal Assembly could ignore constituent demands to take an "all-Yugoslav" position. Largely because most politicians identified such a position with Serbian centralist domination, delegates were held to strict pursuit of regional interests. Discussion of such issues signaled the rekindling of ethnic nationalist conflicts that had been muffled by totalitarianism in the past, and the resolution of the delegate responsibility question indicated ascendancy of nationalist forces. Beginning in 1966, ethnic conflicts sparked frequent demonstrations throughout the country. Bosnia and Hercegovina complained in 1966 that development funding was insufficient; the longstanding rivalry between Serbia and Croatia resurfaced in 1967; and Albanians demonstrated in Kosovo and Macedonia in 1968. A national-liberal coalition of Croatia, Slovenia, and Macedonia fought for additional decentralization and against anticipated Serbian efforts to dominate the federal government. Although that alliance disintegrated in 1969, its liberal approach dominated policy making until 1971. In an effort to regain control of the republics, the LCY decentralized its structure, giving much more decision-making power to the party at the republic level and lower.

In both party and state political structures, the new regional influence enormously complicated federal policy making. Now every decision required consultation and compromise. The FEC began consulting its equivalents in each republic before performing its role in national executive decision making. The compromise process often led to stalemate, especially on the explosive issue of economic development in the richer versus the poorer republics. To streamline the process, Tito intervened in 1969 to form the new Executive Bureau for the party Presidium. The Executive Bureau was a central party organ empowered to mediate disputes among the parties of the republics. (The party Presidium itself, comprising representatives from each republic, was inherently fragmented along regional lines.) Later that year, however, the Executive Bureau was helpless when demonstrations in Slovenia over distribution of World Bank (see Glossary) funds prompted divisive statements by party leaders of other republics and strong Slovenian criticism of the system. In 1970 the Croatian party began a protracted, powerful campaign against the existing federal system, which it described as a tool for Serbian domination of the other republics. The chief goal of the Croatian campaign was to change federal policy so that a single republic could veto any federal action.

Tito again responded by creating a new federal body, this time in the apparatus of the state rather than the party. Like the party's Executive Bureau, the collective State Presidency included the most qualified representatives of each republic and was intended to provide a forum for national compromise, insulated from regional pressures. Meanwhile, the outburst of ethnic factionalism that surfaced in the late 1960s became especially severe in Croatia. Between 1969 and 1971, protracted negotiations for new amendments to the federal constitution only heightened Croatian separatism. The Croatian nationalists, based in the powerful Matica Hrvatska cultural organization, split the Croatian party and launched a massive separatist propaganda campaign that resulted in serious clashes with ethnic Serbs in Croatia.

Political Innovation and the 1974 Constitution

Finally, Tito (himself a Croat) quelled the separatist movement by purging the Croatian party in 1972. The Croatian purge stemmed the demand for veto power by individual republics and paved the way for party recentralization and ratification of the constitutional amendments promoted by Tito. The State Presidency was added to the federal structure with Tito as its head, once again the sole symbol of both party and state leadership. In general, beginning in 1972, interregional consensus came more easily, although members of central party organs still were chosen by regional, not central, decision. In the following years, Tito was able to create a consensual system of interrepublic debate and compromise, with constitutional amendments as required. That process culminated in the 1974 Constitution, which ratified and adjusted preceding changes and attempted to construct a system that would survive Tito's passing.

The 1974 Constitution, which remained in effect through 1990, only partially reversed the extreme decentralization of the early 1970s. With 406 original articles, it was one of the longest constitutions in the world. It added elaborate language protecting the socialist self-management system from state interference and expanding representation of republics and provinces in all electoral and policy forums. The Constitution called the restructured Federal Assembly the highest expression of the self-management system (see Government Structure, this ch.). Accordingly, it prescribed a complex electoral procedure for that body, beginning with the local labor and political organizations (see fig. 12). Those bodies were to elect commune-level assemblies, which then would elect assemblies at province and republic level; finally, the latter groups would elect the members of the two equal components of the Federal Assembly, the Federal Chamber and the Chamber of Republics and Provinces. Like its predecessor, the 1974 Constitution tried to refine the balance between economic and ethnic diversity on the one hand and the communist ideal of social unity on the other.

The new Constitution also reduced the State Presidency from twenty-three to nine members, with equal representation for each republic and province and an ex-officio position for the president of the LCY. The party tried to reactivate its role in guiding national policy through automatic inclusion of the party chief in the State Presidency. That practice was discontinued in 1988, when the political climate called for further separation of party and state functions. This reduced the State Presidency to eight members. The 1974 Constitution also expanded protection of individual rights and court procedures, with the all-purpose caveat that no citizen could use those freedoms to disrupt the prescribed social system. Finally, Kosovo and Vojvodina, the two constituent provinces of Serbia, received substantially increased autonomy, including de facto veto power in the Serbian parliament. This change became

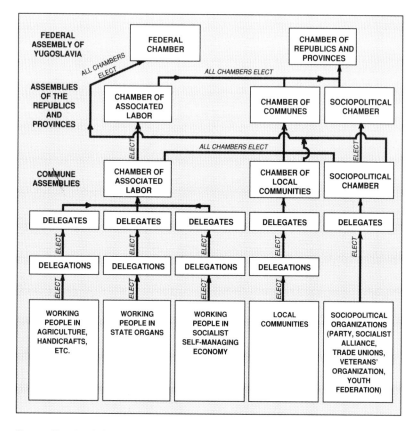

Source: Based on information from Jovan Djordjević (ed.), *Društveno-politički sistem, SFRJ,*
Belgrade, 1975, 462.

Figure 12. The Delegate System of Elections, 1990

a turbulent issue of interrepublic debate in post-Tito Yugoslavia
(see Regional Political Issues, this ch.).

In practice, despite nominal dispersal of power, throughout the
1970s the power of the LCY rested entirely on the personal leadership of Tito and his chief theoretician Kardelj. In 1974 Tito was
elected president for life of the LCY, and the new Constitution
gave him increased powers as state president. The new provision
strengthened the legitimacy of the Yugoslav regime as defender
of Marxism-Leninism.

After personally intervening in the Croatian crisis in 1971, Tito
gradually withdrew from the domestic decision-making process.
He continued making inspirational speeches to party cadres and
appointing officials of the party Presidium, but by 1976 he no longer

presided over meetings of the Presidium or the State Presidency. In the last four years of his life, Tito's contact with day-to-day government operations decreased, and he no longer used his immense prestige to break policy deadlocks.

In 1977 Kardelj attempted to lay the ideological groundwork for a diversified post-Tito political system. In his *The Directions of Development of the Political System of Self-Management,* Kardelj admitted that pluralism was an inevitable fact of Yugoslav political life, but he insisted that this pluralism had nothing in common with the pluralism of the bourgeois democracies of the West. In Yugoslavia, he said, conflicting interests could be accommodated within the scope of the LCY. Kardelj correctly identified one of the strongest forces of pluralism as the principle of self-management of economic and political organizations, which was greatly expanded in the 1974 Constitution. The trend continued in 1976, when the Law on Associated Labor prescribed the basic organizations of associated labor (BOALs) and self-management agreements of enterprises with the government. That law and the Constitution not only provided new building blocks for the Yugoslav economy but also codified political decentralization by removing centralized control and stimulating the growth of nonparty interest groups (see Adjustments in the 1970s, ch. 3). "All-Yugoslav" interests, already endangered by regional differences, suffered further fragmentation with the political reforms of the mid-1970s. Individual communists, theoretically given the role of integrating society for the common good of the working class, succumbed to divided loyalties and weak central leadership.

In 1979 the Presidium, chief executive body of the LCY, began annual rotation of its chairmanship. After Tito died, his power to name Presidium members devolved to a special Presidium commission that included regional party leaders. This additional step toward party decentralization further revealed the unique stature of the former leader. Rotation of the Presidium chairmanship continued through the 1980s on a regular schedule, following the "nationality key" that divided the position equally among the eight federal jurisdictions; the rotation was called "the most elaborate quota system in the world." Although he devised the rotation system to prevent party domination by one individual, Tito placed great importance on a strong central party surviving him. By 1980, however, the centrifugal political forces gradually building in the previous fifteen years had already eroded the single party structure. And the example Tito set in 1948 by abandoning a monolithic world communist movement spoke more loudly for pragmatic diversification than any of his pleas thirty years later for national party unity.

The Early Post-Tito Years

As expected, Tito's death began a new era in Yugoslav politics, but many of the trends of the 1970s continued. Milka Planinc of Croatia was elected prime minister in 1982, amid pledges from all quarters to continue Tito's policies. Much rhetoric proclaimed the need for drastic reform, but formidable bureaucratic inertia always blunted the impetus for change. The divisive issues that Tito had held in check were even more pronounced after his death, and the thoroughly divided power structure that succeeded him could manage only superficially the major problems that escalated through the decade.

Eight amendments were added to the Constitution in 1981. Their main purpose was to consolidate the elements of the rotational government that had been developed at various times in preceding years. Significantly, for the first time in a Yugoslav constitution, the term "collective body" was now used in reference to leadership policy. One 1981 amendment eliminated Tito's office of Yugoslav president for life, the functions of which devolved to the nine-member rotating State Presidency.

The Twelfth Party Congress of 1982, the first without Tito, was expected to lay new political ground and provide strong direction. But all progress was blocked by the familiar regional stalemate between the centralizers and the decentralizers within the party. With no strong figure to act as ultimate arbiter, the Twelfth Party Congress began a new stage of strident, fruitless debate in the LCY. Significantly, the centralizers now based their position not on the Leninist idea of the party as national vanguard but on the pragmatic argument that the country would collapse economically without strong central leadership. Throughout the 1980s, Serbia was the foremost exponent of stronger federal government, while Slovenia and Croatia were the foremost exponents of regional autonomy. With some variation, the same division defined national debate on many other issues.

Reform in the 1980s

In 1982 the new Yugoslav government was faced with a serious economic crisis that included rising unemployment, rising prices, and national debt. In 1983 the national sense of crisis was strong enough that the Federal Assembly passed austerity measures that temporarily curbed spending and controlled inflation (see Managing the Crisis of the 1980s, ch. 3). In 1983 the Long-Term Economic Stabilization Program (also known as the Krajgher Commission Report) was issued, after two years of debate, as the official blueprint for economic reform.

The Krajgher Commission Report was evidence that even in

Federal Assembly (Skupština) building, Belgrade
Courtesy Charles Sudetic

1983 most Yugoslav politicians agreed in theory that development of a market economy was necessary to restimulate growth throughout the country. But in practice this would have meant a drastic reduction in the policy-making role of the LCY, hence a total repudiation of the Tito legacy. Free enterprise also would mean that government agencies at all levels would lose their control of economic affairs. For these reasons, market reform met strong institutional resistance. The alternative reform, a return to Stalinist central planning, had few Yugoslav advocates in the mid-1980s and was totally discredited by the fall of central planning governments across Eastern Europe in the late 1980s.

While the government debated reform, the self-management system further dispersed control over economic and financial resources vital to the national economy. In the 1960s and 1970s, individual enterprises had formed alliances with local party machines, protecting uneconomical industries by giving them disproportionate influence on policy making and eroding regional support for price and wage controls. Many of the short-term austerity measures of 1983 were relaxed by the national government even before their expiration dates. The national political system then drifted into inaction, ignoring the need for fundamental economic reform that had been obvious since 1980.

The Thirteenth Party Congress briefly rekindled activism in 1986 by restating the conclusions of the Long-Term Economic Stabilization Program and by officially recognizing serious economic defects such as insufficient support for the relatively profitable private enterprise sector and unwise investment of foreign capital. The next years produced many official lists of resolutions and targets, all politically unpopular and aimed at imposing short-term austerity in order to effect long-term economic reform. Beginning in 1987, austerity wage freezes and plant closings were met by industrial strikes of increasing magnitude, and for the next two years government policy wavered between hard-line measures (such as threats to use the army to break strikes) and accommodation (such as replacement of unpopular party and state figures in Montenegro). Strikes contributed to the 1988 fall of Prime Minister Branko Mikulić, and they threatened to topple Mikulić's successor, Ante Marković, in 1989.

The 1980s also brought many proposals for political reform, some of which were drastic. Suggestions included abolishing all political parties and running the system through citizens' associations; holding multi-candidate elections within the party; and introducing a full multi-party system that would have meant electoral competition for the LCY. Once the pattern of intraparty debate was established at the 1982 Twelfth Party Congress of the LCY, variations on all these themes appeared in official and unofficial forums throughout the decade. After the Twelfth Party Congress, Najdan Pašić, a Serbian member of the LCY Central Committee, wrote a letter summarizing Serbian reform demands to alleviate the stalemate of Tito's government by consensus. The working group that grew from these demands took three years to produce its "Critical Analysis of the Functioning of the Political System of Socialist Self-Management," to which over 200 individuals contributed. The final report was so nebulous that both sides of the centralization issue claimed it as a victory. In 1984 the League of Communists of Serbia officially demanded repeal of autonomy in Kosovo and Vojvodina, plus reinforced federal government power, liberalized control of economic enterprises, and democratization of the electoral system. The main result of this proposal was angry dissent in Kosovo and Vojvodina. In 1986 a lengthy memorandum by the Serbian Academy of Sciences attacked the 1974 Constitution for blocking Serbian control of its provinces and criticized the party for failure to implement the program of the Krajgher Commission. The memorandum brought polemical responses from Kosovo and Vojvodina, as well as official censure of the academy by the party.

At the Thirteenth Party Congress in 1986, advocates of strong central government gained wide support among all delegations except the Slovenian. There was general agreement that decentralization had led to a dangerous proliferation of narrow, technocratic local interests, beyond the control of the LCY. Centralist forces won a victory when a new party statute transferred election of party Central Committee members from the republic parties to the LCY party congress and gave the national party the right to curb deviation by republican parties. In a massive transition of party power, only 38 of the party's 165-member Central Committee were reelected at the Thirteenth Party Congress.

The Thirteenth Party Congress also formed a commission to write a new series of constitutional amendments. Amendments proposed in 1987 sought to reduce the obstructive influence of decentralized government. The federal planning system was to be strengthened, and the relations of the republics and provinces to the federal government were to be redefined. Several aspects of economic reform were addressed, but the main impetus behind the amendments was the Serbian drive to regain control over its provinces. After twenty-two months of heated regional debate, the amendments were approved by the Federal Assembly. Because of their broad application in economics, government, and the party, they were expected to form the basis for yet another completely new Yugoslav constitution in the early 1990s. The idea of a new constitution was supported most strongly by the Serbs, who saw it as a vehicle to officially ratify their control of Kosovo and Vojvodina and achieve at least parity with the other republics (which had no such problematic semiautonomous provinces). An estimated 6 million people took part in public debate on what finally emerged in 1988 as thirty-nine amendments.

The Leadership Crisis

A political crisis occurred in late 1988 when Prime Minister Mikulić resigned under pressure. Mikulić, who had initiated several austerity programs to reduce rampant inflation, met general disapproval when his programs produced no immediate results. He was also implicated in the Agrokomerc scandal of 1987, the most extensive instance of government and financial corruption in Yugoslavia to that time. In accordance with the constitutional provisions for resignation, the Mikulić government remained in office until a new government, headed by Marković, was selected in the spring of 1989. Marković, who had gained a reputation as an effective economic innovator and moderate politician in Croatia, drew heavy criticism for refusing to take drastic anti-inflation measures and for allowing both the economy and the Kosovo crisis to worsen in his first year in office.

Throughout the turbulent debates of the 1980s, the Yugoslav political system never produced a leader who commanded the respect of all factions. But by the turn of the decade, an end to the leadership crisis appeared possible. Marković, who became prime minister in 1989, clearly belonged to a generation of technocrats intermediate between the Tito generation and the youngest politicians in the country, and some of his economic policies received strong public criticism. But Marković made bold moves toward a Yugoslav market economy in 1990. He received broad public support when he declared that his government would function independently of LCY influence and would be ready for multiparty elections after the LCY split in 1990. More important for the long term, a new generation of leaders began to fill national positions at the end of the 1980s, leaving few figures from Tito's World War II Partisan circle in power. New faces included 1989 State President Janez Drnovšek of Slovenia and Vasil Tupurkovski, a Macedonian member of the FEC. Both in their thirties when elected but with positive national reputations, Drnovšek and Tupurkovski called consistently for pragmatic, drastic reform.

Government Structure

The Yugoslav Constitution of 1974 prescribed no division of powers among the bodies of the federal or republic governments. In practice, however, these entities resembled those of a parliamentary democracy in their division of responsibility. The basic structure and relationships of government institutions remained the same from 1974 through 1990.

Federal Assembly

The 1974 Constitution divided the Federal Assembly (Skupština) into two chambers, the Federal Chamber and the Chamber of Republics and Provinces (see fig. 13). The former contained thirty representatives from each republic and twenty from each province. Representatives were chosen from among delegates elected by organizations such as communes and institutions at the lowest level of the system, giving the chamber elements of a grass-roots constituency. Members of assemblies below the federal level were not eligible for the Federal Chamber. Voting in the Federal Chamber was by simple majority, and the chamber considered all issues where federal authority had an impact on any local organization. Although originally intended to represent individuals and local organizations, delegates tended to vote according to instructions from their respective regional governments.

The Chamber of Republics and Provinces was elected by the assemblies of the republics and provinces. It included twelve delegates from each republic and eight from each province. Voting was by delegation, and unanimity was required on all interregional questions. This requirement meant that all eight political jurisdictions had veto power in any vote. All interregional issues with federal jurisdiction were considered in this chamber. Proposals were forwarded to the assemblies of the republics involved for formation of the regional position that would determine the bloc vote of the national delegation.

Federal Executive Council

The Federal Executive Council (FEC) was responsible for everyday bureaucratic operation of the government (see fig. 14). Using recommendations from the LCY and its own committees, the FEC was the primary sponsor of proposals for deliberation by the Federal Assembly. The FEC consisted of a prime minister and two deputy prime ministers, who were nominated by the State Presidency and ratified by the Federal Assembly, and the heads, or secretaries, of the twelve major federal bureaucracies (the secretariats for agriculture, development, domestic trade, finance, foreign affairs, foreign economic relations, industry and energy, internal affairs, labor, legal and administrative affairs, national defense, and transportation and communication). The secretaries were selected by the prime minister and approved by the Federal Assembly. Four ministers without portfolio were added from republics underrepresented in the other fifteen positions.

The nineteen-member FEC outlined in the 1974 Constitution was reduced from the previous number of twenty-nine; the federal Secretariat for Finance was added in 1988, the secretariats for development and domestic trade in 1989. Although Tito's rotation principle was not observed in determining the nationality of the prime minister or the federal secretaries, a rough balance was maintained.

FEC members formed a variety of committees for resolution of interregional issues preparatory to making recommendations to the Federal Assembly. Five standing committees, one for each of the most troublesome federal issues, included members from both the FEC and the republic executive councils. These committees debated practical aspects of all national problems, making the FEC the most important national center of political debate, compromise, and influence.

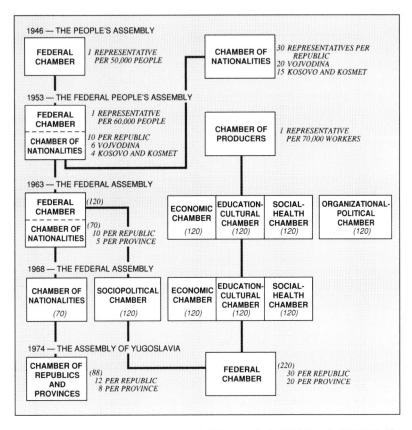

Source: Based on information from Josip Sruk, *Ustavno uredjenje, SFRJ,* Zagreb, 1976, 329–32.

Figure 13. Evolution of the Federal Parliament as of 1990

Legislation was formulated in the FEC—a process that could take a year or more—then sent to the appropriate chamber of the Federal Assembly for debate. In the 1970s, the FEC was second only to Tito himself in producing compromises on controversial issues among opposing republics and second only to the party as a decision-making body. By definition, it controlled all federal bureaucracies and had exclusive access to expert information needed for policy making. The FEC also could determine the scheduling of debate on legislation and policy. After Tito's death, however, regions defended their interests more stubbornly, and party leadership split along regional lines. In negotiations involving party leaders with regional agendas, the FEC increasingly relied on constitutionally prescribed temporary measures, which could not be blocked by dissenting delegations. Such measures remained in effect pending a unanimous resolution, and on many issues they were the only valid legislation for long periods of time. The FEC's failing bargaining power during the 1980s was exemplified by its inability to formulate the practical terms of the Long-Term Program of Economic Stabilization.

FEC members also sat on advisory councils that considered interregional organizational issues. All major social and political organizations, including the LCY, were represented in the councils. Although not prescribed in the Constitution, the councils played a major role in federal policy making after 1973.

State Presidency

Also represented in the federal councils was the third major organ of the Yugoslav national government, the collective State Presidency. Formed by Tito in 1970 to provide all-Yugoslav negotiation of interregional conflicts, the State Presidency became the symbolic replacement for Tito's position as head of state. By 1989 it had evolved from the original twenty-three-member group to an eight-member group, one member of which was elected from each republic and province. A ninth, ex-officio post was held by the president of the LCY Central Committee until late 1988, when the position was abolished to reduce party interference in state institutions. Most republics and provinces elected their representatives to the state Presidency in their assemblies, but in 1989 Bosnia and Hercegovina, Montenegro, and Slovenia held direct popular elections for this post. The position of president rotated yearly, to provide even distribution among the republican and provincial representatives. Beginning with the 1989 president, Janez Drnovšek of Slovenia, the "presidency of the Presidency" was to rotate among the republics and provinces in the following order: Serbia, Croatia, Montenegro, Vojvodina, Kosovo, Macedonia, and Bosnia and Hercegovina, through 1997.

The 1974 Constitution named the State Presidency as "supreme body in charge of administration and command of the armed forces," as well as the main administrator of foreign policy and adviser on domestic policy. The State Presidency controlled its constitutionally prescribed domains through working bodies known as councils of the presidency. Among these were councils for foreign policy, national defense, state security, and protection of the constitutional order. Councils were appointed by the FEC. In practice, the State Presidency deliberated informally, consulting regularly with representatives of other government bodies and developing positions by consensus rather than by the majority vote prescribed in the Constitution. It also met regularly with the LCY

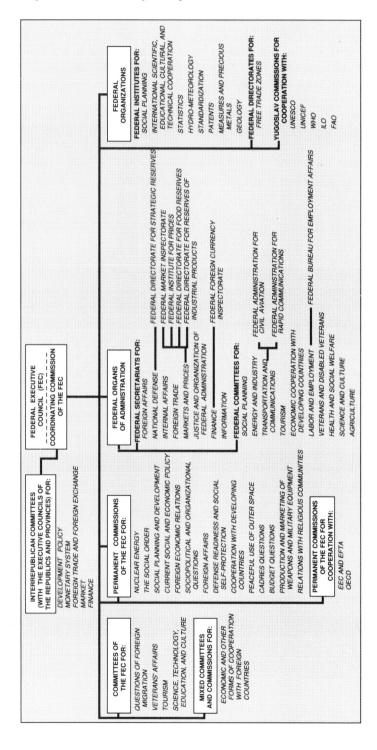

Figure 14. Organization of the Federal Executive Council and Administrative Agencies, 1990

Presidium and regional presidencies. Because its members had no bureaucratic responsibility and because of the prestige left to the institution by Tito, the State Presidency was an important bargaining center for purely political issues that could not be resolved in the Federal Assembly or the FEC. It also initiated all temporary measures passed by the FEC. But the State Presidency had no power to impose compromise; this was not an important weakness when Tito filled the position, but his successors lacked his personal influence.

Court System

Yugoslavia had two national court systems, one for resolution of civil and criminal cases, the other to judge the conformity of national law with the Constitution and the conformity of laws passed by republics and provinces with national law. In 1990 the federal Constitutional Court found recent amendments to the constitutions of all the republics except Montenegro to be at variance with the federal Constitution. The court did not have the authority, however, to take action against such infractions. Its judgments were passed to the Federal Assembly for action. The federal Constitutional Court also resolved disputes of authority between regional bodies or between a regional body and the national government, but it did not act as an appeals court for the regional level. The republics and provinces also had constitutional courts, which dealt with constitutional questions on their level. For national uniformity, the members of the regional constitutional courts held regular consultations on procedures and constitutional interpretations.

The regular court system consisted of the federal, republican, and provincial supreme courts and of local (commune) courts, each resolving civil and criminal cases involving laws at their level of government. Local regular courts included untrained citizens elected by their communes, as well as professional jurists. This provision partially fulfilled the function of trial by jury, which did not exist in Yugoslavia. The Yugoslav system also had no habeas corpus law. Only professional judges served on the regular courts of the republics and the federal Supreme Court. The system also included local- to federal-level self-management courts (courts of associated labor), which heard only cases involving acts of the self-management organizations not involving government law. The military courts completed the Yugoslav justice system (see Courts, Detention, and Punishment, ch. 5).

Each republic and province had its own law code, separate from the federal criminal code. By federal law, political crimes were first tried at district level; then cases could be appealed at the republic and federal levels of the regular court system. The federal Supreme Court was the final court of appeal for lower courts of all types. The chief civil law enforcement officer was the public prosecutor, elected by the Federal Assembly. The republics and provinces had corresponding officers, similarly elected and under the direction of the federal prosecutor.

Local Government and the Communes

Government structure at the republic level was essentially the same as that at the federal level. This included multi-member presidencies headed by a single member designated as president of the republic. In multiethnic republics such as Bosnia and Hercegovina, members of the presidency were allotted and selected by ethnic group. Through 1990 each republic had a three-chamber assembly, including the chambers of associated labor and communes and the sociopolitical chamber. Republic executive councils included a full complement of ministries, including foreign ministries. The governments of the "autonomous" provinces Kosovo and Vojvodina had the same structure; in the years of true autonomy, 1974–88, the provinces' delegates to the federal State Presidency and the federal Chamber of Republics and Provinces took independent positions on some issues. Beginning in 1988, however, Serbia tightened control over the provinces by purging the Kosovo and Vojvodina leagues of communists (hence the government leadership) and inserting pro-Serbian individuals. Amendment of the constitution of Serbia, to which the provinces were bound, overrode the autonomy provisions of the 1974 federal Constitution.

Local government in Yugoslavia was based on the unique institution of the commune, officially defined as "a self-managing sociopolitical community based on the power of and self-management by working-class and all working people." In 1988 Yugoslav local government consisted of about 500 communes. Beginning in the 1950s, the communes held all political authority not specifically delegated to government at the federal or republic level; they were the source of Yugoslavia's claim that, unlike the centralized Soviet system, Yugoslav socialism truly gave power to the workers. Because they generated pockets of political power controlled by local party officials, the communes also contributed to the fractious, unfocused nature of political power throughout the country after the death of Tito. The district, next-highest political level above the commune, controlled law enforcement and elections, but functions such as economic planning, management of utilities, and supervision of economic enterprises were the responsibility of the commune. Workers' councils of industrial enterprises were obliged to submit financial records to the communes to justify the setting of worker wages (see The Economic Management Mechanism, ch. 3).

The commune was also the lowest level in the complex delegate system that ultimately elected members of the Federal Assembly. Workers, sociopolitical organizations, and local communities elected the members of three-chamber commune assemblies, which in turn elected delegates to republic and provincial assemblies and delegates to the Federal Chamber of the Federal Assembly. Delegates to the republic and provincial assemblies elected members of the Chamber of Republics and Provinces of the Federal Assembly, but they had no voice in choosing the Federal Chamber. In practice, individual voters at the commune level chose only from closed lists of delegate candidates, with little regard for capacity to represent a constituency. Although liberalization of the electoral system was frequently discussed, no open nomination process had emerged by 1990. Both commune and republic assemblies had three chambers, each representing a sector of society (associated labor, local communities, and sociopolitical organizations). Because those categories overlapped, some citizens were represented by more than one delegate.

Behind the principle of socialist self-management, prescribed at length in the 1974 Constitution, was the concept that self-managing citizens' organizations would assume complete governmental control and the state would disappear entirely at some point. In practice, however, grass-roots political power shrank in the 1980s, especially as it applied to economic policy. Exercise of this power was blocked by an intermediate layer of political managers, whose selection remained an LCY prerogative at the republic and provincial levels. Given this selection policy, the regional Yugoslav system mainly chose loyal party operatives over competent managers when such a choice was necessary. Given the autonomy of all state agencies below the federal level in Yugoslavia, these political appointees were able to block national reform programs that threatened their elite positions. Yugoslavia had renounced both Stalinist centralized planning and (to a lesser extent) the practice of limiting the best party jobs to a privileged elite, known in communist societies as the *nomenklatura.* Nevertheless, in Yugoslavia a number of inflexible smaller systems deprived industrial and agricultural workers of the decision-making powers guaranteed them by the Constitution to control their own economic destiny. Decision-making bodies were in no way answerable to the workers for their policies. Neither of the chambers of the Federal Assembly, election of whose delegates nominally began at the grass-roots level, represented workers or their organizations as separate interest groups independent of the overall political position of their region.

Nongovernmental Political Institutions

Beginning in 1945, the institutions of the Yugoslav government were overshadowed by the dominating policy input of the single ruling communist party and by a number of party-controlled organizations designed to maintain control of various sectors of society. At the end of the first post-Tito decade, however, this condition changed in two ways. First, major party-controlled organizations such as unions and youth groups took independent positions, and some became rival parties to the LCY. Those that remained closest to the LCY lost membership and influence. Second, the 1990 split of the LCY left that organization without even nominal policy-making control for the first time since 1945. These developments threatened to complete the separation of state from party that had begun in 1948.

League of Communists of Yugoslavia

Through the end of the 1980s, Yugoslavia remained a one-party state. All government officials at national and republic levels, and a very high percentage of local officials, were chosen from among the 2 million members of the League of Communists of Yugoslavia (LCY). The 1974 Constitution described the LCY as "the prime mover and exponent of political activity," using its "guiding ideological and political action" to foster self-management, the socialist revolution, and "social and democratic consciousness." In the process of government reforms in the 1960s and 1970s, the dominance of the LCY began to erode, especially in the area of economic policy. Through the 1980s, however, the LCY remained nominally the primary nongovernmental political institution, with continued heavy influence on matters of political policy at all levels of the federal state. In practical input to policy decisions, the power of the LCY leadership overlapped and often blended with that of the collective State Presidency and the FEC. But party influence and respect in Yugoslav society at large lagged noticeably, and alternative political organizations proliferated. By 1990 the constitutional guarantee for the existence of LCY-sponsored organizations was being used to justify the formation of noncommunist parties without further amendment of the Constitution.

LCY membership decreased slightly in the 1980s. The last increase was recorded in 1982, and in 1988 membership fell below 2 million for the first time since 1979. The death of Tito deprived the party of its only unifying element, and after 1980 the party suffered from the same fragmentation and diffusion of power as government institutions.

Founded in 1919, the party came to power in 1945 and followed the organizational pattern of the communist party in the Soviet Union until the Sixth Party Congress (1952). The first major party decentralization occurred at that time, beginning a long, uneven process of reducing direct party authority in society. The Sixth Party Congress also changed the name of the party from the Communist Party of Yugoslavia (CPY) to the League of Communists of Yugoslavia (LCY), to differentiate it from the other East European communist parties.

Under Tito, a series of pragmatic adjustments were made after 1952 to counteract the decentralization trend, when more control was needed in the central party organ. The first major event in that series was the 1954 condemnation of Milovan Djilas, architect of the 1952 reforms. Beginning in 1963, major structural changes affected the national role of the LCY. Early changes were the introduction of direct channels of influence for self-management groups into policy making (1963) and the mandated separation of top party and state positions (1966). Until the removal of Ranković in 1966, a strong conservative element sought to restore the direct, central role that the party had gradually lost after the split with the Soviet Union. Beginning in 1966, however, the party assumed an atmosphere of open, regionally based disagreement that intensified for the next twenty-five years. In 1969 the failure of the prestigious Executive Bureau of the party Presidium to act as a truly national mediator within the party signaled growing fragmentation in the LCY structure (see Political Evolution after 1945, this ch.). The open rebellion of the Croatian party between 1969 and 1971 had negative repercussions for the LCY, despite Tito's decisive purge. Croatia remained tranquil in the 1970s, but the Serbian and Slovenian parties criticized the national organization periodically. The Serbs were especially restive after passage of the 1974 Constitution. In 1976 Najdan Pašić, in the name of the Serbian central committee, presented a document known as the *Blue Book* to the LCY leadership. That document was a list of damages suffered by the Serbs because of inequities in the Constitution. Tito suppressed the *Blue Book,* but six years later Pašić attracted more attention by suggesting that a commission study problems of government function.

Efforts to streamline Yugoslavia's economic and political systems always involved making changes in the LCY. All factions understood that no meaningful change was possible in those areas without cutting through the cumbersome lines of power held by party elites at all levels. All the major reform efforts of the 1980s (the Pašić letter of 1982, an open call for reform proposals in 1985, and the national working group report and Serbian Academy of Sciences document of 1986) listed party reform as the starting point for political progress (see Reform in the 1980s, this ch.). Nevertheless, in 1990 the LCY was still organized in substantially the same way as it had been at the time of Tito's death. By that time, the LCY was commonly called "not one party, but eight," a description that accurately reflected its fragmentation.

In theory, the national party congress was the highest authority of the LCY; it was mandated to meet at least every five years. Accordingly, the Twelfth Party Congress met in 1982, the Thirteenth Party Congress in 1986, the Fourteenth Party Congress in 1990. The main goal of those congresses was reconciliation of regional differences on reform that would restore the party's leading role in shaping national policy. The 1982 and 1986 congresses each began with hopeful rhetoric and dissolved into renewed regional squabbles. The 1990 congress was the first since 1945 to be labeled "extraordinary" (meaning "emergency"). It was widely viewed as the party's "last chance" for constructive action to improve its sagging national image.

A commission on party statute reform met six months prior to the Fourteenth Party Congress to develop reform proposals for discussion at the congress. This commission reaffirmed the Leninist principle of democratic centralism—meaning that diverse views were to be heard but that the will of the majority would determine policy. The commission also recommended streamlining the party hierarchy for greater accountability. But the vague language of the commission report addressed none of the deep and controversial statutory changes universally acknowledged as necessary. The stimulus for change would thus have to come from a platform adopted by the congress itself. By party law, such a platform was required to precede statutory changes. In fact, prior to the opening of the congress, no formal proposal for party transformation had ever been made.

The Fourteenth Party Congress included 1,688 delegates, of which 994 were elected by local commune party conferences (1 delegate per 2,000 party members). Each of the six republic party organizations then added 60 delegates. The two provincial party organizations added 40 each, and the Yugoslav People's Army (YPA) added another 30. Other party organizations sent a total of 204 delegates. Regional representation was divided as follows: Serbia had 360 delegates; Bosnia and Hercegovina, 278; Croatia, 240; Macedonia, 166; Vojvodina, 157; Slovenia, 139; Montenegro, 123; and Kosovo, 112.

Doctrinal reform was the central task of the Fourteenth Party Congress. The congress voted to relinquish the LCY's monopoly of political power and allow multiparty elections in response to similar moves in neighboring communist countries. But the meeting was cut short when the Slovenian delegation departed in protest of the defeat of its proposal to restructure the LCY as a league of republican organizations freely associated under the national party. The departure of the League of Communists of Slovenia left the national organization weakened and uncertain, especially because national television had revealed acrimonious conflicts in what was supposedly the strongest unifying political force in the country. In the months following the congress, the status of the party remained unknown, as Serbian and other members attempted to reconvene the congress and complete the much-needed new party platform. Both the passage of electoral reforms and the interruption of the congress by the Slovenes dampened Serbian ambitions for using the party to control national politics.

The procedures and structure of the LCY remained largely unchanged during the 1980s. The party was directed between congresses by the Presidium, the twenty-three member steering body for the Central Committee. The Presidium oversaw a variety of commissions and organizations and implemented party policy. Specific Presidium members directed party activities in ideology, organizational development, socioeconomic relations, political propaganda, and international relations. Nationalities were apportioned in the Presidium according to republic and province (three members per republic, two per province, one representing the YPA, plus the president, who was elected by the party Central Committee). Of the Presidium membership, fourteen were full members; the others were ex officio members (one from the YPA, plus the presidents of the party presidiums of each republic and province). Ex officio members could not be directly removed. Because the Presidium thus provided the YPA a direct role in decision making, that organization strongly opposed legalization of other political parties that would not provide it such input (see The Military and the Party, ch. 5). Tito's last major adjustment to the party system had established rotation of major party leadership positions, which after 1979 were assumed by a representative of a different region every one or two years. When Tito died, the Presidium seemed to be increasing its influence on national policy making. That trend ended in 1980, however, when the position of party president was abolished in favor of collective leadership in the Presidium.

In the late 1980s, the Central Committee comprised 165 members. Those individuals were nominated by the central committees of the republics and provinces. The national Central Committee was called into plenary session at irregular intervals to discuss urgent policy questions. In less than one year in 1988–89, ten such sessions—some held consecutively—were called to discuss party reform. Both the Presidium and the Central Committee were targeted in reform agendas; reform efforts removed five Presidium members in 1989, and an 1989 LCY commission proposed reducing the size of the Central Committee to 129 members.

Membership policy for the LCY differed markedly from that for other communist parties. Until the reforms of 1952, Yugoslavia followed the Soviet model. Recommendations for party membership were required from two party members; then a candidate for membership was placed on probation for eighteen months. Both those requirements were dropped in 1952; after that time, nominations also were accepted from nonparty Yugoslavs in good standing. During the 1970s, party membership nearly doubled, despite the large-scale expulsions of the Tito era (170,000 left the party forcibly or voluntarily between 1972 and 1979). Membership reached 2 million in 1980. From 1983 until 1988, however, the number decreased slightly every year, although massive expulsions did not recur after the purge of the Kosovo party following the 1981 riots. About 5 percent of party members left voluntarily in the 1980s, and the percentage of worker and peasant members declined. In 1987 workers constituted only 30 percent of the total membership and 8 percent of the Central Committee, while peasants made up only 3.5 percent of total party membership. Increasing party elitism was indicated by the stable percentage of the intelligentsia, who depended on party membership for upward professional mobility. In the mid-1980s, some 95 percent of top managers and 77.6 percent of professionals in Yugoslavia were party members. In 1980 only 25 percent of party membership was younger than twenty-seven, including only 1 in 200 students.

Authoritative studies and surveys in the 1980s showed that most Yugoslavs, whether party members or nonmembers, viewed the LCY as a practical avenue to success, not as a leading force in the ideology or ethics of the nation. Many LCY members did not participate in political activities, and power positions remained in the same hands for long periods of time. A considerable number of Central Committee members served more than one term, some as many as seven.

Party organization at the republic and province level was identical to that of the national party. A group of executive secretaries of the national Presidium served as the liaison between the national party and the next level in the hierarchy. In the 1980s, the republic and provincial parties were the most important arenas for formulating and expressing the positions of their respective jurisdictions toward national political and economic issues. For example, the central committees of Slovenia and Serbia framed much of the political polemics between the two republics. Slobodan Milošević used the presidency of the Serbian presidium in the late 1980s as a platform to advocate Serbian nationalism and recentralization of party and state institutions. Approval by the Slovenian and Croatian central committees for multiparty local elections in 1990 signaled a major breakthrough toward a true multiparty system in those republics (see Regional Political Issues, this ch.). And the purging of provincial party leaders in Vojvodina and Kosovo under pressure from the Serbian party in 1988 marked a turning point in Serbia's struggle to reassert control over its two provinces.

Thus in 1990 the LCY was decentralized in exercising authority but increasingly elitist in terms of who occupied positions of power in the party organizations. Party configuration was the most formidable obstacle to reform of the national political system, but structural change could come only from a centralized authority whose mere existence would threaten regional elites. Even as actual LCY power waned, Tito's legacy of party policy-making dominance remained the theoretical, paralyzing basis of government operations.

Socialist Alliance of Working People of Yugoslavia

The Socialist Alliance of Working People of Yugoslavia (SAWPY), formerly the People's Front, was the largest and most influential mass organization in Yugoslavia from 1945 through 1990. In 1990 its membership was 13 million, including most of the adult population of the country. The political purpose of this national organization, sponsored by the LCY, was to involve as many people as possible in activities on the party agenda, without the restrictions and negative connotations of direct party control. SAWPY also was chartered as a national arbitration forum for competing cross-regional interests. Although party officials were forbidden to hold simultaneous office in SAWPY, the top echelon of the latter was dominated by established party members. The importance of SAWPY to the party leadership increased as the party's direct control over social and state institutions decreased. It was useful in mobilizing otherwise apathetic citizens during the Croatian crisis of 1971 and the Kosovo crisis of 1987.

The Constitution stipulated a wide variety of social and political functions for SAWPY, including nomination of candidates for delegate at the commune level, suggesting solutions to national and local social issues to assembly delegates, and overseeing elections and public policy implementation. Both individuals and interest groups held membership. The structure of SAWPY was very similar to that of the party, including a hierarchy that extended from national to commune level. SAWPY organizations in the republics and provinces were simplified versions of the national structure.

The national organization was run by a conference of delegates chosen by the regional SAWPY leadership. The conference presidium included members from the party, the armed forces, trade unions, the Youth League of Yugoslavia, and other national organizations. Like the LCY Central Committee, the SAWPY conference established departments to formulate policy recommendations in areas such as economics, education, and sociopolitical relations. Coordinating committees were also active in interregional consultation on policy and mass political action.

In Slovenia, the Socialist Alliance of Working People became an umbrella organization for a number of nonparty organizations with political interests, beginning in 1988. On a lesser scale, similar changes occurred in other republics. This development rekindled the idea that SAWPY might be divorced from LCY domination and reconstituted as a second political party at the national level. Pending such an event, SAWPY was regarded throughout the 1980s as a puppet of the party elite, particularly by virtue of its exclusive control over the nomination of assembly delegates at the commune level.

Trade Unions

The Confederation of Trade Unions of Yugoslavia also was a party-dominated mass organization. It had the constitutional mandate of protecting the rights of workers and preserving the self-management system. It also oversaw selection of delegates to the Federal Assembly from economic enterprises and of delegates to the management bodies of those enterprises. The structure of the confederation was the same as that of the party and SAWPY, but the ruling body, the Council of the Confederation, did not allot positions according to ethnic or regional quotas. Seats on the presidium of the council were held by the national heads of the Yugoslav trade unions and the presidents of regional trade union councils. Party influence in the trade unions remained very strong through the 1980s; virtually all officials were party members, and worker membership in the unions, although voluntary, was considered automatic in many enterprises.

In the Yugoslav self-managed enterprise system, there was no true adversary function for unions or their officials because there was no true distinction between employers and employees.

Agreements were made between worker groups within and among enterprises, cutting across union organizational boundaries (see The Economic Management Mechanism, ch. 3). The function of the unions was to preserve party influence by selecting the members of the workers' councils, to ensure that the enterprise was run according to the self-management laws, and to protect the working environment. Until 1987 union officials also were expected to suppress "work stoppages," but they offered little resistance to the increasing number of strikes between 1987 and 1990.

According to a 1986 national poll, 71 percent of workers identified themselves as either members or officers of a trade union, while 25 percent denied membership. These figures differed considerably from official membership statistics, which claimed a 97 percent enrollment. Other poll results showed a lack of broad, active support of the unions, even among members; the majority of workers polled did not believe that the trade union system was a useful institution in representing their interests, and only a small percentage of members took an active role in the organization. Nevertheless, the presence of a genuine trade union structure controlled at the enterprise level was a significant departure from the enterprise politics of the ''conventional'' communist states.

Youth League of Yugoslavia

The Youth League of Yugoslavia was the training organization for future members of the LCY, SAWPY, and the trade unions. Patterned after the Soviet model of youth indoctrination organizations, the Yugoslav youth group suffered from divided leadership, poor support from the party, and dwindling membership in the 1980s. The very high youth unemployment rate of the late 1980s made the indoctrination of young socialists a difficult task under the best of conditions. The proportion of nonparticipating members doubled between 1981 and 1986. Slovenia, where only 5 percent of youth expressed a desire to become party members in 1986, had the lowest figure for the period. The youth league exerted little influence on state or party politics. However, in 1989 the Slovenian branch of the organization announced plans for transformation into a new political party with mass support, in time for the 1990 Slovenian parliamentary elections.

Veterans' Association

The Federation of Associations of Veterans of the National Liberation War (Savez udruženja boraca Narodno-oslobodilačkog rata—SUBNOR) was an aging, dwindling group of former World War II Partisans. The assemblies of local and republic governments designated seats for SUBNOR representatives. Often used by Tito as a prestigious lever for centralizing party control, SUBNOR in the 1980s espoused the view that modern Yugoslavia had degenerated since the early days of struggle and that new leadership was needed. Although by 1990 few figures of its generation and viewpoint remained in national politics, SUBNOR retained considerable influence in the first post-Tito decade (see Government Organization for Defense, ch. 5).

Regional Political Issues

Throughout the postwar era, each of Yugoslavia's six republics and two provinces maintained its own political posture and agenda, many aspects of which had originated centuries before. Geography, natural resources, religion, nationality, economic policy, and traditional relations with other countries influenced the positions of republics and provinces. In 1987 Pedro Ramet, a scholar of Yugoslav politics, summarized interrepublican political differences thus: ''. . . liberal recentralizers are dominant in the Serbian Party, conservative recentralizers in the Bosnian and Montenegrin Parties, liberal decentralizers in the Slovenian and Vojvodinan Parties, and conservative decentralizers in the Croatian, Macedonian, and Kosovan Parties.'' By 1990 a complex combination of differentiating factors again threatened to divide the federal structure of the Yugoslav state.

Slovenia

Throughout the postwar period, Slovenia was by far the richest per capita, the most ethnically homogeneous, and the most open to political experimentation of the Yugoslav republics. In centuries of close contact with Austria, Italy, and France, it had absorbed much from Western political and economic thought (see The Slovenes, ch. 1). Preservation of hard-won economic advantages was a primary consideration in Slovenia's political posture, especially after the 1974 Constitution prescribed new federal budgeting procedures. Slovenes had always objected to federal levies used to support underdeveloped economies in other republics. By the mid-1980s, Slovenes were highly critical of federal (Serb-dominated) financial policy, especially when the new procedures failed to reduce their payments for support of a deteriorating economy in Kosovo and when rising inflation hurt their economy (see Structure of the Economy, ch. 3).

The combination of Western intellectual influence and increasing pressure for independent solution of economic problems led to formation of many official and unofficial noncommunist political

*Serbian demonstrator
burning photograph
of Tito, Belgrade, 1990
Courtesy Charles Sudetic*

groups in Slovenia, which became the center of a major political controversy in the late 1980s. Several politically significant acts by official and unofficial Slovenian groups posed a clear threat that the republic's substantial industrial, financial, and agricultural resources might be withdrawn from the federation. While loudly opposing the Serbian thrust for centralization and dominance of Kosovo, the Slovenes liberalized their own political system by adding multicandidate elections, open media discussion of all issues, and noncommunist political groups. In 1989 the Slovenian League of Communists endorsed multiparty elections, and in 1990 it renamed itself the Party of Democratic Renewal.

Although Slovenian party president Milan Kučan had led a substantial bloc of moderates as late as 1989, the momentum of new party formation and the failure of compromise with Serbia brought controversial change that threatened to carry the Slovenes farther from the center of the federation. Among amendments added to the Slovenian constitution in late 1989 were provisions limiting the emergency intervention power of the Yugoslav government in Slovenia and affirming Slovenia's right to secede from the federation if ''national self-determination'' were not guaranteed in the next round of constitutional changes. Those amendments were viewed as an alarming precedent by nearly all non-Slovenian political groups, and they were declared at variance with the national constitution by an advisory decision of the Constitutional Court of Yugoslavia a few months after passage.

As economic success and political reform progressed at home, the Slovenes increasingly perceived Serbian nationalism as a major danger. For Slovenes, Serbian nationalism threatened to reinstate external control of economic resources and political processes. At the time of the Fourteenth Party Congress in early 1990, the federal government and the LCY were split between pro-Serbian and pro-Slovenian factions. Slovenian party officials condemned Serbian oppression in Kosovo and the Serbian demand for a one man-one vote national decision-making system, which would allow Serbia to dominate because of its large population. In 1989 the Front for Independent Slovenia appeared with demands for total independence. Slovenia was the first Yugoslav republic ever to hold multiparty elections, in early 1990. At the time of the elections, the Slovenian Social Democratic Alliance was one of only two Yugoslav noncommunist parties to have expanded past republican borders. That group was part of a coalition called Demos, which easily won the first (parliamentary) phase of elections, defeating Kučan's former communists with a platform that included secession from Yugoslavia. In the presidential runoff, the popular reformist Kučan won, making him the first freely elected communist head of government in Eastern Europe and creating a mixed republican government in Slovenia.

Serbia

Serbia was the largest of the Yugoslav republics in population and territory (see table 19, Appendix). Serbs also had the largest total ethnic representation in the other republics. Throughout the twentieth century, the Serbs saw themselves as the basis of whatever Yugoslav federation existed because of their central role in nineteenth-century liberation struggles and in both world wars. After 1945 this concept was represented in a consistent Serbian drive for strong federal government and a strong, centralized LCY. Virtually all the steps in postwar political decentralization diminished Serbian dominance by giving equal status to all republics and weakening federal institutions. Under Aleksandar Ranković, Serbia conducted a Serbianization campaign against ethnic minorities in Vojvodina, Kosovo, and Bosnia and Hercegovina to advance Yugoslav unity. Ranković's fall in 1966 weakened this drive, and the party reforms of the 1960s and 1970s weakened Serbian influence on party appointments in other republics. The long political dominance of Tito, a Croat, also diminished Serbian power.

The 1974 Constitution rekindled the Serbian drive for dominance by limiting Serbian control of Kosovo and Vojvodina, constituent provinces with large non-Slav ethnic groups. By applying the consensus principle to the assemblies of the republics, the 1974 Constitution gave Kosovo and Vojvodina virtual veto power within the Serbian assembly. This was a serious obstacle to Serbian control over Kosovo in the face of a strong Albanian separatist movement in the province. Therefore, recapture of the Serbian provinces became the chief political goal of all Serbian leaders after 1974. In 1980 a new generation of Serbian political leaders appeared, led by the moderate Ivan Stambolić. Stambolić used conciliation and his considerable national stature to seek the approval of the other republics for reducing provincial autonomy. Failing in this effort, Stambolić was displaced in 1987 by his protégé, Slobodan Milošević. As head of the League of Communists of Serbia, Milošević used the nationalist appeal of the Kosovo issue and a national economic crisis to overcome the Stambolić faction. Milošević's ascendancy was a triumph for the concept of a monolithic Serbian communist party permitting no dissent and aiming for ultimate dominance of the LCY.

In 1988 Serbian officials began orchestrating mass demonstrations to support the Serbian position in Kosovo. These demonstrations led to purges of the party leadership in both Kosovo and Vojvodina. The main goal of the purges was to ensure passage of amendments to the Serbian constitution that effectively abolished the autonomy of the provinces in the name of Serbian political unity. Party leaders in other republics condemned both the purges and the amendments. Serbia was expected to make a strong effort to influence a new round of amendments to the federal Constitution, scheduled for 1992, toward recentralizing political institutions under greater Serbian control.

At the end of the 1980s, Milošević completely dominated Serbian politics, using mass demonstrations and media campaigns in every republic except Slovenia to stir support for Serbia against the Kosovo drive for separatism. In 1989 Serbia established direct popular election of its president and assembly delegates, but nomination of all candidates remained under party control. The idea of legalizing opposition parties received little attention by the Serbian party, which through 1990 gave only lip service to pluralism within the party. Nonpolitical alternative groups such as the Writers' Association of Serbia were permitted. By 1990 the dictatorial and manipulative image of Milošević, particularly his unyielding approach to the Kosovo issue, had isolated Serbia politically within the federation. Only Montenegro continued to vote consistently with Serbia on federal issues. By contrast, Milošević's tough nationalist approach to "Serbian unification" made him very popular with his fellow Serbs, who often compared him to Tito. In 1989 Milošević was elected by a wide margin as president of Serbia on a platform of political and economic reform. The Serb-Slovene conflict escalated in 1990 when the Serbian government ordered the severing of commercial ties with Slovenia in retaliation for the Slovenian prohibition of Serbian nationalist demonstrations in Ljubljana.

Kosovo

The province of Kosovo, formerly called Kosovo-Metohija, became the locus of an important political issue during the late 1960s. Removal of the Ranković state security system in 1966 allowed the ethnic Albanian majority in Kosovo to demonstrate for improvement of very poor economic and political conditions. In the next decade, a number of Albanian nationalist groups were active on a small scale in Kosovo. The decentralizing effect of the 1974 Constitution further reduced oppression of Albanians in the province; however, loosening state control increased the scale and visibility of nationalist disturbances in the 1970s. Large-scale demonstrations in 1981 led to a complete purge of the Kosovo party, a harsh security crackdown, and bitter relations between Albania and Yugoslavia (see Foreign Policy, this ch.).

In the 1980s, the gravity of the Kosovo issue increased for several reasons: Kosovo's drive for republic status or total separation increasingly was supported by blatant Albanian intervention; Yugoslavia's richest republics were frustrated by federal investment requirements designed to improve Kosovo's economic situation without any return for their money; and uncontrollable nationalism in one part of the federation threatened to encourage similar bursts of independence elsewhere in the multinational state. The use of the Kosovo issue to reinspire Serbian nationalism was especially worrisome to other republics, while it radicalized most of Yugoslavia's Albanian population. In 1989 Milošević called Kosovo "the heart of Serbia," citing Kosovo's history as the center of the medieval Serbian kingdom that ended in a storied defeat by the Turks in 1389 (see The Serbs and Serbia, Vojvodina, and Montenegro, ch. 1). However, Kosovo had similar historical significance for its largely Albanian population of the late twentieth century; this created an ethnic political struggle that some observers compared to the West Bank situation in the Middle East.

By 1988 intensified political demonstrations and the deadlock of the Serbian and Albanian wings of the Kosovo party provided a

Nationalist Serbs in anti-Tito demonstration, Belgrade, 1990
Courtesy Charles Sudetic

pretext for political intervention by the Serbian government in Kosovo. A thorough Serbianization campaign begun in 1987 had undercut local compromise efforts by removing all party officials showing sympathy for the Kosovan nationalist cause. By one estimate, 485,000 Kosovans were arrested between 1981 and 1987. Civil rights increasingly were suspended. The intervention also eliminated the influence of Azem Vlasi, an ethnic Albanian who had been a strong, moderate spokesman for liberalization in the Kosovo League of Communists. Vlasi and his colleagues were purged in 1989, and their prolonged trial by the Serbian government for counterrevolutionary activities brought strong condemnation from Slovenia and Croatia.

The internal politics of Kosovo were dominated by severe economic backwardness and hatred between the Albanian majority and the Serbian minority. Conditions worsened in the 1980s despite disproportionately high national investment in the region (see Regional Disparities, ch. 3). Although the Serbs claimed that the Albanians ran an organized campaign to drive out Slavs, economic conditions were at least as instrumental in the decline of the Serbian population. Many Albanians also left to seek employment elsewhere. After the purge of 1989, the Kosovo League of Communists and the provincial assembly were puppet organizations controlled from Belgrade—a situation that exacerbated nationalist feeling and protests. In 1990 political control of the province still eluded the Serbian party, which continued its polemics with the Slovenes and Croats over Kosovo policy. An opposition group, the Democratic Alliance of Kosovo, began a propaganda campaign against the Serbs and the League of Communists of Kosovo that year. In 1990 the fragmentation of the LCY at its Fourteenth Party Congress provoked a new series of violent demonstrations against Serbian oppression. The FEC drafted a plan to alleviate the Kosovo crisis, but factions in the Federal Assembly delayed its passage.

Vojvodina

Vojvodina, the second province of the Serbian Republic, occupied a much more favorable economic and geographic position than Kosovo, but its political status was equally ambiguous in the 1980s. This was emphasized in 1981, when ethnic Hungarians demonstrated in support of the Kosovan nationalists. In 1987 the president of Vojvodina rejected categorically Serbia's proposal that provincial autonomy be repealed. In late 1988 mass pro-Serbian demonstrations orchestrated by Milošević in Vojvodina forced resignation of the Vojvodina provincial party presidium, which was replaced by a pro-Serbian group. This move ensured support for the recentralization amendments to the Serbian constitution in 1989. In the Serbian presidential election of 1989, Milošević received a strong majority in Vojvodina, but not in Kosovo. Vojvodinian political leaders of the new regime firmly supported amendment of the Serbian constitution and other pro-Serbian positions. The region had a history of relative stability in the Austro-Hungarian Empire, and the border with neighboring Hungary was tranquil. The ethnic Hungarian population was much smaller (16 percent in 1991, down from 19 percent in 1981) than the Albanian population of Kosovo; the nationality key, which required balanced representation in party and state for the major ethnic groups in Yugoslavia, did not apply to the ethnic Hungarians in Vojvodina, but the province's relative prosperity precluded major political unrest. In 1990 Hungarian activists formed the Democratic Community of Vojvodina Hungarians (DCVH) to advance cultural autonomy and eventual self-rule for the Hungarian minority. Strongly backing a united Yugoslavia, the DCVH advocated equal status for the Hungarian language and publications in Vojvodina and restoration of autonomy for the province rather than independence from Serbia.

Croatia

Like Slovenia, Croatia was a relatively wealthy northwestern republic with longstanding cultural ties to Western Europe and a tolerance for liberal political experimentation. The removal of Ranković in 1966 unleashed a strong Croatian nationalist movement, led by the Matica Hrvatska society. The movement played on Croatian fears of Serbian dominance and sought political reforms that would substantially increase Croatian autonomy, but it clashed with Serbian and Slovenian interests and threatened the unity of the federation. Tito's intervention to purge the nationalist elements of the Croatian party in 1972 moderated the republic's political climate for the next two decades.

The influence of the moderate wing of the League of Communists of Croatia was felt in the Serb-Slovene polemics of the 1980s, when the Croats often attempted to act as mediators and avoid reviving the ancient Serb-Croat nationalist antagonism within their republic. Because 30 percent of the members of the League of Communists of Croatia were Serbs in 1989, a substantial difference of opinion arose by the end of the decade as to Croatia's proper position toward the issues in the Serb-Slovene dispute. The 1989 election of the moderate Ante Marković, a Croat, as a reform prime minister, moderated Croatia's position on some federal issues. Beginning in 1988, however, both official and unofficial Croatian sources were highly critical of the policies of Milošević, particularly his manipulation of party politics in Vojvodina and the staging of demonstrations in the Croatian district of Knin, a Serbian enclave. The issue of the Serbian minority promised further conflict when Vojvodina proposed creation of four autonomous provinces in Croatia, all with large Serbian populations. Croatia strongly supported Slovenia on the Serbian trade embargo issue in early 1990. Such issues caused heated polemics between Serbia and Croatia and between pro- and anti-Serbian factions of the League of Communists of Croatia.

In 1989 the League of Communists of Croatia followed the Slovene party in legalizing opposition parties and establishing multiparty elections. The republic amended its constitution in 1990 to create the statutory basis for such elections. In 1989 the League of Communists of Croatia became the first Yugoslav party organization at any level to hold direct elections of party officials. Among noncommunist groups formed that year were the Association for a Yugoslav Democratic Initiative (which had thirteen affiliates throughout Yugoslavia in 1990), the Croatian Democratic Union, and the Croatian Social Liberal Alliance, all with strong reformist platforms. The Croatian Democratic Union, led by former Tito colleague Franjo Tudjman, won a sweeping victory in the first Croatian ultiparty election in 1990, forming the first postwar noncommunist government in Yugoslavia. Because that coalition had a nationalist and separatist platform, its success intensified the threat of secession and national collapse. Bosnia and Hercegovina feared that Croatia planned a takeover of Bosnian territory that was once part of Croatia. In the election, the reorganized League of Communists of Croatia and the reform Coalition of People's Accord trailed the Croatian Democratic Union, in that order. These developments in Croatia consolidated the "northwest bloc" of Slovenia and Croatia in Yugoslav politics, put those republics into the mainstream of East European political reform, and widened the gap between them and Serbia.

Montenegro

In the divisive late 1980s, the political position of Montenegro remained closer to that of Serbia than did that of any other republic. This was because of a close ethnic connection between the Serbs and the Montenegrin majority of the population and because Montenegrins were the second Slavic minority "persecuted" in Kosovo—giving them an anti-Albanian nationalist cause similar to that of the Serbs. Montenegro's relatively weak economy made it dependent on the continued strength of the federation. Like Serbia, Montenegro was independent through most of the nineteenth century, a factor that influenced the Montenegrin view of nationalism in the twentieth century.

Montenegro was a strong supporter of Serbian constitutional amendments limiting provincial autonomy in 1989, and party speakers consistently criticized Slovenia's independent stance and its position on Kosovo. Internally, some progressive movement occurred in Montenegrin politics at the end of the 1980s. A traditionally conservative government was ousted in 1988, following mass protests of economic and political conditions by workers and students, who received strong support from the Youth League of Montenegro. Six months later the entire central committee of the League of Communists of Montenegro was forced to resign, and a new central committee was named following a second wave of demonstrations against government inaction. The average age of the new central committee was forty, and the party filled many positions with former protest leaders. This removed the remaining members of the Tito generation from power in Montenegro. Nenad Bučin, elected by referendum as Montenegrin representative to the State Presidency in 1989 advocated government participation by noncommunists. Alternative groups were nominally legalized in 1989, but did not immediately receive status or public access equal to that of the Montenegrin communists.

208

*Voting in the first multiparty
election in Croatia, 1990
Courtesy Charles Sudetic*

Bosnia and Hercegovina

In the 1980s, the political positions of Bosnia and Hercegovina (respectively, the northern and southern parts of a region administered as a unit since the eighteenth century) were consistently conservative and cool to the reforms adopted in other republics. This political atmosphere changed dramatically in the late 1980s. The entire political structure of Bosnia and Hercegovina was shaken by the Agrokomerc banking scandal of 1987, which the Yugoslav press compared to the American Watergate scandal. Hamdija Pozderac, vice president and representative of Bosnia and Hercegovina in the national State Presidency, was forced to resign because of his link to Agrokomerc. A number of republic-level officials also resigned, and more than 100 party members were arrested. The scandal revealed corrupt financial dealings of politicians all over Yugoslavia, but public trust was most badly damaged in the republic where the scandal began. After wholesale replacement of political figures, a young group of progressives, led by Bosnia and Hercegovina president Nijaz Djuraković, came to power in 1989.

When the new Yugoslav State Presidency was chosen in 1989, students and progressive members of the republic's Socialist Alliance of Working People exerted pressure for popular election of the new representative from Bosnia and Hercegovina. Although this did not occur, pressure for democratization was a significant new phenomenon. On national issues, Bosnia and Hercegovina reflected its own multiethnic composition of Serbs, Croats, and nearly 40 percent Muslim Slavs. The ethnic balance, which had been maintained by conservative policies until the late 1980s, was threatened by intensification of nationalist movements elsewhere in the federation. By 1990 the republic found itself torn and manipulated by the Serb-Slovene and Serb-Croat conflicts. The official position of Bosnia and Hercegovina in 1990 strongly supported reconciliation of ethnic differences in the federation, while defending the ethnic individuality of the republics against homogenization.

Macedonia

Next to Kosovo, Macedonia was the most economically deprived region of Yugoslavia. Like Kosovo, it was dependent on the richer republics for financial support throughout the postwar period. For the first forty years after World War II, political life remained placid and under the firm control of the local party. But with the explosion of nationalist feeling elsewhere in Yugoslavia in the late 1980s, the presence of substantial Albanian minorities began to complicate regional politics. Strikes and protests against economic conditions began in 1987. After that time, ethnic tensions mounted between Albanians and Macedonians, especially in the Albanian ghettos of Skopje, the capital city. Symbolic acts by Macedonian authorities worsened the situation. In 1989 the Macedonian assembly ratified a constitutional amendment deleting ''Albanian and Turkish minorities'' from the definition of the republic in the 1974 republican constitution. This move, which paralleled the Serbian constitutional limitation of autonomy in its provinces, drew criticism domestically and in other republics for its nationalist overtones. Macedonia also had a centuries-long dispute with neighboring Bulgaria and Greece over the identity and treatment of Macedonian minorities in those countries. This external conflict was unique among the Yugoslav republics, and it added an independent quality to the cause of Macedonian nationalism.

As a small republic with voting power equal to all other republics, Macedonia was pressured and manipulated by both Serbia and Slovenia in the late 1980s. During the late 1980s, Macedonian policy concentrated alternately on allegiance to Serbia and Macedonian nationalism, depending on which of two factions prevailed in the local political establishment. In 1990 the top Macedonian policy makers still strongly supported a united Yugoslavia and opposed legalization of rival parties. However, these policies were increasingly challenged by an independent political faction led by Vasil Tupurkovski, Macedonian representative to the State Presidency of Yugoslavia. In 1990 Tupurkovski's faction moved toward formation of a separate party advocating political reform.

The Public and Political Decision Making

Yugoslavia had a long tradition of open criticism of oppression, corruption, and incompetence in government. Yugoslav governments also had a tradition of selective repression of opposition movements and leaders. As the initial split from Soviet dogma widened through the postwar decades, intellectuals such as Milovan Djilas and Dobrica Ćosić, and groups such as Praxis and the editors of youth newspapers, took advantage of partial constitutional guarantees to criticize their government and society. In the 1980s, selective prosecution for such actions diminished, and by 1990 the Yugoslav public received a wide range of information and opportunities for expressing opinions.

Djilas, Praxis, and Intellectual Repression

The most celebrated instance of dissident repression in postwar Yugoslavia was the case of Milovan Djilas. His often-published heretical political views brought Djilas official denunciation by the LCY and imprisonment in the 1950s and 1960s, despite his earlier close association with Tito. Djilas was released from prison after the Ranković era ended in 1966, but he was harassed long afterward, and similar cases occurred through the following decades. The majority of postwar dissident writers were students and academics whose published material criticized the Yugoslav political system or advocated regional political diversity. Mihajlo Mihajlov, for example, was tried and jailed several times between 1965 and 1975 for propaganda deemed dangerous to the state. In many instances, established writers such as the Serb Dobrica Ćosić were allowed to criticize the regime harshly (Ćosić called Tito a "spiritual nihilist"), while less influential figures were prosecuted for expressing the same ideas.

In 1968 a group of intellectuals connected with the journal *Praxis* began conducting an open polemic with the theories of party ideologist Eduard Kardelj. The group soon gained a substantial audience for its attacks on censorship, bureaucracy, and economic planning mistakes. Because the Praxis group used Marxist argumentation very effectively, many of its ideas were applied by economic and political reformers in the early 1980s. Tito finally succeeded in silencing Praxis in 1975 as part of a crackdown on intellectual dissenters centered in Yugoslav universities.

The most widely publicized dissident trial of the 1980s involved the "Belgrade Six," a group of intellectuals arrested in 1984 for planning a meeting with Djilas (whose views remained officially heretical). The group, which for several years had official permission to meet, received international publicity that eventually forced the government to free three members and reduce the sentences of the others.

Throughout the 1980s, measures to control free speech had a legal basis in the uneven civil rights provisions of the Yugoslav Constitution. The Constitution did not specifically protect privacy of communication from police interference; the ill-defined concepts of "hostile propaganda," "fostering national hatred," and "derogatory statements" were used to silence troublesome protest voices, most often on the sensitive Kosovo issue; and the lack of a habeas corpus principle made arbitrary detention legal. Although criminal trials in Yugoslavia were open to the public, political trials often were closed in the 1980s. Such techniques were used irregularly, but their existence remained a curb on popular expression (see Dissidence, ch. 5).

In the 1980s, the majority of known political prisoners in Yugoslavia were ethnic Albanians involved in the Kosovo liberation movement. In 1987 nearly all prisoners charged with "most serious political criminal acts" were in this category. According to Yugoslav sources, 1,652 people were tried for political crimes between 1981 and 1985. Isolated crackdowns on dissent occurred in Serbia (a political show trial in 1984), Slovenia (army court proceedings against government critics in 1988), and Croatia (a blacklist of Croatian intelligentsia in 1984). But public criticism of the government continued in spite of such measures.

Intellectual Opposition Groups

The writers' associations of several republics developed large followings in the 1980s. The Serbian and Slovenian associations exchanged polemics from opposite sides of the Kosovo issue, echoing the positions of their respective republics. The national Writers' Association of Yugoslavia held only two congresses between 1965 and 1985 because of regional squabbles within the umbrella organization. However, in the late 1980s the Slovenian and Serbian associations expressed similar positions on issues such as diversification of political parties, the danger of dictatorship, and human rights. In 1982 the Writers' Association of Serbia, which was especially well organized and influential, formed the Committee for the Protection of Artistic Freedom in response to the political trial of poet Gojko Djogo. In 1986 the Committee for the Protection of Humanity and the Environment was formed under the auspices of the Serbian association, and it was given legal status by the government. The writers' groups used forums such as press conferences and open letters to express harsh criticism of Yugoslav political life. The 1984 trial of the Belgrade Six caused Ćosić to form the Committee for the Defense of Freedom of Thought and Expression. This group of highly respected intellectuals issued petitions for drastic political change, and, despite being officially illegal, it was able to meet openly because of the stature of its members.

Generally speaking, Serbia produced the most vigorous and varied intellectual dissent of the 1970s and 1980s. Most Serbian intellectuals supported the 1989 amendments to the Serbian constitution, but at the same time many backed Ćosić's demands for democratization of the Serbian system once the two provinces were "reunited" with Serbia. In 1989 the Serbian Writers' Association issued a public appeal that included the following points: abolition of the single-party system and of the LCY's power monopoly; full respect for human rights; equal rights for all citizens before the law; equal rights to vote and be elected to office, irrespective of political affiliation; an independent judiciary; and freedom of the press. In the same year, the Serbian group began criticizing the nationalist position of Milošević, and some factions discussed transforming the association into a political party.

The Media

Throughout the postwar period, the Yugoslav press differed from press institutions in the other East European communist countries because it saw itself primarily as a source of information and only secondarily as an instrument of party control—despite the official party view that the press should be primarily a vehicle of political education. In the 1980s, the expression of independent viewpoints in the Yugoslav press generally grew. In 1981 protests by the journalistic community broke a government-enforced silence about ethnic strife in Kosovo. A new federal press law was passed in 1985 to broaden and standardize the types of information available to the public through the newspapers. During that time the press consistently criticized government political and economic policy, as well as the FEC and the national and regional parties. The State Presidency received less negative comment. However, journalists were required to join the party-controlled League of Journalists of Yugoslavia, and expulsion from the league meant the end of a career. Topics generally closed to objective press discussion in the 1980s were foreign policy, revision of official national history, religious policy, and nationalities policy. In the politically charged period of the Fourteenth Party Congress (January 1990), press restraint decreased noticeably as dissident movements, corruption, and prison conditions received particular attention.

Besides the effect of censorship, the lack of a centralized information system also made the flow of public information through Yugoslavia uneven. Each Yugoslav republic had its own press system, and the media operated as individual self-managed enterprises. Tanjug, the national news agency, acted as the ''official source'' of stories, and its coverage provided guidance in the handling of controversial topics. Because publications were not subsidized, the profit motive made periodicals responsive to reader needs.

All media required the political sponsorship of the national or regional socialist alliances, and each system reflected the national political position of its region. The most extreme example of this in the late 1980s was the daily newspaper *Politika,* published in Belgrade. That daily, an object of great respect since its founding before World War I, came under the complete control of the Milošević government. As the main organ of the Serbian nationalist propaganda campaign based on the Kosovo issue, *Politika* engaged in sharp polemics with *Delo,* the official organ of the Slovenian Socialist Alliance of Working People, and other daily publications. By 1990 other elements of the Serbian media were also controlled by the Milošević faction. In general, the Yugoslav youth press was the most troublesome to political authorities; periodicals in this category discussed all taboo topics without being eliminated, but they were constantly harassed by authorities. One of the most controversial periodicals of the late 1980s was *Mladina,* a Slovenian student weekly whose wide circulation spread the most radical political ideas developed in that republic.

Censorship

The print and broadcast media were nominally free of censorship in the 1980s, but printed material was reviewed by official publication boards that ensured party control. Those boards were able to stop publication of some new radical periodicals, but in 1985 their ban of *Mladina* was overruled by the Slovenian supreme court. Only postpublication censorship was exercised for periodicals, and individual banned issues circulated widely in spite of the system. Over a dozen Croatian magazines and student newspapers were banned because of anti-Serbian positions in the late 1980s. Late in the 1980s, book censorship was loosened and cases of official interference decreased. The list of taboo topics for books was similar to that for periodicals. Foreign dissident writings were widely

First televised Orthodox Easter service, Cathedral of St. Sava, Belgrade, 1990
Courtesy Charles Sudetic

available, as were the writings of Djilas, which still were banned officially in 1990.

For the first time in 1990, political opposition parties received permission to televise their views prior to an election. Slovenian and Croatian self-managed television enterprises reserved air time for all parties participating in elections for the republican assemblies. The stations observed strict equality of time allotment. Commercial purchase of additional time was forbidden, to avoid giving richer parties disproportionate access to the viewing public.

Foreign Policy

With the exception of the first three postwar years, the foreign policy of Yugoslavia emphasized balanced relations between East and West and strong links with as many nonaligned nations as possible. As in domestic politics, a primary motivation for this course was to differentiate Yugoslavia from the members of the Soviet alliance; having made that distinction in all areas by 1952, Tito pragmatically sought commercial and political relations wherever and whenever advantageous. After weathering numerous crises in its relations with both superpowers, Yugoslavia entered the 1990s as titular head of a diminished Nonaligned Movement; political and economic reversals in Eastern Europe and the Soviet Union forced Yugoslavia to move closer to the wealthy West European nations, with the ultimate goal of membership in the European Economic Community (EEC—see Glossary).

The Government Foreign Policy Mechanism

The foreign policy of Yugoslavia was conducted at the highest level by the State Presidency, the president of which was the official representative of the country. The line of authority extended from the president through the FEC to the Secretariat for Foreign Affairs. Nationality quotas for personnel in the secretariat and subordinate levels ensured each republic an equal voice in foreign policy formulation. The quota was also used in making foreign service appointments and staffing embassies abroad—a policy criticized because it did not always permit the most qualified personnel access to foreign policy positions. Committees of the LCY and SAWPY (also apportioned by nationality) also had significant foreign policy input.

Nonalignment

Beginning with its exit from the Soviet sphere in 1948, Yugoslavia sought appropriate alliances to ensure its security. As early as 1953, relations were established with nonaligned Asian countries. In 1954 Tito suggested, then withdrew from, a Balkan alliance with Greece and Turkey. When the colonial empires of the West European nations broke up in the decades following, Yugoslavia became a leader of the bloc of new nations created by that process. The former colonies considered the economic and political success of the Yugoslav nonalignment policy a positive model, and Tito joined Jawaharlal Nehru of India, Sukarno of Indonesia, Kwame Nkrumah of Ghana, and Gamal Abdul Nasser of Egypt as founders of the Nonaligned Movement in the mid-1950s. Founding principles of that movement were opposition to all foreign intervention and peaceful coexistence. The official nonaligned position of Yugoslavia was declared at the Belgrade Conference of Nonaligned Nations in 1961. In the 1950s and 1960s, Yugoslavia's position gave it international prestige because both the United States and the Soviet Union required support from the growing bloc of independent nations it led.

Within the nonaligned group, Yugoslavia leaned strongly toward the Arab nations and supported the Palestine Liberation Organization against Israel—mainly because of Tito's friendship with Nasser and the influence of the large Yugoslav Muslim population. Tito personified Yugoslavia's international position; in the 1960s and 1970s, he traveled worldwide to cement relations in the

Third World. Although Nikita S. Khrushchev had mended Soviet relations with Yugoslavia in the mid-1950s, that relationship was threatened by periodic Soviet expansionism, and Tito successfully sought to balance Western and Soviet influences. Part of that balancing act was development of close relations with China in the 1970s; at that time, China was hostile to the Soviet Union and opening communications with the West, making it an effective counterbalance for Tito. Yugoslav-Chinese relations remained warm through the 1980s.

In the 1970s, Yugoslavia became a moderate force in the Nonaligned Movement, balancing the strong pro-Soviet influence of Fidel Castro (to whom Tito had initially given strong support). Castro's election as chairman of the Nonaligned Movement in 1979 was considered a defeat for Tito. Between 1955 and 1979, the Nonaligned Movement grew from 25 to 117 member countries, largely because of Tito's leadership. When Tito died in 1980, Yugoslavia lost its leadership role to Cuba, and the Nonaligned Movement leaned decidedly toward the Soviet side. But Yugoslavia regained an important role in the eighth summit meeting (1986) of the organization. In 1989 the ninth summit meeting was held in Belgrade, and Yugoslavia became leader of the movement until 1992. In the 1980s, the main Yugoslav role in the Nonaligned Movement was using the provisions of the Helsinki Accords (see Glossary) of 1975 to lobby for easing the Cold War tensions that flared in Europe and mediating conflicts between Third World nations such as Iraq and Iran. Yugoslavia was especially concerned with Middle Eastern events that endangered its oil supply.

Although emphasis changed somewhat, Tito's nonalignment policy remained in place for the entire decade following his death. Although hosting the meeting and regaining chairmanship of the Nonaligned Movement improved Yugoslavia's international standing, many Yugoslavs (especially in Croatia and Slovenia) questioned the value of a leadership position among a group of impoverished nations long after the initial purpose of the movement had changed. The credibility of the movement decreased in the 1980s because of Castro's influence, and by 1990 the disappearance of monolithic communism from Eastern Europe had changed the entire definition of nonalignment. Even in Tito's time, Yugoslavia gained only prestige from its leadership of Third World countries poorer than itself; it lost much money in unrepaid loans to those countries. As the 1990s began, domestic pressures increased to strengthen political and economic ties with Western Europe, which could provide much-needed economic aid.

The Soviet Union

Yugoslav relations with the Soviet Union remained stable in the decade after Tito's death. Through the mid-1980s, Yugoslav policy toward the Soviet Union was partly based on the possibility that one side in an internal Yugoslav ethnic conflict might invite the Soviet Union to intervene, providing a pretext for restoring Yugoslavia to the Warsaw Pact. The 1948 rift with the Soviet Union was repaired by the Belgrade Declaration of 1955, in which the Soviet Union conceded the right of other socialist countries to interpret Marxism in their own way. But in the ensuing three decades, covert Soviet contacts with illegal nationalist and pro-Soviet groups in Yugoslavia kept alive the fear that the Soviet Union might intervene (see Threat Perception, ch. 5).

As a leader of the nonaligned movement, Tito often criticized Soviet policy. His stand against the 1968 Soviet-led Warsaw Pact invasion of Czechoslovakia caused friction, and relations remained uneven throughout the 1970s. That decade culminated in a strong Yugoslav condemnation of the Soviet invasion of Afghanistan in 1979. But in the 1980s, official Yugoslav policy favored political and economic rapprochement, and the Soviet Union remained the country's largest trading partner throughout the period (see Trading Partners, ch. 3). In that decade, the two countries remained ideological rivals in the socialist world, with Afghanistan as the chief subject of Yugoslav polemics against Soviet policy. In 1988 Soviet General Secretary Mikhail S. Gorbachev and Defense Minister Dmitrii Iazov made official visits to reassure the Yugoslavs of continued military and political stability between the two countries. The fall of East European communist governments in 1989 eased the threat that the Soviet Union would invade Yugoslavia under any circumstances and provided an opportunity to shift the emphasis of Yugoslav trade toward the West.

The United States

Tito cultivated positive relations with the United States to balance Soviet influence and to receive the substantial American economic aid that became available after his break with the Soviet Union. Tension periodically resulted from Yugoslav Middle East policy, Tito's frequent support of Soviet causes, and from terrorist acts committed by Yugoslav émigrés in the United States. However, Tito and his successors found important issues upon which to continue friendly relations with the United States through the 1980s. The Yugoslav policy of nonalignment precluded formal security treaties, but protection of Yugoslav soveignty was internationally

Prime Minister Marković with President Bush, Washington, 1990
Courtesy White House Photography Office

understood as part of United States-European policy—especially after President Jimmy Carter made a specific policy statement to that effect in 1978. Tension rose in 1989, when resolutions of the United States Congress condemned Yugoslav human rights policies and were labeled as uninformed interference in internal Yugoslav affairs. The stimulus for this disagreement was Yugoslav policy toward Dobroslav Paraga, an exiled Croatian separatist who became a leader of extremist émigrés in North America. On an official visit to the United States following that exchange, Prime Minister Marković explained Yugoslav reform and human rights policies, and United States officials urged that Yugoslavia follow the contemporary reform pattern of other East European communist countries. Both sides agreed that the visit improved the climate for United States financial support of economic reforms and United States understanding of internal Yugoslav political conditions.

European Neighbors

The issue of Macedonian nationality caused friction between Yugoslavia and neighboring Bulgaria and Greece, which contained large Macedonian minorities. Throughout the postwar period, the Yugoslav press propagandized against Bulgarian expansionist policies toward Macedonia and the failure to recognize Macedonians as a separate nationality in Bulgaria. Although the Bulgarian press reciprocated much more strongly after the 1989 change of government in Bulgaria, the two governments showed little desire to magnify an issue that had been at the center of the Balkan wars before World War I (see The Balkan Wars and World War I, ch. 1).

In the mid-1980s, the Yugoslav press strongly criticized the Greek government for failing to recognize the Macedonian Orthodox Church. But relations with Greece were generally warm in the 1980s, and Yugoslavia backed the Greeks against the Turks on the Cyprus issue early in the decade. For diplomatic reasons, the Yugoslav government did not permit Macedonian nationalist writers to protest Greek discrimination against Macedonians until the 1980s. The other ethnic-based foreign policy dilemma was dealing with Albanian intervention in Kosovo. The enmity between Yugoslavia and Albania began with Tito's repudiation of Stalinism and with personal animosity between Albanian president Enver Hoxha and Tito. Stalinist Albania and revisionist Yugoslavia remained hostile throughout the postwar period, with a brief thaw in the late 1960s. For Albania, economic discontent in adjoining Kosovo was a prime weapon throughout the postwar period in preventing penetration of Yugoslav influence into its closed society and in discrediting Yugoslav economic and political innovations. Albania maintained strong cultural ties with Kosovo (which contained over half as many Albanians as Albania itself), while remaining isolated from the rest of Yugoslavia. Officially, the Yugoslav government strongly condemned Albanian intervention in Kosovo, although the northwestern republics of Croatia and Slovenia insisted that Serbian intransigence was the root of the Kosovo problem.

Relations with Hungary, the other neighbor with a substantial ethnic minority within Yugoslavia, continued without major complication. In light of Hungarian political reforms, new agreements in 1989 and 1990 demilitarized the common border and expanded economic ties, emphasizing regional cooperation that also included Austria.

The Middle East and Western Europe

Yugoslav policy toward the Middle East continued the Tito line through the 1980s, supporting the Palestine Liberation Organization (PLO) and forswearing relations with Israel. This policy continued to be driven by the need to protect sources of oil and other imports from that area. When PLO head Yasir Arafat made an official visit to Belgrade in 1988 to urge that Yugoslavia act as a peacemaker in the Middle East, he was received warmly. In 1989 Israel urged that Yugoslavia accord it diplomatic recognition so that the 1989 summit meeting of the Nonaligned Movement also could be used for advancing peace in the Middle East. Yugoslavia did not do so. At the turn of the decade, Yugoslavia also sought to resume the close relations with Egypt initially established between Tito and Nasser. This was given priority because Egypt had rejoined the League of Arab States and become a major force in regional peace efforts.

By 1990 Yugoslavia's relations with West European nations were defined by the need to participate more fully in European markets and alleviate a grave balance of payments situation. Budimir Lončar, secretary for foreign affairs in the Marković government, was especially active in talks with Italy and the Federal Republic of Germany (West Germany), Yugoslavia's largest West European trade partners in the 1980s, at the turn of the decade (see Foreign Trade, ch. 3). In the case of both countries, past political issues hampered progress: West Germany continued to refuse World War II reparations claims by Yugoslavia, and bad feelings were caused by treatment of the Slovenian minority in Italy. Another problem in the late 1980s was the decline of leftist political parties in West European countries, notably Italy, France, and West Germany; those parties naturally were more sympathetic to Yugoslav positions than the more conservative groups that dominated by 1990. In its relations with the North Atlantic Treaty Organization (NATO), Yugoslavia pressed for designation of the Mediterranean Sea as a "zone of peace" to eliminate the danger posed by American missiles in nearby Italy and to defuse tension in the Middle East.

Yugoslavia made frequent overtures for membership in the EEC to expand markets for its exports in the 1980s and to compensate for increased protectionism within the community. The EEC made clear the requirement that Yugoslavia establish a national multiparty system before admittance would be considered. This increased the incentive to end domination of the LCY and follow the example of liberalization set by 1990 in Eastern Europe. Meanwhile, Yugoslavia built a potential bridge to the EEC by establishing closer ties with members of the European Free Trade Association (EFTA—see Glossary), a group of neutral European nations given special trade status by the EEC (see Trading Partners, ch. 3).

The Political Agenda for the 1990s

As Yugoslavia entered the 1990s, four major political problems remained unsolved: achieving meaningful, nationwide economic reform to save the country from the economic decay that had occurred in the 1980s; finding and institutionalizing procedures for compromise among regions with increasingly diverse political and economic interests; forging useful political relations with Western nations willing to provide economic aid and making foreign policy adjustments to harmonize with new political conditions in Europe; and negating the divisive influence of the rotation system to ensure selection of national leaders competent to focus attention on solving all-Yugoslav issues. Ultimately, resolution of all those problems depended on restructuring the national political system to allow for multiple parties and accurate representation of current economic interest groups; such representation required a breakdown of the traditional regional fiefdoms of party and enterprise groupings.

Because self-managed socialism was the foundation of both economic and political institutions in Yugoslavia, economic and political issues were inseparable in the post-Tito period. For that reason, formation of economic policy was the main driving force of political decision making in the late 1980s and early 1990s. An important aspect of the economic reform issue was the desperate need for an all-Yugoslav program for equitable division of the natural resources distributed so unevenly among the six republics. Without unanimous backing for such a program by all six republics, only the richer republics could function in the market economy specified in reform programs; however, without sufficient motivation to continue their financial contributions to the federation, Slovenia and Croatia would declare economic independence and demolish the national economy.

Because most members of the intelligentsia belonged to the party, criticism and reform proposals from that important quarter were frequently cautious in the 1980s. Although new political energy and diversity in several republics promised the eventual reversal of this tendency and the uprooting of old-line centers of political power, such change had not yet altered the paths of political power in 1990. Historically, the shape of Yugoslav regional political interests changed only in times of common threat (such as invasion or economic disaster) or if a strong leader were skillful and determined enough to focus the attention of all factions on survival of the federation. In 1990 all regions continued to declare their commitment to Tito's federal goal as a matter of common survival. The less wealthy republics—Montenegro, Macedonia, and Bosnia and Hercegovina—adhered most strongly to this line because they obviously could not survive outside the federal structure. Meanwhile, the most powerful republics—Croatia, Serbia, and Slovenia—took advantage of the vacuum in the national leadership to alternate between defending the federation and asserting local sovereignty, depending on political conditions.

But while politicians were swearing allegiance to the Yugoslav nation, the updating and restating of historical conflicts continued into the 1990s, always threatening to overcome constructive political approaches. Long-standing animosities remained between Serbia and Croatia, the Albanian minority and the Macedonians in Macedonia, and the Slavic minority and the Albanian majority in Kosovo (see Macedonia, ch. 1; The Kingdom of Yugoslavia, ch. 1; Kosovo, this ch.).

In 1990 the Serbian-Slovenian split in the LCY severely limited the unifying role of that organization and its policy input to the government. Because the party had played the role of national synthesizer of interests, the LCY split also was the final blow for Tito's concept of mandatory consensus among factions in national decision making. Only the Yugoslav government institutions themselves remained in an all-Yugoslav power role, but those institutions had never been tested on their own merits as the final arbiters of conflicting interests on behalf of the federation as a whole.

Besides the task of wholly remaking the Yugoslav economic structure, the government faced an escalating crisis in Kosovo. In 1990 Kosovo was the most critical of many domestic problems unresolved since the 1980s because of the struggle between the Serbian and the Slovenian factions of the party.

As the 1990s began, the political culture of Yugoslavia was in an unprecedented state of flux. To reach his goal of separating his government completely from communist domination, Prime Minister Marković pushed new laws that would allow national, multiparty elections in 1990. Substantial opposition met his proposals in the Federal Assembly and the State Presidency, however—especially because at the time of the proposed changes only Slovenia and Croatia had committed themselves to a multiparty system at the republic level.

In 1990 each side in the Serbian-Slovenian conflict had goals that, if reached, could threaten or enhance the health of the political culture. On the one hand, a reasonable case was made for a strong, Serb-dominated state as the most efficient way to achieve any truly national program; but on the other hand, that scenario promised little progress toward political reform or pluralism, and it threatened the independence of other republics. Diametrically opposed was the position of Croatia and Slovenia, which included political movements promising a highly diversified political culture, with free input from all parts of society. But the efficacy of such a culture in achieving short-range, drastic national reform was very doubtful. Meanwhile, the new East European spirit of democracy infected all the republics and provinces of Yugoslavia through numerous intellectual and media channels. Republic communist parties, many with young, energetic leadership, liberalized their approach to dissent from within, and dozens of noncommunist political groups challenged every orthodox belief of the old order. Many feared that these events would mean total fragmentation of the political structure and a return to the instability that preceded World War II. But the long, slow process of liberalization that Tito initiated in 1948 was clearly accelerating as the 1990s began.

* * *

A number of useful monographs on the Yugoslav political system appeared in the 1980s. *The Politics of Ethnicity in Eastern Europe,* edited by George Klein and Milan J. Reban, contains a chapter summarizing the ethnic dynamics behind contemporary political institutions. *Yugoslavia: Politics, Economics, and Society* by Bruce J. McFarlane, is a multidimensional account that provides historical background as well as contemporary analysis, stressing the linkage of economic and political issues. Harold Lydall's *Yugoslavia in Crisis* also emphasizes economics as a vital component of the contemporary political crisis, with an in-depth description of economic and political institutions. *The Yugoslavs* by Dusko Doder is an informal cultural description providing much insight to the behavior of Yugoslav groups and institutions. *Yugoslavia in the 1980s,* edited by Pedro Ramet, is a collection of essays on political institutions, domestic issues, foreign policy, and Yugoslav political philosophy. Finally, the essay collection entitled *Yugoslavia: A Fractured Federalism,* edited by Dennison Rusinow, covers official and unofficial political power centers and their roles in the decision-making process at all levels of government. (For further information and complete citations, see Bibliography.)

Chapter 5. National Security

Members of Yugoslav People's Army

IN 1990 THE NATIONAL SECURITY of Yugoslavia reflected various strengths and weaknesses of its history, society, economy, and politics. Adhering to its nonaligned foreign policy, Yugoslavia belonged to no military alliance and maintained an omnidirectional defense posture. Although potential invasion by the Soviet Union remained the primary factor in Yugoslav defense planning, external threats to Yugoslavia were greatly reduced in 1990. The country's military doctrine of Total National Defense (TND) emphasized coordination between a standing army and large numbers of ordinary citizens organized into locally based militia units. TND was designed to counter a massive Soviet-led Warsaw Pact invasion. It used the wartime experience of Yugoslavia's partisan guerrilla fighters as its model.

The armed forces consisted of the Yugoslav People's Army (YPA) and the Territorial Defense Forces (TDF). The YPA, a regular force of more than 180,000 troops, was organized into three armed services—the army, the air force, and the navy. Most soldiers in the YPA were conscripts who were led by a professional officer corps. Apparently an effective fighting force, the YPA generally exercised control over the large, militia-like TDF. The YPA exercised autonomy in military matters and also exerted considerable influence within the League of Communists of Yugoslavia (LCY— see Glossary) and the civilian government.

In 1990 the YPA retained both popular prestige and priority access to national economic resources, but circumstances were changing. Some citizens increasingly viewed the YPA as a vehicle for domination by the Republic of Serbia, while others saw it as the country's only safeguard against divisive interests. Meanwhile, economic stringency obliged the YPA to accept reduced budgets and manpower.

In 1990 the internal threats of nationalism (based on claims of nations and nationalities—see Glossary), separatism, and political and economic crises were more acute than any conceivable external threat to Yugoslavia's national security. The YPA's mission to defend the country's independence against external aggression was undisputed. However, its mission of protecting the constitutional order against change from within aroused controversy. The LCY and the civilian government increasingly looked to the YPA to ensure public order against nationalist and separatist activity and the ensuing political and social crises. The military strongly supported continued survival of the unified federal state. However, like Yugoslav society as a whole, the YPA was beset by ethnic tensions.

Josip Broz Tito, the only modern Yugoslav leader to successfully balance military and political roles, believed that the YPA had to protect the established political and economic system against internal opponents because domestic divisions would weaken the country's defense against external threats. In a time of reduced foreign threats, however, many Yugoslav leaders believed the YPA should restrict its role to external defense, minimizing its internal security functions.

Development of the Armed Forces

The history of the Yugoslav nations and nationalities is full of foreign invasion and subjugation. The Ottoman Empire, Habsburg Empire, and Nazi Germany dominated Yugoslav territories to a greater or lesser extent for most of the last 500 years (see Histories of the Yugoslav Peoples to World War I, ch. 1). Times of relative security and independence resulted from an overall strategic balance among great powers or superpowers in Europe. However, the People's Liberation Army and Partisan Detachments of Yugoslavia, commonly known as the Partisans (see Glossary), were an important part of the Allied effort in World War II. Under Tito the Partisans were largely responsible for the liberation of the country; after liberation they were organized well enough to control Yugoslavia politically. The tenacious struggle of the Partisans established a proud and heroic military tradition that extended long into the postwar era. The National Liberation War of 1941–45, as Yugoslav sources called it, remained the central frame of reference for discussing military affairs in 1990.

Early Development

Nomadic tribes sporadically invaded and conquered the disparate peoples living in South Slav lands from Roman times until the nineteenth century. The Serbs resisted but fell under foreign domination for nearly 500 years after the Ottoman Empire defeated them at the Battle of Kosovo Polje in 1389. Of the peoples forming modern Yugoslavia, only the Montenegrins remained independent through the centuries of foreign domination.

The South Slavs were intensely involved in the military maneuvers, power politics, and alliances in Europe that precipitated World War I. In 1912 Serbia joined its smaller neighbors to drive the Ottoman Empire from Macedonia in the First Balkan War. The following year, Serbia successfully contested Bulgarian claims to that territory in the Second Balkan War. During the world war that followed, Serbia was attacked by Austria-Hungary and Germany on northern and southern fronts, and it paid dearly for its earlier victories. In October 1915, Serbian forces retreated from Belgrade to the Adriatic Sea. Evacuated to Greece to fight under a French command, they eventually participated in the defeat of the Central Powers and liberation of Serbia.

Like other small states during the years between the world wars, the Kingdom of the Serbs, Croats, and Slovenes (as present-day Yugoslavia was then called) sought protection in alliances and collective security arrangements. It allied with Czechoslovakia and Romania and signed a treaty of friendship with France. It joined the Balkan Entente with Romania, Greece, and Turkey in 1934. This pact obligated each signatory to defend existing borders in southeastern Europe against aggression by revisionist powers. Nevertheless, for self-protection Yugoslavia gravitated toward Germany and Italy when the major European powers failed to oppose Axis expansionism in the late 1930s. Yugoslavia declined a belated French offer to conclude a mutual assistance pact in 1937. The policy of accommodation to the Axis powers culminated in Yugoslav accession to the pro-Nazi Tripartite Pact on March 25, 1941.

Outraged at the government's cooperation with Nazi Germany, air force General Dušan Simović led a group of military officers in a swift coup d'état. They declared their objections to, but were careful not to abrogate, the Tripartite Pact. Despite their caution, Germany leveled Belgrade with a massive air strike and began a full-scale ground invasion of Yugoslavia in April 1941, without a formal declaration of war.

World War II

The thirty divisions of the Yugoslav army were not equipped or prepared to meet the fifty-two invading German, Italian, and Hungarian divisions and the Bulgarian forces that invaded Macedonia. Lacking modern equipment and adequate mobility and firepower, the Yugoslav army faced a surprise attack on several fronts by superior and heavily armored and mechanized forces. Yugoslav forces retreated rapidly to the center of the country, attempting to use the mountainous coastal areas as a base and to maintain lines of supply to Greece and the Allies. However, German forces captured the supreme command at Sarajevo on April 17, 1941, and Yugoslavia formally surrendered. Germany, Italy, Hungary, Bulgaria, and Albania annexed or occupied parts of the country.

A small group of officers led by Colonel Draža Mihajlović refused to surrender and continued to resist the occupation from a base in western Serbia. They called themselves the Četnik Detachments of the Yugoslav Army of the Fatherland. The Četnici (sing., Četnik—see Glossary) also represented the royal government-in-exile. They received a British military liaison officer and considerable amounts of British supplies and equipment. However, they avoided attacking the occupiers because they feared reprisals against the noncombatant population. The Četnici believed their military actions could not influence the course of the war, and they waited instead for the Allies to defeat the Axis powers. They were later discredited in Yugoslavia as collaborators because of their unwillingness to resist.

The Communist Party of Yugoslavia (CPY) under Tito also refused to accept defeat. It remained inactive, however, until Germany attacked the Soviet Union on June 22, 1941. Through the Comintern (Communist International), the CPY received orders from the Soviet Union to resist the German occupation. Initially, the military committees of the CPY collected arms and organized available manpower. Then they conducted small armed attacks and acts of sabotage against occupying Axis forces. They waged their military campaign without regard to the fate of civilians living under the occupation—often the occupiers executed large numbers of civilians in retaliation for attacks and sabotage. The difference in strategies and political views quickly brought the Četnici and CPY forces into a state of civil war. The former unsuccessfully attempted to attack Tito's headquarters in November 1941.

The CPY military wing formally became the People's Liberation Army and Partisan Detachments of Yugoslavia (commonly known as the Partisans) on December 22, 1941. With approximately 80,000 fighters, the Partisans fought occupying forces, collaborators such as the Ustaše (see Glossary) in Croatia, and their political opponents, the Četnici. By the end of 1942, the Partisans had grown to 150,000 troops organized into two corps, three divisions, thirty-one brigades, and thirty-eight detachments. Axis occupation forces launched several major offensives to destroy the Partisans, but they failed in each case. Although the Partisans liberated some areas of the country, they generally avoided major engagements with superior forces.

Yugoslavia became an unanticipated theater of war for the Axis. Large German forces were forced to remain there to protect lines of supply to Greece and North Africa during the critical year of 1942. Nearly 600,000 Axis troops, thirty-eight divisions in all, were needed to control the country and thus were unavailable as reinforcements for the pivotal battles of El Alamein and Stalingrad. The occupation of Yugoslavia drained significant Axis manpower and resources from other theaters over a long period of time. Partisan pressure was a factor in Italy's withdrawal from the war in September 1943. When Italy's twenty divisions left Yugoslav territory, Germany had to commit even greater numbers of soldiers to maintain its position there. At maximum strength, the German occupying army included twenty-six divisions.

By late 1943, the Partisans began to resemble a regular army. With captured or abandoned Italian arms, they armed 300,000 combatants in eight corps and twenty-six divisions. At the end of 1943, virtually all Allied military assistance was transferred from the Četnici to the Partisans, whose operations had the potential of hastening the defeat of Germany. From then until the end of the war, the Partisans received over 100 tanks, 300 field guns, 2,000 mortars, 13,000 machine guns, and 130,000 rifles from Britain and the United States. The Soviet Union provided even larger numbers of guns, mortars, and machine guns.

As the Germans retreated from Greece through Yugoslavia and the Soviet Red Army advanced into Romania in 1944, the Partisans cleared most of the German troops from the country while simultaneously battling their domestic Ustaše and Četnik enemies. Tito flew to Moscow to meet Joseph V. Stalin and to coordinate Partisan and Red Army operations on Yugoslav territory. The Red Army wheeled north after entering the country and, together with the Partisans, liberated Belgrade on October 20, 1944. The Red Army pursued the retreating German forces from northeast Yugoslavia into Hungary, leaving the Partisans in control in Yugoslavia. The 800,000 troops of the People's Liberation Army officially became the Yugoslav People's Army (YPA) on March 1, 1945.

Yugoslavia suffered 1.7 million dead during the war, out of a total population of 15 million. Of these, over 300,000 were killed in action. Another 400,000 were wounded. Yugoslav sources claimed that the Partisans inflicted over 450,000 enemy casualties. The amount of Ustaše and Četnik casualties in that total is unknown.

Postwar Development

Demobilization, begun in late 1945, eventually reduced the size of the YPA by half. Disagreements with the Soviet Union soon had an impact on the Yugoslav military establishment. The Soviet Union wanted its junior ally to maintain only a small army and to depend mainly on the Red Army for defense. Although the Soviet Union offered to train that small army, the Yugoslavs rejected this proposal because they were dissatisfied with the quantity and quality of Soviet military assistance. Tito also was angered by Soviet attempts to recruit a network of agents within the Yugoslav military. Upon the break in Soviet-Yugoslav relations in 1948, the Soviet Union withdrew its military advisers.

Yugoslavia's ability to endure the Soviet-led blockade that followed the break was largely result of the loyalty of the YPA to Tito and the country. To ensure control, Tito served as his own minister of defense until 1953. From 1948 until 1954, the YPA maintained a constant state of military alert to repel a possible Soviet invasion to overthrow Tito.

The United States was also a large factor in postwar Yugoslav military policy. President Harry S Truman gave an indirect guarantee of Yugoslavia's security when he declared its continued independence to be a national interest of the United States. The risk of a possible United States response to a Soviet invasion of Yugoslavia outweighed any conceivable gain. Between 1948 and 1955, the United States gave Yugoslavia US$600 million in direct military grants and an equal amount in economic aid, enabling Yugoslavia to devote more of its domestic resources to defense. By 1952 the YPA had grown to 500,000 troops, and defense expenditures consumed 22 percent of the gross national product (GNP—see Glossary). A formal United States Military Assistance Advisory Group (MAAG) was established in Belgrade in 1951. It operated for ten years, disbursing military grants and arranging another US$1 billion in arms sales on favorable terms. At United States urging, Yugoslavia sought a collective security agreement with Greece and Turkey in 1954. Tito withdrew from that grouping before it was formalized, however. Yugoslavia distanced itself from the United States, after Nikita S. Khrushchev repaired bilateral Soviet-Yugoslav ties and Tito became involved in the Nonaligned Movement in the mid-1950s. By the time the MAAG was withdrawn in 1961, military relations with the United States had dwindled to US$1 million in spare parts and ammunition purchased yearly.

Yugoslavia depended heavily on purchases of Soviet arms and equipment during the 1960s and 1970s, but the Soviet threat increased at essentially the same time. The Soviet-led Warsaw Pact invasion of Czechoslovakia in 1968 forced a major change in Yugoslav military doctrine. The surprise, speed, and massive superiority of the invading forces in Czechoslovakia indicated that the relatively small YPA could not successfully use conventional tactics to defend Yugoslav territory against a similar attack. A new doctrine of Total National Defense (TND) was promulgated to permit continuous, unconventional warfare by the entire population against a massive invasion and occupation. After implementing the new doctrine in the early 1970s, Yugoslavia increased its military contacts with countries other than the Soviet Union; in the late 1970s and 1980s, it began to buy more weapons from other sources or to produce them domestically.

National Defense

In 1990 Yugoslav military doctrine specified strategy and tactics to manage most likely security threats. The major problem in national defense was the country's status as a relatively small, nonaligned country in a volatile region dominated by two large military alliances. Yugoslavia constantly measured its military efforts against those of the alliances. But, because battlefield, arms development, and production competition with the larger powers was impossible, Yugoslav doctrine, strategy, and tactics tried to use limited national defense resources in the most efficient way.

Threat Perception

Beginning in 1945, Yugoslavia's geopolitical situation made it more important than size, economic resources, or military power alone would warrant. Wedged between the North Atlantic Treaty Organization (NATO; established in 1949) and Warsaw Pact (established in 1955) alliances in the strategic Mediterranean region, Yugoslavia shared more than half its 3,000-kilometer land border with three Warsaw Pact countries (Hungary, Romania, and Bulgaria) and also bordered two NATO members (Italy and Greece). Neutral Austria to the north and isolationist Albania to the south completed Yugoslavia's borders.

Between 1948 and 1955, the possibility of a Soviet invasion to bring Yugoslavia back into the Soviet orbit remained the largest factor in Yugoslavia's perception of external threat. This scenario involved a possible military intervention in support of pro-Soviet Yugoslavs (see Internal Security, this ch.). Joint Soviet-Yugoslav declarations in 1955 and 1956 prohibited the threat or use of force in relations between the two countries, but the Soviet invasion of Hungary in November 1956 undermined the credibility of those declarations. The Soviet-led Warsaw Pact invasion of Czechoslovakia in 1968 further heightened Yugoslavia's perception of external threat, leading to a dramatic shift in Yugoslav military doctrine (see Military Doctrine, this ch.).

From 1968 until the mid-1980s, many Western and Yugoslav military observers conjectured that if a general conflict erupted between the Warsaw Pact and NATO, the Soviet Union would occupy Yugoslavia. Control of the Yugoslav territory and coastline would split NATO's southern flank and provide the Soviet navy anchorages and direct access to the Mediterranean Sea. Meanwhile, the Soviet Union also menaced Yugoslavia by supporting with varying degrees of enthusiasm Bulgaria's long-standing claim to territory in the Yugoslav Republic of Macedonia.

Albania also contributed to Yugoslavia's perception of threat during the 1970s and 1980s. Albania had a strong interest in the large ethnic Albanian population in Kosovo, economically the most backward region of Yugoslavia. The explosive conditions in Kosovo caused by unemployment, separatist movements, and Serbian repression created a constant possibility of hostilities between the two countries. Albania could block the Strait of Otranto between itself and Italy, denying Yugoslavia access to the Mediterranean Sea. The combined hostility of Albania and Bulgaria posed a further threat to Yugoslavia. After leaving the Soviet orbit in 1961, Albania preserved its military cooperation agreement with Bulgaria, although it abrogated similar agreements with the other Warsaw Pact countries. Continued relations between Albania and Bulgaria hinged largely on their common hostility toward Yugoslavia. Meanwhile, Yugoslavia sought to counteract such proximate threats by maintaining good relations with, and obtaining military technology from, other European neutrals such as Austria, Switzerland, and Sweden.

After Mikhail S. Gorbachev came to power in the Soviet Union in 1985, the perception of Soviet threat to Yugoslavia diminished. Gorbachev's visit to Belgrade in March 1988 apparently allayed many Yugoslav strategic concerns. In a declaration similar to those of 1955 and 1956, the two countries again pledged respect of mutual security.

While in Yugoslavia, Gorbachev addressed the concept of limiting United States and Soviet arms in the Mediterranean region. The Yugoslav reaction to Gorbachev's proposal revealed the influence of the superpower balance in the region on Yugoslavia's perception of its security. Gorbachev's proposal essentially called for the elimination of tactical nuclear weapons from United States forces in Greece and the United States Navy's Sixth Fleet in the Mediterranean. Yugoslavia opposed the proposal because it lacked corresponding reductions in the conventional weapons of the Warsaw Pact in the region. The diminution of NATO and United States strength would have reduced the relative security of Yugoslavia.

In 1990 rapid political change in Eastern Europe, possible Soviet troop withdrawals, and the declining military relevance of the Warsaw Pact combined to decrease Yugoslavia's perception of external threat. A unilateral Soviet invasion had become a virtual impossibility. Moreover, improved relations between Yugoslavia and Hungary, Romania, and Bulgaria made a coordinated Warsaw Pact invasion unlikely.

Military Doctrine

Yugoslavia's Total National Defense (TND) doctrine reconciled the country's domestic and foreign policies with its strategic realities and limitations. Formulated after the 1968 invasion of Czechoslovakia, TND became Yugoslavia's official military doctrine when the National Defense Law of 1969 was published.

Yugoslavia's determination to rely on its own resources and to remain independent and nonaligned conflicted with strategic reality. The invasion of Czechoslovakia showed that the standing conventional forces of a small country could not repulse a surprise attack by a qualitatively and quantitatively superior aggressor. TND was designed to allow Yugoslavia to maintain or eventually reestablish its independent and nonaligned status should an invasion occur.

TND prepared the entire population to contest the occupation of the country and finally to liberate it. The Territorial Defense Forces (TDF) would mobilize the population for this purpose (see Territorial Defense Forces, this ch.). The combat readiness of the TDF meant that the steps of organization and training could be bypassed after the start of hostilities. The TDF would supplement the YPA, giving it greater defensive depth and an armed local population ready to support combat actions. Large numbers of armed civilians would increase the cost of an invasion to a potential aggressor.

The most likely scenario in the doctrine of TND was general war between the Warsaw Pact and NATO in Europe. In such a situation, Yugoslavia would remain nonaligned, and it would not accept foreign troops of either alliance on its territory regardless of threats or inducements. The doctrine did recognize the likelihood that one side or the other might try to seize Yugoslav territory as a forward staging area, to ensure lines of communication, or simply to deny the territory to enemy forces. Such action would be considered aggression and would be resisted. Regardless of ideology, the occupiers would be considered Yugoslavia's enemy, and Yugoslavia would immediately join the opposing side for the specific purpose of liberating its territory.

TND was legally codified in Article 240 of the Constitution of 1974. The article declares that the armed forces consist of the YPA and territorial defense units organized for nationwide armed resistance. It stipulates that any citizen who resists an aggressor is a member of the armed forces. Article 238 declares that no one has the right to acknowledge or sign an act of capitulation, to accept or recognize the occupation of the country, or to prevent other citizens from resisting. To do so is high treason. This provision

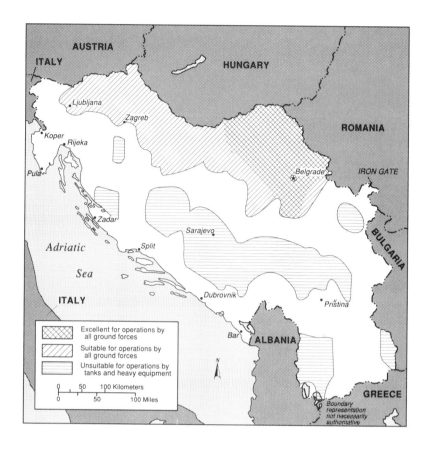

Figure 15. Terrain Considerations in Military Operations

was written to prevent an occupying force from using a Yugoslav faction or group to request and legitimize an invasion. The National Defense Law of 1982 further elaborates these provisions and explicitly states the LCY's responsibility for defense efforts.

Strategy and Tactics

Yugoslav military doctrine assumed an omnidirectional threat, but its strategy and tactics presupposed a heavily armored and mechanized Soviet or Soviet-led Warsaw Pact invasion, entering from the northeast and driving southwest to split the country. Major exercises were held every few years to test the doctrine in action. Special attention went to coordinating combat actions between YPA and TDF units.

Yugoslavia's defense strategies were circumscribed largely by geography and the size and capabilities of its forces (see fig. 15).

However, military leaders believed that their strategy and tactics were appropriate and viable and that their manpower and equipment were sufficient to defend against anticipated threats. Also, the experience of the wartime Partisans proved the effectiveness of TDF units for national defense.

The events of 1968 changed the previously exclusive emphasis on a regular army, conventional war, and the defense of strategic areas in the north of Yugoslavia. The developed northern part of the country was recognized as virtually indefensible. The major cities, industries, and communications networks situated in the northeastern part of the country would be easy strategic targets for a potential attacker, as such assets were in the 1968 invasion of Czechoslovakia.

TND doctrine required the YPA to blunt or at least to slow an enemy invasion in the north. While conventional forces fought defensive actions along a nationwide front, 1 million to 3 million citizen-soldiers would mobilize in TDF units. Small TDF units would engage alongside regular troops in their local areas, with TDF tactics emphasizing mobility and light antipersonnel and antiarmor weapons. The terrain would become increasingly favorable to the defenders as fighting shifted from the northeast to the less developed mountainous and forested areas of the Adriatic littoral and southern Yugoslavia. On this terrain the tanks, mechanized infantry, and self-propelled artillery of a superior enemy force would be less effective.

When possible, TDF units would coordinate their actions with the YPA. This coordination was practiced in several major nationwide maneuvers in the 1970s and 1980s. The TDF units also were capable of continuing action independently under local commanders. According to doctrine, the TDF would resort ultimately to protracted guerrilla warfare against an invading force to turn a blitzkrieg into a costly and lengthy occupation. Independent TDF units would attack occupying forces in as many places as possible and carry out harassing actions, ambushes, and sabotage behind enemy lines. Yugoslav military authorities believed that, based on current estimates of relative military power and the Partisan experience of World War II, 2 million enemy troops would be required to subjugate the country. Such a commitment would deter a potential aggressor from invading Yugoslavia while managing other strategic requirements.

Defense Organization

In 1990 the armed forces consisted of the Yugoslav People's Army (YPA) and the Territorial Defense Forces (TDF) (see fig. 16). The

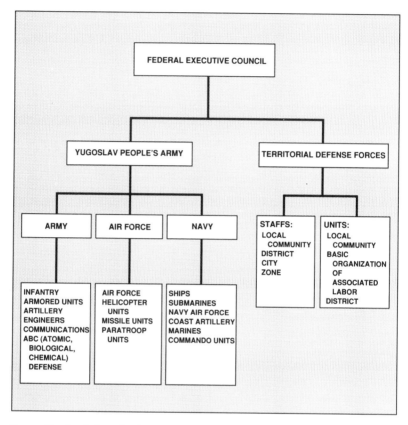

Source: Based on information from "Defense School: The Yugoslav Armed Forces—Bulwark of Our Defense," *Front* [Belgrade], November 28, 1980, in Joint Publications Research Service, *Translations on East Europe*, February 4, 1981.

Figure 16. Organization of the Armed Forces, 1990

professional YPA in turn included three service branches: the army, the air force and air defense, and the navy. The TDF was a large militia force with local units throughout the country. The passing of virtually the entire Partisan generation, beginning with the death of Tito in 1980, removed a major source of inspiration from the Yugoslav military establishment. In 1990 the leadership abilities of the younger officers, who had experienced neither combat nor invasion, remained untested and largely unknown.

Government Organization for Defense

A major issue in the government's organization for defense concerned the position of supreme commander of the armed forces.

From 1941 until his death in 1980, Tito was supreme commander. He achieved legendary stature as a military leader because of his role in directing the wartime Partisans. After Tito's death, no political leader carried the same respect and authority with military commanders.

Since 1980 the powers of the supreme commander have been dispersed within the State Presidency. Article 283 of the Constitution gave the Federal Assembly (Skupština) power to declare war and peace and to ratify military agreements and treaties. However, the State Presidency had direct command of the armed forces. The State Presidency was authorized to make general plans and preparations for defense, to declare that an imminent danger of war existed, to order mobilization, and to declare war in the event that the Federal Assembly could not meet. The State Presidency appointed, promoted, and relieved general officers. Despite these formal powers, however, in 1990 the State Presidency was not deemed likely to exercise immediate control over the armed forces. Because of its lack of military experience and expertise, the State Presidency likely would approve responses to crises and decisions on strategic issues that were proposed at lower levels. Because of its collective nature and annual rotation, the State Presidency could not replicate Tito's role as an actual supreme commander (see State Presidency, ch. 4). As provided in Article 316 of the Constitution, it delegated most of its command responsibilities and administrative duties to the Council for National Defense and the Secretariat for National Defense.

Established before Tito's death, the Council for National Defense was the highest functional link between the State Presidency, LCY leadership, civilian government, and professional military. The council was headed by the president of the State Presidency, according to Article 326 of the Constitution. However, the Constitution did not elaborate on its composition or the exact scope of its work. During most of the 1980s, the eleven-member body included six army generals (among them the secretary for national defense and the chief of the YPA General Staff) and five officials of the government and LCY. The council reviewed national defense issues presented by the secretary and his subordinates. Its decisions were subject to final approval by the State Presidency.

The Secretariat for National Defense organized and supervised the armed forces on a day-to-day basis. The secretary for national defense was always a lieutenant general or admiral who was also a member of the Council for National Defense. National defense was the most highly centralized federal secretariat.

The secretary for national defense exercised full operational control over the armed forces and was, for all practical purposes, supreme commander. He could issue military orders and instructions on behalf of the State Presidency. The importance of this position increased after the death of Tito. The office conferred far greater command authority and administrative autonomy than did its counterparts in other East European communist countries.

Following TND doctrine, the secretary for national defense planned operations on Yugoslav territory and was responsible for the structure, deployment, training, and equipping of the armed forces. All YPA and TDF commanders reported to the secretary for national defense. The three military services each had an assistant secretary to manage their administrative affairs. The assistant secretaries were responsible for budgets, military construction, and regulations. They were also ex officio deputy chiefs of the YPA General Staff.

As principal deputy to the secretary for national defense, the chief of the YPA General Staff used the directorates of the defense establishment to carry out a variety of assigned administrative duties (see fig. 17). In the 1980s, service as chief of staff was apparently a prerequisite for promotion to secretary for national defense.

The Council for Territorial Defense was established in 1980 as part of the Secretariat for National Defense. After the TDF was established in 1968, tensions arose between the regular YPA and the militia-style TDF. At that time, the TDF enjoyed high national prestige. Tito may have viewed the TDF as a hedge against the possible political ambitions of the professional military. During the Croatian nationalist disturbances of 1969–71, national leaders feared that Croatian TDF units would become the basis of an independent Croatian army. Formation of the Council for Territorial Defense effectively brought the TDF under direct control of the secretary for national defense and the YPA. The council included representatives of the secretary for national defense and those of TDF commanders in the republics and provinces. It advised the federal secretary on the organization, training, and requirements of TDF units.

The executive committees of the republics and provinces also had secretaries for national defense, who retained some formal responsibilities. Article 239 of the Constitution required republics, provinces, and communes to organize national defense, territorial defense, civil defense, and internal security measures in their respective jurisdictions. Commissions for TND and social self-protection existed for this purpose in the local government and LCY organs. They had little authority for this purpose, however, beyond coordinating mobilization and providing logistical support for the armed forces.

The Military and the Party

In 1990 more than 100,000 YPA soldiers, airmen, and sailors were members of the LCY and formed party cells in the military. Because party membership was a criterion for officer status, virtually all officers were LCY members. Despite this, LCY control over the YPA was relatively loose. In fact, the large number of military personnel in the LCY made the YPA a powerful constituency with interests claiming full party attention.

As in most communist states, military representation in the party leadership was significant in the 1980s. The LCY committee in the YPA was virtually a military wing of the party. The president of the committee, always a general, was likely eventually to become federal secretary for national defense. The committee held party conferences to elect delegates to represent the YPA at LCY party congresses. YPA party conferences were similar to the regional conferences that elected republic and province delegates to LCY party congresses. The YPA also elected its president, secretary, and fifty party committee members. YPA delegates elected to the Thirteenth Party Congress in 1986 included primarily generals and other officers, but some noncommissioned officers, soldiers, civilian YPA employees, and higher military school cadets also participated.

The LCY committee in the YPA elected fourteen officers to serve on the LCY Central Committee in 1986. Other officers were elected to the Central Committee as representatives of the party in the republics and provinces. By 1986, having steadily increased since the 1970s, the percentage of military leaders in the Central Committee was greater than the percentage of military personnel in the total population. In Central Committee representation, the YPA allotment almost equaled that of the republics and did equal that of the provinces. At various times, the federal secretary for national defense has been a member of the Presidium of the LCY Central Committee.

Tito controlled the YPA by exercising his tremendous personal authority and purging the ranks occasionally, while allowing considerable professional autonomy. Many YPA leaders were loyal Tito compatriots from the Partisan years, although their numbers were declining noticeably by the late 1980s. Even in retirement, many of this group remained politically active within the Federation of Associations of Veterans of the National Liberation War (Savez udruženja boraca Narodno-oslobodilačkog rata—SUBNOR; see Veterans' Association, ch. 4).

Military influence in the political system increased steadily after the early 1970s. The military earned its influence by stabilizing

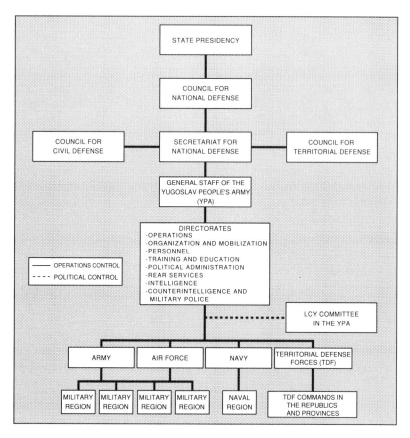

Source: Based on information from Milan N. Vego, "The Yugoslav Ground Forces: A Look at the Past and the Present," *Military Review*, 60, November 1980, 21; and Marko Milivojević, "The Yugoslav People's Army," *Armed Forces*, 6, 1987, 19.

Figure 17. Command and Control of the Armed Forces, 1990

Yugoslavia during critical periods of internal tension. In 1979 its high political profile obligated the YPA to issue a formal disavowal of any intention to assume power after Tito's death. In the 1980s, the constant speculation about the political role of the YPA was due less to the political ambitions of Yugoslav generals than to the many social, economic, and political crises afflicting the state. On several occasions, military leaders felt compelled to warn that the YPA would not allow disunity to cause the dissolution of the Yugoslav state.

The possibility of a "Polish" situation was openly discussed; this term referred to General Wojciech Jaruzelski's 1981 imposition of martial law and communist military dictatorship during a political crisis in Poland. Were the LCY and civilian government unable to solve long-standing problems, the YPA might be seen as the last effective, cohesive force in Yugoslavia, intervening in politics to ensure the survival of the state. A military coup against the LCY was considered unlikely, however, because the YPA was too well integrated into the LCY and the process of government. The interests of the two organizations were more parallel than contradictory. The YPA was, to an extent, the party in uniform. If it acted to rescue party rule, it would actually be demonstrating LCY impotence and further undermining LCY legitimacy.

Armed Services

In 1990 the YPA consisted of the army, air force, and navy. The armed services were organized into four military regions, including the Split Naval Region. The regions were further divided into districts that were responsible for administrative tasks such as draft registration, mobilization, and construction and maintenance of military facilities. Of the YPA's more than 180,000 soldiers, airmen, and sailors, nearly 100,000 were conscripts.

Army

The army led the armed services in personnel. In 1990 the army had 140,000 active-duty soldiers (including 90,000 conscripts) and could mobilize nearly 450,000 trained reservists in wartime. The army comprised several major service branches, including infantry, armor, artillery, and air defense, and smaller support branches, such as the signal, engineering, and chemical defense corps.

The army was organized into three military regions and ten army corps headquarters. The military regions and corps headquarters were responsible for forces and operations in three strategic areas: Slovenia and northern Croatia; eastern Croatia, Vojvodina, and Serbia; and Kosovo and Macedonia. In 1990 the army had nearly completed a major overhaul of its basic force structure. It eliminated its old divisional infantry organization and established the brigade as the largest operational unit. The army converted ten of twelve infantry divisions into twenty-nine tank, mechanized, and mountain infantry brigades with integral artillery, air defense, and antitank regiments. One airborne brigade was also organized before 1990. The shift to brigade-level organization provided greater operational flexibility, maneuverability, and tactical initiative, and it reduced the possibility that large army units would be destroyed in set-piece engagements with an aggressor. The change created many senior field command positions that would develop relatively young and talented officers. The brigade structure also was more appropriate at a time of declining manpower.

Tank brigades comprised two or three battalions. They operated about 750 Soviet T–54 and T–55 tanks, 290 Yugoslav M–84 tanks, and some United States–made M–47 tanks. The LCY held about 550 Soviet T–34 and United States-produced M–4 tanks in storage as reserves. The army's tanks were in many respects its most obsolete forces. The T–54/–55 was a frontline model during the 1960s. The M–47, T–34, and M–4 were tanks of World War II vintage and the early postwar era. Domestic production of the M–84 (basically a version of the Soviet T–72 built under license in Yugoslavia) was slowly providing the army with a late 1970s and 1980s model (see Arms Procurement, this ch.).

Mechanized infantry brigades lacked sufficient mechanization. In 1990 fewer than 1,000 armored combat vehicles and personnel carriers served almost 50,000 troops in frontline infantry units. Far fewer than one-half of all brigades were substantially mechanized. The majority of mechanized units were concentrated in eastern Croatia, Vojvodina, and Serbia along what would be the main axis of a Warsaw Pact invasion of Yugoslavia.

The army had over 400 M–980 armored combat vehicles and 300 M–60P armored personnel carriers produced domestically. The infantry also operated more than 200 Soviet-made BTR–152, BTR–40, and BTR–50 armored personnel carriers, which had been purchased in the 1960s and 1970s. It had 100 M–3A1 half-tracked personnel carriers produced by the United States and a small number of new Romanian TAB–72 armored personnel carriers. Armored reconnaissance vehicles included a few older Soviet BTR–40s, newer BRDM–2 models, and domestic BOV and M–8 vehicles.

Artillery regiments were well equipped with Soviet, United States, and domestic systems. Soviet artillery in these units consisted of approximately 1,000 towed 122mm howitzers, 130mm guns, 152mm gun/howitzers, and 155mm howitzers. There were about 700 older United States 105mm and 155mm towed guns and domestically produced models such as the M–65 in the artillery regiments. Towed pieces were very important for operations in the country's mountainous terrain. Artillery units operated Soviet 100mm and 122mm and Yugoslav-produced 105mm M–7 self-propelled guns. Those units had over 6,000 82mm and 120mm mortars, including a self-propelled 82mm mortar mounted on an M–60PB variant of the standard armored personnel carrier.

Artillery units operated several battlefield missile systems, including 160 128mm YMRL–32 and M–63 multiple-rocket launchers.

Soldiers of the Yugoslav People's Army in field exercise
Courtesy Embassy of Yugoslavia, Washington

The arsenal included four launchers for Soviet FROG–7 surface-to-surface missiles. First fielded in 1967, the unguided FROG–7 had a range of 100 kilometers.

Antitank regiments had towed antitank guns, recoilless rifles, and Soviet antitank guided missiles. Antitank guns included 75mm, 90mm, and 100mm models. They were Soviet produced with the exception of the 90mm M–63B2, which was manufactured domestically. The recoilless rifles were manufactured domestically and included 57mm, 82mm, and 105mm models. Two self-propelled 82mm recoilless rifles could be mounted on an M–60PB armored personnel carrier. Antitank guided missiles were the Soviet AT–1 and AT–3. They were used in both antitank and infantry units, but because of their early vintage, effectiveness against advanced armor was uncertain. The four-wheeled BOV–1 armored reconnaissance vehicle could be equipped with six AT–3 launchers to serve as a highly mobile antitank platform.

Larger army units had considerable tactical air defense assets, designed to defend major troop concentrations against enemy air strikes. The ground forces had four surface-to-air missile, regiments and eleven antiaircraft artillery regiments. The former operated Soviet SA–6 mobile medium-range surface-to-air missiles as well as large numbers of shorter-range portable SA–7 and vehicle-mounted SA–9 missiles. Short-range systems also were employed in infantry units.

Yugoslav antiaircraft artillery regiments operated over 5,000 guns. Self-propelled gun systems included the Soviet-made 57mm dual ZSU–57–2 gun systems and the domestically produced triple 20mm BOV–3 and dual 30mm BOV–30. Large numbers of towed antiaircraft guns of many calibers were in the inventory. Of both domestic and foreign origin, they included pieces purchased from the United States, Czechoslovakia, Switzerland, and Sweden.

In general, the army's major deficiencies were its lack of adequate firepower and mobility. Infantry units were insufficiently mechanized to maneuver on a modern battlefield, and tank forces were largely outdated. Using equipment from the Soviet Union, the United States, and other countries, the army had serious logistical problems, including irregular ammunition supply and maintainance of many nonstandard weapons systems. The army lacked sufficient fire support from the air force, although by 1990 the latter was acquiring additional ground attack aircraft and helicopters to perform this mission. The army emphasized developing or obtaining more effective vehicle-mounted and portable antitank guided missiles and antiaircraft missiles. A shortage was evident in advanced target designation systems, including infrared sights and laser range finders.

Air Force

In 1990 the air force included more than 32,000 personnel; because of the professional and technical requirements of the service, fewer than 4,000 were conscripts. The air force operated over 400 combat aircraft and 200 armed helicopters. It was responsible for transport, reconnaissance, and rotary-wing aircraft as well as the national air defense system. The primary air force missions were to contest enemy efforts to establish air superiority over Yugoslavia and to support the defensive operations of the army and navy. Most aircraft and missiles were produced domestically or supplied by the Soviet Union.

The air force had twelve squadrons of domestically produced ground attack fighters. The ground attack squadrons provided close air support to army operations. They were equipped with 165 new Orao-2, Super Galeb and Jastreb, and older P–2 Kraguj fighters. In 1990 gradual procurement of more Orao-2 fighters was facilitating replacement by the older fighters in ground attack squadrons. Many ground attack fighters were armed with AGM–65 Maverick air-to-surface missiles purchased from the United States. Others were armed with Soviet AS–7 and AS–9 missiles. The air force also had seventy armed Mi-8 helicopter gunships to provide added mobility and fire support for small ground units. A large number of reconnaissance aircraft were available to support army operations. Four squadrons of seventy Galeb, Jastreb, and Orao-1 fighters were configured for reconnaissance missions.

The air force provided limited transport for the army. It had two squadrons with over thirty Soviet-made Yak-40, An-12, and An-26 transport aircraft. It had seven helicopter transport squadrons with Soviet Mi-8 and domestic Partisan helicopters. In 1990 the air force transport aircraft and helicopters could transport only part of the men and equipment of the army's airborne brigade.

The air force had a limited role in supporting the navy in coastal defense operations. It operated one squadron of Soviet-made Ka-25 and Ka-28 antisubmarine warfare helicopters and two squadrons of Mi-8 and Partisan transport helicopters in support of navy missions.

The air force conducted a large pilot training program with almost 200 Galeb, Jastreb, and UTVA–75/–76 aircraft. The propeller-driven UTVA trainers had underwing pylons capable of carrying light weapons loads. A new UTVA Lasta trainer was under development in 1990. After practicing instrument and night flying, gunnery, bombing, rocket firing, and aerial maneuvers in the Lasta, student pilots progressed to the Super Galeb. Twenty Partisan helicopters were used for pilot training.

The air force had nine squadrons of 130 Soviet-made MiG-21 interceptors for air defense. First produced in the late 1950s, the MiG-21 was largely obsolete in 1990 and represented a potential weakness in Yugoslavia's air defense. The MiG-21s were armed with Soviet AA–2 air-to-air missiles of a similar vintage and some more modern AA–8 missiles as well as twin 30mm cannons. The air force acquired one squadron of new Soviet MiG-29 interceptors in 1989, possibly as an initial step toward modernizing its interceptor squadrons. One Yugoslav aircraft manufacturer also was developing a new domestic multirole fighter to replace the MiG-21.

The air force controlled additional capable ground-based air defense forces, which were upgraded in the mid-1970s. They included eight battalions of Soviet SA–2 surface-to-air missiles; six battalions of more modern SA–3 missiles; fifteen regiments of antiaircraft artillery; and a network of early warning radars and command, control, and communications equipment dispersed at sites around the country. The best-defended sites were those with strategic military value, including government army headquarters, industrial infrastructure, major population centers, ports, and airports.

Navy

In 1990 the navy had 10,000 sailors (4,400 conscripts), including 2,300 in twenty-five coastal artillery batteries and 900 marines in one light naval infantry brigade. This was essentially a coastal defense force with the mission of preventing enemy landings along the country's rugged 1,500-kilometer shoreline or coastal islands and of contesting an enemy blockade or control of the strategic Strait of Otranto. Its capabilities were limited by a lack of operational time at sea and infrequent live-fire exercises.

Minor surface combatants operated by the navy included nearly eighty frigates, corvettes, submarines, minesweepers, and missile, torpedo, and patrol boats in the Adriatic Fleet. The entire coast of Yugoslavia was part of the naval region headquartered at Split. The naval region was divided into three smaller naval districts and a riverine flotilla with major bases located at Split, Šibenik, Pula, Ploče, and Kotor on the Adriatic and Novi Sad on the Danube. The fleet was organized into missile, torpedo, and patrol boat brigades, a submarine division, and minesweeper flotillas. The naval order of battle included four frigates, three corvettes, five patrol submarines, twenty-eight minesweepers, and fifty-eight missile, torpedo, and patrol boats. One antisubmarine warfare helicopter squadron was based at Divulje on the Adriatic for coastal operations. It employed Soviet Ka-25, Ka-28, and Mi-8 helicopters and domestic Partisan helicopters. Some air force fighter and reconnaissance squadrons supported naval operations.

During World War II, the Partisans operated many small boats in raids harassing Italian convoys in the Adriatic Sea. After the war, the navy operated numerous German and Italian submarines, destroyers, minesweepers, and tank-landing craft captured during the war or received as war reparations. The United States provided eight torpedo boats in the late 1940s, but most of those units were soon obsolete. The navy was upgraded in the 1960s when it acquired ten Osa-I class missile boats and four Shershen-class torpedo boats from the Soviet Union. The Soviet Union granted a license to build eleven additional Shershen units in Yugoslav shipyards developed for this purpose.

In 1980 and 1982, the navy took delivery of two Soviet Koni-class frigates. In 1988 it completed two additional units under license. The Koni frigates were armed with four Soviet SS–N–2B surface-to-surface missile launchers, twin SA–N–4 surface-to-air missiles, and antisubmarine rocket launchers. The Yugoslav navy

Officer inspecting paratrooper equipment
Courtesy Embassy of Yugoslavia, Washington

developed its own submarine-building capability during the 1960s. In 1990 the main combat units of the submarine service were three Heroj-class patrol submarines armed with 533mm torpedoes. Two smaller Sava-class units entered service in the late 1970s. Two Sutjeska-class submarines had been relegated mainly to training missions by 1990. At that time, the navy had apparently shifted to construction of versatile midget submarines. Four Una-class midgets and four Mala-class swimmer delivery vehicles were in service in the late 1980s. They were built for use by underwater demolition teams and special forces. The Una-class boats carried five crewmen, eight combat swimmers, four Mala vehicles, and limpet mines. The Mala vehicles in turn carried two swimmers and 250 kilograms of mines.

The navy operated ten Osa I-class and six Končar-class missile boats. The Osa I boats were armed with four SS–N–2A surface-to-surface missile launchers. In 1990 domestic Kobra boats were scheduled to begin replacing the Osa I boats. The Kobra was to be armed with four SS–N–2C launchers or eight Swedish RBS–15 antiship missile launchers. Armed with two SS–N–2B launchers, the Končar-class boats were modeled after the Swedish Spica class. The navy also operated fifteen Shershen-class torpedo boats and eleven Yugoslav-built units.

249

Patrol boats were operated primarily for antisubmarine warfare. The inventory included three Mornar-class corvettes with antisubmarine rocket launchers and depth charges. The Mornar class was based on a French design from the mid-1950s. Seventeen Mirna inshore patrol boats and thirteen older Kraljevica submarine chasers also were available.

The navy's mine warfare and countermeasures capabilities were considered adequate in 1990. It operated four Vukov Klanac-class coastal minehunters built on a French design, four British Ham-class inshore minesweepers, and six 117-class inshore minesweepers built in domestic shipyards. Larger numbers of older and less capable minesweepers were mainly used in riverine operations. Other older units were used as dedicated minelayers.

The navy used amphibious landing craft in support of army operations in the area of the Danube, Sava, and Drava rivers. They included both tank and assault landing craft. In 1990 there were four 501-class, ten 211-class, and twenty-five 601-class landing craft in service. Most of them were also capable of laying mines in rivers and coastal areas.

. The coastal artillery batteries had both surface-to-surface missiles and guns. They operated the Soviet-designed SS–C–3 and a truck-mounted, Yugoslav-produced Brom antiship missile. The latter was essentially a Yugoslav variant of the Soviet SS–N–2. Coastal guns included over 400 88mm, 122mm, 130mm, and 152mm artillery pieces obtained from the Soviet Union, the United States, Germany (immediately after World War II), and Yugoslav manufacturers.

Territorial Defense Forces

The Territorial Defense Forces (TDF) were formed in 1968 as an integral part of the TND doctrine (see Military Doctrine, this ch.). TDF units were a vehicle for mobilizing able-bodied civilian males and females to participate in national defense. Between 1 million and 3 million Yugoslavs between the ages of fifteen and sixty-five would fight under TDF command as irregular or guerrilla forces in wartime. In peacetime, however, about 860,000 TDF troops were involved in training and other activities.

As originally formed, the TDF was highly decentralized and independent. TDF units were organized and funded by the party and governments in the republics, provinces, and communes. The units were commanded by TDF commanders, but they were responsible to both regional LCY leadership and the nearest YPA command. The formation of TDF units strained the budget, personnel, logistics, and training resources of the YPA without giving

Member of Territorial Defense Forces
Courtesy Embassy of Yugoslavia, Washington

it direct control over them. Because of its high initial priority, the TDF also became a rival of sorts and detracted from the status and prestige of the YPA.

Tension between the TDF and the YPA persisted throughout the 1970s. The possibility that one republic might form its TDF units into an independent army capable of opposing the YPA brought gradual centralization of the TDF. The process culminated in the establishment of the Council for Territorial Defense under the control of the secretary for national defense in 1980 (see Government Organization for Defense, this ch.).

Additional changes made republic and province TDF commanders directly responsible to the chief of the YPA General Staff. Active-duty and reserve YPA officers assumed command of TDF units throughout the country. It became increasingly apparent that the YPA would direct TDF units in combat, except in enemy-controlled areas or in case of a disruption in the chain of command.

Despite losing control over their TDF organizations, the republics and provinces continued to bear the financial burden of supporting them. Those jurisdictions were still required to provide infrastructure and logistical support to TDF units operating on their territory. During the 1980s, the cost of the TDF was estimated at approximately 1 percent of GNP annually.

The TDF concept focused on small, lightly armed infantry units fighting defensive actions on familiar local terrain. The typical unit was a company-sized detachment organized by more than 2,000 communes, neighborhood factories, and other enterprises. These units would fight in their home areas, maintaining local defense production essential to the overall war effort. The TDF also included some larger, more heavily equipped units with wider operational responsibilities. TDF battalions and regiments operated in regional areas with older artillery and antiaircraft guns and some obsolete armored vehicles. Using their mobility and tactical initiative, these units would attempt to alleviate the pressure of enemy armored columns, air strikes, and air assaults on smaller TDF units.

In coastal regions, TDF units had naval missions. They operated some obsolete gunboats in support of navy operations. They were organized to defend strategic coastal areas and naval facilities against enemy amphibious landings and raids. They also trained some divers for use in sabotage and other special operations.

The TDF was helped by the fact that most of its male citizen-soldiers were onetime YPA conscripts who had completed their term of compulsory military service. But TDF recruitment was somewhat limited by the YPA desire to include as many recently released conscripts as possible in its reserve. Other sources of TDF manpower lacked prior military service and required extensive basic training.

Military Manpower

Articles 172 and 241 of the Constitution of 1974 declare military service and defense of the country to be the supreme duty and honor of every citizen. In 1990 more than 4 million Yugoslavs were in the YPA, the reserve, the TDF, or civil defense.

The Yugoslav people generally held favorable opinions of military personnel because of the identification with the Partisans who liberated the country in World War II. However, memories of Partisan activities had dimmed noticeably by 1990. By that time, the popularity and prestige of the YPA had begun to diminish, and military careers had grown less attractive, even among the most patriotic parts of society.

The Military and Society

For most of the 1980s, the YPA was considered the strongest unifying institution in the country. The military played a fundamental role in preventing the dissolution of the federal state after the death of Tito and the dramatic rise of ethnic tensions in the 1980s. By 1990, however, serious problems had developed in YPA ranks and in its relationship to society as a whole.

The YPA remained very popular in Serbia in the 1980s. A former secretary for national defense served as president of Serbia in 1984, and a retired chief of the YPA General Staff held that position in 1988. The predominantly Serbian leadership of the YPA made high-profile appeals for national unity and public order. To non-Serbs, however, these calls seemed to be demands for greater centralism to the detriment of the federal system.

The YPA faced growing criticism and antimilitary attitudes from civilians of other nationalities. Although the organization remained unified, divisive tensions paralleled Yugoslavia's growing social problems. Nationalist movements in several regions of the country posed the most immediate threat: to many observers, ethnic strife complicated the YPA missions of defending against external threats and suppressing internal ones. Beginning in the mid-1980s, the civilian press, especially in Slovenia, subjected the military to unprecedented criticism and scrutiny. It called the YPA an undemocratic institution that favored Serbs over other nationalities. Investigative reports described the use of military labor to build expensive villas for the LCY and YPA leadership. The press questioned the use of military force in situations of internal unrest.

Slovene reporters revealed Yugoslavia's role as an intermediary in Swedish arms sales to Libya and Iraq (see Arms Sales, this ch.). The controversial story led to a military investigation of the reporters and an effort to silence public criticism of the YPA (see Courts, Detention, and Punishment, this ch.). In 1988 a former secretary for national defense asserted that hostile elements were tarnishing the military's reputation and stirring ethnic unrest among military personnel. Alleged uprisings plotted by ethnic Albanians in the YPA were mentioned prominently in his speech. He claimed that attacks on the YPA destabilized the country's constitutional order by undermining one of its most important institutions.

In the 1980s, physical attacks on YPA personnel increased. In 1985 alone, thirty attacks were reported. Nineteen soldiers were attacked during mass demonstrations protesting the arrests of the journalists who had publicized the arms deal with Libya and Iraq. While asserting that most attacks were motivated by nationalists and separatists, the military did not reveal that the majority of incidents involved recent, non-Serbian YPA conscripts. For example, in 1987 an ethnic Albanian conscript murdered four soldiers in a federal army garrison in Serbia in what may have been an ethnically motivated incident.

As in all Yugoslav institutions, the delicacy of the ethnic balance in the YPA had a serious impact on the military's effectiveness. Article 242 of the Constitution requires that the senior YPA command and officer corps reflect proportional representation of all nations and nationalities. However, the proportion of Serbs in the YPA was higher than that in the total population. In 1983 Serbs made up more than 57 percent of the YPA officer corps. And an even higher percentage of Serbs reportedly occupied the high command positions. Virtually every former secretary for national defense or chief of the YPA General Staff was a Serb. Among the other nationalities, Montenegrins had a strong military tradition and close ties to Serbia. They made up over 10 percent of the officer corps but only 3 percent of the total population. Croats and Slovenes were the most seriously underrepresented nationalities in the YPA officer corps. They made up only 15 and 5 percent, respectively, of all officers and 20 and 8 percent, respectively, of the civilian population. Croats met some discrimination in the YPA because of lingering doubts about their loyalty to the Yugoslav state. Muslims, Albanians, Macedonians, and Hungarians constituted a small fraction of the officer corps. Serbian officers and noncommissioned officers commanded YPA forces that included mostly non-Serbian soldiers. Serbian officers tended to have a strong

Military Museum at Kalemegdan, Belgrade

all-Yugoslav outlook, whereas the non-Serbian conscripts they commanded brought with them a strong bias toward their own region. Nationalism was particularly intense among the increasing number of ethnic Albanian conscripts from Kosovo.

Every YPA unit included soldiers of each nationality. With the exception of the Serbs, conscripts usually were not trained or stationed in their home republics or provinces. This practice ensured troop loyalty during internal security actions by the army. For example, Macedonian soldiers would likely have fewer reservations about using force to restore order among the population of Kosovo than against their fellow Macedonians.

Because the YPA was assigned the role of maintaining the federal Yugoslav state, nationalist friction among members of the armed forces was an especially important problem. By 1990 this situation raised serious questions as to whether the YPA could contain ethnic tension in its own ranks, much less the entire country. As in other facets of Yugoslav life, Tito's leadership had inspired cooperation toward unified military achievement; following his death, fundamental ethnic hostilities began to surface. Doubts also arose about the dependability of troops from certain nationalities in defending Yugoslavia against external attack. In 1990 such doubts fell especially on the Croats, ethnic Albanians, and Slovenes because of political and economic conditions that had emerged in their regions in the 1980s (see Regional Political Issues, ch. 4).

A series of Croatian demands for military autonomy brought forceful suppression of the Croatian separatist movement by Serb-dominated YPA forces in 1971 and 1972. The Croats sought permission to perform compulsory YPA service in their home republic, instead of automatically being assigned elsewhere, and some even demanded formation of a separate army in their republic. The latter demand, with its implications for Croatian independence, prompted YPA intervention to keep the republic in the federal state. This crisis demonstrated the extent of the ethnic fault line in the YPA. In the decades following the massive Croatian collaboration with the Nazis in World War II, Croatian officers and soldiers had largely restored the group's reputation for military reliability. But the separatist crisis of 1971–72 resuscitated doubts about Croatian loyalty. In the aftermath of the crisis, many Croatian officers who either actively or tacitly supported Croat nationalists were purged from the YPA; this purge heightened Croatian hostility toward the national military establishment.

In 1981 similar tensions existed in Kosovo. Ethnic Albanians there complained that YPA forces used excessive brutality in suppressing the massive nationalist uprisings that year. Periodic disturbances lasted throughout the 1980s (see Kosovo, ch. 4). Setting an ominous precedent for the future, the residents of Kosovo actively resisted YPA intervention and the semipermanent occupation of their province by YPA detachments. In 1987 the YPA held large-scale maneuvers in Slovenia. Because the Slovenes had also made serious demands for political and economic autonomy in the 1980s, those maneuvers seemed a possible prelude to YPA intervention in that republic. Some observers feared that, under the weight of nationalism, the YPA might eventually degenerate into rival armed ethnic militias fighting a civil war.

Recruitment and Service Obligations

Conscription was the principal source of soldiers in Yugoslavia. All male citizens were subject to conscription, regardless of ethnic group. The ethnic breakdown of YPA conscripts closely approximated the ethnic composition of the population as a whole. By law, twelve months of military service was compulsory. Young men registered for conscription on their seventeenth birthday. Usually inducted in the spring or fall after their nineteenth birthday, young men remained eligible for the draft until age thirty. In 1990 about 2.8 million males in this age-group were fit for military service, out of an estimated national population of 23.5 million. Within this group, about 180,000 reached the normal induction age of nineteen every year. Between 60 and 70 percent of the 180,000 were drafted in their first year of eligibility. By law men between the ages of eighteen and fifty-five could be drafted in the event of war or imminent threat of war. About 5 million males were eligible for service under this category.

Treatment of conscientious objectors was harsh, and no form of alternative service was available for those who refused. Article 214 of the federal criminal code provided for imprisonment for one to ten years for avoiding military service. In time of war or immediate danger of war, the penalty for refusing to serve ranged from five years in prison to capital punishment.

Even after the reduction in the size of the YPA in the late 1980s, the ratio of soldiers to civilians remained high. By the late 1980s, a new military obligation law had shortened the term of conscription from fifteen to twelve months. Military policy makers did not reduce the term of service willingly, but demographic factors had left no alternative.

Young males working abroad reduced the number of potential conscripts for the YPA, although this problem was less acute in the 1980s than in the 1970s. A limited number of exemptions were based on physical disability or family hardship. Students enrolled in or preparing to enter a university program also received deferments. University graduates were unlikely to serve a full year in the military. Many fulfilled their service requirement by receiving reserve officer commissions upon graduation from a university. Yugoslav sources reported that 20,000 reserve officers were commissioned annually through the TDN and university training programs.

Although not ordinarily subject to conscription, women served in the military in several capacities. Beginning in 1983, women were allowed to volunteer for noncombat duty as communications, medical, and clerical personnel. They also served in the reserves and could be drafted into the YPA during war or imminent threat of war, upon a special order of the secretary for national defense. A large percentage of TDF personnel were women.

Between 1987 and 1990, financial and demographic factors gradually reduced the number of YPA personnel from 266,000 to 180,000. The economic rationale was apparent: in a time of extreme national economic crisis and lessening international tension, the military was a natural target for budget cutting. At the same time, by 1990 Yugoslavia's population growth was relatively slow at 0.6 percent annually. Because the ethnic Albanians of Kosovo accounted for most of this small increase, maintaining force strength in the YPA would mean inducting higher percentages of this potentially disruptive segment of the population—a course not favored by Yugoslav military policy makers in the late 1980s.

Noncommissioned officers (NCOs) were generally selected from two sources. Commanders could recommend that soldiers attend an NCO school upon completing basic training. Other qualified youths could apply to an NCO school directly from civilian life. NCO candidates graduated with the rank of sergeant. They signed up for three- to nine-year tours of duty.

Commissioned officers were trained primarily in higher military schools run by the three service branches (see Military Training and Education, this ch.). Particularly well-qualified NCOs who passed the officer examination could also receive commissions. Civilians with technical specialties such as engineering or medicine could be commissioned directly from civilian life.

Retirement in the YPA was mandatory after forty years of service or at age sixty, except for those in the general officer ranks. Service in the reserves began on completion of active duty. Conscripts and NCOs were obligated until age fifty-five, and warrant officers and commissioned officers were obligated until age sixty. Women served in the reserves until age fifty. NCOs could enter the reserves as junior (second) lieutenants after completing a reserve officer course. During war or imminent threat of war, the secretary for national defense could extend reserve service obligations. Promotion and other advancement generally came more slowly in the reserves than in the active service.

Organized civil defense was another form of citizen participation within the national defense establishment. Beginning in the late 1960s, the emphasis on the TDF and local defense drained personnel from the extensive civil defense and urban evacuation program already in existence. Nonetheless, in 1989 civil defense units included about 2 million adults not included in the YPA, its reserve, or the TDF. The Council for Civil Defense was a joint military and civilian body within the Secretariat for National Defense. It brought representatives of the secretary for national defense together with military and government officials from each republic or province. The former provided assistance and advice to the latter as they formed civil defense organizations at every level of government in the republic or province.

Civil defense originally was directed at planning for the mass evacuation of large cities and defense against atomic, biological, or chemical (ABC) attack. It later acquired other major wartime reconstruction and reconstitution responsibilities, such as fire fighting, provision of public health, sanitation, emergency shelters, evacuation, and civil engineering. Civil defense units also were involved in damage recovery from natural or man-made disasters and other national emergency situations.

Military Training and Education

In 1990 about one-half of all conscripts came from rural backgrounds. They tended to adapt well to the rigors of military life. Many conscripts lacked significant technical training or mechanical experience prior to entering military service. This factor, combined with a relatively short time of service, impeded training beyond basic military skills. Article 243 of the 1974 Constitution guaranteed the equality of all national languages in the armed forces. However, that article also stated that a single, unspecified language could be used for military training and command. In practice, Serbo-Croatian was the only language used in the armed forces.

Conscription was instituted at the time of maximum Soviet threat in 1948. Many seventeen-year-olds received premilitary training prior to induction. This training was intended to give youths some basic military knowledge so that they could enter the YPA prepared to fight. In 1990 reserve NCOs and officers still conducted regular premilitary drills in intermediate schools.

Basic YPA training was conducted in special training units. Based on the TND doctrine, training covered both conventional military operations and unconventional guerrilla warfare tactics developed by the wartime Partisans. Basic training included twenty weeks of individual physical conditioning, military drill and discipline, weapons familiarization and range firing, political indoctrination, and squad and platoon tactical exercises. Soldiers participated in more advanced training in the units to which they were permanently assigned at the end of basic training. They were involved in larger unit maneuvers and exercises up to the brigade level. Some troops received specialist training in their permanent units, while others were sent to technical schools.

Economic stringency limited expenditures on realistic live-fire exercises, large-scale maneuvers, and extensive education. The YPA also was required to supply conscript labor for many large-scale civilian construction projects. YPA units and military engineers worked on roads, bridges, railroads, tunnels, coal mines, and water supply systems. These activities detracted from conventional military training time.

Officer Education

Several higher military schools served as the main training source for officers of the various service branches. Secondary-school students and a certain number of qualified active-duty NCOs could apply for competitive admission to those institutions. Applicants were required to have good "moral-political" qualities, a term generally interpreted to mean membership in the Youth League of Yugoslavia (the official youth organization sponsored by the LCY). By 1990, however, Yugoslav youth showed diminished enthusiasm both for party activity and for a military career; applications to higher military schools dropped accordingly.

Cadets in the military schools normally followed a three- to five-year curriculum designed for line officers or for military engineers. Each combat arm and technical or administrative branch of the YPA had at least one higher military school. Once commissioned into active duty, graduates were required to remain in service for six to ten years. Military pilots had a fifteen-year obligation. After being assigned to a permanent unit, young officers learned most of their basic duties on the job. After several years of active service, they were selected for specialist training. Some commissioned officers in technical fields such as communications and aviation maintenance were sent directly to advanced training programs. Outstanding senior captains, majors, and lieutenant colonels were chosen to attend a higher military academy for two years of advanced study in tactics and operations. Selected colonels attended a one-year command-and-staff program. Naval officers below rear admiral attended similar courses at the Higher Naval Academy in Split. In 1990 some Yugoslav officers were selected to attend prestigious Soviet military academies, which were similar to command-and-staff or war colleges in the United States.

Reserve Training

Reserve training was limited by law. Reservists were eligible for periodic temporary call-up to active duty for training. But reserve soldiers were not required to train more than two months in any year or more than six months total during their entire reserve obligation. Officers were not required to train more than twelve months during their obligation. All reservists remained subject to periodic training until the last five years of their obligation. They were compensated for wages forfeited during temporary active duty. Failure to respond to a call-up without a proper waiver was a criminal offense prosecuted in military courts. Reservists could be arrested and tried for crimes or breaches of military discipline while in an active-duty status.

Military Life

Yugoslavia's socialist self-management system was defended by the one institution in the country that did not practice self-management (see Socialist Self-Management, ch. 3). It was believed that the independence implicit in self-management was contradictory to the essential military principles of command, subordination, and discipline.

Soldiers received free military housing, meals, and health care, plus a small monthly payment for personal expenses. They spent a considerable amount of time producing their own food. Larger military units raised and slaughtered livestock and grew various staple crops. The stipulated average workweek of a YPA soldier was forty-two hours; however, training exercises and maneuvers could extend that time. Soldiers were entitled to fifteen to twenty-one days of regular leave during the active-duty period. Some received extra leave privileges for good conduct. Overall, the standard of living of the average soldier was below that of his civilian counterpart. This was not a serious concern, however, because military service was both mandatory and relatively brief.

Although they lacked the privileges of self-management, soldiers had a special right to complain to their immediate superiors about unsatisfactory working and living conditions. They could appeal an unfavorable decision to a higher officer within thirty days.

Military law stipulated that regular meetings of military units and facilities would discuss housing, health care, and other conditions of military life. Like other citizens, soldiers voted for delegates to serve in commune, republic or province, and federal assemblies. These delegates represented their service post and not their home region.

The majority of soldiers came directly to the service from school, but if they were employed prior to conscription, they had the right to return to their former jobs. Military service brought with it a fairly generous disability allowance as well as death benefits to a soldier's family.

Unlike soldiers, officers received sufficient pay and allowances to live in better circumstances than their civilian counterparts. Officer pay was determined by a combination of factors, including rank, length of service, marital status, and number of dependents. Officers received generous allowances for travel, family separation, cost-of-living differentials, and other hardships. Air crews and airborne officers received hazardous duty pay, and medical doctors, engineers, and technicians with special skills or training received extra incentive pay to stay in the service.

Promotions were awarded rapidly and equitably. Active-duty performance was evaluated as either favorable or unfavorable. A favorable rating was further classified as adequate, good, outstanding, or especially outstanding. Officers were rated after one year of service and every three years thereafter until the tenth year of service. After ten years of service, they were evaluated every four years.

Officer benefits were generous. Leave amounted to thirty days every year. Officers with more than twenty-five years of active-duty service or older than age fifty received an additional ten days per year. In most cases, retirement pay was more than fifty percent of active-duty pay. Nevertheless, inadequate military housing was a common problem that lowered morale among officers.

Ranks, Insignia, and Uniforms

Ranks in the YPA were updated by the Army Law of 1982. According to that law, the YPA had five categories of ranks, including general officers, senior officers, junior officers, NCOs, and soldiers. The lowest three enlisted ranks wore one, two, and three red chevrons, respectively, on a background of olive-green, blue-gray, or black—corresponding, respectively, to the ground forces, air force, or navy. In the army and air force, the upper enlisted ranks wore single thin yellow-gold chevrons with one, two, three, and four yellow-gold stars, respectively. The two classes of warrant officer wore two yellow-gold chevrons with one and two gold stars, respectively.

The lowest three navy ranks were indicated by one, two, and three red chevrons, respectively. Petty officers second class (roughly equivalent to petty officers first class) wore one red chevron and one red star. The upper three enlisted ranks wore two, three, and four yellow-gold chevrons and one yellow-gold star, respectively. Warrant officers wore one broad and one narrow yellow-gold chevron and one yellow-gold star, chief warrant officers (warrant officers first class) wore a second narrow yellow-gold chevron and one yellow-gold star.

Insignia for commissioned officers were worn on shoulder boards in colors corresponding to their service branch: olive-green for the army, blue-gray for the air force, and black for the navy. Shoulder boards were piped with single and double yellow-gold braid, respectively, for junior and senior officers of the army and air force. Shoulder boards of navy officers were not piped. General officers of all three services wore shoulder boards piped with twisted gold cord.

In the army and air force, the four junior officer ranks wore shoulder boards with one, two, three, and four small yellow-gold stars, respectively. The shoulder boards of the three senior officer ranks bore one, two, and three large yellow-gold stars, respectively. General officers of both army and air force wore a crossed sword and cannon, with one, two, three, and four gold stars, respectively. Tito was the only person to hold the rank of marshal, and the position was abolished shortly after his death. Junior and senior naval officers wore shoulder boards with yellow-gold stripes and one yellow-gold star. In rank sequence, the stripe configurations of junior officers were one broad, one broad and one narrow, two broad, two broad and one narrow, three broad, three broad and one narrow, and four broad stripes.

The four senior naval officer ranks wore one broad band and one, two, three, and four broad gold stripes, respectively, each with one gold star on the shoulder boards. The shoulder boards of the naval dress uniform were like those of the army and air force, distinguished by an anchor representing the branch (see fig. 18).

Soldiers and NCOs were issued uniforms. Soldiers had field and service uniforms, while NCOs were authorized a dress uniform as well. Because they held conscript or enlisted ranks, military school cadets wore soldiers' uniforms. Soldiers' winter and summer uniforms were made of light or heavy wool and cotton in olive-green, blue-gray, and black for army, air force, and navy, respectively. Navy conscripts and enlisted men also had summer white uniforms.

COMMISSIONED OFFICERS

YUGOSLAV RANK ARMY AND AIR FORCE	GENERAL ARMIJE	GENERAL-PUKOVNIK	GENERAL-POTPUKOVNIK	GENERAL-MAJOR	PUKOVNIK	POTPUKOVNIK	MAJOR	KAPETAN I KLASE	KAPETAN	PORUČNIK	POTPORUČNIK
UNITED STATES RANK TITLES	GENERAL	LIEUTENANT GENERAL	MAJOR GENERAL	BRIGADIER GENERAL	COLONEL	LIEUTENANT COLONEL	MAJOR	CAPTAIN		1ST LIEUTENANT	2D LIEUTENANT
YUGOSLAV RANK NAVY	ADMIRAL FLOTE	ADMIRAL	VICEADMIRAL	KONTRAADMIRAL	KAPETAN BOJNOG BRODA	KAPETAN FREGATE	KAPETAN KORVETE	PORUČNIK BOJNOG BRODA	PORUČNIK FREGATE	PORUČNIK KORVETE	POTPORUČNIK
UNITED STATES RANK TITLES	ADMIRAL	VICE ADMIRAL	REAR ADMIRAL	REAR ADMIRAL (LOWER HALF)	CAPTAIN	COMMANDER	LIEUTENANT COMMANDER	LIEUTENANT	LIEUTENANT JUNIOR GRADE	ENSIGN	

WARRANT OFFICERS AND ENLISTED PERSONNEL

YUGOSLAV RANK ARMY AND AIR FORCE		ZASTAVNIK I KLASE	ZASTAVNIK	STARIJI VODNIK I KLASE	STARIJI VODNIK	VODNIK I KLASE	VODNIK	MLADI VODNIK	DESETAR	RAZVODNIK	VOJNIK
UNITED STATES ARMY RANK TITLES		CHIEF WARRANT OFFICER W-2	WARRANT OFFICER W-1	COMMAND SERGEANT MAJOR	SERGEANT MAJOR OF THE ARMY	FIRST SERGEANT	SERGEANT FIRST CLASS	MASTER SERGEANT	STAFF SERGEANT	SERGEANT	CORPORAL	PRIVATE / PRIVATE 1ST CLASS	BASIC PRIVATE
UNITED STATES AIR FORCE RANK TITLES		NO RANK	NO RANK	CHIEF MASTER SERGEANT OF THE AIR FORCE	CHIEF MASTER SERGEANT	SENIOR MASTER SERGEANT	MASTER SERGEANT	TECHNICAL SERGEANT	STAFF SERGEANT	SENIOR AIRMAN / SERGEANT	AIRMAN / AIRMAN 1ST CLASS	AIRMAN BASIC
YUGOSLAV RANK NAVY		ZASTAVNIK I KLASE	ZASTAVNIK	STARIJI VODNIK I KLASE	STARIJI VODNIK	VODNIK I KLASE	VODNIK	MLADI VODNIK	DESETAR	RAZVODNIK	VOJNIK
UNITED STATES RANK TITLES		CHIEF WARRANT OFFICER W-2	NO RANK	FLEET FORCE MASTER CHIEF PETTY OFFICER OF THE NAVY	MASTER CHIEF PETTY OFFICER	SENIOR CHIEF PETTY OFFICER	CHIEF PETTY OFFICER	PETTY OFFICER 1ST CLASS	PETTY OFFICER 2D CLASS	PETTY OFFICER 3D CLASS	SEAMAN / SEAMAN APPRENTICE	SEAMAN RECRUIT

Figure 18. Military Ranks and Insignia, 1990

All soldiers wore neckties of the same colors except in summer, when the uniform shirt was worn with an open collar.

There were several variations on the basic soldier's uniform. Women's uniforms were of the same style as those for men, except that a skirt was substituted for trousers. Airborne troops wore an olive-green beret instead of the standard garrison or service cap. The naval infantry wore distinctive blue and white sleeve patches and black berets with anchor and wreath emblems. Mountain troops wore distinctive stiff field caps with semirigid visors and earflaps. They wore loose winter shirts under which additional layers could be worn. The shirt itself had a lining and a collar that could be turned up to cover the neck and chin. The trousers worn by mountain troops extended just below the knee, with a strap and buckle closure. Leather leggings, heavy wool socks, and foul-weather capes also were worn by the mountain troops.

Officers had to procure their own field, service, dress, and full dress uniforms. They wore insignia on the lapels of the field uniform shirts. The service uniform differed only in some details from the basic dress uniform. The shirt buttons of the dress uniform were yellow-gold instead of the service color. The trousers, jackets, and overcoats were piped along the seams with distinctive service colors—red for army, blue for air force, and black for navy. The dress cap visor showed the same piping as the officer's shoulder boards. The general officer's dress cap had a chin strap of twisted gold cord. Other officers wore plain plastic or leather chin straps. Full dress uniforms were blue and were worn with a yellow-gold sash belt lined with the appropriate service color. Cap emblems all included a red star with yellow-gold rays, given distinctive configurations according to branch. Air force officers had the red star perched on the wings of an eagle with a sword clenched in its talons. Airborne officers had the red star resting on a silver parachute against a blue background. Cap emblems for general officers showed the same gold wreath as the shoulder boards.

Defense and the National Economy

From 1948 until well into the 1980s, Yugoslavia devoted a considerable proportion of its national resources to defense. By all indicators, the economy was fairly military oriented, considering the country's modest overall level of development. Yugoslavia's nonaligned foreign policy made a high military budget necessary because the country had no alliances guaranteeing military assistance. But the Yugoslav situation resembled that of other communist states, such as Cuba, the Democratic People's Republic of Korea (North Korea), and Vietnam, which also received considerable amounts of Soviet arms and military equipment without being members of the Warsaw Pact.

On several occasions in the 1980s, the YPA leadership stated that the country's economic crisis and diminished resource allocations to the military directly affected the quality of YPA weapons, equipment, and personnel, thereby weakening YPA ability to provide a reliable defense against external threats. Yet critics of the YPA contended that the military still spent the major portion of the country's resources and that military spending was a major factor in the economic crisis that persisted and worsened in Yugoslavia through the 1980s.

In 1990 much of the YPA weapons inventory was obsolete. In previous years, weapons had been stockpiled from both foreign acquisition and domestic production. But for long periods, Yugoslavia's nonaligned status precipitated partial embargos by both East and West. NATO and the Warsaw Pact were cautious about selling Yugoslavia advanced weapons that could reach hostile third parties. By 1990 Yugoslavia had strengthened its domestic arms manufacturing, and that year it claimed that 80 percent of its new weapons came from that source. But both sources remained problematic; imports were expensive and politically vulnerable, yet domestically produced weapons were generally of lower quality. Also, importing equipment from many different manufacturers complicated standardization, maintenance, and logistics. Critics complained that arms purchases abroad and domestic military production were too expensive and were incompatible with long-term economic stabilization. The military, however, argued that arms procurement helped with the acquisition or development of technologies of value in the production of civilian goods.

Military Budget

In the early 1980s, the military budget of Yugoslavia held steady between US$2 billion and US$2.5 billion, despite the country's severe economic stringency. The expanded internal security mission of the YPA was probably the compelling factor in higher defense spending in the mid-1980s (see Internal Security, this ch.). Nevertheless, the Krajgher Commission's Long-Term Economic Stabilization Program required the YPA to cut expenditures by 5 percent in both 1986 and 1987. The 1987 military budget was US$2.7 billion, with cuts absorbed largely in reduced manpower (see Recruitment and Service Obligations, this ch.). At that time, Yugoslav defense expenditures dropped below those of every non-Soviet Warsaw Pact state and of neighboring NATO countries Italy and Greece. In 1988 the military budget increased to US$2.8 billion and to over US$4.4 billion in 1989. Yet these increases failed to match the national inflation rate, and defense spending declined in real terms.

In postwar Yugoslavia, the burden of the military budget on the national economy was traditionally a heavy one. In 1952, at the height of spending to meet the Soviet threat to Yugoslavia, 22 percent of the country's GNP was dedicated to fielding a 500,000-man regular army. That figure subsequently decreased, but throughout the Tito years it remained relatively high by world standards.

The military budget as a proportion of federal government expenditures also reflected the high priority of defense. The federal government routinely dedicated 50 percent to 60 percent of its annual outlay to defense. In the 1980s, this ratio was consistently the highest or second highest in the world. In 1987, however, spending cuts temporarily dropped the defense share of total federal expenditures to just under 30 percent. In Yugoslavia this measurement overstated the burden of military spending somewhat because many government expenditures were made at the republic, province, or commune level, rather than at the federal government level. Even considering that factor, however, defense remained the largest component of federal government spending.

Arms Procurement

In 1990 Yugoslavia remained dependent on the Soviet Union for most of its heavy armaments and complex weapons systems, including tanks, armored vehicles, antitank and antiaircraft missiles, and ships. Until the late 1980s, this created a dangerous situation in which Yugoslavia's principal arms supplier was also the country's greatest apparent external threat. Therefore, in 1990 Yugoslav arms procurement policy aimed to expand purchases from the other Warsaw Pact states, the United States, and neutral European countries, as well as to increase domestic production. Despite significant progress, self-sufficiency in arms supply remained elusive for both economic and technological reasons. Yugoslavia's domestic arms industry remained relatively small, and in 1990 it faced declining export markets.

Arms Imports

Immediately after World War II, Yugoslavia received a substantial amount of Italian military equipment as war reparations. The Yugoslav arms industry used captured German and Czechoslovak weapons as models in manufacturing its own small arms and infantry equipment. The United States, France, and Britain also supplied arms after the war. After Yugoslavia broke with the Soviet

Union in 1948, Yugoslavia depended heavily on the United States for military assistance. A United States Military Assistance Advisory Group (MAAG) was active in Yugoslavia until 1961, managing a total of about US$600 million in military aid. In conjunction with the flow of United States weapons, many Yugoslav officers came to the United States for training during that period. Yugoslavia received World War II-vintage equipment and some more up-to-date systems, including M-4 Sherman and M-47 Patton tanks, M-2 and M-3 half-tracked personnel carriers, artillery, and F-86 Thunderflash fighter-bombers. Some of this equipment was still in service or held in reserve in 1990. After the Belgrade Declaration of 1955 improved bilateral relations, the Soviet Union became Yugoslavia's main supplier of arms and equipment. In the 1960s, Yugoslavia received Soviet T-34 and T-54/-55 tanks, first-generation antitank guided missiles, Osa-class missile boats, and MiG-21 fighters. In the 1970s, the Soviet Union sold Mi-4 and Mi-8 helicopters and SA-2 and SA-6 surface-to-air missiles. Since 1985 Yugoslavia has received a license to produce a domestic version of the Soviet T-72 tank for its own use and for export. In the late 1980s, Yugoslavia was one of only a few countries to be sold the new Soviet MiG-29 fighter. At an estimated cost of US$20 million per aircraft, however, the MiG-29 was considered too expensive for Yugoslavia to purchase more than a few as models for its own aircraft industry.

Purchases from the Soviet Union had the advantage of sparing Yugoslavia the scarce hard-currency (see Glossary) reserves required as payment by Western suppliers. The Soviet Union also provided generous credit and repayment terms. Civilian authorities in Yugoslavia voiced serious concerns about the political influence gained by the Soviet Union from such favorable terms. Arms sales and frequent contacts had the potential to build a constituency favorable to the Soviet Union in the YPA and its leadership. In any event, the situation in 1990 preserved some of Yugoslavia's previous dependency on good relations with the Soviet Union.

In the late 1980s, economic stringency forced postponement of some major military purchases from Western countries. Yugoslavia investigated purchase from other suppliers of mobile missile systems for defense against armor, aircraft, and ships. Antitank, antiaircraft, and antiship missiles were relatively cheap alternatives to domestic manufacture of more tanks, interceptors, and ships.

When possible, Yugoslavia sought to establish licensed domestic production of foreign weapons systems. In general, Western countries placed more restrictions on licensing agreements and offered less generous terms than the Soviet Union because the former saw such deals strictly as profit-making transactions. In all cases, Yugoslavia refused to accept political conditions on the use or resale of imported arms. In the early 1980s, negotiations to supply Yugoslavia with modern United States-manufactured TOW anti-tank guided missiles broke down after the revelation that Yugoslavia had violated the terms of a prior transfer by sending M–47 tanks to the new revolutionary regime in Ethiopia in the early 1980s.

In the 1970s and 1980s, Yugoslavia expanded significantly its arms cooperation with countries outside the Soviet and United States spheres. In cooperation with Swiss firms, Yugoslavia produced a multiple-use 20mm antiaircraft cannon and incorporated the imported Snecma engine into its own M–980 armored combat vehicle. The Yugoslav M–60P armored personnel carrier used an Austrian engine. Cooperation with other nonaligned countries was extensive. With India and Egypt, Yugoslavia traded spare parts for Soviet weapons and aircraft. With Swedish assistance, Yugoslav engineers developed laser range finders for sale to Egypt and for domestic installation on Soviet-made tanks. Yugoslavia bought many systems from two Soviet Warsaw Pact allies, Czechoslovakia and Poland. The Yugoslav 128mm YMRL–32 multiple-rocket launcher, with thirty-two tubes and automatic reloader, was modeled after Czechoslovak and Romanian versions of the Soviet BM–21. Yugoslavia purchased MiG–21 fighters made under Soviet license in Czechoslovakia; Czechoslovak M53/59 truck-mounted antiaircraft guns; and T–55 tanks and An-2 and An-28 transport aircraft built under Soviet license in Poland.

According to the United States Arms Control and Disarmament Agency, between 1967 and 1976 the Soviet Union supplied 93 percent of Yugoslavia's arms purchases, Poland and France supplied 2 percent each, the Federal Republic of Germany (West Germany) and Czechoslovakia supplied 1 percent each, and the United States supplied less than 1 percent. In that period, arms made up 5 to 6 percent of the country's total imports. The situation changed considerably in succeeding years as the Soviet Union's supply role diminished. Between 1983 and 1987, Yugoslavia bought US$600 million in arms abroad. The Soviet Union supplied 75 percent of this amount and the United States 23 percent, with the remaining 2 percent supplied by ten other countries. In 1985 economic stringency reduced arms imports to US$30 million, less than 0.25 percent of total imports. By 1987 that figure had rebounded to US$210 million.

Domestic Arms Production

Beginning in the mid-1970s, Yugoslavia made considerable progress in replacing imports with cheaper domestically manufactured military equipment. As Yugoslav military equipment approached the quality of European equipment, international sale of such products became a potential source of hard currency for the Yugoslav economy (see Arms Sales, this ch.). By 1990 Yugoslav industry was providing about 80 percent of basic military equipment and some advanced systems. But that figure included mostly infantry weapons, antitank systems, armored vehicles, boats and ships, and relatively simple components. Although the objective was to keep pace with the best armaments in NATO and Warsaw Pact inventories, this goal was hindered by the tremendous financial and technological obstacles facing all of Yugoslav industry in 1990. The Yugoslav arms industry upgraded or modernized existing systems when possible, extended the service life or improved the effectiveness of major weapons systems, and shared research and development breakthroughs with civilian industry to maximize economic impact. Yugoslav arms industries operated somewhat differently from other economic enterprises. Article 281 of the Constitution empowered the federal secretary for national defense to regulate associated labor and self-managed organizations involved in defense production and research. A 1979 law on domestic defense industries consolidated many enterprises producing arms and other military equipment. It also provided the federal secretary for national defense more direct control over the activities of those enterprises. Domestic defense production in the 1970s had been hampered by the relative autonomy of many highly interdependent industries. As many as 240 loosely associated enterprises produced necessary parts for a single complex weapons system. The 1979 law weakened the principle of self-management in defense production enterprises, citing their special role in national security. The law severely circumscribed the right of employees to set prices for their products. This provision allayed military concerns about the inflation and escalating arms costs caused by worker wage demands. Workers continued the formal process of setting prices, but only under strict guidelines issued by the secretary for national defense. The secretary also prepared an arms import program. Funds from the defense budget had to be allocated if foreign exchange earnings from arms exports did not match the cost of arms imports. The secretary was responsible for arranging credit or payment terms with foreign governments or suppliers.

The army was the first priority in Yugoslavia's arms procurement plans. The most urgent requirements were replacement of obsolete armored equipment and improvement of mobile defense infantry weapons, including antitank and antiaircraft systems, to compensate for infantry manpower cutbacks. In 1990 Yugoslavia also was developing its own military aircraft and helicopters. Improved target detection and designation systems were sought.

In the late 1970s, the Soviet Union granted Yugoslavia a license to build the T-72 tank. The Yugoslav version, designated M-84, went into serial production in the late 1980s. According to Yugoslav sources, the M-84 had a computerized fire control system, electronics, and a laser range finder comparable to those of advanced NATO and Warsaw Pact models. It featured protection against armor-piercing shells, a low silhouette, and a defensive alarm system to warn the crew when the vehicle was illuminated by enemy radar, infrared, or laser target designators.

By contrast, the Yugoslav M-980 armored combat vehicle was an entirely domestic design. When initially fielded in 1975, it was one of the world's most advanced models, rated on a par with the Soviet BMP-1 or French AMX-10. The amphibious M-980 carried an eight-man infantry squad, a driver, and a gunner. It was armed with Soviet AT-3 antitank guided missiles, a 20mm cannon, and a 7.92mm machine gun and was powered by a Snecma diesel engine. The Yugoslav BOV was a particularly versatile domestic armored reconnaissance vehicle configured with a number of mounted antitank and antiaircraft weapons systems.

Yugoslavia produced its first fighter aircraft in 1950 and followed it with many trainers and experimental aircraft in later years. In the mid-1960s, the Galeb and Jastreb fighters were the first domestically manufactured jet aircraft. In the 1970s, Yugoslavia produced the Super Galeb light attack aircraft and began to work jointly with Romania to develop its first sophisticated domestic fighter/attack aircraft, the Orao. A single Rolls Royce Mk 632 Viper turbojet engine powered the Super Galeb, which carried two twin 23mm cannons, 57mm and 128mm rockets, and cluster bombs. Its total ordnance load capability was 2,000 kilograms. The Orao incorporated both domestic and foreign technology, including twin Rolls Royce Mk 633-41 Viper turbojet engines. The initial prototype was ready in 1974, and serial production began in 1980. Performance of the Orao was very similar to that of the Alpha jet used by NATO forces.

Although it represented a considerable advance for Yugoslav military aviation, the Orao had some significant shortcomings. It was limited to subsonic performance, carried a relatively light weapons load of 2,500 kilograms, lacked air-to-air missiles, and offered a short combat radius of 400 kilometers. By 1990 fewer than 100 had been built, and plans to build a new multirole fighter cast doubt on the future of the Orao program.

In the 1980s, the Ivo Lola Ribar Machine Industry of Belgrade began manufacturing French Aérospatiale SA–342 Gazelle helicopters under license. Called the Partisan, this was the first domestically produced rotary-wing aircraft. It could carry four launchers for AT–3 antitank guided missiles.

In 1990 Yugoslavia had a solid technological and manufacturing base for producing other weapons systems; the main weak points of this base were in electronics and guidance technologies. Yugoslavia cooperated with Sweden to produce laser range finders and gun sights. Its arms industries used Soviet, Czechoslovak, and United States models to achieve self-sufficiency in rifles, machine guns, light antiarmor rockets, mortars, and artillery pieces and to provide a substantial portion of boats and landing craft used by the YPA. The Soviet Osa class served as a design model for Yugoslav missile boats, which were powered by British turbine engines and armed with French-supplied Exocet antiship missiles. The Yugoslav 501-class landing craft was a versatile platform capable of transporting three tanks and two platoons of troops or two eight-gun artillery batteries. It also could serve as a coastal minelayer. But in 1990, Yugoslavia still relied on the Soviet Union and a number of Italian, Spanish, Swiss, and Swedish arms firms for weapons and electronics to outfit the ships and boats built in Yugoslav shipyards.

Domestic production of antitank systems was a high priority because such systems were not easily available elsewhere. The Soviet Union was reluctant to provide Yugoslavia its more advanced antitank guided missiles, which might be used later against its own main battle tanks. The United States had declined to sell TOW missiles because Yugoslavia had failed to abide by the terms of previous arms transfers.

Foreign Military Relations

Working relationships with the military establishments in a wide range of foreign countries were an important facet of Yugoslavia's nonaligned foreign policy. Maintenance of such links guaranteed flexibility in dealing with unforeseen events and provided maximum access to advanced foreign military technology. However, by 1990 foreign military ties had become a major source of domestic political controversy.

The Yugoslav military had a long-standing relationship with its Soviet counterpart. Between 1945 and 1948, the Soviet military had a strong formative influence on the new YPA. The Soviet model was followed in organization, training, and even uniform style. The Soviet Union built some of the first military infrastructure, including airfields, command posts, and coastal gun emplacements, for the Tito government. Although damaged by Yugoslavia's 1948 break with the Soviet Union, military ties were renewed quickly after Soviet-Yugoslav relations were normalized in 1955. Annual bilateral exchanges began between the general staffs of the two countries.

Although such cooperation gave the Soviet Union considerable influence with the Yugoslav military, Yugoslavia rebuffed Soviet requests for formal naval base access and airfield landing rights, offering instead case-by-case consideration. Landing rights were granted Soviet aircraft during the 1967 and 1973 Middle East wars. Yugoslavia established a regular contract to maintain and repair Soviet submarines and submarine tenders in its shipyard at Kotor. Military ties to other countries, including the United States, served to balance these accommodations to the Soviet Union. The secretary for national defense last made an official visit to Washington in 1984.

Warship Visits

Warships from the Soviet Union and the United States made occasional port calls in Yugoslavia, but such visits sometimes aroused controversy. After an incident involving the United States aircraft carrier *Saratoga* in 1987, Yugoslavia amended its federal law to prohibit foreign warships from using nuclear power or carrying nuclear weapons from entering its territorial waters. The revised law also placed new restrictions on foreign port calls, limiting foreign countries to four formal visits of ten days or fewer each year. No more than three combat and two auxiliary ships of the same nation were allowed to enter Yugoslav waters during a six-month period. Maximum displacements for visiting ships were also set at 10,000 tons for combatants and 4,000 tons for submarines and auxiliary vessels. The carefully worded new law aimed visitation limits at the Mediterranean Squadron of the Soviet navy and displacement limits at the United States Navy's Sixth Fleet.

Arms Sales

In 1990 Yugoslavia was among a small group of less developed countries with industrial economies actively developing arms export industries. In the international arms market, competition from larger countries was formidable. A civilian government organization, the Directorate for Supply and Procurement, managed foreign sales programs. In the late 1980s, arms exports averaged over US$400 million per year, exceeding US$500 million per year twice between 1977 and 1987. However, the amount fluctuated by as much as 40 percent from year to year. Yugoslavia sold almost US$2 billion worth of weapons to Iraq in its war with Iran during the 1980s. In that decade, Yugoslav arms sales exceeded those of Warsaw Pact countries Hungary, the German Democratic Republic (East Germany), and Bulgaria; NATO members Belgium and the Netherlands; and neutral countries Austria, Sweden, and Switzerland. They were less than those of Warsaw Pact countries Poland, Czechoslovakia, and Romania and NATO countries Spain and Italy. Arms accounted for an average of 4 percent of total Yugoslav exports annually and as much as 6 or 7 percent in some years. In all, Yugoslav arms went to sixty-seven countries in 1990, but the Middle East and North Africa were the prime markets. Many top customer countries were members of the Nonaligned Movement. Among other weapons and equipment, Yugoslavia exported ammunition, antiarmor and antitank weapons systems, frigates, missile boats, and Mala swimmer delivery vehicles. A proposed expansion for the 1990s was to include foreign sale of the Orao ground attack fighter and the Partisan helicopter.

In the 1980s, Yugoslav weapons sales to troubled regions of the world became an important ethical issue for many citizens, especially in Slovenia. They objected to the lack of Federal Assembly oversight and public information about the country's arms industries and their dealings abroad. In the early 1980s, Yugoslavia apparently helped a Swedish firm avoid Sweden's strict arms export laws. It posed as the ultimate recipient of Bofors 40mm L/70 antiaircraft guns and artillery pieces that were subsequently reexported to Libya and Iraq. The incident revealed the extent of Yugoslav involvement in the international arms market. In 1988 the situation became a cause célèbre in Slovenia when the Slovenes who had revealed Yugoslavia's role were arrested and tried for divulging military secrets.

Military Exchanges

Yugoslavia conducted active military exchanges with a number of countries, including the United States, the Soviet Union, other NATO and Warsaw Pact countries, and several countries in North Africa and the Middle East. Reciprocal military visits with the United States were frequent in the late 1970s, a period of intense United States concern about the direction of post-Tito Yugoslavia. The United States secretary of defense visited Yugoslavia in 1977 to discuss possible arms sales and training for YPA officers in the United States. He and the Yugoslav secretary for national defense exchanged visits the following year. They discussed possible transfer of antitank, antiship, and air-to-surface missiles, aircraft engines, communications equipment, and an integrated naval air defense system. Of these, only the sale of Maverick air-to-surface missiles was completed. The chairman of the United States Joint Chiefs of Staff visited Yugoslavia in 1979 and 1985, and the secretary of defense returned there in 1982. These visits included discussions of the general strategic situation in Europe and the long-standing Yugoslav interest in buying advanced arms from the United States.

Despite the Soviet Union's role as Yugoslavia's leading arms supplier, relatively few high-level military exchanges occurred between the Soviet Union and Yugoslavia. A 1988 visit by the Soviet minister of defense to Belgrade was the first since 1976; the Yugoslav secretary for national defense returned this visit in 1989. Both visits featured discussion of increased military cooperation.

Yugoslavia had many contacts with countries in North Africa and the Middle East, with special attention to Libya, Egypt, and Ethiopia. Several high-level exchanges occurred with the Libyan armed forces in the late 1970s and 1980s. As a result, Libya purchased Yugoslav armored personnel carriers, small arms, patrol boats, and ammunition, as well as training for Libyan officers in Yugoslavia. Egypt and Yugoslavia established a military cooperation program in 1984. Reciprocal general staff visits in 1988 and 1989 elaborated the Yugoslav role in training Egyptian soldiers and upgrading older Soviet arms and equipment in the Egyptian inventory. In 1988 the Yugoslav secretary for national defense visited Ethiopia to promote military-industrial cooperation between the two countries.

Other significant military visits included reciprocal exchanges of high-ranking officers with India in 1979 and 1984 and with Angola in 1979 and 1986. Like Yugoslavia, each of those countries had large numbers of Soviet weapons systems that were the stimulus for military cooperation. Angola also expressed interest in Yugoslav aircraft and pilot training.

Internal Security

The internal security situation in Yugoslavia threatened national security in 1990. Internal ethnic tensions were a potential hindrance to defense against external threats. As was demonstrated in World War II, such discord could be exploited by an aggressor to overcome the Yugoslav armed forces and occupy the country. Even without external pressures, open civil war among different nationalities seemed a real possibility in 1990. Ethnic Albanians in Kosovo, Croats, and Slovenes felt that internal security provisions were applied against them with unwarranted severity. After the fall of East European communist regimes in 1989, the internal forces aroused by such suspicions and resentments overshadowed any external threat to national security.

Although ordinary crime was an increasing problem in Yugoslav society of the 1980s, political crime or dissidence was more widely publicized. Dissident activities ranged from peaceful protest and publication to the sensational politically motivated violence, assassination, and terrorism that had marked the country's history (see The Public and Political Decision Making, ch. 4). In the 1980s, nationalism was the force behind the most visible dissident activity. Deemed a threat to the unity of the Yugoslav federation, the advocacy of nationalism was officially considered criminal. Military courts exercised jurisdiction in all cases of dissidence because all forms of such activity were considered a threat to national security. In the 1980s, civilian internal security forces proved unable to manage large-scale political unrest effectively; they depended increasingly on YPA intervention in internal security matters.

Dissidence

Official Yugoslav sources reported that political offenses increased dramatically during the 1980s. Each year several hundred individuals were arrested on political charges. Those arrested generally were either intellectuals arguing for greater freedom of expression or nationalists agitating for change in the composition of the federal republic. Violent incidents were rare when compared with peaceful expressions of dissident political ideas.

The Yugoslav Constitution of 1974 guarantees the citizen many basic rights and freedoms, including petition (Article 157); opinion (Article 166); press, media, speech, expression, association, and assembly (Article 167); movement and abode (Article 183); inviolability of the home (Article 184); and confidentiality of communication (Article 185). Nevertheless, throughout the 1970s and 1980s writers, poets, sociologists, philosophers, and ordinary citizens received harsh punishments for exercising the basic political freedoms guaranteed by the Constitution as well as by international conventions to which Yugoslavia was a signatory. Major loopholes in the civil rights language of the Constitution legalized prosecution for undefined activities inimical to the established constitutional order (see Djilas, Praxis, and Intellectual Repression, ch. 4). By 1990 many proposals for a new constitution called for elimination of the vague language that had allowed selective prosecution. Given the open political climate in other East European states by 1990, Yugoslav government and LCY officials became increasingly sensitive to descriptions of Yugoslavia as a police state. Internal and external political events pressured the government and party toward competing with politically unacceptable opinions and ideas rather than imposing prison sentences on those who expressed them.

The federal criminal code of 1977 contained one chapter on petty offenses against the social system and security of the country. It included a number of political offenses and so-called "verbal crimes," another catchall category under which many types of opposition could be thwarted. Any article, pamphlet, or speech advocating changes in the socialist self-management system, disrupting the unity of nations and nationalities, or maliciously or untruthfully portraying sociopolitical conditions in the country was punishable by one to ten years in prison (Article 133). Also known as the Law on Hostile Propaganda, this was the most infamous and frequently applied criminal law against political activity. A conviction on charges of hostile propaganda did not require the prosecution to prove that the article, pamphlet, or speech in question was malicious or untruthful.

Article 133 carried a mandatory three-year sentence in cases with foreign involvement. Preparing, possessing, or reproducing such material for dissemination could bring a prison term of five years. A sentence for violating Article 133 usually was followed by a ban on public appearance and expression for several years. The law criminalized open criticism of the one-party political system, the LCY, or Tito; possession of unsanctioned historical treatises or émigré newspapers; granting of interviews or writing of works published abroad; authoring of political graffiti; and circulation of petitions to delete Article 133 from the federal criminal code. The Law on Hostile Propaganda was applied strictly against Yugoslav workers abroad, who often returned with émigré literature or newspapers in their possession. A less serious category of "verbal crime" was described as damaging the reputation of the state or its leaders and spreading false rumors. Such activity was punishable by short prison terms of one or two months.

In the wake of the Kosovo unrest in 1981, more than 2,000 ethnic Albanians, many of them students and instructors at the University of Priština, were arrested on charges of damaging official reputations. About 250 people received sentences under Article 133 for terms of one to fifteen years. Another 250 people received fines or sentences of sixty days for lesser "verbal crimes." Although some violent clashes had occurred, most convictions were for shouting or painting slogans on walls or distributing pamphlets or poems.

Several other laws criminalized peaceful political or nationalist association and assembly. Such activities included participation in hostile activity (Article 131), incitement to national hatred (Article 134), association for the purpose of hostile activity (Article 136), and counterrevolutionary endangering of the social order (Article 114). The maximum sentence among those provisions was eight years in prison. Yugoslavs abroad who contacted émigré political parties or nationalist groups or who participated in demonstrations inside the country have been sentenced under these laws. After the Croatian nationalist crisis of 1969–71, over 500 Croats were sentenced using those provisions. Article 134 in particular was applied to silence individuals who raised the political, economic, or cultural grievances of a particular nation or nationality or who complained of discrimination against such a group. The provision was used to prevent the public use of national flags and songs representing the ethnic groups of the Yugoslav federation.

In the absence of legal means of peaceful political expression, many individuals and groups resorted to violence. Several nationalist organizations maintained armed paramilitary or terrorist units. Their actions had the negative effect of justifying government repression of peaceful as well as violent dissidents. Nationalist groups aimed bombing and sabotage attacks at official targets in Yugoslavia and abroad.

The secret police relentlessly pursued underground nationalist groups. In 1984 twenty-three Croats identified with the separatist Croatian Militant Unity group were convicted for allegedly smuggling arms into the country and perpetrating a series of bombings. The next year, six Macedonians were imprisoned for a campaign of bombings during the early 1970s.

After two decades of unrest, ethnic Albanians in Kosovo increasingly turned to violence. They occasionally used firearms and explosives against the security forces, occupying YPA troops, and Serbs in Kosovo. This development indicated the adverse consequences of universal military training in a tense ethnic situation. Many ethnic Albanians involved in violent activity apparently had learned to handle weapons in the army or in the TDF. One group in Kosovo hijacked a government vehicle carrying small arms.

Courts, Detention, and Punishment

Arrest without warrant was standard procedure. Detainees had the right to know the reasons for their arrest within twenty-four hours, by which time their families were to be informed of their whereabouts. Under Article 178 of the Constitution, a prisoner could be held three days before a judge was required to decide whether further detention was permissible. The court could detain individuals for three months without charging them with a criminal offense. The federal Supreme Court had the power to extend imprisonment by an additional three months without charging the individual with a crime. The judiciary lacked sufficient independence to ensure impartial justice for all citizens. Judges were subject to party discipline by the LCY, through which they had reached office. Most judges were appointed only after receiving party approval of their "moral-political suitability." The State Presidency directly appointed and dismissed judges and prosecutors (see Court System, ch. 4).

Twelve major federal prisons were operated throughout the country. Even party veterans admitted that prison conditions were worse under the LCY-dominated government than they were under the old regime. Amnesty International received occasional reports of psychological and physical abuse applied to obtain confessions from detainees. That organization estimated that at least several hundred political prisoners were held in Yugoslavia in any given year of the 1980s. Thousands of other citizens were punished by more insidious means. The government often revoked or denied passports, or it dismissed suspicious individuals from employment in their chosen profession.

The military had a separate court system, which included the Office of the Military Prosecutor and the Supreme Military Court. Military courts tried cases involving criminal offenses by armed forces personnel and cases otherwise connected with military service. The most serious offenses in this category were desertion, dereliction of duty, and activities contrary to military morale. Article 221 of the Constitution also granted military courts jurisdiction over certain criminal offenses committed by civilians but related to national defense. They could impose sentences, including the death penalty, for criminal offenses that undermined the economic or military strength of the country in times of war or imminent danger of war. In the 1980s, military courts were increasingly used for proceedings against civilians because they could be conducted in closed sessions. The State Presidency appointed and dismissed military judges and prosecutors, as it did for civil courts.

In a highly publicized case in 1988, two young Slovenian journalists and a noncommissioned officer were arrested by military authorities and accused of illegally possessing secret military information. The journalists had recently published an article critical of the Yugoslav role as intermediary in Swedish arms sales to Libya and Iraq. When a military court in Ljubljana found them guilty of revealing military secrets, thousands of Slovenes protested the trial, and a rash of physical attacks on YPA personnel followed the verdict.

Internal Security Forces

Internal security forces were instrumental in establishing and maintaining the communist-controlled Yugoslav state after World War II. They were responsible for identifying and prosecuting Ustaše leaders and others who collaborated with occupying German and Italian forces during World War II. But alleged collaboration became a pretext for reprisals against political opponents such as the Četnici and others who did not support Tito's Partisans. Many, including Četnik leader Draža Mihajlović and Croatian Roman Catholic archbishop Alojzije Stepinac, were executed or imprisoned after summary trials.

After the break in relations with the Soviet Union in 1948, the Yugoslav government feared that the Soviet Union might find or create a group within Yugoslavia to request Soviet intervention to assist it in "preserving socialism." The Yugoslav security agency investigated more than 50,000 alleged "Cominformists" (from Cominform—see Glossary), or pro-Soviet party members, who were subsequently purged from the party. Several thousand were eventually jailed, either without trials or after show trials. They were interned in political prisons at Goli Otok in the Adriatic, at Sremska Mitrovica in Vojvodina, and at Stara Gradiška in Bosnia. Others were subjected to administrative punishment or petty harassment.

In 1948 the Soviet Union formed an orthodox CPY in exile to rally Tito's opponents and to topple him. To support this movement, an estimated 200 to 300 Yugoslav "Cominformists" took up residence in Moscow. The YPA was an important target of their anti-Tito propaganda. The CPY in exile held meetings outside the Soviet Union and clandestine party congresses inside Yugoslavia. During this time, Yugoslav internal security forces exercised great power and directed much of it at the YPA. Security agents exposed many real or suspected Soviet operatives in high positions in the YPA, and some of those accused were executed. The resulting bitterness and rivalry between the internal security forces and the YPA survived for decades afterward.

In 1966 a major purge of the Yugoslav internal security forces benefited the military in this rivalry. The chief of the secret police—the Directorate for State Security (Uprava državne bezbednosti—UDB)—Aleksandar Ranković, was involved in the behind-the-scenes struggle to be next in line to Tito. Allegedly on orders from Ranković, the UDB covertly monitored the telephone calls of all major party leaders, including Tito. When Ranković was dismissed in 1966, however, the official announcement mentioned only his responsibility for UDB brutality and repression of Kosovo's Albanian population. The military equivalent of the UDB, the Military Counterintelligence Service (Kontraobaveštajna služba—KOS) was instrumental in exposing UDB activities. The UDB was purged, its name was changed to the State Security Service (Služba državne bezbednosti—SDB), and a YPA general became its chief. In its new form, the agency retained substantial secret police powers.

The YPA has maintained some control over the civilian security service since the 1966 purge. After the Croatian nationalist unrest of 1971, a general became federal secretary for internal affairs (the secretariat controlling the SDB), and another became federal public prosecutor. Using such appointments, the military controlled the internal security forces until 1984. In 1990 a former chief of the YPA General Staff was federal secretary for internal affairs.

During the 1980s, the SDB actively pursued its mission of identifying and neutralizing émigré organizations in foreign countries to inhibit their efforts to establish contacts and support inside Yugoslavia. A small number of émigré groups of various political persuasions and nationalities committed violent acts against Yugoslav interests abroad. Those acts sometimes included assassinations of Yugoslav diplomats or representatives abroad. Special attention went to pro-Soviet Yugoslav exiles, whose activities against the Yugoslav government were well supported by Soviet funds. Believing that such groups threatened public order, the SDB and its clandestine foreign intelligence units used various means to counter their activities. The SDB monitored the activities of the pro-Soviet CPY organization, which advocated overthrow of Tito, in Yugoslavia and other countries. In 1974 thirty-two Montenegrins convicted of organizing a CPY congress received prison terms of up to fourteen years. A long investigation of this case ended in the arrest of a Soviet diplomat in 1976.

Another major task of the SDB was to monitor Croatian organizations in Austria, Sweden, France, West Germany, Canada, and the United States. Surveillance of these groups provided evidence for prosecuting Yugoslavs who contacted them when abroad and then returned home. The SDB reportedly abducted and assassinated prominent émigrés. A former YPA colonel who escaped imprisonment as an alleged "Cominformist" in 1948 was seized in Romania in 1976, clandestinely returned to Yugoslavia, and jailed. As many as twenty troublesome émigrés may have been killed in Europe by the SDB, by other Yugoslav operatives, or by their paid agents since the early 1970s. In 1981 two West Germans and one Yugoslav were convicted for murdering an émigré in West Germany. They were allegedly paid a large sum to kill a former SDB agent who defected from the security service while abroad. However, the Yugoslav government contended that most violence against émigrés was committed by rival émigré organizations, not by the SDB.

Organization for Internal Security

The Council for the Protection of the Constitutional Order was the highest government organization responsible for internal security matters. Its chairman was the president of the collective State Presidency, and its membership included the federal secretary for internal affairs, the federal secretary for national defense, and other military, party, and civilian officials. Under the Constitution, the State Presidency has the authority to order the use of the armed forces in peacetime to ensure internal security. It can suspend any provision in the Constitution if necessary for defense and security during war or imminent danger of war.

Considerable police and paramilitary power was concentrated in the Secretariat for Internal Affairs, which supervised the work of subordinate secretariats for internal affairs in the republics and provinces. Besides the SDB, the federal secretariat included the Office of the Federal Public Prosecutor, who in turn controlled public prosecutors in the republics.

The SDB was responsible for identifying and neutralizing subversive elements regarded as threats to the constitutional order and the socialist self-management system. Both violent groups and peaceful dissidents were included in this broad category. Plainclothes SDB agents investigated and monitored such groups and infiltrated their ranks. One of the SDB's most effective weapons was the concept of social self-protection. It was the equivalent of the TDF in internal security matters. Article 173 of the Constitution declared the duty of all citizens to participate in social self-protection by reporting immediately to the SDB their knowledge of "hostile activities," including ordinary crime, political offenses, and terrorism.

The Secretariat for Internal Affairs also controlled a federal paramilitary force, the People's Militia, which numbered more than 15,000 troops. This force operated numerous BOV–M armored vehicles equipped with machine guns, water cannons, smoke and tear gas launchers for crowd control and riot situations, armored personnel carriers, and helicopters. These internal security troops were well paid, heavily indoctrinated, experienced, and reliable. They could be deployed in times of political unrest or disorder when the local police were expected to side with the populace against federal authorities. The People's Militia provided security for the 1984 Winter Olympics in Sarajevo. The Secretariat for Internal Affairs also controlled 15,000 troops in border guard units. In coastal areas, the border guards operated sixteen patrol boats in 1990.

The secretariats for internal affairs in the republics and provinces controlled the militia (regular police) forces in their territory. In 1990 there were an estimated 40,000 professional law enforcement officers. They were responsible for maintaining government communications, issuing travel documents to citizens, and registering foreign residents. The average militia officer was male, twenty-two years of age, and had completed his secondary education in special schools operated by the Secretariat for Internal Affairs. Select militia officers were later sent for a university education.

The militia were organized into stations and substations in larger cities. They were involved in routine law enforcement as well as more sensitive cases involving ethnic groups. Cases ranged from physical attacks and harassment to homicide. In Priština, site of a major university and a center of Albanian ethnic dissidence, every confrontation with authority had the potential to erupt into large disturbances between ethnic communities. In 1990 that city had seven militia stations and four substations, serving a population of 400,000.

The Military in Domestic Peacekeeping

The YPA became involved in internal security when unrest in Kosovo escalated in 1981. Under a declaration of national emergency, the army intervened to stop demonstrations by ethnic Albanians beyond the control of the LCY, People's Militia, and local militia. Hundreds of citizens were injured, and some were killed during the YPA's suppression of the demonstrations. Some reports indicated that one-fourth of the YPA's total manpower remained in Kosovo to maintain order throughout the 1980s. The YPA presence added to local resentment; demonstrations resumed in 1987 and continued through 1990.

Use of military force against the domestic population to maintain order aroused controversy. Top government and party leaders, rank-and-file military, and government critics expressed varying opinions. Political leaders expected the military to ensure the unity of Yugoslavia and preserve its constitutional order against internal threats. Yet the internal security mission put the YPA under great stress because it was not structured or equipped for such activity. In Kosovo the YPA suffered consistent intense hostility from the ethnic Albanian population, including armed attacks by local militants. Some officers believed involvement in ethnic problems put the army in a dangerous position of opposing large segments of society. More important, they believed that such involvement might weaken or divide the YPA. Many in this group preferred to stay in the barracks and concentrate on defense against foreign aggression. Outside critics of the YPA also argued that its only legitimate role was external defense and that the army was a bulwark of the excessive centralism opposed by many citizens. The YPA seemed to be involved in all Yugoslavia's political and social crises. Some citizens looked to it for solutions; others viewed it as part of the country's problems.

The controversy surrounding the role of the YPA in 1990 meant that the political and social tensions of Yugoslavia had finally begun to affect the last bastion of all-Yugoslav solidarity. Significant reduction in the threat of foreign invasion and the urgent need for reduction in a high military budget also brought major changes in actual Yugoslav military practice—although in 1990 the World War II-vintage doctrine of civilian defense forces and preparation for invasion remained in place. At the policy level, Yugoslavia's nonaligned military position remained firm; greater emphasis on domestic arms manufacture and reduced reliance on the Soviet Union and other suppliers strengthened that position. Meanwhile, Yugoslav security forces continued to monitor dissident activity at home and abroad. As nationalist political activism grew in the 1980s, the role of the security forces increased, particularly in turbulent Kosovo. By 1990, however, the democratization of neighboring countries and the pluralization of Yugoslav society exerted substantial pressure to abolish laws that justified arbitrary prosecution of domestic dissident activity. Many observers believed that the fragmentation threatened by reduced control of nationalist activity might become a justification for military intervention in national politics or for expanded use of the YPA in quelling civil disturbances.

*   *   *

In *Yugoslavia's Security Dilemmas* and numerous articles, Marko Milivojević shows that he is a leading student of Yugoslav security and military affairs. A number of Yugoslav authors describe well the country's military history and doctrine. Walter R. Roberts's *Tito, Mihailović, and the Allies, 1941–1945,* a vital work on Yugoslavia during World War II, was revised and updated in 1987. Although articles by former YPA officer and émigré Milan N. Vego are somewhat dated, they offer firsthand experience with the subject. The Radio Free Europe/Radio Liberty reports on external security matters are useful sources of up-to-date information on external security matters. The *Daily Report: East Europe* of the Foreign

Broadcast Information Service is important for obtaining translations of illuminating articles from the Yugoslav military press. The United States Arms Control and Disarmament Agency's annual report *World Military Expenditures and Arms Transfers* is a source of data on the economics of national defense in Yugoslavia. Amnesty International reports provide reliable coverage of the internal security and human rights situation in the country. (For further information and complete citations, see Bibliography.)

Appendix

Table 1. Metric Conversion Coefficients and Factors

When you know	Multiply by	To find
Millimeters	0.04	inches
Centimeters	0.39	inches
Meters	3.3	feet
Kilometers	0.62	miles
Hectares (10,000 m²)	2.47	acres
Square kilometers	0.39	square miles
Cubic meters	35.3	cubic feet
Liters	0.26	gallons
Kilograms	2.2	pounds
Metric tons	0.98	long tons
....	1.1	short tons
....	2,204	pounds
Degrees Celsius	9	degrees Fahrenheit
(Centigrade)	divide by 5 and add 32	

Table 2. Life Expectancy by Republic and Province, 1952 and 1982

	Bosnia and Hercegovina	Croatia	Kosovo	Macedonia	Montenegro	Serbia Proper *	Slovenia	Vojvodina	All Yugoslavia
Males									
1952	52.6	59.1	48.6	54.9	58.4	59.1	63.0	58.3	56.9
1982	68.2	66.8	67.4	68.6	71.9	69.3	67.2	67.0	67.8
Females									
1952	52.6	59.1	48.6	54.9	58.4	59.1	63.0	58.3	56.9
1982	73.5	74.4	70.6	72.2	76.5	74.0	75.1	73.6	73.5

* Serbia proper is the Republic of Serbia excluding the provinces of Kosovo and Vojvodina.

Source: Based on information from Dušan Miljković (ed.), *Jugoslavija, 1945–1985*, Belgrade, 1986, 218.

Table 3. Birth Rates and Mortality Rates by Republic and Province, 1947 and 1984

	Bosnia and Hercegovina	Croatia	Kosovo	Macedonia	Montenegro	Serbia Proper[1]	Slovenia	Vojvodina	All Yugoslavia
Birth rate[2]									
1947	35.1	22.4	38.5	35.0	28.9	23.1	22.4	24.4	26.7
1984	16.9	14.1	31.0	20.0	17.3	14.0	14.7	12.8	16.4
Infant mortality rate[3]									
1947	125.6	112.0	133.2	136.1	41.0	91.2	81.3	129.7	102.2
1984	28.9	15.8	63.1	49.5	22.4	24.1	15.7	12.0	28.9
Total mortality rate[4]									
1947	12.8	13.5	13.0	13.7	6.9	11.1	13.5	15.2	12.8
1984	6.3	11.8	5.8	7.3	6.1	10.1	10.9	11.7	9.3

[1] Serbia proper is the Republic of Serbia excluding the provinces of Kosovo and Vojvodina.
[2] Live births per 1,000 individuals.
[3] Per 1,000 live births.
[4] Per 1,000 individuals.

Source: Based on information from Dušan Miljković (ed.), *Jugoslavija, 1945–1985*, Belgrade, 1986, 200.

Table 4. Population by Ethnic Group, 1948 and 1981

Ethnic Group	1948	1981
Serbs	6,547,117	8,140,452
Croats	3,784,353	4,428,005
Muslim Slavs	808,921	1,999,957
Slovenes	1,415,432	1,753,554
Albanians	750,431	1,730,364
Macedonians	810,126	1,339,729
Yugoslavs [1]	n.a.	1,219,045
Montenegrins	425,703	579,023
Hungarians	496,492	426,866
Gypsies	72,736	168,099
Turks	97,954	101,191
Slovaks	83,626	80,334
Romanians	64,095	54,954
Bulgars	61,140	36,185
Vlachs	102,953	32,063
Ruthenians	37,140	23,285
Czechs	39,015	19,625
Italians	79,575	15,132
Ukrainians	n.a.	12,813
Germans	55,337	8,712
Russians	20,069	4,463
Poles	n.a.	3,043
Greeks	n.a.	1,639
Austrians	n.a.	1,402
Jews	n.a.	1,383
Other	19,883	17,645
TOTAL	15,772,098	22,424,711 [2]

n.a.—not available.
[1] No ethnic identity claimed.
[2] Includes individuals not reporting or not reporting under prescribed census headings.

Source: Based on information from Yugoslavia, Savezni zavod za statistiku, *Statistički godišnjak Jugoslavije, 1989,* Belgrade, 1990, 122.

Table 5. Ethnic Structure of Republics and Provinces, 1981
(in percentages)

Ethnic Group	Bosnia and Hercegovina	Croatia	Kosovo	Macedonia	Montenegro	Serbia Proper [1]	Slovenia	Vojvodina	All Yugoslavia
Serbs	32.0	11.5	13.2	2.3	3.3	85.4	2.2	54.4	36.3
Montenegrins ...	0.3	0.2	1.7	0.2	68.5	1.4	0.2	2.1	2.6
Macedonians ...	0.1	0.1	0.1	67.0	0.2	0.5	0.2	0.9	6.0
Slovenes	0.1	0.6	—	—	0.2	0.1	90.5	0.1	7.8
Croats	18.4	75.1	0.5	0.2	1.4	0.5	2.9	5.4	19.8
Muslim Slavs ...	39.5	0.5	3.7	2.1	13.4	2.7	0.7	0.2	8.9
Yugoslavs [2] ...	7.9	8.2	0.2	0.7	5.3	4.8	1.4	8.2	5.4
Albanians	0.1	0.1	77.4	19.8	6.3	1.3	0.1	0.2	7.7
Hungarians	—	0.6	—	—	—	0.1	0.5	19.0	1.9
Other	1.6	3.1	3.2	1.4	1.4	3.2	1.3	9.2	3.6
TOTAL [3]	100.0	100.0	100.0	100.0	100.0	100.0	100.0	100.0	100.0

— means negligible.
[1] Serbia proper is the Republic of Serbia excluding the provinces of Kosovo and Vojvodina.
[2] No ethnic identity claimed.
[3] Figures may not add to total because of rounding.

Source: Based on information from Leonard Cohen and Paul Warwick, *Political Cohesion in a Fragile Mosaic*, Boulder, Colorado, 1983, 164.

Table 6. *Estimated Pension Recipients, 1965, 1982, and 1988*

	1965	1982	1988
Old-age	314,000	650,000	934,000
Disability	311,000	623,000	780,000
Survivor	224,000	487,000	621,000

Source: Based on information from Yugoslavia, Savezni zavod za statistiku, *Statistički godišnjak Jugoslavije, 1989,* Belgrade, 1990, 406.

Table 7. *Level of Education by Republic and Province, 1953 and 1981*
(in percentages of persons age ten or older)

Level	Bosnia and Hercegovina	Croatia	Kosovo	Macedonia	Montenegro	Serbia Proper[1]	Slovenia	Vojvodina	All Yugoslavia
1953									
No schooling	67.2	30.5	71.2	50.7	47.2	44.5	15.2	28.4	42.1
Primary (four years)	26.1	58.0	22.8	40.3	40.9	43.2	68.2	56.5	46.0
Primary (eight years)	2.4	4.8	1.9	3.5	5.7	4.0	4.5	6.5	4.2
Secondary	4.1	7.3	2.3	3.8	5.3	7.0	11.2	7.5	6.6
Higher education	0.3	0.7	0.1	0.3	0.5	0.8	0.8	0.5	0.6
Total[2]	100.0	100.0	100.0	100.0	100.0	100.0	100.0	100.0	100.0
1981									
No schooling	25.2	13.5	27.9	17.5	17.5	18.7	3.6	13.4	17.3
Primary (four years)	24.3	31.9	17.1	27.8	24.6	29.8	22.4	21.2	26.8
Primary (eight years)	24.2	19.2	34.4	28.1	23.1	18.8	32.5	31.7	24.2
Secondary	21.7	28.3	15.3	21.2	28.3	25.1	34.5	27.1	25.5
Higher education	4.3	6.4	3.3	5.1	6.2	6.4	5.9	5.1	5.6
Total[2]	100.0	100.0	100.0	100.0	100.0	100.0	100.0	100.0	100.0

[1] Serbia proper is the Republic of Serbia excluding the provinces of Kosovo and Vojvodina.
[2] Figures may not add to total because of rounding.

Source: Based on information from Dušan Miljković (ed.), *Jugoslavija, 1945–1985*, Belgrade, 1986, 199.

Table 8. Schools Teaching Minority Languages, 1987

Language	Primary Schools	Secondary Schools
Albanian	1,221	112
Bulgarian	40	n.a.
Hungarian	151	25
Italian	27	7
Romanian	31	2
Turkish	66	14
Other *	40	4

n.a.—not available.
* Czech, Russian, Slovak, and Ukrainian.

Source: Based on information from Yugoslavia, Savezni zavod za statistiku, *Statistički godišnjak Jugoslavije, 1989,* Belgrade, 1990, 373.

Table 9. Literacy Rate by Republic and Province, 1948 and 1981

Republic or Province	1948	1981
Bosnia and Hercegovina	55.1	85.5
Croatia	84.4	94.4
Kosovo	37.5	82.4
Macedonia	59.7	89.1
Montenegro	73.6	90.6
Serbia proper *	72.6	88.9
Slovenia	97.6	99.2
Vojvodina	88.2	94.2
YUGOSLAVIA	74.6	90.5

* Serbia proper is the Republic of Serbia excluding the provinces of Kosovo and Vojvodina.

Source: Based on information from Dušan Miljković (ed.), *Jugoslavija, 1945–1985,* Belgrade, 1986, 199; and Joseph Rothschild, *East Central Europe Between the Two World Wars,* Seattle, 1974, ix.

Table 10. Medical Personnel and Hospital Beds, Selected Years, 1955–87

	1955	1965	1975	1987
Physicians				
Specialists	n.a.	9,714	13,466	24,897
Other	n.a.	5,729	10,747	20,972
Total physicians	8,136	15,443	24,213	45,869
Medical workers	n.a.	53,150	95,004	145,372
Hospital beds	68,165	112,958	127,645	142,427

n.a.—not available.

Source: Based on information from Yugoslavia, Savezni zavod za statistiku, *Statistički godišnjak Jugoslavije, 1989,* Belgrade, 1990, 400.

Table 11. Government Budget, 1988
(in billions of dinars)*

	Republic, Province, and Commune	Federal
Schools	128	0
Defense	50	5,247
Public health and social welfare	334	1,184
Government	3,234	454
Other	3,402	712
TOTAL	7,148	7,597

* For value of the dinar—see Glossary.

Source: Based on information from *The Europa World Year Book, 1990,* 2, London, 1990, 2976.

Table 12. Employment in Selected Enterprise Categories,
1975, 1985, and 1988
(in thousands of workers)

Enterprise Category	1975	1985	1988
Manufacturing and mining	1,819	2,529	2,716
Agriculture and fishing	177	233	246
Construction	492	608	584
Transport and communications	346	441	459
Commerce	476	641	676
Handicrafts	170	254	278
Education and culture	354	429	449
Health and social welfare	239	376	420
Other	685	1,005	1,056
TOTAL	4,758	6,516	6,884

Source: Based on information from Yugoslavia, Savezni zavod za statistiku, *Statistički godišnjak Jugoslavije, 1989,* Belgrade, 1990, 144.

Table 13. Indexes of Production in Selected Nonpriority Industries,
Selected Years, 1952–90
(1987 = 100)

Industry	1952	1960	1970	1980	1990
Finished wood products	5	17	44	98	103
Construction materials	13	30	50	105	101
Food	5	26	48	88	96
Beverages	3	14	40	96	99
Paper products	3	11	42	86	102
Tobacco products	29	41	55	92	87

Source: Based on information from Yugoslavia, Savezni zavod za statistiku, *Statistički godišnjak Jugoslavije, 1989,* Belgrade, 1990, 280.

Table 14. Indicators of Agricultural Development, 1975, 1985, and 1988

	1975	1985	1988
Tractors [1]			
State	26	32	33
Private	200	850	1,033
Total tractors	226	882	1,066
Livestock [1]			
State	458	863	924
Private	4,981	4,412	4,153
Total livestock	5,439	5,275	5,077
Cultivated area [2]			
State	1,535	1,695	1,741
Private	8,466	8,146	8,077
Total cultivated area	10,001	9,841	9,818

[1] In thousands.
[2] In thousands of hectares.

Source: Based on information from Yugoslavia, Savezni zavod za statistiku, *Statistički godišnjak Jugoslavije, 1989,* Belgrade, 1990, 250.

Table 15. Value of Selected Exports, 1986, 1987, and 1988 (in billions of dinars) *

Commodity	1986	1987	1988
Food and live animals	341	680	2,455
Nonfuel crude materials	171	435	1,801
Mineral fuels and lubricants	80	170	520
Chemicals	478	996	2,982
Textiles	151	326	1,326
Iron and steel	153	524	2,014
Nonferrous metals	189	519	2,113
Machinery and transport equipment	1,381	2,683	5,127

* For value of the dinar—see Glossary.

Source: Based on information from *The Europa World Year Book, 1990,* 2, London, 1990, 2977-78.

Table 16. Value of Selected Imports, 1986, 1987, and 1988
(in billions of dinars) *

Commodity	1986	1987	1988
Food and live animals	296	529	2,126
Nonfuel crude materials	483	877	3,765
Mineral fuels and lubricants	925	1,659	6,055
Chemicals	707	1,553	5,958
Textiles	152	363	1,087
Iron and steel	292	508	1,650
Machinery and transport equipment	1,483	2,904	9,340

* For value of the dinar—see Glossary.

Source: Based on information from *The Europa World Year Book, 1990,* 2, London, 1990,
2977–78.

Table 17. Principal Trading Partners, 1988
(in billions of dinars) [1]

Country	Imports [2]	Exports [3]
Austria	1,569	1,127
Czechoslovakia	1,183	1,380
France	1,450	1,281
Iraq	1,642	1,034
Italy	3,582	4,922
Poland	1,134	1,283
Soviet Union	4,569	6,145
United States	1,901	1,892
West Germany	5,898	3,728
Other	11,449	10,089
TOTAL	34,377	32,881

[1] For value of the dinar—see Glossary.
[2] Cost, insurance, and freight.
[3] Free on board.

Source: Based on information from *The Europa World Year Book, 1990,* 2, London, 1990,
2977–78.

Table 18. Debt Data, 1984, 1986, and 1988
(in millions of United States dollars)

	1984	1986	1988
Gross national product	44,274	64,664	49,782
International reserves	1,732	2,189	3,074
External debt, excluding IMF *	17,691	19,414	20,373
Principal repayments	1,567	1,540	1,773
Net flows	-120	-886	52
Interest payments	2,338	1,777	1,401

* IMF—International Monetary Fund.

Source: Based on information from World Bank, *World Debt Tables, 1989–90,* Washington, 1990, 21.

Table 19. Area and Population of Republics and Provinces, 1981

Republic or Province	Area [1]	Population	Capital
Bosnia and Hercegovina	51,129	4,124,008	Sarajevo
Croatia	56,538	4,601,469	Zagreb
Kosovo	10,887	1,584,441	Priština
Macedonia	25,713	1,912,257	Skopje
Montenegro	13,812	584,310	Titograd
Serbia proper [2]	55,968	5,694,464	Belgrade
Slovenia	20,251	1,891,864	Ljubljana
Vojvodina	21,506	2,034,772	Novi Sad
TOTAL	255,804	22,427,585	

[1] In square kilometers.
[2] Serbia proper is the Republic of Serbia excluding the provinces of Kosovo and Vojvodina. The total area of the Republic of Serbia is 88,361 square kilometers, and the total population of the republic is 9,313,677.

Source: Based on information from *The Europa Year Book, 1990,* 2, London, 1990, 2974.

Bibliography

Chapter 1

Adamček, Josip. "Ekonomsko-društveni razvoj u sjeverozapadnoj Hrvatskoj u 16. i 17. stoleći." Pages 15–40 in Mirjana Gross (ed.), *Društveni razvoj u Hrvatskoj*. Zagreb: Sveučilišna naklada Liber, 1981.

_____. "Seljačka buna 1573." Pages 41–58 in Mirjana Gross (ed.), *Društveni razvoj u Hrvatskoj*. Zagreb: Sveučilišna naklada Liber, 1981.

Alexander, John. *Jugoslavia Before the Roman Conquest*. London: Thames and Hudson, 1972.

Barker, Elisabeth. *Macedonia*. London: Royal Institute of International Affairs, 1950.

Bogdanović, Dimitrije. *Knjiga o Kosovu*. Belgrade: Srpska akademija nauka i umetnosti, 1986.

Burg, Steven L. *Conflict and Cohesion in Socialist Yugoslavia*. Princeton: Princeton University Press, 1983.

Clissold, Stephen. *Yugoslavia and the Soviet Union, 1939–1973*. London: Oxford University Press, 1975.

Clissold, Stephen (ed.). *A Short History of Yugoslavia*. Cambridge: Cambridge University Press, 1966.

Crankshaw, Edward. *Khrushchev: A Career*. New York: Viking Press, 1966.

Črnja, Zvane. *Kulturna historija Hrvatske*. Zagreb: Epoha, 1965.

Cviić, K.F. "The Nature of Government and Politics in Yugoslavia." Pages 345–63 in George Schöpflin (ed.), *The Soviet Union and Eastern Europe*. New York: Facts on File, 1986.

Dedijer, Vladimir, et al. *History of Yugoslavia*. New York: McGraw-Hill, 1974.

Denitch, Bogdan. "Yugoslavia: The Limits of Reform," *Dissent*, 36, Winter 1989, 78–85.

Deutscher, Isaac. *Stalin*. New York: Oxford University Press, 1967.

Djilas, Milovan. *Land Without Justice*. New York: Harcourt Brace, 1958.

_____. *The Unperfect Society*. New York: Harcourt, Brace and World, 1969.

Djordjević, Dimitrije (ed.). *The Creation of Yugoslavia, 1914–1918*. Santa Barbara, California: Clio Books, 1980.

Dragnich, Alex N. *The First Yugoslavia*. Stanford, California: Hoover Institution Press, 1983.

Dvornik, Francis. *Byzantine Missions among the Slavs.* New Brunswick, New Jersey: Rutgers University Press, 1970.

_____. *The Making of Central and Eastern Europe.* Gulf Breeze, Florida: Academic International Press, 1974.

_____. *The Slavs: Their Early History and Civilization.* Boston: American Academy of Art and Sciences, 1956.

_____. *The Slavs in European History and Civilization.* New Brunswick, New Jersey: Rutgers University Press, 1962.

Ekmečić, Milorad. ''Serbian War Aims.'' Pages 20–31 in Dimitrije Djordjević (ed.), *The Creation of Yugoslavia, 1914–1918.* Santa Barbara, California: Clio Books, 1980.

Freidenreich, Harriet Pass. *The Jews of Yugoslavia.* Philadelphia: Jewish Publication Society of America, 1979.

Gati, Charles. *Hungary and the Soviet Bloc.* Durham, North Carolina: Duke University Press, 1986.

Germany. Foreign Ministry. *Documents on German Foreign Policy, 1919–1945.* Washington: GPO, 1949.

Gömöri, George. ''The Political and Social Setting of the Contemporary Arts.'' Pages 547–64 in George Schöpflin (ed.), *The Soviet Union and Eastern Europe.* New York: Facts on File, 1986.

Gross, Mirjana (ed.). *Društveni razvoj u Hrvatskoj.* Zagreb: Sveučilišna naklada Liber, 1981.

Guldescu, Stanko. *History of Medieval Croatia.* The Hague: Mouton, 1964.

Herodotus. *The Persian Wars.* New York: Modern Library, 1942.

Hoptner, J.B. *Yugoslavia in Crisis, 1934–1941.* New York: Columbia University Press, 1962.

Ilustrirana povijest Hrvata. Zagreb: Stvarnost, 1971.

Ionescu, Ghita. *Communism in Rumania.* London: Oxford University Press, 1964.

Kann, Robert A. *A History of the Habsburg Empire.* Berkeley: University of California Press, 1974.

Lampe, John R. ''Unifying the Yugoslav Economy, 1918–1921: Misery and Early Misunderstandings.'' Pages 139–56 in Dimitrije Djordjević (ed.), *The Creation of Yugoslavia, 1914–1918.* Santa Barbara, California: Clio Books, 1980.

Littlefield, Frank C. *Germany and Yugoslavia, 1933–1941.* Boulder, Colorado: East European Monographs, 1988.

Logoreci, Anton. ''A Clash Between Two Nationalities in Kosova.'' Pages 185–94 in Arshi Pipa and Sami Repishti (eds.), *Studies on Kosova.* Boulder, Colorado: East European Monographs, 1984.

Macartney, Carlile Alymer. *Hungary: A Short History.* Edinburgh: University Press, 1962.

McDonald, Gordon C., et al. *Yugoslavia: A Country Study.* (DA Pam 550–99.) Washington: GPO for Foreign Area Studies, The American University, 1971.

Mićunović, Veljko. *Moskovske godine, 1956–1958.* Belgrade: Jugoslovenska revija, 1984.

———. *Moskovske godine, 1969–1971.* Belgrade: Jugoslovenska revija, 1984.

Omrćanin, Ivo. *Diplomatic and Political History of Croatia.* Philadelphia: Dorrance, 1972.

Pipa, Arshi. "The Other Albania: A Balkan Perspective." Pages 164–73 in Arshi Pipa and Sami Repishti (eds.), *Studies on Kosova.* Boulder, Colorado: East European Monographs, 1984.

Pipa, Arshi, and Sami Repishti (eds.). *Studies on Kosova.* Boulder, Colorado: East European Monographs, 1984.

Popović, Nenad. *Yugoslavia: The New Class in Crisis.* Syracuse, New York: Syracuse University Press, 1968.

Remington, Robin Alison. "Nation Versus Class in Yugoslavia," *Current History,* 86, No. 11, November 1987, 365–68, 386–87.

Roberts, Allen. *The Turning Point: The Assassination of Louis Barthou and King Alexander I of Yugoslavia.* New York: St. Martin's Press, 1970.

Rogel, Carole. *The Slovenes and Yugoslavism, 1890–1914.* Boulder, Colorado: East European Quarterly, 1977.

Rostovzeff, M. *Rome.* Oxford: Oxford University Press, 1960.

Rothenberg, Gunther. *The Military Border in Croatia, 1740–1881.* Chicago: University of Chicago Press, 1966.

Rusinow, Dennison. *The Yugoslav Experiment, 1948–1974.* Berkeley: University of California Press, 1977.

Rusinow, Dennison (ed.). *Yugoslavia: A Fractured Federalism.* Washington: Wilson Center Press, 1988.

Schöpflin, George (ed.). *The Soviet Union and Eastern Europe.* New York: Facts on File, 1986.

Seton-Watson, Robert William. *The Southern Slav Question.* New York: Howard Fertig, 1969.

Sherman, Laura Beth. *Fires on the Mountain.* Boulder, Colorado: East European Monographs, 1980.

Singleton, Fred. *A Short History of the Yugoslav Peoples.* Cambridge: Cambridge University Press, 1985.

———. *Twentieth-Century Yugoslavia.* New York: Columbia University Press, 1976.

Staar, Richard F. *Communist Regimes in Eastern Europe.* Stanford, California: Hoover Institution Press, 1988.

Stanojević, Stanoje. *Istorija srpskoga naroda.* Belgrade: Altera, 1989.

Stanovičić, Vojislav. "History and Status of Ethnic Conflicts."

Pages 23–40 in Dennison Rusinow (ed.), *Yugoslavia: A Fractured Federalism.* Washington: Wilson Center Press, 1988.

Stokes, Gale. "The Role of the Yugoslav Committee in the Formation of Yugoslavia." Pages 51–65 in Dimitrije Djordjević (ed.), *The Creation of Yugoslavia, 1914–1918.* Santa Barbara, California: Clio Books, 1980.

Sulimirski, Tadeusz. *The Sarmatians.* New York: Praeger, 1970.

_____. "Sarmatians in the Polish Past," *The Polish Review,* 9, No. 1, Winter 1964, 13–66.

Toynbee, Arnold. *Constantine Porphyrogenitus and His World.* London: Oxford University Press, 1973.

Trifunović, Lazar. *Yugoslavia from Prehistory to the Present Day: Monuments of Art.* Belgrade: Jugoslovenska knjiga, 1988.

Ulam, Adam. *Titoism and the Cominform.* Cambridge: Harvard University Press, 1952.

United Kingdom. Admiralty. Naval Intelligence Division. *Yugoslavia, 2: History, Peoples, and Administration.* London: 1944.

Vasiliev, A.A. *History of the Byzantine Empire.* Madison: University of Wisconsin Press, 1952.

Vucinic, Wayne. "The Formation of Yugoslavia." Pages 184–95 in Dimitrije Djordjević (ed.), *The Creation of Yugoslavia, 1914–1918.* Santa Barbara, California: Clio Books, 1980.

West, Rebecca. *Black Lamb and Grey Falcon.* New York: Viking Press, 1943.

Williams, Stephen. *Diocletian and the Roman Recovery.* New York: Methuen, 1985.

Wolff, Robert Lee. *The Balkans in Our Time.* Cambridge: Harvard University Press, 1956.

Chapter 2

Albert, Hartmut. "Kosovo 1979, Albania 1980." Pages 103–21 in Arshi Pipa and Sami Repishti (eds.), *Studies on Kosova.* Boulder, Colorado: East European Monographs, 1984.

Alexander, Stella. *Church and State in Yugoslavia since 1945.* Cambridge: Cambridge University Press, 1973.

Auty, Phyllis. "Yugoslavia: Introduction." Pages 283–93 in G.F. Cushing et al. (eds.), *Contrasts in Emerging Societies: Readings in the Social and Economic History of South-Eastern Europe.* London: Athlone Press for the University of London, 1965.

Banac, Ivo. *The National Question in Yugoslavia: Origins, History, Politics.* Ithaca: Cornell University Press, 1988.

Bartl, Peter. "Kosovo and Macedonia as Reflected in Ecclesiastical

Reports." Pages 23–40 in Arshi Pipa and Sami Repishti (eds.), *Studies on Kosova*. Boulder, Colorado: East European Monographs, 1984.

Basta-Nadaški, Ljubica. "Women's Maternity Health Care and Welfare, 1976–86," *Yugoslav Survey* [Belgrade], 29, No. 3, 1988, 145–54.

Bečin, Aleksandar, and Milosav Milosavljević. "Social Work Centres," *Yugoslav Survey* [Belgrade], 28, No. 1, 1987, 117–34.

Blagojević, Dušan, and Dragoljub Vujica (eds.). *Moslems in Yugoslavia*. Belgrade: Review of International Affairs, 1985.

Bogavać, Snežana. "Jugosloveni, napolje?" *Borba* [Belgrade], June 30–July 1, 1990, 6.

Breznik, Dušan. "The Population of Kosovo," *Yugoslav Survey* [Belgrade], 30, No. 4, 1989, 3–28.

Breznik, Dušan, and Nada Raduški. "The Economic and Professional Composition of the Labor Force, 1961–1981," *Yugoslav Survey* [Belgrade], 29, No. 3, 1988, 3–24.

Burg, Steven L. *Conflict and Cohesion in Socialist Yugoslavia*. Princeton: Princeton University Press, 1983.

Čelić, Džemal. "Islam and the Cultural Heritage of Yugoslavia." Pages 47–62 in Dušan Blagojević and Dragoljub Vujica (eds.), *Moslems in Yugoslavia*. Belgrade: Review of International Affairs, 1985.

Cerović, Z. "Reke teku uzalud," *Borba* [Belgrade], May 8, 1990, 9.

Cohen, Leonard, and Paul Warwick. *Political Cohesion in a Fragile Mosaic*. Boulder, Colorado: Westview Press, 1983.

Cushing, G.F., et al. (eds.). *Contrasts in Emerging Societies: Readings in the Social and Economic History of South-Eastern Europe*. London: Athlone Press for the University of London, 1965.

Dempsey, Judy. "Religion in the Soviet Union and Eastern Europe." Pages 583–89 in George Schöpflin (ed.), *The Soviet Union and Eastern Europe*. New York: Facts on File, 1986.

Denitch, Bogdan. "Yugoslavia: The Limits of Reform: Economic Crisis, Nationalism, Inner Strife," *Dissent*, 36, Winter 1989, 78–85.

Djurdjić, Rajko. "U Skupštini," *Nin* [Belgrade], No. 2053, May 6, 1990, 22.

Doder, Dusko. *The Yugoslavs*. New York: Vintage, 1979.

Ducellier, Alain. "Genesis and Failure of the Albanian State in the Fourteenth and Fifteenth Centuries." Pages 3–22 in Arshi Pipa and Sami Repishti (eds.), *Studies on Kosova*. Boulder, Colorado: East European Monographs, 1984.

Duraković, Nijaz. "National Question of Moslems in Yugoslavia." Pages 21–46 in Dušan Blagojević and Dragoljub Vujica (eds.),

Moslems in Yugoslavia. Belgrade: Review of International Affairs, 1985.

Filipović, Nedim. "Forming of Moslem Ethnicon in Bosnia and Hercegovina." Pages 1-20 in Dušan Blagojević and Dragoljub Vujica (eds.), *Moslems in Yugoslavia.* Belgrade: Review of International Affairs, 1985.

Gapić, Marija. "Pension and Disability Insurance of Farmers," *Yugoslav Survey* [Belgrade], 28, No. 4, 1987, 135-44.

Grozdanić, Sulejman, and Srdjan Janković. "Literature of the Moslems of Bosnia and Hercegovina in Oriental Languages." Pages 63-75 in Dušan Blagojević and Dragoljub Vujica (eds.), *Moslems in Yugoslavia.* Belgrade: Review of International Affairs, 1985.

Halpern, Joel M. *A Serbian Village.* New York: Harper and Row, 1967.

"Higher Education and Doctorates Conferred," *Yugoslav Survey* [Belgrade], 30, No. 1, 1988, 157-60.

Jancar, Barbara. "Environmental Protection: The Tragedy of the Republics." Pages 224-45 in Pedro Ramet (ed.), *Yugoslavia in the 1980s.* Boulder, Colorado: Westview Press, 1985.

_____. "The New Feminism in Yugoslavia." Pages 201-23 in Pedro Ramet (ed.), *Yugoslavia in the 1980s.* Boulder, Colorado: Westview Press, 1985.

Jončić, Koča. *Nationalities in Yugoslavia.* Belgrade: Jugoslavenska stvarnost—medjunarodna politika, 1982.

Jovanović, Dragan. "Demonstracija je, ipak, bilo," *Borba* [Belgrade], May 8, 1990, 9.

Jovanović, M. "Conservative Peasants." Pages 307-13 in G.F. Cushing et al. (eds.), *Contrasts in Emerging Societies: Readings in the Social and Economic History of South-Eastern Europe.* London: Athlone Press for the University of London, 1965.

Jovičić, Vladimir (ed.). *Serbia.* Belgrade: Jugoslovenska revija, 1982.

Karadžić, Vuk. "The Peasant Nation." Pages 296-99 in G.F. Cushing et al. (eds.), *Contrasts in Emerging Societies: Readings in the Social and Economic History of South-Eastern Europe.* London: Athlone Press for the University of London, 1965.

Klančir, Djurdjica. "Tiha, prljava rabota," *Danas* [Ljubljana], No. 415, January 30, 1990, 74-5.

Logoreci, Anton. "A Clash Between Two Nationalities in Kosovo." Pages 185-94 in Arshi Pipa and Sami Repishti (eds.), *Studies on Kosova.* Boulder, Colorado: East European Monographs, 1984.

Macura, Miloš. "The Problem of Natality in Kosovo." Pages 190-97 in Ranko Petković (ed.), *Kosovo: Past and Present.* Belgrade: Review of International Affairs, 1989.

Milačić, Tomislav (ed.). *Handbook on Yugoslavia.* Belgrade: Federal Secretariat of Information, 1987.

Miljka, Dušan. "Hoće li papa kleknuti u Jasenovcu," *Nin* [Belgrade], No. 2053, May 6, 1990, 9–11.

Miljković, Dušan (ed.). *Jugoslavija, 1945–1985.* Belgrade: Savezni zavod za statistiku, 1986.

Miller, Robert F. "Church and State in Yugoslavia: Exorcising the Spectre of 'Clerico-Nationalism'," *South Slav Journal* [London], 10, Summer 1987, 9–29.

Milosavljević, Milosav. "Social Welfare, 1974–1986," *Yugoslav Survey* [Belgrade], 29, No. 3, 1988, 119–44.

Nikolić, Milenko, and Tomislav Bogavać. *Educational Policy in Yugoslavia.* Belgrade: Jugoslovenska stvarnost, 1980.

Obradović, Josip. "Socijalna struktura i obrazovna reforma," *Sociologija* [Belgrade], 25, No. 4, October-December 1983, 397–417.

Palošević, Abidin. "Agricultural Land," *Yugoslav Survey* [Belgrade], 29, No. 3, 1988, 59–70.

_____. "Land Policy," *Yugoslav Survey* [Belgrade], 30, No. 1, 1989, 79–93.

Penev, Goran, and Nada Raduški. "The Non-Agricultural Population," *Yugoslav Survey* [Belgrade], 28, No. 3, 1987, 3–24.

"Penzija za sve zemljoradnike," *Bilten za akreditovane novinare* [Belgrade], No. 20, April 4, 1990, 6.

Perovic, Marina (ed.). *Tanjug International Press Center Handbook, 1989–1990.* Belgrade: Tanjug International Press Center, 1989.

Petković, Ranko (ed.). *Kosovo: Past and Present.* Belgrade: Review of International Affairs, 1989.

Petranović, Branko, and Momčilo Zečević. *Jugoslovenski federalizam: ideje i stvarnost,* 2. Belgrade: Prosveta, 1987.

Petrović, Ruža, and Marina Blagojević. "Migrations of Serbs and Montenegrins from Kosovo and Metohija," Pages 258–69 in Ranko Petković (ed.), *Kosovo: Past and Present.* Belgrade: Review of International Affairs, 1989.

_____. *Seobe Srba i Crnogoraca sa Kosova i iz Metohije.* Belgrade: Srpska akademija nauka i umetnosti, 1989.

Pipa, Arshi. "The Other Albania: A Balkan Perspective." Pages 239–55 in Arshi Pipa and Sami Repishti (eds.), *Studies on Kosova.* Boulder, Colorado: East European Monographs, 1984.

_____. "The Political Situation of the Albanians in Yugoslavia with Particular Attention to the Kosovo Problem," *East European Quarterly,* 23, No. 2, June 1989, 159–81.

Pipa, Arshi, and Sami Repishti (eds.). *Studies on Kosova.* Boulder, Colorado: East European Monographs, 1984.

Pižurica, Olga. "Educational-Pedagogical Service," *Yugoslav Survey* [Belgrade], 28, No. 1, 1987, 109–16.

Poček, Branko. "Disability Insurance Benefits, 1980–85," *Yugoslav Survey* [Belgrade], 27, No. 3, 1986, 143–49.

_____. "Inpatient Health Care," *Yugoslav Survey* [Belgrade], 27, No. 3, 1986, 149–54.

Popović, Božidar. "The Housing Policy and Housing," *Yugoslav Survey* [Belgrade], 29, No. 3, 1988, 89–118.

Potkonjak, Nikola. "Elementary and Secondary School Teachers," *Yugoslav Survey* [Belgrade], 30, No. 1, 1989, 112–18.

_____. "Secondary Education," *Yugoslav Survey* [Belgrade], 27, No. 3, 1986, 111–42.

Prifti, Peter. "Kosovo's Economy: Problems and Prospects." Pages 125–61 in Arshi Pipa and Sami Repishti (eds.), *Studies on Kosova*. Boulder, Colorado: East European Monographs, 1984.

Radivojević, Biljana. "Mortality," *Yugoslav Survey* [Belgrade], 30, No. 1, 1989, 67–78.

Ramet, Pedro. *Nationalism and Federalism in Yugoslavia, 1963–1983.* Bloomington: Indiana University Press, 1984.

_____. "The Rock Scene in Yugoslavia," *Eastern European Politics and Societies,* 2, Spring 1988, 396–410.

_____. "Yugoslavia 1987: Stirrings from Below," *South Slav Journal* [London], 10, Fall 1987, 21–35.

Ramet, Pedro (ed.). *Yugoslavia in the 1980s.* Boulder, Colorado: Westview Press, 1985.

Rapi, Djerdj. "Promene u strukturi porodice na selu u SAR Kosovo," *Sociologija sela* [Belgrade], 24, Nos. 91–94, 1986, 79–93.

Remington, Robin Alison. "Nation Versus Class in Yugoslavia," *Current History,* 86, No. 11, November 1987, 365–68, 386–87.

Repishti, Sami. "The Evolution of Kosova's Autonomy." Pages 195–232 in Arshi Pipa and Sami Repishti (eds.), *Studies on Kosova*. Boulder, Colorado: East European Monographs, 1984.

Rothschild, Joseph. *East Central Europe Between the Two World Wars.* Seattle: University of Washington Press, 1974.

Rusinow, Dennison. *The Yugoslav Experiment, 1948–1974.* Berkeley: University of California Press, 1977.

Rusinow, Dennison (ed.). *Yugoslavia: A Fractured Federalism.* Washington: Wilson Center Press, 1988.

Samardžić, Radovan. *Religious Communities in Yugoslavia.* Belgrade: Jugoslovenska stvarnost, 1981.

Schöpflin, George (ed.). *The Soviet Union and Eastern Europe.* New York: Facts on File, 1986.

Šekelj, Laslo. "Yugoslavia: A Party State in Crisis," *Studies of Comparative Communism,* 21, Fall-Winter 1988, 389–98.

Seroka, Jim. "Contemporary Issues and Stability in Socialist Yugoslavia," *Journal of Communist Studies,* 2, No. 6, June 1986, 127–44.

Seroka, Jim, and Vukašin Pavlović. "Yugoslav Trade Unions and the Paralysis of Political Decision-Making," *Eastern European Politics and Societies,* 1, Spring 1987, 277–94.

Shoup, Paul. "The Government and Constitutional Status of Kosova: Some Brief Remarks." Pages 233–38 in Arshi Pipa and Sami Repeshti (eds.), *Studies on Kosova.* Boulder, Colorado: East European Monographs, 1984.

Simić, Snežana, et al. (eds.). "Assessment of the Effects of Cost-Sharing in Yugoslavia," *Medical Care* [Belgrade], 26, February 1988, 148–58.

Šimonović, Ivan. "Socialism, Federalism, and Ethnic Identity." Pages 41–57 in Dennison Rusinow (ed.), *Yugoslavia: A Fractured Federalism.* Washington: Wilson Center Press, 1988.

Singleton, Fred. *Twentieth-Century Yugoslavia.* New York: Columbia University Press, 1976.

Sirotić, Sonja. "Basic Indexes of Household Conditions," *Yugoslav Survey* [Belgrade], 28, No. 4, 1987, 75–84.

Škrlj, M. "Programme Base for the Prevention of Drug Abuse in Yugoslavia," *Bulletin on Narcotics* [Belgrade], 38, January/June 1986, 105–12.

Srdjić-Djaković, Ljubica. "Repatriation of Yugoslav Migrant Workers," *Yugoslav Survey* [Belgrade], 28, No. 2, 1987, 3–12.

Stanovčić, Vojislav. "History and Status of Ethnic Conflicts." Pages 23–40 in Dennison Rusinow (ed.), *Yugoslavia: A Fractured Federalism.* Washington: Wilson Center Press, 1988.

Stipetić, Vladimir. *Yugoslavia's Agriculture, 1945–1975.* Belgrade: Socialist Thought and Practice, 1975.

Stoianovich, Traian. *A Study in Balkan Civilization.* New York: Knopf, 1967.

Stojakov, Svetislav. "Ten Years of the Changes in Education and Upbringing," *Socialist Thought and Practice,* 25, May 1985, 58–72.

Tkalac, I. "Feudal Conditions in Croatia." Pages 329–30 in G.F. Cushing et al. (eds.), *Contrasts in Emerging Societies: Readings in the Social and Economic History of South-Eastern Europe.* London: Athlone Press for the University of London, 1965.

"Tko izazava 'sveti rat?' " *Glas koncila* [Zagreb], April 22, 1990, 2.

Todorović, Gordana. "Basic Population Projections by Age and Sex, 1981–2021," *Yugoslav Survey* [Belgrade], 28, No. 2, 1987, 13–24.

Tomc, Gregor. "Classes, Party Elites, and Ethnic Groups." Pages 59–77 in Dennison Rusinow (ed.), *Yugoslavia: A Fractured Federalism.* Washington: Wilson Center Press, 1988.

"Uskrsnuće Uskrsa," *Glas koncila* [Zagreb], April 22, 1990, 1–4.

Van der Voort, Theodore. "Orthodoxy in Serbia," *Frontier,* March–April 1988, 8–11.

Wilkinson, John Gardner. "Village Life and Trade." Pages 366–71 in G.F. Cushing et al. (eds.), *Contrasts in Emerging Societies: Readings in the Social and Economic History of South-Eastern Europe.* London: Athlone Press for the University of London, 1965.

Wolff, Robert Lee. *The Balkans in Our Time.* Cambridge: Harvard University Press, 1956.

Woodward, Susan L. "Reforming a Socialist State: Ideology and Public Finance in Yugoslavia," *World Politics,* 61, January 1989, 267–305.

Yugoslavia. Savezni zavod za statistiku. *Statistički godiñjak Jugoslavije, 1988.* Belgrade: 1989.

_____. Savezni zavod za statistiku. *Statistički godišnjak Jugoslavije, 1989.* Belgrade: 1990.

Zimmerman, William. *Politics and Culture in Yugoslavia.* Ann Arbor: Center for Political Studies, Institute for Social Research, University of Michigan, 1987.

Chapter 3

"Acceleration of Inflation into Hyperinflation: The Yugoslav Experience in the 1980s," *Economic Analysis and Workers' Management,* No. 21, 1987.

Alton, Thad P., et al. *Occasional Papers Nos. 105–109 of the Research Project on National Income in East Central Europe.* New York: LW International Financial Research, 1989.

Artisien, Patrick. "Joint Venturing in Yugoslavia: Twenty Years of Liberalization," *Multinational Business* [London], Autumn 1987, 12–24.

Babic, Mate, and Emil Primorac. "Some Causes of the Growth of the Yugoslav External Debt," *Soviet Studies* [Glasgow], 38, No. 1, January 1986, 69–88.

Bajt, A. "Trends and Cycles in the Yugoslav Stabilization," *Est-Ouest* [Trieste], No. 4, 1985.

"Better Year Forecast for Yugoslavia," *Motor Ship* [Surrey, United Kingdom], 69, September 1988, 82–86.

Bicanic, Ivo. "Fractured Economy." Pages 120–55 in Dennison Rusinow (ed.), *Yugoslavia: A Fractured Federalism.* Washington: Wilson Center Press, 1988.

Bukowski, Charles J. "Politics and Prospects for Economic Reform in Yugoslavia," *Eastern European Politics and Societies,* 2, Winter 1988, 94–114.

Bukowski, Charles J., and Mark A. Cichock (eds.). *Prospects for Change in Socialist Systems.* New York: Praeger, 1987.

Burkett, John P. "Stabilization Measures in Yugoslavia: An Assessment of the Proposals of Yugoslavia's Commission for Problems of Economic Stabilization." Pages 561–74 in United States Congress, 99th, 2d Session, Joint Economic Committee, *East European Economies: Slow Growth in the 1980s.* (Country Studies on Eastern Europe and Yugoslavia, 3.) Washington: GPO, 1986.

Burkett, John P., and Borislav Skegro. "Are Economic Fractures Widening?" Pages 142–55 in Dennison Rusinow (ed.), *Yugoslavia: A Fractured Federalism.* Washington: Wilson Center Press, 1988.

Chernyshev, V. "Ekonomika Yugoslavii v 80–e gody: problemy razvitiia," *Voprosy ekonomiki* [Moscow], No. 11, 1989, 108–16.

Cochrane, Nancy J. "Yugoslav Agricultural Performance in the 1980s and Prospects for 1990." Pages 575–94 in United States Congress, 99th, 2d Session, Joint Economic Committee, *East European Economies: Slow Growth in the 1980s.* (Country Studies on Eastern Europe and Yugoslavia, 3.) Washington: GPO, 1986.

"A Convertible Dinar Is Just the Beginning," *Bloc,* 2, No. 2, April–May 1990, 21.

Denitch, Bogdan. "Yugoslavia, the Limits of Reform: Economic Crisis, Nationalism, Inner Strife," *Dissent,* No. 36, Winter 1989, 78–85.

"Economics Endanger Bulgaria, Politics Endanger Yugoslavia," *The Woodrow Wilson Center Report,* 2, No. 3, November 1990, 2–3.

"EFTA Will Help Yugoslavia," *Vjesnik* [Zagreb], November 12, 1989. Joint Publications Research Service, *East Europe Report.* (FBIS–EEU–89–183.) January 9, 1990, 6–9.

The Europa World Year Book, 1990, 2. London: Europa, 1990.

"Foreign Debt and Efforts to Increase Exports," *South Slav Journal* [London], April 1988, 87.

Knyazev, Yuri. "A Convertible Dinar," *Business in the USSR* [Paris], No. 3, July-August 1990, 52–53.

Loncarevic, Ivan. "Prices and Private Agriculture in Yugoslavia," *Soviet Studies* [Glasgow], 39, No. 4, October 1987.

Lydall, Harold. *Yugoslavia in Crisis.* Oxford: Clarendon Press, 1989.

_____. *Yugoslav Socialism: Theory and Practice.* Oxford: Clarendon Press, 1984.

McFarlane, Bruce T. *Yugoslavia: Politics, Economics, and Society.* London: Pinter, 1988.

Marer, Paul. "Economic Policies and Systems in Eastern Europe and Yugoslavia: Commonalities and Differences." Pages 595–633 in United States Congress, 99th, 2d session, Joint Economic Committee, *East European Economies: Slow Growth in the*

1980s. (Country Studies on Eastern Europe and Yugoslavia, 3.) Washington: GPO, 1986.

Milivojevic, Marko. "Yugoslavia's Increasing Economic Dependence on Comecon in the 1980s," *South Slav Journal* [London], 9, No. 4, Fall-Winter 1986, 39–51.

Mirkovic, Damir. "Sociological Reflections on Yugoslav Participatory Democracy and Social Ownership," *East European Quarterly*, 21, No. 3, September 1987, 319–32.

Peters, Tim. "Conflict Regulation in Yugoslavia," *South Slav Journal* [London], 10, No. 1, Spring 1987, 19–24.

Ramet, Pedro (ed.). *Yugoslavia in the 1980s*. Boulder, Colorado: Westview Press, 1985.

Remington, Robin Alison. "Nation Versus Class in Yugoslavia," *Current History*, 86, No. 11, November 1987, 365–68, 386–87.

Robinson, Sherman, Laura D. Tyson, and Mathias Dewatripont. "Yugoslav Economic Performance in the 1980s: Alternative Scenarios." Pages 543–60 in United States Congress, 99th, 2d Session, Joint Economic Committee, *East European Economies: Slow Growth in the 1980s*. (Country Studies on Eastern Europe and Yugoslavia, 3.) Washington: GPO, 1986.

Rusinow, Dennison. "Yugoslavia: Enduring Crisis and Delayed Reforms." Pages 52–69 in United States Congress, 101st, 1st Session, Joint Economic Committee, *Pressures for Reform in the East European Economies*, 2. Washington: GPO, 1989.

Rusinow, Dennison (ed.). *Yugoslavia: A Fractured Federalism*. Washington: Wilson Center Press, 1988.

Seroka, Jim. "Contemporary Issues and Stability in Socialist Yugoslavia," *Journal of Communist Studies*, 2, No. 6, June 1986, 128–31.

Singleton, Fred. *Twentieth-Century Yugoslavia*. New York: Columbia University Press, 1976.

Singleton, Fred, and Bernard Carter. *The Economy of Yugoslavia*. New York: St. Martin's Press, 1982.

Staar, Richard F. *Communist Regimes in Eastern Europe*. (5th ed.) Stanford, California: Hoover Institution Press, 1988.

Stankovic, Slobodan. *The End of the Tito Era: Yugoslavia's Dilemmas*. Stanford, California: Hoover Institution Press, 1981.

"Tito's Other Legacy," *Banker* [London], 139, June 1989, 74–75.

United States. Congress. 99th, 2d Session. Joint Economic Committee. *East European Economies: Slow Growth in the 1980s*. (Country Studies on Eastern Europe and Yugoslavia, 3.) Washington: GPO, 1986.

_____. Congress. 101st, 1st Session. Joint Economic Committee. *Pressures for Reform in the East European Economies*, 2. Washington: GPO, 1989.

"Whether Darkness Looms," *Danas* [Zagreb], July 25, 1989. Joint Publications Research Service, *East Europe Report.* (FBIS-EEU-90-006.) September 22, 1989, 26-29.

Woodward, Susan L. "Reforming a Socialist State: Ideology and Public Finance in Yugoslavia," *World Politics,* 61, January 1989, 267-305.

World Bank. *World Debt Tables, 1989-90: External Debt of Developing Countries.* Washington: 1990.

Yugoslavia. Savezni zavod za statistiku. *Statistički godišnjak Jugoslavije, 1989.* Belgrade: 1990.

(Various issues of the following periodicals were also used in the preparation of this chapter: *Business East Europe; Ekonomska politika* [Belgrade]; Foreign Broadcast Information Service, *Daily Report: East Europe; Journal of Commerce; Nafta* [Belgrade]; *Népszava* [Budapest]; Radio Free Europe/Radio Liberty, *Report on Eastern Europe* [Munich]; *Wall Street Journal;* and *Washington Post.)*

Chapter 4

Banac, Ivo. *The National Question in Yugoslavia: Origins, History, Politics.* Ithaca: Cornell University Press, 1984.

Beloff, Nora. "Yugoslavia and the West," *Est-Ouest* [Trieste], 17, No. 4, 1986, 149-67.

Biberaj, Elez. "Yugoslavia: A Continuing Crisis?" *Conflict Studies* [London], 225, October 1989, 1-22.

Bukowski, Charles J. "Politics and Prospects for Economic Reform in Yugoslavia," *East European Politics and Societies,* 2, Winter 1988, 94-151.

Bukowski, Charles J., and Mark A. Cichock (eds.). *Prospects for Change in Socialist Systems.* New York: Praeger, 1987.

Burg, Steven L. *Conflict and Cohesion in Socialist Yugoslavia.* Princeton: Princeton University Press, 1983.

Cviic, Christopher. "Religion and Nationalism in Eastern Europe: The Case of Yugoslavia," *Millennium,* 14, No. 2, Summer 1985, 195-206.

Denitch, Bogdan. "Yugoslavia: The Limits of Reform: Economic Crisis, Nationalism, Inner Strife," *Dissent,* 36, Winter 1989, 78-85.

Djordjević, Jovan (ed.). *Društveno-politički sistem, SFRJ.* Belgrade: 1975.

Doder, Dusko. *The Yugoslavs.* New York: Random House, 1978.

Gruenwald, Oskar, and Karen Rosenblum-Cale (eds.). *Human Rights in Yugoslavia.* New York: Irvington, 1986.

Jugoslovenski pregled. *Constitutional System of Yugoslavia.* Belgrade: Jugoslovenska stvarnost, Jugoslovenski pregled, 1980.

Klein, George, and Milan J. Reban (eds.). *The Politics of Ethnicity in Eastern Europe.* Boulder, Colorado: East European Monographs, 1981.

Linden, Ronald H. "The Impact of Interdependence: Yugoslavia and International Change," *Comparative Politics,* 18, No. 1, January 1986, 211–34.

Lydall, Harold. *Yugoslavia in Crisis.* Oxford: Clarendon Press, 1989.

McFarlane, Bruce J. *Yugoslavia: Politics, Economics, and Society.* London: Pinter, 1988.

Magas, Branko. "Yugoslavia: The Spectre of Balkanization," *New Left Review* [London], No. 174, March-April 1989, 3–31.

Milivojevic, Marko. "Yugoslavia's Security Dilemmas and the West," *Journal of Strategic Studies,* 8, No. 9, September 1985, 284–306.

Pavlowitch, Stevan K. *The Improbable Survivor: Yugoslavia and Its Problems, 1918–1988.* Columbus: Ohio State University Press, 1988.

Pipa, Arshi. "The Political Situation of the Albanians in Yugoslavia with Particular Attention to the Kosovo Problem: A Critical Approach," *East European Quarterly,* 23, No. 2, June 1989, 159–81.

Ramet, Pedro. "The Limits of Political Change in a Communist Country: The Yugoslav Debate, 1980–1986," *Crossroads,* 3, No. 23, November 1987, 67–79.

_____. *Nationalism and Federalism in Yugoslavia, 1963–1983.* Bloomington: Indiana University Press, 1984.

Ramet, Pedro (ed.). *Yugoslavia in the 1980s.* Boulder, Colorado: Westview Press, 1985.

Remington, Robin Alison. "Nation Versus Class in Yugoslavia," *Current History,* 86, No. 11, November 1987, 365–68, 386–87.

Rusinow, Dennison (ed.). *Yugoslavia: A Fractured Federalism.* Washington: Wilson Center Press, 1988.

Sekelj, Laslo. "The Communist League of Yugoslavia: Elite of Power or Consciousness?" *Socialism and Democracy,* 6, Spring-Summer 1988, 115–34.

Seroka, Jim. "Contemporary Issues and Stability in Socialist Yugoslavia," *Journal of Communist Studies,* 2, No. 6, June 1986, 127–44.

_____. "Prognosis for Political Stability in Yugoslavia in the Post-Tito Era," *East European Quarterly,* 22, No. 2, June 1988, 173–90.

Seroka, Jim, and Vukašin Pavlović. "Yugoslav Trade Unions and the Paralysis of Political Decision-Making," *Eastern European Politics and Societies*, 1, Spring 1987, 277–94.

Singleton, Fred. *A Short History of the Yugoslav Peoples*. Cambridge: Cambridge University Press, 1985.

Smiljkovic, Rados. *Interesi i političke akcije u samoupravljanju*. Belgrade: Naučna knjiga, 1987.

Sruk, Josip. *Ustavno uredjenje, SFRJ*. Zagreb: Informator, 1976.

Staar, Richard F. *Communist Regimes in Eastern Europe*. (5th ed.) Stanford, California: Hoover Institution Press, 1988.

Yugoslavia. *The Constitution of the Socialist Federal Republic of Yugoslavia*. Belgrade: Dopisna delavska univerza, 1974.

Zaninovich, M. George. "A Prognosis for Yugoslavia," *Current History*, 88, No. 11, November 1989, 393–96, 404–405.

(Various issues of the following periodicals were also used in the preparation of this chapter: Foreign Broadcast Information Service, *Daily Report: East Europe; New York Times;* Radio Free Europe/Radio Liberty, *Report on Eastern Europe* [Munich]; *South Slav Journal;* and *Washington Post*.)

Chapter 5

Amnesty International. *Yugoslavia: Prisoners of Conscience*. London: 1982.

Bebler, Anton. "Yugoslavia's Positions and Policies on Arms Control and Disarmament," *International Spectator* [Rome], 24, No. 2, April-June 1989, 94–101.

Clare, Joseph F., Jr. "Whither the Third World Arms Producers?" Pages 23–28 in United States, Arms Control and Disarmament Agency, *World Military Expenditures and Arms Transfers, 1986*. Washington: GPO, 1987.

"Defense School: The Yugoslav Armed Forces—Bulwark of Our Defense," *Front* [Belgrade], November 28, 1980. Joint Publications Research Service, *Translations on East Europe: Political, Sociological, and Military Affairs*. February 4, 1981, 44.

The Europa World Year Book, 1988, 2. London: Europa, 1988.

Horhager, Axel. "Yugoslavia's Defense: The Logic of Politics," *International Defense Review*, 9, October 1976, 733–38.

Ilijev, Bogoljub. "Yugoslavia's Contribution to the Victory over Fascism," *Socialist Thought and Practice*, 20, July-August 1980, 53–67.

Jane's All the World's Aircraft, 1989-90. (Ed., John W.R. Taylor.) Surrey, United Kingdom: Jane's Information Group, 1990.

Jane's Armour and Artillery, 1987-88. (Ed., Christopher F. Foss.) London: Jane's, 1987.

Jane's Fighting Ships, 1989-90. (Ed., Richard Sharpe.) Surrey, United Kingdom: Jane's Information Group, 1990.

Jane's Infantry Weapons, 1989-90. (Ed., Ian V. Hogg). Surrey, United Kingdom: Jane's Information Group, 1989.

Karber, Phillip A., and Jon L. Lellenberg. "Yugoslav Security after Tito," *Strategic Review,* 8, Spring 1980, 44-58.

The Military Balance, 1989-1990. London: International Institute for Strategic Studies, 1989.

Milivojević, Marko. "Yugoslavia's Security Dilemmas and the West," *Journal of Strategic Studies,* 8, September 1985, 284-306.

_____. "The Yugoslav People's Army," *Armed Forces,* 6, 1987, 15-19.

_____. "The Yugoslav People's Army: Another Jaruzelski on the Way?" *South Slav Journal* [London], 11, Summer–Autumn 1988, 1-18.

Milivojević, Marko (ed.). *Yugoslavia's Security Dilemmas.* New York: St. Martin's Press, 1988.

Miller, Morton S. "Conventional Arms Trade in the Developing World, 1976-86: Reflections on a Decade." Pages 19-24 in United States, Arms Control and Disarmament Agency, *World Military Expenditures and Arms Transfers, 1988.* Washington: GPO, 1989.

Ramet, Pedro. "Yugoslavia and the Threat of Internal and External Discontents," *Orbis,* 28, Spring 1984, 103-21.

Ramet, Pedro (ed.). *Yugoslavia in the 1980s.* Boulder, Colorado: Westview Press, 1985.

Rawleigh, G. "Yugoslavia/France: Supersonic Combat Aircraft," *FBIS Science and Technology Perspectives,* 5, No. 5, May 31, 1990, 7-8.

Remington, Robin Alison. "Political-Military Relations in Post-Tito Yugoslavia." Pages 56-75 in Pedro Ramet (ed.), *Yugoslavia in the 1980s.* Boulder, Colorado: Westview Press, 1985.

Roberts, Walter R. *Tito, Mihailovic, and the Allies, 1941-1945.* Durham, North Carolina: Duke University Press, 1987.

Snitch, Thomas H. "East European Involvement in the World's Arms Market." Pages 117-21 in United States, Arms Control and Disarmament Agency, *World Military Expenditures and Arms Transfers, 1972-1982.* Washington: GPO, 1984.

United States. Arms Control and Disarmament Agency. *World Military Expenditures and Arms Transfers, 1972-1982.* Washington: GPO, 1984.

_____. Arms Control and Disarmament Agency. *World Military Expenditures and Arms Transfers, 1986.* Washington: GPO, 1987.

_____. Arms Control and Disarmament Agency. *World Military Expenditures and Arms Transfers, 1988.* Washington: GPO, 1989.

Vego, Milan N. "The Yugoslav Ground Forces: A Look at the Past and the Present," *Military Review,* 60, November 1980, 14–27.

_____. "The Yugoslavian Navy: A Critical Review," *United States Naval Institute Proceedings,* 104, September 1978, 127–33.

Yugoslavia. *The Constitution of the Socialist Federal Republic of Yugoslavia.* Belgrade: Dopisna delavska univerza, 1974.

(Various issues of the following periodicals were also used in the preparation of this chapter: Foreign Broadcast Information Service, *Daily Report: East Europe;* and Radio Free Europe/Radio Liberty, *Report on Eastern Europe* [Munich].)

Glossary

Četnik (pl., Četnici)—Name derived from the Serbian word for detachment; in full, Četnik Detachments of the Yugoslav Army of the Fatherland. Given to several Serbian resistance groups in World War II organized to oppose occupying Nazis and Croatian collaborators. Avoiding large-scale conflict with the invaders, the Četnici mostly fought the communist Partisans (*q.v.*) of Josip Broz Tito. The most important Četnik group was led by Draža Mihajlović.

collectivization of agriculture—The process of imposing state control of agriculture by forming privately held land into socially owned and managed farms.

Comecon (Council for Mutual Economic Assistance)—A multilateral economic alliance headquartered in Moscow. Members in 1990 included Bulgaria, Cuba, Czechoslovakia, the German Democratic Republic (East Germany), Hungary, Mongolia, Poland, Romania, the Soviet Union, and Vietnam. Also referred to as CMEA or CEMA.

Cominform (Communist Information Bureau)—An international communist organization (1947–56) including the communist parties of Bulgaria, Czechoslovakia, France, Hungary, Italy, Poland, Romania, the Soviet Union, and Yugoslavia (expelled in 1948). Formed on Soviet initiative, it issued propaganda advocating international communist solidarity as a tool of Soviet foreign policy.

Cyrillic—Alphabet ascribed to missionaries Cyril and Methodius (ninth century), developed from Greek for church literature in Russian. The official alphabet of the Soviet Slavic republics, Yugoslavia excepting Croatia and Slovenia, and Bulgaria, it was one of the three principal alphabets of the world.

dinar—Yugoslav national currency unit consisting of 100 paras. Devalued frequently after 1980. In 1980 exchange rate was YD24.9 per US$1; in 1985, YD270.2 per US$1; and in 1988, YD2,522.6 per US$1. In 1990 new ''heavy'' dinar was established, worth 10,000 old dinars; 1990 exchange rate was fixed at 7 dinars per West German deutsche mark. New rate January 1991 was YD10.50 per US$1.

Dual Monarchy—Popular name for the Habsburg Empire after the 1867 Ausgleich (Compromise) that united Austria and Hungary under a common monarch; arranged to bolster the waning influence of Austria in Europe. Also known as the Austro-Hungarian Empire.

EC (European Community)—A group of three primarily economic communities of West European countries, including the European Economic Community (EEC—*q.v.*), the European Atomic Energy Community (Euratom or EAEC), and the European Coal and Steel Community (ECSC). Executive power rested with the European Commission, which implemented and defended the community treaties in the interests of the EC as a whole. Also known as the European Communities.

EEC (European Economic Community)—The ''Common Market'' of primarily West European countries organized to promote coordinated development of economic activities, continuous and balanced expansion, increased stability, and closer relations among member states. Methods included elimination of customs duties and import restrictions among member states and a common customs tariff, a common commercial policy toward outside countries, and a common agricultural and transport policy.

EFTA (European Free Trade Association)—Created in 1960 to bring about free trade in industrial goods and expansion of trade in agricultural goods among member countries. In 1990 members included Austria, Finland, Iceland, Norway, Sweden, and Switzerland. The Joint EFTA-Yugoslavia Committee was established in 1978 to expand trade and industrial cooperation with Yugoslavia.

GATT (General Agreement on Tariffs and Trade)—An integrated set of bilateral trade agreements among nations, formed in 1947 to abolish quotas and reduce tariffs. Yugoslavia became a member of GATT in 1965, when its tariff and trade regulations were brought into line with international practices.

GDP (gross domestic product)—A measure of the total value of goods and services produced by a domestic economy during a given period, usually a year. Obtained by adding the value of profits, employee compensation, and depreciation of capital from each sector of the economy.

GMP (gross material product)—The value added by the productive sectors before deduction of depreciation. GMP excludes the value of services in the nonproductive sectors such as defense, public administration, finance, education, health, and housing. Also known as social product.

GNP (gross national product)—The sum of the gross domestic product (GDP—*q.v.*) and the income received from abroad by residents, minus payments remitted abroad to nonresidents.

Green Plans—A series of federal government agricultural plans in Yugoslavia for the period 1973 through 1985, aimed at stimulating agricultural production. They provided for large foreign and domestic investment in agriculture and incentives for private agriculture.

hard currency—Currency freely convertible and traded on international currency markets.

Helsinki Accords—Signed August 1975 by all European countries except Albania, plus Canada and the United States, to endorse general principles of international behavior, especially in economic, environmental, and humanitarian issues. Helsinki Accords is short form for the Final Act of the Conference on Security and Cooperation in Europe (CSCE).

IMF (International Monetary Fund)—Established with the World Bank (*q.v.*) in 1945, a specialized agency affiliated with the United Nations and responsible for stabilizing international exchange rates and payments. Its main business is providing loans to its members when they experience balance of payments difficulties.

LCY (League of Communists of Yugoslavia)—Until 1990 the sole legal political party of Yugoslavia. Each republic and province had a separate organization, such as the League of Communists of Macedonia. Until 1952 called the Communist Party of Yugoslavia (CPY). In 1990 the national organization split at the Fourteenth Party Congress; some republic parties took different names, e.g., the Serbian party changed its name from League of Communists of Serbia to Socialist Party of Serbia. All the republic communist parties remained intact (although reduced in membership) and ran candidates in the multiparty 1990 republic elections.

market socialism—The economic system introduced in 1963 in Yugoslavia based on worker-managed enterprises, using domestic and foreign market forces as a management guide.

nation and nationality—Juridically important distinctions that played significant roles in Yugoslav political life, in spite of legislation that gave full equality to minorities in culture, public life, and language. The term *nation* was used in reference to ethnic groups whose traditional territorial homelands lay mostly within the modern boundaries of Yugoslavia, i.e., the Croats, Macedonians, Montenegrins, Muslim Slavs, Serbs, and Slovenes. The term *nationality,* or *national minority,* designated groups in Yugoslavia whose homelands were outside Yugoslavia; the largest of these were the Hungarians and the Albanians.

pan-Slavism—A nineteenth-century intellectual movement that sought to unite the Slavic peoples of Europe based on their common ethnic background, culture, and political goals.

Partisans—Popular name for resistance forces led by Josip Broz Tito during World War II. In December 1941, adopted formal name People's Liberation Army and Partisan Detachments.

Serbia proper—The part of the Republic of Serbia not including the provinces of Vojvodina and Kosovo; the ethnic and political core of the Serbian state.

social product—*See* GMP (gross material product).

social sector—The sector of the Yugoslav economy in which assets were socially owned and self-management governed economic activity.

Ustaše (sing., Ustaša)—From the word *ustanak,* meaning uprising or rebellion. An extremist Croatian movement that began as an interwar terrorist organization, then adopted fascist guidelines and collaborated with German and Italian occupation forces in World War II. The movement's genocidal practices against Serbs, Muslims, Jews, and other minorities in Croatia and Bosnia and Hercegovina caused animosities that lasted long after the war.

World Bank—Informal name used to designate a group of three affiliated international institutions: the International Bank for Reconstruction and Development (IBRD), providing loans to developing countries; the International Development Association (IDA), providing credits to the poorest developing countries on easier terms than the IBRD; and the International Finance Corporation (IFC), supplementing IBRD activity by loans to stimulate private enterprise in less developed countries. The three institutions are owned by the governments of the countries that subscribe their capital. To participate in the World Bank group, member states must first belong to the International Monetary Fund (IMF—*q.v.*).

Index

specific national branches), 6, 18, 30, 107, 108-10; number of members, 108; persecution of priests, 108

East Germany. *See* German Democratic Republic

EC. *See* European Community

ecology, 101

economic blockade, 46, 126, 232

economic crisis, 163-65; and military spending, 266

economic disparities, 163

economic enterprises, 198; bankruptcy of, xxxiii-xxxiv

economic issues, 222

economic planning, 128, 134-35; "indicative," 134; problems with, 134-35; process of, 134; "social," 134

economic problems, 62-63, 123, 126

economic reforms, xxvi, xxxii, xxxv, 48, 50, 92, 180-83; attempts to block, 52, 175; austerity measures under, 180, 181, 182, 183; of banking, 137; components of, 129-30; effect on workers, 93; and ethnic rivalries, 50, 222; goals of, 129, 139; under Marković, xxxii-xxxiii, 123-24; of 1965, 129-30, 155; problems under, 51, 222

economic reforms of 1990, 165-67; bankruptcy laws strengthened, 165-66; effects of, 166; monetary reform, 165; phase one, 166; phase two, 166-67; price controls removed, 165; resistance to, 166-67; wage austerity program, 165, 182

economy: development of, 125-26; in the 1920s, 32-33; under German occupation, 124; state control of, 125

education, 113-16; church schools, 86; under communist government, 48; higher, 116; history of, 113-14; Islamic, 83; languages used in, 73, 114, 115; level attained, 114, 115; secular, 83; student-teacher ratio, 114-15; of women, 83, 100, 113

education, primary, 114-15; attendance, 114; enrollment, 114; languages used in, 115; student-teacher ratio, 114

education, secondary, 115; curriculum reform in, 115; languages used in, 115; number of students in, 115; spending on, 115; student-teacher ratio in, 115

EEC. *See* European Economic Community

EFTA. *See* European Free Trade Association

Egypt, 216, 269; exports to, 160; imports from, 156; military exchanges with, 275; relations with, 221

El Alamein, Battle of, 230

elections, multiparty, xxvii, xxxvi, xxxviii, 201-2, 207-8, 223

electrical power, 91; hydroelectric, 148-49; nuclear, 149; production of, 146; transmission grid, 146

emigration, 104

émigrés: assassinations of, 281-82; subversive activities of, 281

Emona (*see also* Ljubljana), 6

employment: peasant migration for, 92; rate, 102; of women, 100

Energoinvest, 160

Energoproekt, 160

energy, 146-50; consumption, 146-47; generation of, 91, 146, 148-49; shortage of, 146

Enlightenment: influence on Slovenian nationalism, 8-9; spread to Serbs, 21

Ethiopia, 269; military exchanges with, 275

ethnic composition, xxix, 70-72

ethnic groups (*see also under individual groups; see also* South Slavs), 6-16, 30-31; categories of, 70; education of, 115; equal rights for, 71-72; histories of, 6-7; nationalities, 70; nations, 70, 73-90

ethnic rivalries, xxvi; between Croats and Serbs, 73-74; sparked by economic reform, 50

ethnographic history, 69-70; complexities of, 70; of South Slavs, 69

Europe, Eastern: relations with, 219-20; trade with, 44, 126, 143

Europe, Western: credits and loans from, 126; relations with, 221; trade with, 158

European Community (EC), xli; ceasefires arranged by, xxx, xxxi, xxxix; recognition by, of Croatia and Slovenia, xxxix-xli

European Economic Community (EEC): commercial agreement with, 52, 158; Common Agricultural Policy of, 158; economic sanctions threatened by, xxxiv; goal of membership in, xxiii, xxviii, xxxiv, 158, 165, 216, 221; loan from, xxxiv; obstacles to membership

Published Country Studies

(Area Handbook Series)

550-65	Afghanistan		550-87	Greece
550-98	Albania		550-78	Guatemala
550-44	Algeria		550-174	Guinea
550-59	Angola		550-82	Guyana and Belize
550-73	Argentina		550-151	Honduras
550-169	Australia		550-165	Hungary
550-176	Austria		550-21	India
550-175	Bangladesh		550-154	Indian Ocean
550-170	Belgium		550-39	Indonesia
550-66	Bolivia		550-68	Iran
550-20	Brazil		550-31	Iraq
550-168	Bulgaria		550-25	Israel
550-61	Burma		550-182	Italy
550-50	Cambodia		550-30	Japan
550-166	Cameroon		550-34	Jordan
550-159	Chad		550-56	Kenya
550-77	Chile		550-81	Korea, North
550-60	China		550-41	Korea, South
550-26	Colombia		550-58	Laos
550-33	Commonwealth Caribbean, Islands of the		550-24	Lebanon
550-91	Congo		550-38	Liberia
550-90	Costa Rica		550-85	Libya
550-69	Côte d'Ivoire (Ivory Coast)		550-172	Malawi
550-152	Cuba		550-45	Malaysia
550-22	Cyprus		550-161	Mauritania
550-158	Czechoslovakia		550-79	Mexico
550-36	Dominican Republic and Haiti		550-76	Mongolia
550-52	Ecuador		550-49	Morocco
550-43	Egypt		550-64	Mozambique
550-150	El Salvador		550-35	Nepal and Bhutan
550-28	Ethiopia		550-88	Nicaragua
550-167	Finland		550-157	Nigeria
550-155	Germany, East		550-94	Oceania
550-173	Germany, Fed. Rep. of		550-48	Pakistan
550-153	Ghana		550-46	Panama

550-156	Paraguay	550-53	Thailand
550-185	Persian Gulf States	550-89	Tunisia
550-42	Peru	550-80	Turkey
550-72	Philippines	550-74	Uganda
550-162	Poland	550-97	Uruguay
550-181	Portugal	550-71	Venezuela
550-160	Romania	550-32	Vietnam
550-37	Rwanda and Burundi	550-183	Yemens, The
550-51	Saudi Arabia	550-99	Yugoslavia
550-70	Senegal	550-67	Zaire
550-180	Sierra Leone	550-75	Zambia
550-184	Singapore	550-171	Zimbabwe
550-86	Somalia		
550-93	South Africa		
550-95	Soviet Union		
550-179	Spain		
550-96	Sri Lanka		
550-27	Sudan		
550-47	Syria		
550-62	Tanzania		